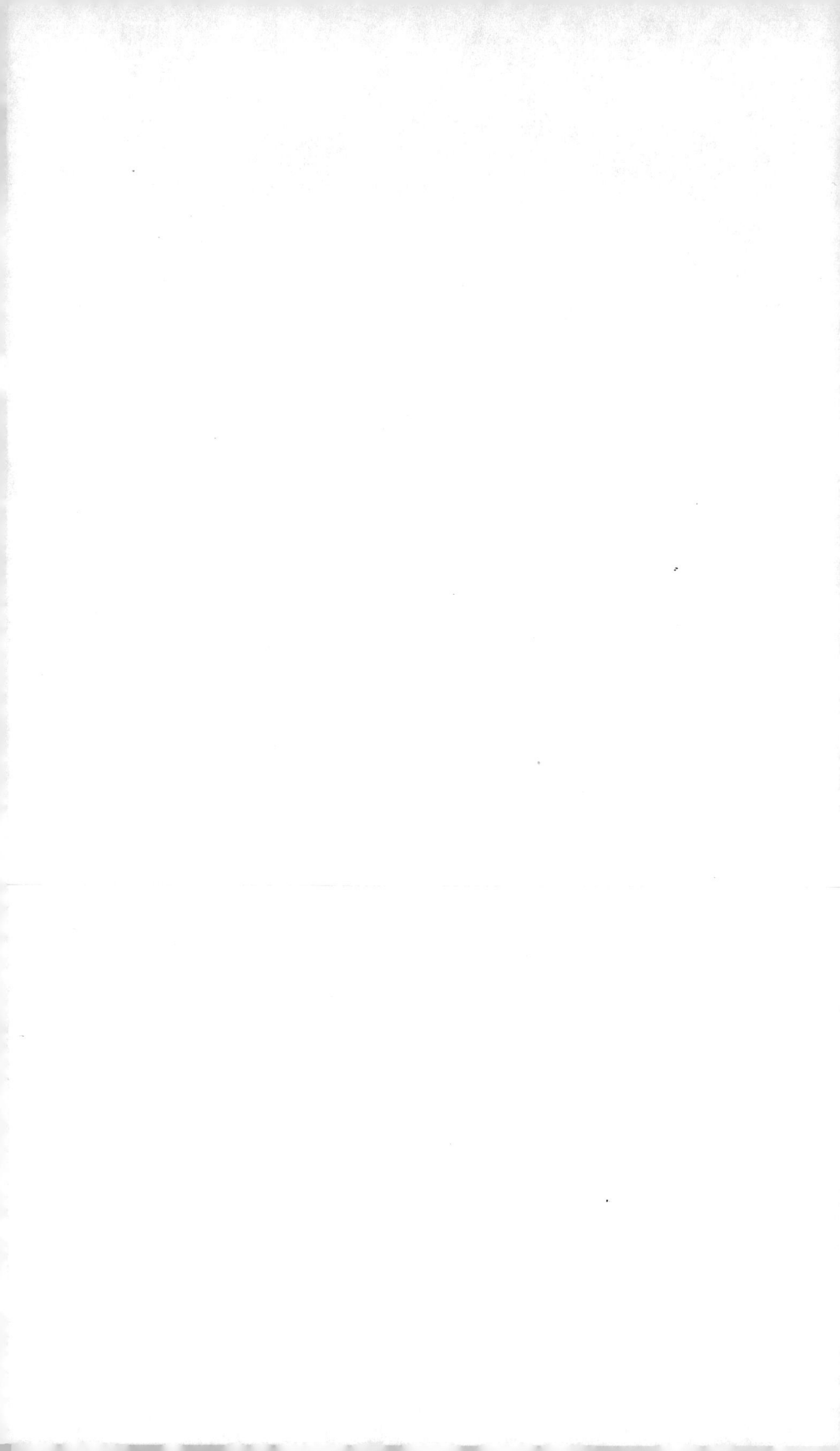

A Benedictine Martyrology

A
𝔅𝔢𝔫𝔢𝔡𝔦𝔠𝔱𝔦𝔫𝔢 𝔐𝔞𝔯𝔱𝔶𝔯𝔬𝔩𝔬𝔤𝔶

BEING A REVISION OF

REV. PETER LECHNER'S AUSFÜHRLICHES
MARTYROLOGIUM DES BENEDICTINER-ORDENS
UND SEINER VERZWEIGUNGEN

BY

ALEXIUS HOFFMANN, O. S. B.

COLLEGEVILLE, MINNESOTA
ST. JOHN'S ABBEY
1922

𝔓𝔢𝔯𝔪𝔦𝔰𝔰𝔲 𝔖𝔲𝔭𝔢𝔯𝔦𝔬𝔯𝔲𝔪

Nihil obstat
ALCUINUS DEUTSCH, O.S.B.
.Censor dep.

Imprimatur
+ JOSEPHUS F. BUSCH
Ep. S. Clodoaldi

Jan. 19, 1920

Preface

The German original, of which the present volume is a translation and revision, with some omissions and additions, was the work of Father Peter Lechner, O.S.B., who compiled it in order to supply his monastery of Scheyern, in
Bavaria, with a condensed martyrology, or menology, for reading at table
every day of the year. No attempt was made to write a detailed life of the
persons commemorated: only the most significant facts and such as were conducive to edification were selected. In preparing the present volume, the
revisor has made no departure from the spirit of the original. Some entries
have been slightly abbreviated and several added, especially the names of several victims of the French Revolution, whose process of beatification has been
introduced in Rome. For the accommodation of students of Benedictine history, a number of additional references and notes has been added at the foot of
each page.

The book is not a martyrology in the strict sense of that term either in
content or in style. The Roman Martyrology contains the names of only such
persons—Saints or Blessed—to whom public veneration may be shown. Fr.
Lechner's work, however, admits a number of others who never have received
public veneration, but whose virtues were preserved in pious memory in certain
branches or houses of the Order. It is not claimed that all the persons mentioned were Benedictines by monastic profession, or vows. The author thus
justifies his introduction of Saints who followed the rule of St: Columban: "The
disciples of St. Columban receive mention in this Martyrology for two reasons:
first, because their rule and manner of life resembled that of St. Benedict, and,
secondly, because all the Columban monasteries gradually passed over to the
observance of the rule of St. Benedict. The disciples of St. Columban were at
all times regarded as Benedictines. Many would be surprised if St. Gall, for
instance, were not considered a Benedictine, although he lived according to the
rule of St. Columban." With much better reason place was allotted to the
Saints and Blessed of the several reforms and branches of the Order—such as
the Order of Citeaux, of Camaldoli, of Vallombrosa, of Monte Oliveto, of Monte
Vergine, of Fiore, of Pulsano, of La Trappe, of the Celestines and the Humiliati,
and the Congregations of Cava and Cluny—all of which adopted the Rule of
St. Benedict as their constitution. The same may be said of the military
Orders—Knights Templars, Knights of Alcantara, Montesia and St. Stephen.
In addition, the names of a few eminent benefactors are commemorated, as
well as memorable incidents in the history of the Order.

As this work is intended chiefly for edification and does not claim to be a
critical study—Mabillon, Menard and the Bollandists must be consulted for
critical dissertations—no special effort has been made to correct or change anything beyond a few inaccuracies which may possibly be charged to typo-
graphers.

A word as to the genesis of this Martyrology. In preparing his book, Fr.
Peter Lechner took as a basis a "Kirchen-Kalender des Benediktiner Ordens"
published anonymously by the abbey of Donauwoerth in Bavaria in 1786. The
late Fr. Pirmin Lindner, O.S.B., a well known Benedictine literary historian,
mentions P. Bernard Stocker, O.S.B. (†1806), a monk of Donauwoerth, as the

author.(Schriftsteller des Ben. Ordens in Bayern. vol. 2. 1880). Fr. Lechner admitted that the selection was made with care and discrimination, but considered the sketches too brief and matter-of-fact. For the purpose of supplying this deficiency, he prepared his Martyrology, which was published by B. Schmid at Augsburg in 1855 with the sanction of the ordinariate of the archdiocese of Muenchen-Freising. It is an octavo volume of 536 pages; each day of the year has on an average four entries.

Father Peter Lechner, D.D. was born at Pfaffenhofen in Bavaria on March 7, 1805, studied at Landshut and Munich and was ordained December 9, 1827 at Augsburg. On November 1, 1838 he entered the monastery of Scheyern, which had recently been restored; made profession on November 1, 1839; was prior from 1842-1847, and was associated with the early Benedictines at St. Vincent's near Latrobe in Pennsylvania from 1847-1851, when he was recalled to his abbey in Europe. He died July 26, 1873. Fr. Pirmin Lindner mentions forty-one works of this pious and industrious religious.

In compliance with the decrees of Pope Urban VIII, the translator and editor of the present volume declares that where the title of Saint, Blessed or Venerable is given to persons not officially recognized as such by the Holy See, it is done simply to indicate in what esteem the persons honored with such titles were held in the past and what titles are given them in hagiographical sources. In no instance is there a desire or intention to anticipate the decision of the Holy See, to whose correction this volume is most humbly submitted.

—The Revisor.

Collegeville, Minnesota

Sept. 24, 1922.

January

1

1. **St. Clarus**, abbot of St. Marcel at Vienne, in France, received his early training in the monastery of Ferreol, and was appointed abbot of St. Marcel by Bishop Cadoldus. During his last illness he foretold that after the death of six bishops dire disasters would befall Vienne at the hands of the Saracens, and his prophecy was fulfilled. Several days before his death he saw, in a vision, St. Blandina, who made known to him its approach. He yielded up his spirit while the brethren stood at his bedside chanting the words: "Let every spirit praise the Lord." He passed away in 660 and was buried in the church of St. Blandina; many miracles wrought at his intercession testified to the sanctity of his life. His veneration was approved December 1, 1903.

2. **St. Frodobert**, first abbot of Moutier-la-Celle near Troyes, was a native of Troyes and at an early age was received among the clergy of the diocese. Burning with a desire for a perfect life, he entered the monastery of Luxeuil, where he edified all by his meekness and simplicity of heart. Several years later he was invited to found a monastery in his native diocese on grounds granted by King Clothair I. This was the beginning of Moutier-la-Celle (founded ab. 650), over which Frodobert presided with great piety and prudence. He died in the night between the last day of December and January 1 of the year 673.

3. **St. Odilo** (de Mercoeur), sixth abbot of Cluny, received the Benedictine habit at the hands of St. Majolus, abbot of that celebrated monastery. At the age of twenty-nine years he was selected by Majolus to share the duties of his office. Three years later, after the death of Majolus (994), Odilo was chosen as his successor. His piety and rare gifts attracted universal attention, and he became one of the most influential men of his day. He accompanied the emperor St. Henry II to Rome, for that monarch's solemn coronation. After his return he spent several years in visiting the numerous houses of the great congregation of which he was the head, and everywhere restored order or exhorted the brethren to maintain good discipline where it had not suffered. So great was his love for the poor, that during the famine which afflicted the country in 1016 he not only distributed all the food and grain of the monastery but even sold sacred vessels, altar plate and other valuable possessions in order to relieve the sufferers. It was this son of St. Benedict who introduced the annual observance of All Souls' Day in his monastery,—an observance which in the course of time was adopted throughout western Christendom. In 1030 he declined an appointment to the espiscopal see of Lyons. During the last five years of his life he was afflicted with a painful illness, of which he died on New Year day 1049, having governed

---

Clarus: Mab., Buch., Chev., Acta S. Sedis, XXXVI, 424.
Frodobert: Mab. Vita ascribed to Abbot Adso, in the Bollandists. Chev., Buch. Other forms of the name: Flodobert, Frobert. Ana. Bolland. V, 59-66.

Cluny for nearly fifty-six years.   He was at the time conducting a visitation
of the monastery of Souvigny.

4. St. William (*supra Regulam*), abbot of St. Benigne at Dijon, was born
962 at Novara in Italy.   He was a monk at Lucedio (Lucedia) in Piedmont,
but passed over to the Congregation of Cluny, where his abilities were soon recognized by abbot Majolus, who appointed him prior of St. Saurin (Saturnin)
and, some time later, abbot of St. Benigne.   Many houses were either reformed
or founded by this zealous champion of the Holy Rule.   His advice was sought
by eminent persons both in Church and State.   He gladly served every one
and taught the brethren that it was better to give than to take.   The monastic schools, in particular that of Fecamp in Normandy, were endowed with
new life by Abbot William.   While at Fecamp he was summoned to
receive the reward of his faithful labors in 1031.   Notwithstanding protests
on the part of the monks of Dijon, the remains were interred in the abbey
church of Fecamp.

2

1 St. Adalard (Adelard), abbot of Corbie in Picardy, was the grandson
of Charles Martel, and in his early youth was received among the monks of
Corbie, where he was distinguished for his humility and prudence.   In order
to shun the temptations of the royal court, he joined the community of Monte
Cassino, but was prevailed upon to return and was elected abbot of Corbie.
Like many other prelates of his day, he was required to serve in political ca-
pacities; in 810 he became tutor of Bernard, the son of Pepin, and governed
northern Italy in his name.   Louis the Pious listened to false accusations
against the Saint and banished him to the monastery of St. Philibert on
an island at the mouth of the Loire, together with his brother Wala and his sister Gundrada.   He was recalled seven years later (821) and in 823 was permitted to return to his monastery, where he spent the remaining years of his
life.   Never ceasing to be active in spreading the kingdom of God, he founded
the monastery of New Corbie (Corvey) in Westphalia (823).   Late in 826 he
was befallen by a serious illness; having been anointed by his disciple, bishop
Hildeman of Beauvais, and fortified with the Holy Viaticum he died on the
second day of January 827.

2. St. Blidulph, monk of Bobbio, in Italy, rebuked the Lombard king
Ariowald (625-636) for adhering to the errors of Arianism and was severely
wounded by one of the king's retinue.   To the amazement of all, he recovered
in a short time, returned to his monastery and died in 630.

3. Bl. Gundrada, sister of Abbots Adalard and Wala (q.v.), withdrew
from the perils of the court to save her soul in the monastery of St. Radegundis

Odilo: Mab., St. Peter Damian. Life by Odilo Ringholz, Bruenn, 1885. But., Kir. Lex.,
    Cath. Enc., S. & M. 1887, 15 etc. Olo is another form of the name.
William: Mab., Chev., Buch., Stad., O. Ringholz in S. & M., 1882, III. 2. 363, 383.
Adalard: Paschasius Radbert, Kir. Lex., Cath. Enc., But. The name is also written Adelard,
    Adelhard, Adelhart.
Blidulph: Jonas of Bobbio, Stad. Another form of the name is Bladulph.

at Poitiers. She shared the exile of her brothers, but breathed her last in the house in which she had consecrated her life to God, in 824.

3

1. **St. Blitmundus**, abbot of St. Valery in Picardy, was in his infancy stricken with an ailment that paralyzed all his limbs. Having recovered his health at the intercession of St. Valery (Walaric), he resolved to live for God alone and entered the monastery over which the Saint presided as abbot. To this dignity Blitmundus was elevated after the saintly abbot's death in 622 (see Dec. 12). The community being dispersed by wars, Blitmund betook himself to Bobbio in Italy to live under the direction of Abbot Attala (see March 10). When peace had been restored in his own country, he returned and reorganized his abbey, laboring incessantly in the interest of his brethren and of the faithful in the vicinity. His useful life was crowned by a holy death in 650.

2. **St. Bertila,** nun and recluse at Maroeul, diocese of Arras, in France, obtained the consent of her husband to lead a life of virginity and after his death founded a monastery in honor of Our Lady at Maroeul, where she received the veil and lived as a recluse to the day of her death in 687.

3. **SS. Aimo (Aymo) and Odo,** abbots of St. Martin at Tulle, France, were ornaments of the Order and bright examples of religious life in the course of the twelfth century.

4. **Bl. Bernarius,** brother of St. Adalard (see Jan. 2) of Corbie, shared in his trials and sufferings. He died in the monastery of Lerins, off the southern coast of France, in 830.

5. Establishment of the **Military Order of St. Julian de Pereiro** by two brothers, Ferdinand and Gomez, in 1156, to defend Spain against the Moors. This body was approved as the Order of **Knights of Alcantara** by Pope Alexander III in 1177 and observed the Cistercian Rule.

4

1. **St. Rigobert,** archbishop of Rheims (721-722) and abbot of Orbais, was a zealous promoter of the common life among his clergy. Having incurred the displeasure of Charles Martel, he was banished, but was recalled by Pepin. In the meantime a certain Abbot Milo, a layman, had been appointed to the see of Rheims. Rigobert was not permitted to exercise the functions of the

Gundrada: Mab., Chev.
Blitmund: H. Menard, Stad. Other forms of the name are Blidmundus, Blimond.
Bertila: H. Menard, Stad., Chev., Bolland. Hagiographia Latina, p. 192. Another form of the name is Bertilia.
Aimo, Odo: Mab.
Bernarius: Mab., Stad.(on January 2.).
Knights of St. Julian: Henr., Cath. Enc. "Alcantara."

episcopal office and bore this humiliation with edifying patience. His residence was the village of Gernicourt, about five miles from Rheims; there he
built a church in honor of St. Peter and spent the remainder of his life in prayer and mortifications. He died in 733 and was buried in the church that he
had built. Later his remains were removed to the church of Our Lady in
Rheims by Archbishop Fulco.

2. St. Libentius (Lievizo I) was archbishop of Bremen and Hamburg
and successor of Archbishop Adalgag, upon whose invitation he had come to
the North from Italy. After his election to the episcopal office in 988, he edified
the clergy of his cathedral, all of whom were monks, by his love of retirement
and spirit of mortification. Like his predecessors, he undertook to extend
the spiritual conquest among the pagan inhabitants of the Scandinavian countries, but was prevented by the wars between King Sueno of Denmark and
Eric of Sweden from achieving permanent success. He died in 1013.

3. Bl. Roger was a native of England, but, following a divine inspiration, left his country and became a Cistercian monk in the abbey of Lorroy
in Berry, in France. On account of his holy life his superiors chose him as
the head of a colony sent out to found the monastery of Elan in the diocese of
Rheims. As abbot of that house, he governed the community with great
gentleness and prudence. He was remarkable for his compassion for the
sick and suffering. The resources of his house were so slender that he and his
brethren lived in extreme poverty, yet were always contented. Renowned
for his rare spiritual insight and the gift of prophecy, he passed to a better
life in 1175.

5

1. St. Convoyon, the first abbot of Redon in Brittany, was a
native of Comblessac in the diocese of St. Malo, where he was born in 788.
The bishop of Vannes received him among his clergy and appointed him archdeacon. Obeying an impulse to lead a more perfect life, he set out with five
clerical companions and took up his abode in a secluded locality near Redon.
The hermit Gerfrid, who had lived for several years in the abbey of St. Maur-
sur-Loire, prevailed upon him to adopt the Rule of St. Benedict. Within
a short time, Convoyon's community grew in numbers and many of the faithful commended themselves to their prayer. He did not confine his labors to
the brethren whom he governed, but inveighed fervently against certain simoniacal bishops and even journeyed to Rome to lay his complaints before
Pope Leo IV. Upon his return to Brittany in 848, he lived in peace till the
invasion of the Normans in the reign of Charles the Bald. His monastery
having been laid waste by the invaders, he established himself in a house built
for him at Plelan by the prince Solomon, where he spent his time in pious exercises to the day of his death in 868. His remains were subsequently
removed from Plelan to Redon. In some places the feast is celebrated on
December 28.

Rigobert: Mab., But., Chev., Buch. Robert is another form of the name.
Libentius: Adam of Bremen, Mab. Ebeling says he was canonized shortly after his death.
Roger: Rusca, Stan.
Convoyon: Mab., Chev., Stad., Acta S. Sedis I. 655.

2. **St. Gaudentius**, bishop of Gnesen, who is by some supposed to have been a brother of St. Adalbert (see Apr. 23), was a monk in the monastery of SS. Boniface and Alexius in Rome and was one of the missionaries secured by Adalbert for the evangelization of Bohemia. He accompanied Adalbert on many of his missionary journeys and was finally appointed bishop of Gnesen. His death occurred in 1006 and his body rests at Prague.

3. **Bl. Paula**, a Camaldolese nun at St. Margaret in Florence, was blessed with the gift of meditation and contemplation in a high degree. Her deep love of God and of human souls impelled her to exhort remiss priests and monks to edify the people by more exemplary lives. Never ceasing to pray for the conversion of sinners and to practice rigorous mortifications, she slept in peace in 1368.

4. **Bl. Alachrinus**, a Cistercian monk of Casamari (diocese of Veroli) in Italy, was created a bishop by Pope Innocent III and was sent as legate to Germany by Honorius III. He flourished about 1216.

5. **Balderic**, abbot of St. Peter at Salzburg, was the successor of Abbot Reginbert, who was consecrated bishop of Brixen in 1125. Several miracles were wrought at his intercession, and he was favored with visions. He died in the year 1147.

6

1. **St. Peter**, the first abbot of Canterbury, accompanied St. Augustine from Rome to England in 596 and was shortly after his arrival appointed abbot. On his way to the continent he suffered shipwreck in the bay of Ambleteuse on the northern coast of France in 606. His body was recovered and interred at Boulogne.

2. **St. Erminold**, abbot of Lorsch and Pruefening, was born in Suabia about the year 1075 and received his early training in the abbey of Hirschau. In 1110 he was nominated abbot of Lorsch, a celebrated monastery in the principality of Hessia; but, upon learning that the appointment had been secured by a gift made to the emperor, he left Lorsch and returned to Hirschau, unwilling to continue in a position which had been secured for him through simony, as he believed. Bishop St. Otto of Bamberg invited him to become the first abbot of the newly founded abbey of Pruefening in Bavaria. Accompanied by several monks Erminold set out for his new abode in 1114. During the seven years spent at Pruefening, he was known for his boundless charity to the poor, for whose relief he sacrificed the greater part of the possessions of his abbey. His insistence upon strict observance of the Rule encountered

Gaudentius: Mab., Buch. Slavic form of the name: Radzyn, Radim. Kir. Lex. "Gnesen."
Paula: Pzovius, Fortunius.
Alachrin: Bucelin, Stad.
Baldric: Chronicles of Salzburg, Lindner (Monasticon Salzb.)
Peter: Mab., Chev., Stan.

opposition from some of the religious; one of the malcontents laid violent hands upon the abbot and inflicted a wound of which he died on this day in 1121.

3. **Bl. Albert**, of the counts of Schoenberg, became a monk at Breitenau, in the diocese of Mainz, lived a humble and devout life and died in the year 1132.

4. **Bl. Frederic**, prior of St. Vaast at Arras, was a count of Verdun, made a gift of all his earthly possessions to the diocese of Verdun and entered the monastery of St. Vannes (Viton) about the year 1000. In his humility he did not shrink from performing the most lowly services in the house. Abbot Richard found no one better qualified to be the prior of St. Vaast than Frederic. After many years of meritorious labor he was summoned to his eternal reward in 1022.

7

1. **St. Tillo**, a monk of Solignac, in the diocese of Limoges, was carried off as an infant by robbers and exposed for sale in the Low Countries, where he was bought by St. Eligius, who baptized him and sent him to Solignac to receive an education. When Eligius had been consecrated bishop of Noyon, Tillo professed as a monk at Solignac and was a model religious. After the death of Eligius (659) he left the monastery and took up his abode as a hermit in the mountainous region of Auvergne, where he spent the remaining forty years of his life in prayer. He expired at the age of ninety years in 700 and enjoyed veneration in several of the eastern provinces of France.

2. **Bl. Vitalis** (de Mortain), founder and abbot of the Cistercian monastery of Savigny, in the former diocese of Coutances, at first was a hermit. While ruling his community, he also devoted himself to the conversion of sinners by preaching and prayer. He died in the choir just as he was about to pronounce the blessing over the lector about 1120.

3. **Bl. Albert**, a Camaldolese hermit of Monte Alceto near Siena, died in 1181 in the odor of sanctity after leading a life in seclusion on Monte Toricelli.

4. **Ven. Anno**, abbot of Micy and of Jumiege, was a lover of poverty and of mortification, refreshing his guests with wine while he and the brethren contented themselves with water. After governing his house, which he had rescued from total ruin, for the space of thirty years, he died in the reputation of sanctity in 973.

Erminold: Mab., Raderus, Stan., Chev., Buch.
Albert: Mab.
Frederic: Mab., Stad.
Tillo: Mab., Stad., But.
Vitalis: Boll., Chev. He is also commemorated on January 6 and September 16. Vita in Ana. Boll. I.I. 355-420.
Albert: Razzi, Stad.
Anno: Mab.

5. **Ven. Louis de Blois**—commonly known as Ludovicus Blosius—abbot of Liessies in Hainault, was a scion of the noble houses of Blois and Chatillon and was born in 1506. The years of his boyhood were spent as a page at the court of the archduke Charles, who afterwards was Emperor Charles V. At the age of fourteen he secured his dismissal and entered the Benedictine monastery at Liessies. After completing his studies at Louvain, he was chosen by the agged abbot of Liessies to assist him in bearing the burdens of his office. Upon the abbot's death two years later, Louis became his successor although but twenty-four years of age. From the very beginning of his religious life—even as a novice—his most ardent wish had been to restore the declining discipline of his house. To accomplish this purpose he wrote the *Speculum Monachorum* which was read to the brethren in the refectory. The wars of 1537 and 1538 interrupted his salutary efforts at reform and compelled him to withdraw to the monastery of Ath. Having returned to Liessies, he tempered the severity of his contemplated reform in many points and secured the approval of Pope Paul III in 1545. No inducement could tempt him to exchange his monastic cell for the episcopal chair of Cambrai. He died in 1566 and left a number of excellent ascetical treatises which are still widely read. Saints Ignatius of Loyola and Francis de Sales warmly recommended his writings.

8 ·

1. **St. Erhard**, bishop at Regensburg and a brother of St. Hidulph, bishop of Trier, was educated at the abbey of St. Emmeram in Regensburg. As bishop he labored zealously for the welfare of the people and founded the monastery of Niedermuenster for nuns. According to one account, he spent some time in the Vosges mountains, where he baptized and restored the eyesight of St. Odilia. He died in the eighth century and was canonized by Pope Leo IX during a visit of that Pontiff to Regensburg in 1052. He is venerated as the patron saint of the diocese of Regensburg, where his feast is celebrated on January 19.

2. **St. Wulsin**, bishop of Sherburne in England, was the first abbot of Westminster abbey, and was promoted to the see of Sherburne by St. Dunstan in 940. He at once installed Benedictine monks in his cathedral chapter, and labored faithfully and unceasingly at the conversion and improvement of the flock committed to his charge. His character was marked by singular modesty and humility; he was averse from all display, as was apparent from his pontifical insignia which were still shown at Sherburne a century after his death. He died in 958 (others say 1001, or 973) exclaiming with the first martyr, St. Stephen: "I see the heavens open and Jesus at the right hand of God."

3. **Bl. Peter Aldobrandini** (surnamed *Igneus* or *Ignitus*), cardinal bishop of Albano, a Vallumbrosan monk, was one of the disciples of St. John Gual-

Blosius: Boll., Kir. Lex., Cath. Enc., Ziegelbauer, George de Blois: A Benedictine of the XVI. Century (tr. by Lady Lovat.)
Erhard: Boll., AA. SS., Stad. Chev. says he was only a Chorepiscopus. Other forms of the name: Erard, Errard, Erchard. Battandier: Ann. Pontif. 1903. 410.
Wulsin: William of Malmesbury. Fleming: Calendar of English Saints. Stan., But., Lingard, Chev. Latin form: Vulsinus.

bertus. His efforts as a preacher were mainly directed against the prevailing vice of simony. When Bishop Peter of Pavia was accused of simony, the zealous monk testified to his guilt by publicly undergoing the ordeal of fire in the city of Florence. Subsequently he was appointed prior at Passiniano and abbot at Ficedo, and in 1073 was created a cardinal and bishop of Albano by Pope Gregory VII. In this capacity he was dispatched on important ecclesiastical business to France and Germany. He died at Florence in 1089.

4. Bl. Thorfinus, a Cistercian monk, was bishop of Hammar in Norway. He was a native of Denmark and a monk of Thosan near Bruges in Flanders. On account of the holiness of his life he was selected to govern the see of Hammar. His fearless defence of the rights of the Church resulted in persecutions, in consequence of which he was compelled to leave his see. He retired to his monastery and died in 1284.

9

1. St. Brithwald, archbishop of Canterbury (692–731), was of noble, if not royal lineage, and was born about the middle of the seventh century; but neither the place nor the exact date of his birth is known. He was abbot of Reculver in the county of Kent and was elected to succeed Theodore of Tarsus in the primatial see of Canterbury. For some time he was opposed to St. Wilfrid of York and even caused him to be deposed from his see, but made amends when the innocence of the latter had been established. After governing his church faithfully in difficult times, he rested from his labors in 731.

2. St. Adrian, abbot of St. Peter's at Canterbury, an African by birth, was abbot of Nerida near Naples and was selected by Pope Vitalian to fill the see of Canterbury. His humility forbade him to accept the honor and he recommended St. Theodore, a learned Greek monk living in Rome. The Pope agreed, but charged Adrian to accompany him as an adviser. While traveling through France, Adrian was detained as a spy by Ebroin, major of the palace of the king of Neustria and Burgundy. Satisfied that his suspicions were groundless, Ebroin permitted him to proceed on his way. Having reached England, he was appointed abbot of St. Peter's, and devoted all his energies to the conversion of the people, the establishment of schools, the introduction of the Roman rite, and the promotion of good discipline in his monastery. After thirty-nine years of unremitting labor he was called to his reward in 710.

3. St. Maurontius, abbot of Glonne (or Florent-le-Vieul), in the former diocese of Anjou, was honored as a saint immediately after his death in 695, and his feast was annually observed. In a vision, St. Hermeland, abbot of a monastery in Brittany, saw his soul borne to heaven by angels.

Peter Ign: Stad., Buch., Chev., Kir. Lex., Cath. Enc.
Thorfinus: Stad., Molanus, Chev.(Thorphin). Gams: Series Epp. Other forms of the name: Torphinus, Trophimus.
Brithwald: Ven. Bede, Stan., But., Dugdale: Monasticon, Chev. Other forms of the name: Bertwald, Berthewald, Brithewald.
Adrian: Ven. Bede, William of Malmesbury, Stan., But., Chev.

10

1. **St. Agatho**, Pope, was, before his elevation to the chair of Peter, a monk in the abbey of St. John the Baptist (or of St. Hermes) at Palermo. He succeeded Pope Domnus in the government of the Church (678) at the time when the heresy of the Monothelites was distressing the East. In a synod held in Rome, St. Wilfrid, who had taken recourse to Pope Agatho after he had been unjustly deposed from the see of York by Archbishop Theodore of Canterbury, was vindicated and restored to his see. This Pope also convoked the Sixth General Council (III of Constantinople), which condemned the Monothelite heresy (680); but he died before the acts of the Council could be submitted for his signature, in 681, at the age of one hundred years. He was remarkable for his affability and charity and wrought so many miracles that he was styled Thaumaturgus. He is venerated in both the Latin and the Greek Church.

2. **St. William** (de Donjeon), a Cistercian and archbishop of Bourges, was of the family of the Counts of Nevers and was born in the castle of Arthel about 1150. For his early education he was indebted to his uncle Peter, archdeacon of Soissons; having successively filled a canonicate in Soissons and Paris, he sought rest for his soul in the Order of Grammont, but did not feel at peace till he had received the Cistercian habit at Pontigny, where he shone by his humility and charity. Both as abbot of Fontaine-Jean and later of Chalis, he edified his brethren by his eminent virtue. In 1200 he was elected archbishop of Bourges, where he labored with much zeal in the eradication of abuses and valiantly defended the liberties of the Church against the aggressions of Philip II., king of France. While preaching against the Albigenses he was prostrated by a fever and died in 1209. He was canonized in 1218. At present his feast is celebrated on the 19th of January in the Cistercian Order, although January 10 is the day of his death.

3. **St. Ithamar**, bishop of Rochester in England, and successor of St. Paulinus both in office and holiness of life, received the crown of his labors in 655.

4. **St. Aldus**, monk of Bobbio and hermit, was one of the glories of the Church in northern Italy in the eighth century. At first he was interred in the chapel of St. Columban, but was later removed to the cathedral.

5. **St. Sethrida**, abbess and virgin, daughter of Anna, king of the East Angles and of St. Hereswida, closed her holy career in the year 670 at Faremoutier-en-Brie in France.

6. **Bl. Benincasa**, the eighth abbot of Cava, near Naples, who is said to have sent one hundred of his monks for the foundation of the abbey of Mon-

Agatho: But., Stad., Kir. Lex., Cath. Enc.
William: Stad.,Buch., Gams, Roman Martyrology. Vita (hitherto unpublished) in Ana. Bolland. III. 271-361.
Ithamar: Ven. Bede, Barrett, Chev., Stan.(June 10).
Aldus: Boll.
Sethrida: Ven. Bede, Fleming, Stan., Chev. Another form of the name: Sethryda.

reale in Sicily, died in 1194, after faithfully ruling his monastery for twenty-four years.

11

1. **St. Taso**, abbot of St. Vincent on the river Voltorno in the former kingdom of Naples, and a brother of St. Tato, was the successor of St. Paldo, first abbot of that monastery. Displeased with his vigorous maintenance of discipline, the monks caused him to be deposed and elected his brother Tato in his stead, a proceeding that was condemned by Pope Gregory II., who inflicted severe canonical punishments upon the insubordinate religious. Taso was restored to office and ruled his house wisely and firmly to the year 729, when he was rewarded for his sufferings with a crown of glory.

2. **St. Antimus**, one of the first abbots of Brantome near Perigord on the Drome, in France, died about the year 795.

3. **St. Tethwius**, monk of Redon in Brittany and disciple of St. Convoyon, was remarkable for his spirit of prayer and mortification. On one occasion, while he ws driving a heavily laden wagon, one of the servants of the monastery fell beneath the wheels and was bruised; the Saint prayed for the injured man, who in a short time recovered from his injuries. During five years Tethwius was afflicted with paralysis and blindness. His death occurred in the year 870.

4. **St. Lohemellus**, one of the first associates of St. Convoyon in the monastery of Redon in Brittany, was distinguished for knowledge, prudence and piety, and his sanctity was attested by miracles. His death falls in the year 870.

5. **Brother Peter** of Coblentz, Cistercian monk of Hemmenrode, by his prayers obtained the gift of meditation, an exercise in which he had experienced discouraging difficulties. One day, when he was beset by violent temptations, he prostrated himself before the crucifix and begged Our Lord to help him in his need; the crucified Savior, says his biographer, extended his arms, drew him to His bosom, and from that moment Peter was no more troubled by the tempter. Desirous of saving souls, he accompanied Bishop Theodore to Livonia, where he preached the Gospel to the pagans. He reaped the twofold reward of a true monk and a zealous missionary and died at Villers in Brabant about the year 1250.

6. In the Cistercian Order, on this day are commemorated all the holy bishops and abbots of that Order.

Benincasa: Tabulae Cavenses, Guillaume: Abbaye de Cava.
Taso: His Life by Autpert, Stad.
Antimus: Mab., Chev. Also called: Antivius.
Tethwius: Mab., Chev. Other forms of the name: Tetwin, Tethwinus.
Lohemell: Mab. Stad. gives him no title.
Peter of Cob.: Henr., Stad.
Cist. Sts.: Henr,

12

1. **St. Victorian,** first abbot of Montaragon near Osca in Spain, was at first a hermit. Being joined by a number of other devout men, he established a religious community, which he ruled as abbot. According to an epitaph composed by the poet Fortunatus he was abbot of Asana for sixty years. After his holy death in 566, his remains were removed from one place to another, till they found a permanent resting place at Montaragon.

2. **St. Benedict Biscop,** abbot of Wearmouth and Jarrow in England, was an Angle of noble birth and possibly of the royal race of the Lindisfari. He was a thane of King Oswy of Northumberland, but left his court at the age of twenty-five and set out on a pilgrimage to Rome. Returning from a second pilgrimage to the tombs of the Apostles, he became a monk at Lerins, where he remained two years. While visiting Rome a third time, he met St. Theodore— who had been appointed archbishop of Canterbury—and St. Adrian and accompanied them to his native land, where he was appointed abbot of the monastery of SS. Peter and Paul at Canterbury. Two years later (671), he laid down the burdens of his office, and made a fifth pilgrimage to Rome, whence he returned with books, pictures and relics. With the generous assistance of King Egfrid he founded the monasteries of Wearmouth and Jarrow, in which he had the monks instructed in ecclesiastical discipline and in the Roman rite and chant. The church of Wearmouth was built by masons brought over from the continent and was probably the first stone church in England. During the three years preceding his death he was afflicted with sickness. When he was aware that the end of his life was approaching, he summoned the brethren to his bedside, gave them his last fatherly exhortation and died after receiving the Holy Viaticum in the year 690.

3. **St. Ailred,** Cistercian abbot of Rievaulx (Rieval), in England, was the son of noble parents and was born in 1109. Attracted by his learning and piety, King David of Scotland selected him to be the master of his household. "His virtue shone with bright lustre in the world—particularly his meekness, which Christ declared to be His favorite virtue and the distinguishing mark of His true disciples."(Butler). The honors showered upon him by both king and courtiers did not, however, make him vain. To the surprise of all, he bade farewell to the king and became a Cistercian monk at Rievaulx, a monastery that had been but recently founded (1132) in the diocese of York. Nine years later he was elected abbot of Revesby, and in the following year, of Rievaulx, the community of which was composed of three hundred monks. His meekness and charity shone here even more brightly than while he mingled with the court. He died in 1166 and was deemed worthy by the General Chapter of 1250 to be counted among the saints of the Cistercian Order.

4. Commemoration of a number of monks of Lindisfarne who perished at the hands of the Danes in 793.

Ben. Biscop: Ven. Bede; also his Life of the Abbots of Wearmouth, translated by Rev. P. Wilcock, Sunderland, Eng. 1818; reprinted 1910. Stan., But., Buch.
Ailred: Le Nain, But., Capgrave, Henr. Other forms of the name: Aelred, Elred.
Monks of Lindisfarne: Alcuin, Henry of Huntingdon.

5. The learned **William** (a S. Theodorico) abbot of St. Thierry, diocese of Rheims, in France, and a native of Liege, was a great admirer of St. Bernard of Clairvaux and followed in his footsteps by resigning his abbey and becoming a Cistercian monk at Ligny, where he spent his life in prayer and austerities till the Lord summoned him to join his brethren in heaven in 1148. He was a distinguished theological writer and was the first to combat the errors of Abelard.

13

1. **St. Servus Dei** (Servio Deo), a Spanish monk, suffered death for the faith at Cordova in the reign of the Caliph Abderrhaman in 852. He suffered martyrdom together with St. Gumesind.

2. **Bl. Berno,** the first abbot of Cluny, was a native of Burgundy, and became a monk at the monastery of St. Martin at Autun. He founded the abbey of Gigny, ruled it as its first abbot and reformed the abbey of Beaume, which was made subject to his jurisdiction in 895. In 910 he was chosen first abbot of the famous monastery of Cluny, which had been founded by Duke William of Aquitaine. When prostrated by the illness that was to be his last, he invited several bishops to his bedside, resigned his office into their hands, expressed his regret that he had governed his community so unworthily and instructed the monks to choose his successor. He died in 926 or 927 and was buried near the altar of St. Benedict in the church of Cluny.

3. **Bl. Stephen,** a monk of Verdun, was abbot of St. Lawrence at Liege. When he had been appointed to that office and had learned that the abbot of St. Lawrence was still living, he refused to accept the dignity and took his place among the monks. Eventually he was elected abbot, ruled his monastery with scrupulous care for thirty-three years, and died in 1061. According to one authority, he was a canon of St. Denis at Liege before he entered the monastery of St. Vannes at Verdun.

4. **Bl. Juetta** (Juta, Ivetta), widow and recluse of Huy in Belgium, was remarkable for her seriousness and fervent piety even as a child. After the death of her husband, she spent eleven years ministering to the sick in the lepers' hospital at Huy, after which she dwelt for thirty-six years as a recluse near the church, lamenting her venial sins, and subjecting her body to many austerities. Blessed with the gift of contemplation and repeatedly favored with ecstatic raptures, she expired in the peace of the Lord in 1228.

5. The two laybrothers, **Benedict Kantwerk** and **Peter Michl,** and Sister **Martha Wansing,** members of the St. Benedict Mission Society of St. Ottilien in Bavaria, were slain at the missionary station of Pugu in East Africa by hostile Arabs in 1889.

Wm. of St. Thierry: Kir. Lex., Cath. Enc., Hurter: Nomenclator.
Servus Dei: Roman Martyrology, Eulogius.
Berno: Mab., Stad., Kir. Lex. ("Clugny").
Stephen: Mab., Stad.
Juetta: Molanus, Stad., Steele: Anchoresses of the West.
Benedict Kantwerk, etc.: S. & M. 1889, 137, 297.

14

1. **St. Peter Urseolus** (Orseoli), doge of Venice and monk at Cuxa, was born at Rivoalto, in the province of Udine, in 928, of noble Venetian parents. In 976 he was chosen to succeed the doge Peter Candiano, but only accepted the office because he believed he might be able to serve his native land. As pious as he was skilful in ruling the republic, he was a zealous patron of churches and monasteries. The doge's palace and the church of San Marco were rebuilt at his expense, and he bestowed large sums of money upon the poor and the sufferers from a fire that had devastated the city. Induced by the abbot Guarinus of Cuxa in Catalonia, he left Venice secretly (987), entered that monastery and edified all by his humility, fervor in prayer and charity. He that once had ruled a powerful commonwealth was now appointed to the office of sacristan, in which capacity he served humbly and faithfully. For several years previous to his death he was permitted to live as a recluse, devoting himself to penitential practices and prayer. After nineteen years spent in religious life, he closed his eyes in death on January 10, 987. With the approval of the bishop of Elne he was venerated as a saint as early as the eleventh century, and this veneration was sanctioned by Pope Clement (1731), who also appointed the 14th day of January for his feast.

2. **St. Guarinus**, (Garinus, Varinus), Cistercian monk at Hautcombe (Altacumba) in Savoy, spent several years in a solitude; but feeling called to renew the fervor of monks, he entered the monastery of Hautcombe and induced the brethren to adopt the reform of St. Bernard of Clairvaux. In 1138 he was chosen bishop of Sitten (Sedunum) in southern Switzerland, but declined the election. Pope Innocent II., however, commanded him to accept the office and he complied. St. Bernard, in a letter, praised Guarinus for submitting and consoled the monks of Hautcombe, who regretted the loss of their spiritual father. As bishop, Guarinus with his clergy boldly combatted certain ecclesiastical abuses and reformed the morals of the people. He labored devotedly in the service of his Heavenly Master and yielded up his holy soul into the hands of his Creator in 1140.

3. **Bl. Theodemar**, at one time chaplain to the empress Agnes, the wife of Emperor Henry III., sought rest for his soul in the abbey of Monte Cassino under the rule of Abbot Oderisius. He was distinguished for his devotion to Our Blessed Lady, experienced many heavenly consolations, and died about the year 1090.

4. At Troyes in France, the Military Order of **Knights Templars**, with the Cistercian Rule, was approved on this day. The Order was suppressed in 1312 by Pope Clement V.

15

1. **St. Maurus**, a disciple of St. Benedict, was born in 510 and at the age of twelve years was entrusted by his father Equitius to the pious care of our

---

Peter Urseolus: Mab., Roman Martyrology (Jan. 10)., Kir. Lex., Cath. Enc., S. & M. 1901. 71,etc.
Guarinus: St. Bernard, Stad., Buch., Chev.
Theodemar: A. Wion, Mab.
Knights Temp.: Bullar. Rom., Kir. Lex., Cath. Enc.

Holy Father St. Benedict. Recognizing the high qualities of his disciple, St. Benedict reposed great confidence in him and was supported by him in the government of the twelve houses established about Subjaco. It was here that on one occasion, as St. Gregory relates (L. Dial. II), God testified to the eminent sanctity of his servant. The youthful Placidus, while drawing water, had fallen into the stream and was on the point of drowning, when Maurus, in obedience to the command of St. Benedict, fearlessly walked out upon the waters and saved the child. When St. Benedict left Subjaco for Monte Cassino, St. Maurus was among those that accompanied him. Within a few years of its establishment Monte Cassino was so well known, that envoys of the bishop of Le Mans are said to have requested the holy Founder to send some of his monks to that diocese. St. Maurus, it is said, was chosen to lead the little company of brethren that was to bear the light of the Holy Rule into Gaul, 543. Upon his arrival at Le Mans, he learned that the bishop at whose invitation the monks had come was dead and that his successor was not willing to receive them. Accordingly he left that city and passed over into Anjou, where Florus, a high official at the royal court, granted him grounds for the monastery of Glanfeuil, which in later times was known as S. Maur-sur-Loire. When the burden of advancing age prevented him from extending his active solicitude to details in the government of the monastery, he chose Bertulf, the son of Florus. as his assistant, (581), and from this time lived in a cell near the church, constantly intent upon preparing himself for death. An epidemic of some kind depopulated the country, and it is said that within five months one hundred and sixteen monks of Glanfeuil were carried off by the disease, so that only twenty-four remained. St. Maurus himself died on January 15, 583, at the age of seventy-two years.

2. **St. Bonitus** (Bonus, St. Bonet), bishop of Clermont in Auvergne, was born of noble parents in 624 and was chancellor under King Sigbert of Austrasia. In 680 he was appointed governor of Provence and administered that office with great wisdom, diligence and justice. Bishop Avitus of Clermont at the point of death recommended his brother Bonitus as his successor and Bonitus was consecrated bishop. Doubts regarding the regularity of his elevation to the see of Clermont induced him to resign the see and to exchange his episcopal robes for the habit of a monk at Manlieu. He died four years later, in the year 710, at Lyons.

3. **St. Ceolwulf**, first king of Northumbria, devoutly served God even while he governed his people, and found great delight in the reading of edifying books. Venerable Bede dedicated his Ecclesiastical History to this pious monarch. After ruling Northumbria for the space of eight years, he renounced the throne in favor of Edbert, became a monk at Lindisfarne and faithfully served the King of Kings to the day of his death in 760.

Maurus: St. Gregory the Great: Dialog. l. II. Mab., Stad., But., Cath. Enc. As to his canonization, see Battandier: Ann. Pontif. 1903, 409.
Bonitus: Mab., But., Chev., Buch.
Ceolwulf: William of Malmesbury, Matthew of Westminster, Stad., Lingard, Chev., Buch.

16

1. St. Furseus (Fursy), abbot of Lagny, in the diocese of Paris, was of noble descent and born in Ireland, where he ruled a monastery for some time, but on account of political disorders in his native land passed over to England with his brothers, Foilan and Ultan, and founded the monastery of Knobbersbury in Suffolk, entrusting its government to his brother Foilan, while he with Ultan retired into a solitude. Failing to find peace there, he crossed over to France, where, with support from king Clovis II and his majordomo Erconwald, he founded the monastery of Lagny near Paris (641). While conducting the building of a monastery at Perronne he died at Froheins in the diocese of Amiens in 650. Erconwald brought the remains to Perronne and built a basilica in which they were entombed. St. Furseus was selected as patron saint of Perronne.

2. St. Honoratus, second abbot of Subjaco, died about the year 596. In the introduction to the life of St. Benedict by St. Gregory the Great, Honoratus is mentioned as one of those from whom information was obtained regarding St. Benedict. ("Honorato etiam, qui nunc adhuc cellae ejus (S. Ben.) in qua conversatus fuerat, praeest.").

3. The devout Joanna was a laysister in a Camaldolese monastery at Bagnorea in Italy and died in the reputation of sanctity in 1105. Her veneration was approved by Pius VII on April 12, 1823.

4. Sugerius (Suger), abbot of St. Denys near Paris since 1122, was at first a monk of that monastery and was chosen its abbot while he was in Italy. He was appointed prime minister by King Louis VI and during the absence of Louis VII in the East was regent of the realm. Religious discipline suffered in his monastery during this period, since secular persons from all parts flocked to St. Denys to consult with the abbot, who, by force of circumstances, was more of a statesman than an ecclesiastic. He appears also to have affected considerable magnificence in his surroundings, for St. Bernard rebuked him in unmistakable terms, whereupon Suger confined himself to his abbey and labored zealously to restore good order. His efforts in this direction were so successful that even the Cistercians admitted: "He puts us all to shame!" When he felt the hour of his dissolution approaching, he ordered the brethren to carry him to the chapter hall, where he implored them to forgive him for all his shortcomings. At peace with the world and with God, he died in 1152.

17

1. St. Sulpitius, surnamed Pius, was a native of Bourges, in France, and even as a child gave promise of his future greatness by spending hours of prayer in churches by night and by his charity to the poor. This

---

Furseus: Ven. Bede, Mab., Buch., But., Chev.
Honoratus: St. Gregory the Great: Dialog. l. II.
Joanna: Razzi, Ferrari.
Suger: Stad., Cath. Enc., Kir. Lex. Gervaise: Life of Suger.

unusual conduct on the part of a page at the royal court—for such was Sulpitius at the time—moved the archbishop of Bourges to enroll him among
the clergy. King Clothair II appointed him superior of his court chaplains
(abbas castrensis). In 624 he was elected archbishop of Bourges. He made
no change in his accustomed manner of life, which resembled that of a monk
rather than of a prelate, allowed no silver plate on his table and divided his
time between prayer and the discharge of his episcopal duties. He founded
several monasteries, one of which, at the confluence of the Eure and the Au-
ron, he is said to have governed as abbot. Towards the end of his mortal career he sought this haven of calm and expired in 644. In later centuries this
house was known as St. Sulpice and belonged to the Congregation of St. Maur.
He is invoked for protection against harm by fires.

2. **S. Brithwold** (Brithwald), abbot of Glastonbury, was promoted to
the episcopal see of Wilton in England in 996, and discharged the duties of
his office with apostolic zeal to the year 1045, when he entered into the joy of
the Lord.

3. **St. Richmirus** (Ricmir, Rigomer), a native of the diocese of Tours,
was ordained a priest by Bishop Bilgert of Mans and permitted to establish
a monastery near Cour de Manche, but later removed to a more favorable spot
on the river Gundrid, where he founded another house in which he ruled over
forty monks. He set his brethren an example of sincere humility, shared with
them labor in the fields and was content with the coarsest food. Adorned with
the gift of miracles, he died in the year 710. His monastery was suppressed
under bishop Gauziolenus.

4. **SS. Anthony, Merulus** and **John**, three monks of St. Andrew's in
Rome, died in the course of the sixth century, distinguished for lives of extraordinary virtue.

5. **St. Mildgytha** (Milgith) was the daughter of St. Ermenburga and of
the royal race of Mercia in England. Like her sisters, St. Milburga and St.
Mildred, she was favored with a vocation to the religious life and the place
chosen for her retreat was a Northumbrian monastery, the name of which is not
known. An ancient record merely says: "St. Milgith lies in Northumbria,
where her miraculous powers were often exhibited and still are." The year
of her holy death is said to be 676.

18

1. **St. Diey** (Deicolus, Deicola), abbot, left Ireland with St. Columban
and went first to the country of the East Angles and afterwards to Luxeuil,
in France. When Columban was exiled from the latter country, Diey would
have gone with him but was prevented by infirmity and old age. Diey now

---

Sulpitius: Mab., Roman Martyrology, But.
Brithwold: William of Malmesbury, Stan. (Jan. 22), Chev. Another form of the name Bright-
    wold.
John, Anthony, Merulus: Mab.
Mildgytha: Stad., Stan., But. (Milgithe), Dunbar, Fleming, Eng. Mart.

took up his abode at Lure, where a certain Werfar made him a gift of a chapel and a parcel of land, on which, in the course of time, he erected a monastery for the devout brethren who gathered about him to live under his rule (616). When he was no longer able to perform the duties of his office, he counselled the brethren to elect his disciple Columbin, who had come with him from Ireland, as their abbot; lived for some time in a cell close to the monastery and there spent the remainder of his days. On his deathbed he exhorted the brethren to continue in harmony and fraternal charity and died in the arms of Columbin in 625.

2. St. Anthony, a monk of Monte Cassino, was one of the disciples of St. Maurus and is said to have accompanied the latter to France. It is stated in the chronicles of Monte Cassino that, in 1119, Pope Calixtus II visited the monastery of Glanfeuil and at the request of the Cassinese monks in his retinue and of the abbot of Glanfeuil, consecrated the abbey church and transferred to it the remains of SS. Anthony and Constantinian, the associates of St. Maurus on his journey to France shortly before the death of our Holy Father St. Benedict.

3. Bl. Beatrice, daughter of the margrave Azo IX of Este in northern Italy, abandoned the splendors of her father's court and took vows as a nun at the monastery of St. Anthony in Ferrara in 1254. Here she led a holy life in humility and simplicity of heart, till she was bidden to enter the palace of her heavenly Spouse in the year 1262. Remarkable cures were obtained through her intercession. Her veneration was approved in 1774.—She is not identical with the Beatrice whose memory is celebrated on May 10.

4. Establishment of the Order of **Knights of Montesia** in Spain by King James of Aragon in 1317. The first members were survivors of the suppressed Order of Knights Templars. The Order of Montesia was approved by Pope John XXII.

19

1. St. Blaithmaic, abbot of Hy or Iona, an island off the southwestern coast of Scotland, was of noble Irish descent and secretly fled to a monastery to consecrate himself entirely to the service of God. Resisting all efforts of his parents to remove him, he remained and was chosen abbot. Burning with a desire for martyrdom, he made several attempts to visit strange lands, but was always prevented by his monks. Finally, however, he contrived to escape with several disciples and made his way to Iona, "the sacred isle of Columba". Danish pirates made an incursion into the island, and found Blaithmaic at the altar, vested in his priestly robes, for he had just celebrated Holy Mass. Upon his refusal to reveal where the shrine with the relics of St. Columba was concealed, they fell upon him and hewed him into pieces with their swords in 823.

Dicy: Mab., Chifflet, But., O'Hanlon, Roman Martyrology. Other forms of the name: Deicola, Deel, Diel, Dichuil.
Anthony: Chron. Cass. IV. 64, Stad.
Beatrice: Roman Martyrology, Stad., Buch.
Knights of Montesia: Henr., Cath. Enc.
Blaithmaic: Walafrid Strabo, O'Hanlon. Other forms of the name: Blaitmaic, Blatmac.

2. **St. Wulstan,** (Wolstan or Ulfstan), bishop of Worcester, in England, a native of Warwickshire, was reared in the practices of Christian piety. Once when he was tormented by a temptation suggested by the sight of a lewd dance, he threw himself into a thorny thicket and bewailed his weakness for having even for a moment found pleasure in seeing the performance. Turning away from the world, he entered upon a course of study at the monastery of Evesham and completed it at Peterborough. Both his father and mother took the religious habit, while Wulstan was received among the clergy of Worcester. The bishop ordained him and offered him a prosperous parish near the city; but Wulstan felt called to the monastic life and entered the monastery at Worcester, where he was remarkable for the innocence and sanctity of his life. In 1062, when Bishop Alred was transferred to York, Wulstan was selected to succeed him in the see of Worcester. He governed his diocese with great prudence, although he was not possessed of great learning. Although William the Conqueror (1066) deprived the English clergy of the positions of honor which they held, Wulstan succeeded in maintaining himself in the see of Worcester. After ruling his people for thirty-two years, he died in 1095 and was canonized in 1203.

3. **St. Lomer,** (Laudomarus or Launomarus), abbot, in his boyhood kept his father's sheep, at the same time pursuing studies under the direction of a certain priest. He was ordained a priest and made a canon of the church of Chartres. After some years he retired into a neighboring forest to lead the life of a hermit; but when he found himself surrounded by a number of eager disciples, he built the monastery of Corbion (St. Laumer or Moutier-au-Perche) about 575. Far famed for his spirit of prayer and the gift of miracles, he entered through the gates of eternity in 593 at Chartres, in the house of the bishop.

20

1. **St. Maurus,** bishop of Cesena, in Italy, was elevated to the episcopal dignity for his exemplary life as a religious. Even while a bishop he would retire to a cell in the neighboring forest of Spaziano to spend Lent there in prayer and tears. He died November 21, 946 and was buried in his beloved solitude.

2. **Bl. Benedict,** a Vallumbrosan hermit at St. Lawrence in the diocese of Fiesole, Italy, attained such a high degree of perfection that he was permitted to live as a hermit. During the last year of his life, he appeared in the monastery as usual to celebrate the feast of Christmas with the brethren, and exhorted them to remain faithful to the Lord, whom they had promised to serve. Having returned to his cell, he knelt in prayer and expired in the year 1107.

3. **Ven. Daniel,** abbot of the Cistercian monastery of Cambron in Hainault, received his religious training from St. Bernard, by whom he was also

Wulstan: William of Malmesbury, Florence of Worcester, Capgrave, Stan., But. Battandier:
    Ann. Pontif. 1903, 413.
Lomer: Mab., But.
Maurus: St. Peter Damian, Roman Martyrology, Stad.
Benedict: Locatelli in Boll. AA. SS.

appointed abbot. So unworthy did he consider himself of the office, that he would not have the brethren call him abbot. He observed moderation in all things and is said never to have satiated himself at a meal and to have partaken sparingly even of bread. The year of his death is 1191.

4. **Christian**, second abbot of the Scots abbey at Wuerzburg, passed to his eternal reward in 1179, leaving behind him the reputation of a holy life.

21

1. **St. Meinrad**, hermit, was born 805 in Wuerttemberg, was educated at the abbey of Reichenau and received the order of holy priesthood. He put on the religious habit and spent some years at Reichenau, where his kinsman, Erlebald, was abbot; then presided over a school at Oberbollingen on Lake Zurich, and finally resolved to lead an eremitical life on Mount Etzel near the present monastery of Einsiedeln in Switzerland. Seven years he dwelt in solitude, occupied with fasts, prayer and contemplation. His hermitage was soon frequented by numbers of the faithful, who came to venerate a miraculous image of the Blessed Virgin which had been given to him by Abbess Hildegarde of Zurich. This induced him to penetrate farther into the forest to the spot where the abbey of Einsiedeln now stands. Here he built a chapel, in which the image was exposed for the veneration of the pilgrims. He had been living here for twenty-six years, when he was slain by robbers who were aware that the visitors to the shrine had made offerings in token of gratitude for favors received. The year of his death is variously given — about 863. He was canonized by Benedict IX in 1039.

2. **St. Maccallan** (Maccallin), abbot of St. Michael at Thierache, in Belgium, was a native of Ireland who crossed over to the continent and became a monk at Vasour (or at Gorze) in the diocese of Namur. He was elected abbot of Vasour, was installed by the bishop of Metz and blessed by the bishop of Liege. The abbey of St. Michael was entrusted to his supervision and the bishop of Laon invited him to reform that of St. Vincent in his episcopal city. Conspicuous for his zeal and holiness of life he was called to render an account of his faithful stewardship in 978.

3. **St. Ermenburga**, widow and abbess, was the daughter of Prince Ermenred of the royal race of Kent. King Egbert had caused her two brothers, Ethelred and Ethelbright, to be assassinated and made amends in a measure by granting her a considerable parcel of land on the isle of Thanet, where she established the monastery of Minster, or Minstrey. She was its first abbess and died about 670.

Daniel: Henr.
Christian: Stad., Ben. Annals.
Meinrad: Herman Contractus, Trithemius, Burgener.
Maccallan: Frodoard, O'Hanlon. Other forms of the name: Malkalen, Makkalen.
Ermenburga: William of Malmesbury, Fleming, Stad., Chev., Stan. on Nov. 19 calls her St.
    Domniva.

4. **Ven. Alban** (Bartholomew) Roe, a native of Suffolk in England, was converted to the Catholic faith through a visit to a prisoner at St. Alban's, studied at the English College at Douai, professed at the monastery of Dieulward in 1612 and after his ordination went to the English mission in 1615. He labored with great courage and success until he was arrested and banished. His zeal, however, brought him back to England, where he was again arrested in 1625 and kept in prison, with slight interruptions, for seventeen years. The persecuting Parliament tried and condemned him for being a priest, and he was executed at Tyburn the day after the sentence had been pronounced, on January 21, 1641. His companion in martyrdom was Thomas Green, who was also a priest. They were drawn on the same hurdle to the place of execution; on the way they heard each other's confession and they were hanged simultaneously on the same gibbet amidst demonstrations of popular sympathy.

5. **Michael**, Camaldolese hermit at Florence, was the first to use the form of prayer called *Corona Domini*, * and closed his pious life about 1552.

6. The celebrated **Congregation of St. Maur** was approved on this day by Pope Urban VIII in 1627. Didier de la Cour had established the Congregation of St. Vannes in Lorraine in 1601 and a number of monasteries in France accepted his reform. Political considerations moved the General Chapter of 1618 to authorize the French houses to effect a separate organization, which became known as the Congregation of St. Maur and rendered valuable services by the literary labor of its monks down to the time of the French Revolution, when all its houses were suppressed. The modern Congregation of France considers itself the legitimate successor of the Congregation of St. Maur, which gave the Church and letters such men as Mabillon, d'Achery, Martene, Montfaucon and many others.

22

1. **St. Dominic**, abbot at Sora in the former kingdom of Naples, was born at Foligno and during his childhood was remarkable for his sedate behavior. He received a careful education, was ordained a priest and left his native town never to return. First he entered a monastery in the Sabine country, but was permitted to live as a hermit in a cavern at some distance from the house. Margrave Hubert prevailed upon him to establish a monastery at Scandriglia in Umbria. When this work was accomplished, Dominic founded the monastery of St. Peter de Lacu in the territory of the lords of Valva, and another at Sangro, where he also engaged in missionary work among the people in the neighborhood. One of his converts granted him grounds for a monastery near Sora. Here the Saint spent the last years of his life and calmly expired at the age of eighty years in 1031. He was invoked for protection against harm from storms, fevers and poisonous serpents.

Alban Roe: Stan., Challoner: Missionary Priests, Gillow: Bibliog. Dict. of Eng. Cath. vol. V., Cath. Enc.
Michael: Stad., Razzi.
*The *Corona Domini* was a kind of rosary, consisting of 33 Paters in honor of the 33 years of Our Lord's earthly life, and of 5 Aves in honor of the Five Wounds (Stadler).
Dominic: Cardinal Alberic in Mab., Boll., Stad. Vita (hitherto unpublished) in Ana. Bolland. I. 279-322.

2.   Bl. Walter, baron of Bierbeke, a Cistercian monk of Hemmenrode in Brabant, was a soldier before he put on the cowl of a monk.   An experience at a tournament prompted him to abandon a soldier's life and devote himself to the service of God.   He cherished a deep veneration for the Blessed Virgin, in whose honor he fasted every Friday and on every vigil of a feast of Our Lady.   To ensure his salvation he became a monk at Hemmenrode, where, on account of his cheerfulness and piety, he was given charge of the guests' house. He is said to have died at Villers in 1222.

23

1.   St. Ildephonse, bishop of Toledo in Spain, entered the monastery of Agali in that city.   His unusual gifts were discovered by Bishop Eugene, who sent him to Seville to be educated under the eyes of the archbishop, St. Isidore.   While still a deacon he was chosen abbot of Agali.   Being skilled in music he composed two Masses in honor of SS. Cosmas and Damian.   His character was above reproach and his eloquence of the highest order, so that, after the death of Bishop Eugene, he was chosen to succeed him in the see of Toledo.   He had a singular devotion to the Blessed Virgin and to St. Leocadia, the patron saint of his diocese.   Among his writings is a treatise on the perpetual virginity of the Blessed Virgin.   St. Ildephonse died in 667.

2.   St. Barnard, bishop of Vienne in France, was born at Lyons, received an excellent education, and was for some time at the court of Charlemagne, where he exercised a beneficial influence by his exemplary life. In deference to the wishes of his parents he married.   At the death of his parents he inherited their possessions and applied these to the foundation of the monastery of Ambournay, where, with the consent of his wife, he became a religious.   Although he was the founder of the house, he declined every distinction and took his rank among the brethren.   In 817 he was elected bishop of Vienne, in which capacity he befriended sinners and the poor, who had access to him at all times.   For reasons that are not known, he sided with the sons of Emperor Louis against their father, a mistake which he later bitterly regretted.   Whenever he sought for seclusion, he repaired to the monastery of Romans, which he had founded, to refresh himself in prayer and meditation.   After ruling his church for thirty-two years he withdrew to that monastery, where he died, lying on a penitential robe, in 843, at the age of sixty-four years.   On his death-bed he heard a voice which said: "Come, thou art expected."   His veneration was approved by the Holy See on December 1, 1903.

3.   Alphonse of Burgos, a monk of Montserrat in Catalonia, had been a prominent member of the court of emperor Charles V., before he became a religious.   After a life spent in faithful observance of the Holy Rule, he died in the odor of sanctity in 1524.

Walter: Caesarius of Heisterbach, Guido of Clairvaux, Stad.("Gualterius").

Ildephonse: Mab., But., Cath. Enc., Kir. Lex. calls the monastery Agli.

Barnard: Mab., Breviary of Vienne, Ana. Boll. XI. 402-415, Acta S. Sedis, XXXVI. 424.
    Bernard is another form of the name.

Alphonse: Hist. of Montserrat, Stad.

24

1. **St. Bertram,** abbot of St. Quentin in Picardy, was a monk of Luxeuil, and lived under the wise spiritual guidance of St. Eustasius. When St. Audomar had been consecrated bishop of Terrouane, Abbot Walbert of Luxeuil sent the three monks, Bertram, Bertin and Mummolin, to assist him in his labors. God blessed their toil with abundant success. After some time they settled on the spot on which the abbey of St. Omer subsequently was built, and organized a monastic community which rapidly grew in numbers. With great difficulty they succeeded in founding the monastery of Sithiu, of which Bertin (Sept. 5) was appointed the first abbot. In 659 Mummolin was elected bishop of Noyon and Tournay, and appointed Bertram abbot of St. Quentin. Bertram died about the year 680.

2. **Bl. Macarius,** first abbot of the Scots monastery at Wuerzburg, was a native of Ireland, and had at an early age entered the Scots monastery at Regensburg. According to Trithemius, Bishop Embrico of Wuerzburg, at the suggestion of an Irish monk named Christian, abbot of St. James' Scots monastery at Regensburg, founded a monastery for Irish monks in his episcopal city, and Macarius was appointed the first abbot. He is said to have been well versed in the divine law and to have been renowned even in Ireland for his learning. Always cheerful, ever on his guard against anything that might soil the purity of his heart, he lived like an angel among mortals and died a holy death in 1153. Trithemius records the legend that angels sang sweet melodies at the hour of his death.

3. **Bl. Felix** (O'Dullany), bishop of Ossory in Ireland, was a monk of the Cistercian abbey of Jerpoint (Geriponte) in the same country. Both as monk and bishop he was given to prayer and mortifications. The year of his death is uncertain, ranging between 1172 and 1202.

4. **Arno,** archbishop of Salzburg, was abbot of St. Peter's in that city before he was raised to the see of St. Rupert (785). Duke Thassilo II employed him in several diplomatic missions to the court of Charlemagne. His principal merit is the apostolic zeal with which he personally and with the support of others labored for the conversion of the Carinthians, Slavonians and Hungarians. In recognition of his services, Charlemagne secured the archiepiscopal pallium for him from Pope Leo III. Having ruled his diocese for thirty-six years, he slept in the peace of the Lord in 821.

25

1. **St. Praejectus,** bishop of Clermont in Auvergne, was educated by St. Genesius, archdeacon of Clermont, and presided over the parish of Issoire.

Bertram: Mab., Stad., Chev. Other forms of the name: Ebertramus, Ebertrannus, Bertrand, Bertramnus.
Macarius: Ben. Annals, Ranbeck, Irish Eccl. Record, Jan. 1895, Chev. Buch.
Felix: Henr., O'Hanlon, Annals of Kilkenny.
Arno: Chron. of Salzburg, Stad., Kir. Lex., Chev. Also called Arn.

In 666 he was elected bishop. Not only did he edify his people by his virtues, but he built monasteries, numerous churches and hospitals in his diocese. While on his way to the court of Childeric II., he met the Abbot Amarinus of Doroang, whom he persuaded to accompany him. On their return they were attacked by assassins who first slew Amarin, believing him to be the bishop, and after discovering their error, also took the life of Praejectus, in the year 674.

2. **St. Poppo**, abbot of Stablo near Liege in Belgium, laid down the arms with which he had served his earthly master and resolved to devote himself to the service of God. After making pilgrimages to several holy places, he became a monk at St. Thierry near Rheims, and was regarded by his brethren as a model of humility and of every other virtue that should adorn the true religious. He was successively steward and prior at St. Vaast near Arras, abbot of St. Vannes, of Beaulieu, and finally of the two abbeys of Stablo and Malmedy, which were always ruled by one abbot. Preferring the monastic life to distinguished positions either in Church or State, he declined the nomination to the see of Strassburg. He was selected to restore discipline in the monasteries at Trier and Marchiennes, in the latter of which he died in 1048. The remains were entombed at Stablo.

3. **Bl. Joel**, abbot of Pulsano near Monte San Angelo in the former kingdom of Naples, ruled his abbey for thirty-three years and died about 1190. His body lies in the abbey church of Pulsano, where he has been venerated ever since his death.

4. **Bl. Conhojarn**, who was remarkable for his love of prayer and for miracles wrought at his intercession, died as a monk of Redone in Brittany about 868.

5. **Bl. Adelviva**, the mother of St. Poppo of Stablo, withdrew from the world after the death of her husband and joined a community of nuns at Verdun, where she died about the year 1000.

6. **Ven. Agrinus** was for a short time bishop of Langres, but resigned his see and became a monk at St. Benigne in Dijon, where he died two years later, in 913.

7. **Dida**, abbess of St. Peter's at Lyons, was instructed in a vision by St. Bonitus, bishop of Clermont, to procure the translation of his remains from Lyons to Clermont, and died in the eighth century.

Praejectus: Mab., But., Buch. Another form of the name is Projectus. Ana. Boll. II. 239-242.
Poppo: Mab., But., Stad., Chev., Buch.
Joel: Stad. calls him "Saint".
Conhojarn: Mab. Migne calls him Saint and gives 888 as the date of his death.
Adelviva: Martyrol. Gallicanum, Dunbar, Stad.
Agrinus: Mab., Stad. Another form of the name is Argrinus.
Dida: Suppl. to Gallican Martyrology.

26

1. **St. Theorigitha**, virgin and nun at Barking, England, suffered much from ailments during nine years, but bore the affliction patiently in view of the reward held out to those imitating the patience of the greatest of all sufferers, who died that all men might live. Consoled and strengthened by heavenly delights, she bade farewell to the things of time and entered into the joys of eternal life about 710.

2. **St. Alberic**, abbot and one the founders of Citeaux, was one of the principal pupils of St. Robert, by whom also he was appointed prior of Molesme. When many of the monks grew restive under the strict rule of Robert, and the latter retired to found Citeaux, he was accompanied by Alberic. Robert was shortly after recalled to Molesme, and Alberic was elected abbot of Citeaux. It was under this abbot that the Cistercians, as the new Order was called, adopted the white habit in token of their special devotion to the Blessed Virgin Mary, to whom they also dedicated all their churches. On his death-bed Alberic began to recite the litany and expired while saying the words: "Holy Mary, pray for us." The year of his death is 1107.

3. At Wittow on the Island of Ruegen in the Baltic Sea a number of **Cistercian nuns** were slain by pagan invaders and received the twofold crown of virginity and of martyrdom in the fourteenth century.

4. **Bl. Hazeka** lived as a recluse near the monastery of Sichem or Sittichenbach in Thuringia, wearing the garb of the Order for thirty-six years under the direction of the Cistercian monks and sanctifying her life by work and prayer. She died in 1261, was buried in the monastery of Sichem and enjoyed almost universal veneration after her death.

27

1. **St. Theodoric**, bishop of Orleans, was born at Chateau-Thierry of distinguished parents and educated in the monastery of Pierre-le-Vif, of which his uncle, Raynald, was abbot. It appears that he was already a monk and a priest when King Robert, in recognition of his virtue and merit, summoned him to his court, admitted him to his councils and nominated him bishop of Orleans. This promotion caused some dissatisfaction, which led to disorderly scenes at his consecration in 1016. He was charged with a number of misdeeds, of which he was acquitted in an investigation conducted by Archbishop Fulbert of Chartres. A cleric, by the name of Odalric, hired a band of assassins who made an unsuccessful attack upon Theodoric's life. The bishop's only act of revenge was a generous Christian pardon. In the discharge of his duties he called a council to combat the errors of the heretics who were seriously menacing the faith of his people. Never for a moment forgetful of his monastic

Theorigitha: Ven. Bede, Matthew of Westminster, Stan. Another form of the name is Theoritgida.
Alberic: Sigebert of Gemblours, Henr., Buch., Chev., Cist. Chronik XV (1903).
Nuns at Wittow: Henr.
Hazeka: Boll., Stad. Other forms: Haseka, Haseque.

vows, he frequently betook himself to the monastery of St. Pierre-le-Vif near Sens to gather new strength for his arduous day's work. During his last visit, while he was at prayer in the church on the feast of St. Sebastian, he heard a voice in a vision, saying: "Fear not, Theodoric, for a mansion is prepared for thee in Heaven, where St. Sebastian abides in triumph." He was on his way to Rome when he was overtaken by death in the year 1022 at Tonnerre, where he was buried in the church of St. Michael.

2. **St. Emmerius**, abbot of Bannoles in Catalonia, was a native of France. Without informing his aged parents of his intentions, he left home secretly with a companion, Patricus, to live in a solitude. A great prince, probably Charlemagne, was making his way through France on a warlike expedition against the Saracens and invited Emmerius to accompany his forces. Upon his return, Emmerius built a monastery at Bannoles, where he directed an exemplary community of monks. His only nourishment was bread and water, and his charity to the poor knew no bounds. After some time his mother Candida joined him and lived in a small cell near the monastery to the time of her death. The year of his holy death is unknown (8th or 9th century); his body was interred in the church dedicated to the Blessed Virgin and St. Stephen.

3. **Bruno**, a Cistercian monk, for many years confessor to the nuns of St. Antoine de Champs at Paris, was a pronounced enemy of idleness and useless conversation. He died in 1227, while returning from a pilgrimage to the Holy Land. According to the Cistercian Martyrology, he died in Greece, whither he had gone as a missionary. Miracles wrought at his tomb attested his sanctity.

28

1. **St. Amadeus**, at first Cistercian abbot of Hautcombe, was chosen to govern the episcopal see of Lausanne in Switzerland and shone among his contemporaries by his learning, the holiness of his life and particularly by his devotion to the Blessed Mother of God. He died September 27, 1159, but his memory is celebrated on the present day. Pope Clement XI approved his veneration in the Cistercian Order in 1710. At the request of the Bishop of Grenoble, the veneration of St. Amadeus was approved in that diocese by Pope Pius X on December 9, 1903.

2. **Richard**, Cistercian abbot of Vaucelles near Cambray, was a native of England and was elected abbot in 1152. His biographers say that he was a prudent, intelligent man, whose countenance revealed the peace and joy prevailing in his heart. In his intercourse with all men he was kind and unassuming. As abbot he prudently combined severity with mildness, and always maintained admirable discipline. Under his rule, the monastery prospered

---

Theodoric: Mab., Chev., Buch. French form of the name: Thierry.
Emmerius: Boll., Chev.
Bruno: Thomas of Chantimpre, Seguin.
Amadeus: Cist. Suppl. to the Roman Martyrology, Chev., Acta S. Sedis XXXVI. 424.

both materially and spiritually. He died in 1160; in view of the miracles reported at his tomb, Pope Alexander III permitted his remains to be exposed for public veneration in 1179.

3. **Boso**, a monk of Clairvaux, was one of the earliest disciples of St. Bernard. In religion he found that peace of heart which neither prosperity nor adversity can destroy. Although bent by age and enfeebled by austerities, he claimed no relaxation from the rigors of the Rule and scrupulously employed every moment of time. At the hour of his dissolution, his features were overcast with a radiance in which all recognized a sign of his approaching happiness. He died towards the close of the twelfth century.

29

1. **Pope Gelasius II** (1118-1119), who as John Cajetanus, so called either because Gaeta was his native city or because he was descended from the family of the Gaetani, was a professed monk of Monte Cassino. On account of his learning and familiarity with the Latin language, Pope Urban II created him a cardinal and chancellor of the Holy See. While this Pope was besieged on an island in the Tiber by adherents of the anti-pope Guibert, Cardinal John remained by the side of the lawful Pontiff. He was one of the trusted advisers of Pope Pascal II and defended him against the attacks of certain overzealous prelates who charged him with heresy for signing a document which gave the emperor control of papal and episcopal elections. After the death of Pope Pascal, the cardinals, fearing that Emperor Henry V would force his candidate upon them, secretly assembled in Rome, and elected the chancellor, Cardinal John, to fill the chair of Peter. No protest on his part availed against the unanimity of the Sacred College. When the news of the election had spread in the city, a number of imperialists under the leadership of Cincio Frangipani forced their way into the monastery where the election had taken place, laid violent hands upon the new Pope, threw him to the ground, stamped upon him and placed him in confinement, from which he was delivered by the people. Despite the fact that the emperor besieged Rome, Gelasius escaped and took up his abode at Gaeta, where he was ordained priest and received episcopal consecration. His first public act was to excommunicate Henry V and the anti-pope Gregory (Maurice Burdinus). Another attempt to take possession of his person was made by the Frangipani, whereupon Gelasius fled to France, was welcomed at Cluny and there died in 1119, having governed the Church in turbulent times for one year and five days.

2. **St. Charles**, Cistercian abbot of Villers in Brabant, descended from the counts of Seyn, was a soldier, but exchanged the coat of mail for the cowl of a monk for the love of God and the salvation of his soul. With several of his companions-in-arms he entered the abbey of Hemmenrode. When the monastery of Heisterbach was to be organized, Charles was selected as best qualified for the undertaking. Somewhat later he was elected abbot of Villers,

but accepted only in obedience to the command of the General Chapter. Secular princes repeatedly had recourse to his offices as a peacemaker and held him in high esteem. He found the greatest happiness in striving to follow Christ by a humble, mortified life. When some one asked him how he could content himself with the simple, insipid food served in his monastery, he replied: "I season it with vigils and manual labor, and the expectation of something better in the life to come." He died while engaged in reforming the abbey of St. Agatha in 1212.

3. Himmana, a Cistercian abbess at Salsines near Namur in Belgium, and sister of Conrad of Hostaden, archbishop of Cologne, governed her nuns with much wisdom and exemplified her precepts by the practice of every virtue. She died in 1257, having been abbess for nearly thirty years.

30

1. St. Bathildis, queen of France and nun at Chelles, was born in England, but was in her childhood brought over to France, where she was purchased as a slave by the majordomo Erchinbald, who was so powerfully attracted by her virtues and natural good qualities that he placed his household in her charge and even offered to marry her when his wife died. Bathildis fled and did not return till she learned that he had married again. About this time King Clovis II saw her, freed her from servitude and made her his queen in 649. Six years later Clovis died, and Bathildis ruled France during the minority of her sons, Clothair, Childeric and Thierry. Among the beneficial measures adopted during her regency were the abolition of slavery and the proscription of simony among the clergy. She also founded seven monasteries, among them those of Corbie and Chelles, and probably also Jumiege, Jouarre and Luxeuil. About 666 she decided to lay down the regency and withdraw to her foundation for nuns at Chelles. She chose the last place among the sisters, and delighted in serving the sick and the poor with her own hands. Her fortitude was tried by sickness, but she bore it with joy and resignation. Fifteen years she had spent in Chelles as a nun, when she was admitted to the enjoyment of her heavenly reward in 680. She was venerated as a saint immediately after her death and was canonized by Pope Nicholas I. In the Roman Martyrology she is mentioned on January 26.

2. St. Adelgundis, abbess of Maubeuge in Hainault, was the daughter of a Frankish noble, Walbert, and even as a child displayed unusual virtue. Declining to give her hand to an earthly bridegroom, she consecrated herself exclusively to Christ, and prevailed upon her parents to distribute their temporal possessions among the poor and the churches. After the death of her parents she received the veil of a sacred virgin at the hands of the holy bishops Aubert and Amandus and founded the monastery of Maubeuge, which she ruled as abbess. God favored her with the gift of fervent prayer and other

Charles: Chron. of Villers, Chev., S. & M. XXX(1910).
Himmana: J. Meyer. Stad. gives 1287 as the year of her death. Chev. calls her Bl. Imaine de Loss; died 1270.
Bathildis: Mab., But., Cath. Enc., Buch.

spiritual delights.   Towards the end of her life she suffered much from calumnies, and her body was afflicted with cancer.   Humbling herself beneath the
hand of God in the midst of these sufferings, which only served to cleanse her
soul from all earthly dross, she expired in the year 684.

3.   **St. Adelelm**, abbot of St. John at Burgos, Spain, was a native of
Poitou.   After the death of his parents, he abandoned the military career, disposed of his possessions in charities to the poor and made a pilgrimage to Rome.
Upon his return, he became a monk at Chaise-Dieu, where he was successively
master of novices and abbot.   Queen Constantia, the wife of Alphonse VI of
Castile and Leon, invited him to her realm to preach against the religion of the
Moors and to revive monasteries.   For this purpose she granted him lands upon
which he built the monastery of St. John.   Here he served God and ministered
to the wants of the poor, edifying all by his apostolic courage and his good
works.   On his death-bed he confessed his sins to the bishop of Pampelona and
died in the year 1097.   The city of Burgos chose him as its patron saint.

4.   **St. Haberilla**, a disciple of St. Gall, was at first an anchoress, but
later was made abbess of Mehrerau in Switzerland, where she lived and died
in the practice of poverty and mortification in the seventh century.

5.   **St. Amnichadus**, a monk from Ireland, closed his holy life at Fulda
in Germany in 1043.   His sanctity was attested by miracles wrought at his
tomb.

31

1.   **St. Bobinus**, a monk of Moutier-la-Celle and bishop of Troyes, rebuilt the monastic church, embellished the tomb of the first abbot, St. Frodobert, and was a pattern of every Christian virtue for his flock.   His death occurred about the year 790.

2.   **Bl. Eusebius**, monk and recluse on Mount St. Victor in the canton
of Grisons (Graubuendten), Switzerland, was a native of Ireland, for some
time lived at St. Gall's and, in the reign of Charles the Bald,went to the canton
of Grisons, where that monarch had built a church in honor of St. Victor.   After spending thirty years in solitude, communing with God alone, he died in
the year 884.

3.   **Bl. Stephen IV**, Pope, born about 720, was a monk in the monastery
of St. Chrysogonus at Rome and was chosen to succeed Pope Paul I in 768.
His reign of three years fell in stirring times, when unworthy men were thrust
forward as candidates for the papacy.   A council held in the Lateran forbade

Adelgundis: Mab., But., E. Leroy: Histoire de Ste A., Valenciennes.
Adelelm: Mab.
Haberilla: Chron. of Constance. She is also called Habrilia.   Chev., S. Haller: Die hl. Haber-
    illa, (1880), Stad.
Amnichadus: Marianus Scotus, Mab., O'Hanlon.   Chev. calls him St. Anincat.
Bobinus: Vita S. Frodoberti in Boll., Chev. Also called Bodinus.
Eusebius: Ekkehard, Mab., Chev. calls him Blessed.

laymen to be elected popes or to take part in their election, and only cardinals were to be chosen popes. He died in 771 and is called a saint in some martyrologies.

4. **Mary a Matre Dei**, Cistercian abbess at Pinto in Spain, had taken the veil as a nun in the monastery of St. Mary Magdalen at Yepez, but had been sent as abbess to the newly founded (1529) house at Pinto near Madrid. After an exemplary life she died in the sixteenth century—the year is not recorded. As miracles were reported to have been wrought at her intercession, and her remains were found incorrupt when her tomb was opened long after her death, she was venerated by some as "blessed".

5. **Peter**, a laybrother of Villers in Brabant, kept the flesh in subjection by mortification, and was so highly favored with ecstasies and visions that he seemed to have anticipated some of the bliss of heaven while he was still walking among men. The year of his death is unknown. According to de Ram he lived in the thirteenth century.

Stephen IV.: Mann: Hist. of the Popes, Cath. Enc., Kir. Lex.
Mary a Matre Dei: Henr.
Peter: Chron. of Villers, Stad. Chev. assigns him to the XII century.

February

1

1. **St. John de la Grille**, a Cistercian monk and bishop of St. Malo, shone brightly by his sanctity, zeal and learning. He is praised as an ornament of the world of learning, as the Elias of his age, as a zealous bishop, a consoler of the afflicted and a successful peacemaker. It is said that he incurred the displeasure of a neighboring bishop for introducing Canons Regular, and at the advice of St. Bernard journeyed to Rome to explain his course of action. The decision was unfavorable to him, and he betook himself for some time to Clairvaux. A second visit to Rome, however, resulted in complete vindication. He died in 1160, and his veneration was authorized by Pope Leo X in 1517. His tomb was surrounded by a grating or grill, hence his surname *de la Grille* or *du Gril*.

2. **St. Clarus**, monk of Seligenstadt and hermit, was possessed of considerable erudition and for some years took great delight in literary pursuits. Reflecting, however, upon the emptiness of learning and its perils to the soul, he quitted his books and devoted himself to contemplation and prayer. With the approval of his superiors he withdrew to a cell near the monastery, where he spent thirty years in spiritual exercises, fasting and mortification. Endowed with the gift of prophecy, he died in 1043. Monastic chroniclers relate that five monks of Seligenstadt, who died in the same year, heard angelic voices when Clarus' soul winged its way heavenward.

3. **Ven. Evrard**, archbishop of Sens and formerly a monk and abbot of the monastery of St. Columba in the same city, was a prudent and pious bishop who ruled his church for five years. While the Normans were ravaging the country in 888 and were laying siege to Sens, he rested from his labors and slept in peace.

4. The bishops and abbots **Ansologus** and **Savolus** of Salzburg, 650-678 and 678-692 respectively, are commemorated on this day for their zeal in preaching the word of God and for their exemplary lives.

5. **Gaufridus**, a Cistercian, bishop of Chartres and apostolic legate, is highly praised by St. Bernard in the treatise *De Consideratione* for his love of poverty, conscientiousness, charity and zeal for the cause of the Church. Peter the Venerable, in a letter addressed to Gaufrid, says: "Although I am more or less beholden to all bishops, I reserve a place for you in the numerous recesses of my heart." He died in the reputation of sanctity about 1160.

6. In Tuscany is commemorated the establishment of the Order of **Knights of St. Stephen** by duke Cosmo de Medici with the Rule of St.

John: Also called J. de Chatillon. Chev., Stad., Martyr. of France.
Clarus: Trithemius, Chron. of Hirsau.
Evrard: Chron. of S. Pierre le Vif., Chev.
Ansologus: Lindner: Monasticon Salzb. calls him Anzologus, with uncertain date.
Gaufrid: Baronius, Bernard of Bonavalle, Chev. (Geoffroy de Leves, d. 1149). Ana. Bolland. I. 355-420.

Benedict in 1562. The Knights pledged themselves to defend the Catholic faith and to clear the Mediterranean Sea of corsairs.

2

1. **St. Lawrence**, archbishop of Canterbury, a native of Rome and monk of the monastery of St. Andrew in the latter city, was one of the companions of St. Augustine, who was sent to England by Pope Gregory the Great in 596. Several years later, Lawrence was sent back to Rome to submit a report on the progress of the mission and to secure additional laborers. Highly pleased with all that he heard, the Pope bade Lawrence hasten back to England, having supplied him with sacred vessels, books and relics. After St. Augustine's death (604), Lawrence was deemed best qualified to succeed him in the see of Canterbury. This honor brought with it some suffering for Lawrence, particularly after the death of King Ethelbert (619), whose wayward son Eadbald led a scandalous life and refused to heed the admonitions of the archbishop. Difficulties that arose in various parts of England discouraged the Roman missionaries to such a degree that the three prelates, Lawrence, Justus and Mellitus decided to leave and return to Rome. During the night preceding the departure, Lawrence in a vision saw St. Peter, who sternly rebuked him for his weakness and commanded him to remain. He died shortly after, in the year 619, and was buried in the church of the abbey of SS. Peter and Paul.

2. **St. Marquard**, bishop of Hildesheim and martyr, had, before his elevation to the episcopal office, been a monk at New Corbie and abbot of Seligenstadt and had preached the faith to pagans. He was slain by the Normans at Ebsdorf in Saxony in the year 880.

3. **St. Hadeloga**, abbess of Kitzingen, was a daughter of Charles Martel. At an early age she renounced the pleasures of the world and devoted herself to the service of God in religious life. She founded a monastery for nuns at Kitzingen, and governed it to the time of her death about 770. Her foundation existed down to the year 1544, when it was suppressed by the margrave of Brandenburg, because the nuns refused to accept the doctrines of the Reformers.

4. **St. Sicharia** lived a life of humility, chastity and piety at Orleans in the sixth century. Her name occurs in old Roman martyrologies.

3

1. **St. Anschar**, archbishop of Bremen and Hamburg was born of noble parents in France in 801. He was educated in the monastic school of Corbie

---

Knights of St. Stephen: Bullarium Magnum.
Lawrence: Ven. Bede, Wm. of Malmesbury, Stan.
Marquard: Stad., Kir. Lex.
Hadeloga: Ben. Annals, Stad.
Sicharia: Ven. Bede, Ado, Notker.

in Picardy under the eyes of the abbot St. Adalard and of Paschasius Radbertus. At the age of fifteen he was clothed with the religious habit and at once seriously applied himself to the study of perfection. Five years later he was sent to New Corbie in Saxony (Westphalia) to preside over the schools of that abbey, which had but recently been founded. A few years later his yearning to preach the tidings of the Redemption to the heathen was fulfilled. At the suggestion of the exiled King Harold of Denmark, Anschar and the monk Autbert were designated to undertake the conversion of the Danes. In 826 they landed and established a missionary post at Haddeby, where they bought a number of pagan children who were to form the nucleus of Christianity in that region. Disabled by sickness, Autbert returned to New Corbie and died shortly after. The converted King Harold aroused discontent by his intemperate zeal and was banished for a second time. Anschar, too, was compelled to withdraw for a time. Next, Anschar, accompanied by the monks Withmar and Gislemar, passed over to Sweden, where in the course of two years their toil was rewarded with numerous conversions. Returning to Saxony in 831 to report on the progress of his mission, Anschar was appointed abbot of New Corbie by Louis the Pious, but found his new duties little to his taste. About this time the emperor contemplated the erection of the archiepiscopal see of Hamburg, which was to serve as a missionary base and nominated Anschar as the first archbishop (832), to which Pope Gregory added the title of a papal legate. From Hamburg, Anschar sent missionaries into Denmark, Norway and Sweden. In 845 Hamburg was destroyed by the Normans. Nothing daunted, Anschar, who had been compelled to flee, returned and rebuilt his churches and schools. In 848 the sees of Hamburg and Bremen were united. After another visit to the far North, where the missions had been languishing for some time, he returned to his see and devoted the closing years of his life to the sanctification of his own soul by austerities and charitable works. Lamented by all his spiritual children, he died at Bremen in 865.

2. **St. Wereburg**, abbess of Chester in England, was the daughter of King Wulfer of Mercia and of his wife, St. Ermenilda. After her father had embraced the Christian religion, she asked his permission to enter the religious state. Having received the veil at the hands of St. Ediltrudis at Ely, she became a model to all her sisters in religion. In compliance with a request of her uncle, King Ethelred, she restored discipline in a number of communities and founded the monasteries of Trentham, Hambury and Wedon. She prayed many hours of the day on her knees, ate but one meal daily and practiced many other mortifications. After visiting all the houses entrusted to her care, she died at Trentham about the year 700. Eight years later her body was found incorrupt.

3. **St. Hadelin**, abbot of Celles in the diocese of Liege, was a native of Aquitaine and left his home to become a monk at Solignac. Together with his abbot, St. Remaclus, he retired to a solitude near Cugnon, and after the elevation of Remaclus to the see of Mastricht, was ordained a priest. Yielding once more to a desire for a life of retirement, he entered the community at

---

Anschar: Rembert, Adam of Bremen, Kir. Lex., Cath. Enc. Also called Ansgar.
Wereburg: Ven. Bede, Higden, Chev.

Stablo, whither Remaclus also followed him, but subsequently he withdrew to a solitude near Dinant where, with generous assistance from Pepin of Heristal, he founded the monastery of Celles, and died after a holy life in 690. He is represented as clad with a black cloak, bearing in his hand a staff surmounted by a cross upon which a dove is perched; also as a priest wearing the sacerdotal garments, bearing a book in his right and a staff in his left hand.

4. St. Bellendis, nun at Morselle, in the diocese of Malines, was the daughter of the noble Odolard, a military officer in the service of the duke of Lorraine. Being disinherited by her father, she left the world, became a nun at Morselle and, when that monastery was destroyed, returned to her home at Marbek and devoted herself to works of piety and charity. She was called to receive the imperishable crown in 702.

4

1. St. Rabanus Maurus, archbishop of Mainz, was born in that city in 776 and was educated at Fulda. His excellent qualities of heart and mind gave promise of a brilliant future. After receiving the order of deaconship, his abbot sent him to Tours to hear the lectures of Alcuin, one of the ablest scholars of the age. Upon his return to Fulda, he was appointed to direct its schools, founded a library and filled the chair of Holy Scripture. Shortly after his ordination, the abbey of Fulda was the scene of dissensions between Abbot Rutgar and the monks. Rabanus undertook to reconcile the warring parties, but met with no success and decided to make a pilgrimage to the Holy Land. In the meantime, a new abbot, Egil, had calmed the troubled waters and Rabanus returned. In 822 he was elected Egil's successor and in the space of twenty years brought Fulda to the pinnacle of its prosperity. In 842 he resigned his office and lived in retirement on a neighboring hill. But his day's work had not yet been done; in 847, despite all his protests, he was elected archbishop of Mainz. During the nine years of his episcopate he held several councils, lived as simply as a monk and was known for his boundless charities, particularly during the famine of 850. He died in 856, and was buried in the monastery of St. Alban at Mainz, but in 1515 the remains were removed to Halle.

2. St. Rembert, archbishop of Bremen and Hamburg, was born near Bruges in Flanders, and in his childhood attracted the notice of St. Anschar who sent him to the monastery of Turnhold to be educated. He accompanied Anschar to the northern missions and served with such zeal and prudence that the great Apostle of the North on his deathbed recommended Rembert as his successor saying: "Rembert is more worthy to be a bishop than I to be a deacon." He was accordingly elected archbishop in 865, became a monk of New Corbie and lived according to the Rule of St. Benedict. Not content with cultivating the field entrusted to him by Anschar, he turned his attention to

---

Hadelin: Notker, Stad.
Bellendis: Mab. Other forms of the name: Berlendis, Bellande.
Rabanus: Rudolph, Trithemius. His writings in Migne, P. L. The name is also written Rhabanus, Hrabanus. Kir. Lex., Cath. Enc.

the conversion of the Slavs and Wends. He is said to have sold precious altar plate to ransom prisoners from the Normans, and to have driven these invaders out of Frisia, for which reason he was held in high veneration in that country. Having appointed his associate Adalgar as his successor, he died on July 11, 888. The Roman Martyrology commemorates him today, because on this day he was elected archbishop.

3. **St. Vulgisus,** bishop and abbot of Lobbe in the diocese of Liege, was a man of eminent merit and sanctity and died in the year 737.

5

1. **St. Modestus,** a missionary bishop in Carinthia, was at first a monk of Exeter in England, and was sent by St. Virgil of Salzburg to preach the Gospel to the Carinthians. He labored with unflagging zeal under the protection of Our Lady whom he chose as the heavenly patroness of his missions. His death occurred in the year 780.

2. **St. Bertulph,** abbot of Renty in the province of Artois, was a German and the son of pagan parents. Early in life he left his home and received baptism in the diocese of Terrouane. For some years he was steward to Count Wambert, who entertained such a high opinion of his fidelity that he treated him as a brother and made him a gift of an estate at Renty, which the latter accepted subject to the condition that he might build a monastery on the grounds. He carried out the project and, although a layman, ruled the community. He was noted for his charity, generosity and recollection. When the hour of his death approached, he received the Sacraments, delivered a final and fervent exhortation to the brethren, and departed in peace in 705. During the invasion of the Normans, his remains were removed and, after being interred at various places, at last were deposited in a monastery on Mont Blandin at Ghent in Flanders.

3. **St. Aleidis,** abbess of Villich near Bonn, archdiocese of Cologne, was the daughter of Count Megingoz and his wife Gerberta. In her youth, she became a nun at St. Ursula in Cologne, where the rule of St. Jerome was observed. Her parents founded a monastery for women at Villich and invited Aleidis to direct the community. It was the wish of her parents that the nuns observe the Rule of St. Benedict, but Aleidis was reluctant to comply. Only after the death of her mother did she consent to make the change under the guidance of her sister Bertha, abbess of St. Mary's at Cologne. Her moderation and strength of character enabled her to overcome all difficulties connected with the arduous undertaking. Her own example was the most powerful means to lead her sisters on the path of virtue. When, after her father's death, she received her share of the inheritance, she provided for the support of fifteen poor persons out of the revenues of one of her estates and of fifteen

Rembert: Adalgar, Stad., Cath. Enc.("Rimbert"), Kir. Lex.("Hamburg").
Vulgisus: Mab., Martyr. of France.
Modestus: Chron. of Salzburg, Ben. Annals.
Bertulph: Life by a monk of Mont Blandin.

others out of the resources of the monastery. With motherly solicitude and tenderness she observed the progress of the children attending the monastic school and spurred them on to renewed efforts by little acts of kindness. After her sister Bertha's death, she was elected abbess of St. Mary's in Cologne by archbishop Heribert. There, too, she swayed her community by her high sense of duty and considerate attention to the needs of the sisters, particularly of the sick. Prostrated by illness on February 3, she spent the few remaining days of her edifying career in careful preparation for the journey to her heavenly home and expired on February 5, in the year 1015. Her remains were entombed at Villich.

6

1. St. Amandus, bishop of Mastricht, was born near Nantes in France. At the age of twenty years he retired to a monastery on the little island of Oye and resisted his father's persuasions to abandon his resolution of serving God alone. For five years he dwelt in a small cell near the cathedral at Bourges and received instructions in the spiritual life from St. Austregisil. After returning from a pilgrimage to Rome he was consecrated as a missionary bishop without a see and was sent to preach the faith to the unbelievers. His first field of labor was Ghent, in Flanders, where the people were still addicted to idolatry. Insult and maltreatment were the rewards of his preaching among this benighted people. Having returned to France, he incurred the illwill of King Dagobert whom he had rebuked for his sinful life, and was expelled from the country. Although the king regretted the measure and invited Amandus to return, the latter refused and turned his steps towards Carinthia, where his efforts met with little success. About 649 he was appointed bishop of Mastricht, but grew discouraged when he saw that he could not effectually check the disorders in that place and resigned his see in favor of St. Remaclus. For some time he resumed his missionary labor; finally retired to the abbey of Elnon which he had founded, and ruled it as its abbot during the last four years of his life. He died at the age of eighty-six years in 675. Besides Elnon he also founded the monasteries of St. Peter and of St. Bavo at Ghent and helped SS. Gertrude and Itta to establish the monastery at Nivelles. The monastery of Elnon was subsequently known as St. Amand.

2. St. Ina, king of Wessex, England, was the son of Kenred and succeeded his grandfather Ceadwalla, when the latter renounced the throne. He is considered as the founder of the monastery of Glastonbury and the restorer of that of Abingdon. For the purpose of securing privileges for his pious foundations, he visited Rome, where he built a church in honor of Our Lady and established a school. It was this monarch who introduced into England the custom of paying the Romescot, or Peter's Pence, in token of recognition of the authority of the Holy See. About the year 720 he visited Rome a second time, abdicated his throne and lived as a monk to the day of his death about the year 730. He was buried in the church of S. Maria in Saxia in the Anglo-Saxon quarter near the Vatican.

Aleidis: Mab., Other forms of the name: Adeleidis, Adelheidis.
Amandus: Mab., But., Stad., C. E., Kir. Lex.
Ina: William of Malmesb., Stad. Other forms: Ini, Inna.

3. St. Relindis, sister of St. Harlindis and abbess of Eyk, or Maaseyk, in the Netherlands, was educated in the choicest accomplishments of a lady in her time at Valenciennes in Hainault. Not long after the return of the two sisters from the monastic school to their home, they prevailed upon their parents to build a monastery, and assisted personally in the work of construction. The holy bishops Willibrord and Boniface blessed both of them as abbesses and they jointly governed the community. After the death of Harlindis, Relindis ruled the house alone and remained faithful to her purpose to the hour of her death in the eighth century.

4. St. Andrew, abbot of Elnon in Flanders, a disciple of St. Amandus, was chosen by the latter as his successor in Elnon, and died after zealously governing the monastery in 689.

7

1. St. Romuald, founder of the Order of Camaldoli, was descended from the noble family of the Honesti and was born about 956. Although he was brought up according to the principles of the world and enjoyed its pleasures, he felt divine grace at times stirring him to strive for higher things and to do some heroic act for the love of God. One day he was the unwilling witness of a duel in which his father killed a relative. Romuald was so profoundly shocked that he fled to the monastery of S. Apollinare in Classe near Ravenna where he did voluntary penance for forty days. At the close of that period he begged to be received as a monk and was vested with the Benedictine habit. The monastery had been recently reformed by St. Majolus, and yet did not seem strict enough for Romuald. Some of the brethren resented injudicious corrections administered by him; the result was that for the sake of peace, he was permitted to leave and to make his abode near Venice under the guidance of a hermit Marinus. About this time, the doge Peter Orseolo left Venice to become a monk in Catalonia, and was accompanied, among others, by Marinus and Romuald. While the doge entered the monastery of Cuxa, Marinus and Romuald, who were shortly joined by several disciples, lived in a hermitage near the monastery. In the meantime, Romuald's father had, in expiation of his crime, retired from public life and entered a monastery, but began to waver in his resolution, whereupon Romuald speedily returned to Italy to confirm him in his purpose. He settled in the marshy district surrounding Ravenna and founded a monastery of which he was chosen abbot. Here, too, his severity soon led to misunderstandings, in consequence of which he left and resigned his office into the hands of Pope Silvester II at Tivoli. After several other attempts to found religious houses he decided to be a missionary in Hungary, but repeated attacks of illness bade him desist from this enterprise. For seven years he lived as a hermit on Mount Sitria. In 1012 he arrived at Vallombrosa, and shortly after moved into the diocese of Arezzo where one Maldolus granted him an estate (*Campus Maldoli*) on which he built several hermitages which became the cradle of the Order of Camaldoli. Here he died on June 19, 1027. Clement VIII appointed February 7 for his

---

Relindis: Mab.   Also called Reinula, Remula, Rilind's.
Andrew: Mab.

feast. The Rule of the Camaldolese is that of St. Benedict; the garb of the hermits is white, even the cowl or choir cloak.

2. **Leonius,** who had been abbot of Lobbe, was selected to revive the abbey of Sithiu, which had declined from its primitive splendor. In his efforts at reform he laid powerful stress on the observance of silence. While accompanying King Louis VII on a Crusade to the Holy Land, he died in the year 1163.

3. On this day is commemorated the last visit of St. Scholastica to St. Benedict (543) when, as St. Gregory relates, the holy patriarch's sister procured a prolongation of their pious conference by praying for a heavenly intervention in the shape of a storm which prevented St. Benedict from returning to his monastery on Monte Cassino.

4. **Rainer,** a Cistercian laybrother at Villers in Brabant, entered the monastery at an advanced age and spent his life in penitential exercises and faithful observance of the Rule to the day of his death in 1220.

8

1. **St. Paul,** bishop of Verdun in Lorraine, in his youth received a careful education, but feeling an impulse to seek the kingdom of Heaven by following in the footsteps of his Savior, renounced all earthly prospects and betook himself to a solitude in the Vosges Mountains, where he dwelt as hermit with several associates. While visiting the monastery of Tholey, he was convinced by the abbot of that house of the superiority of the monastic to the eremitical life and begged to be admitted to the community. Upon the expiration of his novitiate, he was given charge of the school and directed it so ably that it soon began to attract wide attention. Among his pupils was Grimo, grandson of King Dagobert. After the death of bishop Ermenfrid of Verdun, Paul was chosen as his successor, a choice which he declined to accept until the king's emissaries forcibly led him to Verdun. As bishop he renewed religious life throughout his diocese and provided for the sustenance of the canons, whose resources were so meager that the canonical hours could barely be sung with the decorum befitting a cathedral. He maintained a friendly correspondence with such eminent and saintly prelates as bishops Desiderius of Cahors, Arnulph of Metz, Eligius of Noyon and Cunibert of Cologne. After this death, about 650, he was entombed in the church of St. Saturnine, which he had built.

2. **St. Elfleda,** abbess of Strenshall (Streaneshalch or Whitby) in England. After her father, King Oswy of Northumberland had defeated King Penda of Mercia, he sent Elfleda to be educated by St. Hilda, abbess of Hortle-

---

Romuald: St. Peter Damian.
Leonius: Ben. Annals.
Rainer: Chron. of Villers.
Paul: Mab., Stad. Gams, according to whom Paul was bishop of Verdun 641-648 and possibly later.

pool. Two years later, she accompanied Hilda to the newly founded monastery of Strenshall, where she shone by her exemplary life and was elected abbess after Hilda's death in 680. After governing her house with great success she died in the year 716.

3. **Bl. Jodocus** (Jordanus) **Palmieri**, monk of the congregation of Monte Vergine in Italy, spent his life in incessant praise of God and led many by his example to follow Christ by embracing the religious state. He died in the reputation of sanctity in 1543.

4. **Amulwinus** was abbot of Lobbe, and is supposed by some to have been also a bishop. After a pious and meritorious life he died in 770. His remains were removed to the abbey of Binghen in Hainault in 1409.

9

1. **St. Alto**, abbot of Altomuenster in Bavaria, was of Irish or Scotch origin. He came from his native land to Bavaria, made his abode in a forest to the east of Augsburg, where he preached to the people, and sanctified his own soul by meditation, austerities and manual labor. Pepin the Short, edified by his holiness of life, granted him a part of the forest and Alto built a monastery in which he soon found himself surrounded by a number of pious aspirants to perfection. St. Boniface dedicated the church and installed Alto as abbot in 750. Ten years later he was deemed fit to receive the crown of everlasting life. Many miracles were wrought at his tomb. His foundation became known as Alto-Muenster (Alto's monastery).

2. **St. Ansbert**, archbishop of Rouen, was the son of respected parents at Chaussi, in France. His father provided him with a suitable education and wished him to marry Angadrema, daughter of Robert, chancellor of the realm. Angadrema was afflicted with a disease, said to have been leprosy, and retired to a monastery where she was eventually cured. Ansbert, who had in the meantime succeeded to the office of chancellor, seriously thought of following her example and applied for admission to the abbey of Fontenelle, where he received the habit at the hands of St. Wandregisil and was ordained priest. Both Wandregisil and his successor regarded him as the most exemplary of all the monks, and when abbot Lambert was appointed bishop of Lyons, Ansbert was made abbot of Fontenelle. In the discharge of his onerous duties he displayed admirable moderation, always avoiding the extremes of severity and excessive leniency, winning the love of his monks by kindness rather than by harshness. Having been appointed archbishop of Rouen in 683, he devoted himself to his duties with singular zeal, preaching the word of God, visiting his diocese and relieving the poor and afflicted. Calumniators contrived to have him exiled to the abbey of Hautmont, where he edified all by his fasts and constant prayer. Shortly after receiving notice that he might return to his see

---

Elfleda: William of Malmesb. Also called Elfreda, Aelfled.
Jodocus: Menard, Wion.
Amulwin: Trithem., Molanus.
Alto: Mab., C. E. The English Calendar mentions him on September 5.

unmolested, he passed to a better life in 698. In compliance with his own wish, his remains were interred at Fontenelle, but in the year 1002 they were carried to Mont Blandin at Ghent.

3. **St. Marianus**, first abbot of the Scots monastery of St. James at Regensburg, came from Ireland in the reign of Emperor Henry IV, and betook himself to Regensburg, where the abbess Willa received him hospitably. He established himself in a house near the church of St. Peter, where he formed a community of his countrymen, and governed them as abbot. His favorite pursuits were prayer and the study of Holy Scripture. A copy of the Epistles of St. Paul, beautifully written with his own hand, is extant in Vienna. He died in 1088, and after his death was honored as a saint. He is not to be confounded with another Irish monk of the same name, who died in 1082.

4. **Bl. Murcherad,** who lived as a recluse in Regensburg, was the first Scot or Irishman to settle in Bavaria, and is regarded as the founder of the Scoto-Hibernian monasteries in that country. His life was spent in seclusion and prayer, and closed in the year 1080.

5. **Erizzo** (Ericius), a Vallombrosan monk and disciple of St. John Gualbert, was the fourth general of that Order and was noted for miracles and exceptional holiness of life. He died in the year 1094.

10

1. **St. Scholastica**, abbess, sister of our Holy Father St. Benedict, was born at Nursia about 480, and ruled a community of nuns at Plumbariola in the vicinity of Monte Cassino. Little is known of her life. St. Gregory the Great records a single incident, that indicates the power of her intercession with Heaven. It was her custom every year to meet St. Benedict at a spot between Monte Cassino and Plumbariola, and discourse with him on heavenly subjects, joined, no doubt, with conferences on questions touching religious life and practice. On one such occasion she was so deeply engrossed by the conversation that she was loathe to depart, and begged him to prolong the meeting throughout the night. St. Benedict was reluctant to remain and represented to her that he must go back to his monks. But Scholastica insisted and, when she observed that her persuasions failed to move him, had recourse to prayer. Clouds soon covered the sky and poured down a torrent of rain that prevented St. Benedict from leaving the house. Heaven had favored her and the conversation was continued through the hours of the night until dawn. Three days later, St. Benedict saw her soul in the shape of a dove winging its flight heavenward. Her life work was done and she was resting with the Saints. This was in the year 543. St. Benedict laid her in a tomb prepared for himself. According to one account her remains were carried to Mans in France in 660, and enshrined in a silver reliquary. The city of Mans

Ansbert: Aigrad of Fontenelle, Mab., Vita in Ana. Bolland. I. 178-191.
Marianus: Barrett, C. E., Chev.(B. Muiredach), O'Hanlon(St. Muredhac).
Murcherad: Bl. Marianus, Chev.(Moucherat).
Erizzo: Also called Ericus.

chose her as its patron saint. She is represented as an abbess with a book, staff and dove.

2. **St. Austreberta**, first abbess of Pavilly, in the archdiocese of Rouen, the daughter of the count palatine Badefrid and his wife Framenhildis, was born at Terrouane in Artois in the year 630. Earthly pleasures held no attraction for her; hence she begged the saintly Audomar, bishop of Terrouane, to confer the veil upon her that she might lead the life of a virgin consecrated to God. For some time she lived in retirement in her home but in 656 entered the monastery of Port on the Somme, of which she was deemed worthy to be elected abbess. With difficulty could St. Philibert, abbot of Jumieges, in 670 persuade her to assume the government of the newly founded monastery of Pavilly, which she ruled with gentle firmness. Her humility is illustrated by the following incident. While visiting the dormitories during the night, her steps caused a noise which drew upon her a rebuke from the prioress who was not aware that it was Austreberta. The prioress ordered her to kneel before the cross and atone for her carelessness. Great was the astonishment of the nuns when they found their abbess still kneeling in prayer early in the morning. The Lord called her to receive the reward of the faithful servant in 703.

3. **B. Arnaldus** de Catani was the successor of Abbot Stephen in the government of the abbey of S. Justina at Padua and presided over his community from 1209-1246, when the tyrannical Ezzelino da Romano, leader of the Ghibellines in Italy, threw him into a gloomy dungeon in which he lay for eight long years and died in 1255. He was noted for his purity of soul and body. His remains were first interred at Asolo, but in the sixteenth century were removed to the church of St. Justina in Padua.

4. **Eusebius**, a Camaldolese monk, who had at one time been ambassador of the king of Spain to the doge of Venice, while attending Holy Mass conceived the resolution to serve the Lord of lords and become a monk in the monastery of S. Michael di Murano at Venice, where his charity, obedience and patience endeared him to all. He died in the year 1509.

5. **Paganus**, monk of St. Nicholas in the city of Catania in Sicily, lived during the great Western Schism and shed lustre upon the Church by the beauty of his virtues. After his death in 1423, many experienced the power of his intercession.

6. **Ven. Jarento**, abbot of St. Benigne at Dijon, was a peacemaker among princes and assisted in the suppression of schisms. This faithful steward of his divine Lord was called to receive his recompense in the year 1111.

Scholastica: Greg. the Great, Adrewald, Stad.
Austreberta: Mab., Surius. Also called Austreberga.
Arnaldus: Chron. of S. Justina, Chev. Also known as Arnaldus Cataneus.
Eusebius: Wion, Menard, Stad.
Paganus: Octav. Cajetan.
Jarento: Ben. Annals, Stad., Chev. Also called Geranus.

11

1. **St. Benedict of Aniane**, abbot and earliest reformer of the Benedictine Order, was the son of count Aigulf of Maguelone and was born in Languedoc, in France, in 750. His name was originally Witiza. While accompanying Charlemagne on an expedition to Italy, his brother was drowned in
the Ticino despite his efforts to save him from peril. This misfortune determined Witiza to think more seriously of the affairs of the soul and he became a
monk in 774 at St. Seine. On account of his eminent natural gifts and monastic virtues, he was appointed cellarer, and after the abbot's death was chosen
as his successor. Unfortunately, the brethren were little in sympathy with
his efforts to renew the discipline of the house in conformity with the letter
of the Holy Rule. Therefore he left the monastery about 776 and founded that
of Aniane. Numerous grants of land and other donations enabled him to
provide for a large community. This house became the centre of a great monastic revival in France. Benedict drew up a concordance of all the known
monastic rules to serve as a basis for his reform, one of the chief aims of which
was to procure uniformity by general adoption of the Rule of St. Benedict,
with special modifications demanded by the exigencies of the times. Although
rigorous in his observance of the letter of the Rule, he mitigated its severity
in several particulars for his brethren, but the flesh of quadrupeds was to be
banished from the table. Upon invitation of Louis the Pious, he undertook
to reform all the monasteries in Aquitaine, and after the death of Charlemagne
he was commissioned to supervise all the monasteries of the empire. His
residence was to be the abbey of Cornelimuenster, founded by Louis after his
accession to the throne. Benedict's influence was particularly felt at the synods
of Aachen in 816 and 817, when rules were drawn up with which all monasteries were expected to conform. Although the measure failed, the intentions
of Benedict were honorable and sincere. He died at Cornelimuenster in 821.

2. **St. Ardagnus**, abbot of Tournus in Burgundy, ruled his monastery
with fatherly solicitude and prudence for twenty-eight years and died 1056.
His biographers make special mention of his generosity to the poor during a
wide-spread famine.

3. **St. Adolph**, bishop of Osnabrueck in Westphalia, while visiting the
Cistercian monastery of Kamp, was so deeply touched by the devotion of the
monks who were taking the discipline, that he abandoned the ways of the world
and became a religious. In 1200 he was drawn from his solitude to be bishop
of Osnabrueck. He was noted for his love of prayer and for his charity.
After ruling his diocese for twenty-two years, he died in 1222.

4. **St. Caedmon**, monk of Strenshall in England, though illiterate, was
possessed of a wonderful poetical talent. "One night, when the servants of

Benedict: Ardo Smaragdus, Kir. Lex., Herder: Con. Lex., Chev., But.(Feb. 12).
Ardagnus: Falko, Chifflet in Mab. Ardanus is another form of the name. Chev.(Ardaing).
Adolph: Caesarius of Heisterbach, Kir. Lex. gives year of death 1224, Cath. Enc., Chev.
    Strunck: Die Heiligen Westfalens, II.

the monastery were gathered about the table for good fellowship, and the harp was passed from hand to hand, Caedmon, knowing nothing of piety, left the company for shame, and retired to the stable, as he was assigned that night to the care of the draught-cattle. As he slept, there stood by him in a vision one who bade him sing. ' I cannot sing and therefore I left the feast.' ' Sing to me, however, sing of Creation,' said the vision. Thereupon Caedmon began to sing in praise of God verses which he had never heard before." Hence he was called Cantor Theodidactus (taught by God). Being a man of prayer, he was invited to enter the double monastery of which St. Hilda was abbess. Signing himself with the sign of the Cross, he died in 680.

5. Bl. Heluisa, a recluse at Coulombs, diocese of Chartres, though wealthy, respected and educated, found peace for her soul in a life of prayer and mortification to the day of her departure from this life in 1033.

6. Bl. Henry, first abbot of the Cistercian monastery of Witskeld—or *Vitae Scholae*—in northern Jutland, was a disciple of St. Bernard, founded the monastery aforesaid in 1158, and enjoyed the favor of King Waldemar I of Denmark who endowed the house. Its church is said to have been one of the most beautiful in the North. A model of virtue, he died in the course of the twelfth century.

12

1. St. Benedict, bishop of Albenga, in Italy, was a scion of the family of the Revelli and was born near Tabia, whither his parents had taken refuge during a pestilence. After living as a monk in the monastery of S. Maria dei Fonti and dwelling for some time as a hermit on the island of Galinaria, he was made bishop of Albenga, and died in the year 900, reputed for a holy life and the gift of miracles. At the time of his death he was outside of his diocese, but his remains were taken back first to Albenga and were finally interred in the abbey in which he had professed. The city of Albenga chose him as its patron.

2. St. Ethelwold, bishop of Lindisfarne in England, at first served among the clergy in the diocese of Lindisfarne, subsequently was prior of Melrose in Scotland, and abbot of that monastery. Elected to the see of Lindisfarne, he governed it for sixteen years. He had a stone cross made by skilled sculptors; a book of the Gospels written by his order and adorned with gold and precious stones fell into the sea while it was being borne to a place of concealment during the Danish invasion of 875, but was recovered intact. Ethelwold died in 740.

Caedmon: Bede, Gurteen: Epic of the Fall of Man. Other forms: Cedmon, Ceadmon. Cath. Enc., Stan.(February 10).
Heluisa: Mab., Chev.(Helvise).
Henry: Seguin, Stad.
Benedict: Boll. Acc. to Ughelli (Italia Sacra IV), he died on February 13.
Ethelwold: Florence of Winchester, Stan.

3. **St. Goslin,** second abbot of St. Solutor near Turin in Italy, died in the year 1061. Miracles that took place at the time of the discovery of his remains in 1472 bore witness to the sanctity of his life.

4. **St. Humbelina,** widow, abbess of Julley in Burgundy, was a sister of St. Bernard of Clairvaux. Like St. Scholastica, she emulated her famous brother in humility and every other virtue that constitutes religious perfection and entered the regions of eternal delight in 1136.

5. **Stephen,** cardinal and bishop of Palestrina, previously a Cistercian monk at Clairvaux, was distinguished for his contempt of the world, his love of poverty and his charity to the poor. He died in 1158.

6. Commemoration of all the saintly **Doctors** and **Masters** of the spiritual life, whose writings and teachings have led the children of St. Benedict to the heights of perfection.

13

1. **St. Gregory II.,** Pope, whose parents, Marcellus and Honesta, were members of the Roman nobility, received his early training in the Lateran monastery, which was inhabited by the monks of Monte Cassino after the destruction of that monastery. He occupied several offices of importance in the Roman Church before his elevation to the papal chair. Thus, he was almoner under Pope Sergius I, also papal librarian; as deacon he was selected to accompany Pope Constantine to Constantinople to discuss the canons of the Quinisext council with Emperor Justinian II. After his election to the supreme pontificate, he displayed marvelous activity. He deposed the heretical patriarch John VI of Constantinople, restored the ruinous walls of Rome and prevailed upon King Luitprand to ratify the grants of that monarch's ancestors to the Holy See. He also reestablished Monte Cassino. and appointed abbot Petronax the first superior of the monastery. The northern countries of Europe are deeply indebted to this pontiff, for it was he who consecrated SS. Corbinian and Boniface bishops and commissioned them to evangelize Germany. Two councils held during his pontificate issued legislation condemning concubinage and the heresy of the Iconoclasts. At the instigation of Emperor Leo the Isaurian several attempts were made upon his life, but he escaped all harm. After ruling the Church with great courage and fidelity during sixteen years, he died on February 10, 731. In the Roman Martyrology he is commemorated on the present day.

2. **St. Stephen,** an abbot at Rieti in Italy, lived and died in the sixth century. Though lacking learning, he nevertheless displayed much circumspection and wisdom in ruling his monastery. He despised earthly possessions, loved retirement and prayer. Those who wronged him he regarded as his

---

Goslin: Boll., Chev. Other forms: Goselinus, Guselinus.
Humbelina: Mart. Rom., Henr. Other forms: Humberga and Humberta. Chev. gives 1141 as the year of her death.
Stephen: Ughelli, Chev.
Gregory II: Anastas. Bibl., Cedrenus, Lives of Popes, But.

dearest friends and forgave them sincerely. St. Gregory the Great relates
that when a malicious neighbor set fire to the granary in which Stephen's
monks had just stored the season's crop, and some one exclaimed: "Alas,
Stephen, what has happened to you?" he replied: "Let me rather say, Alas,
what has happened to him that did me this ill turn?" He died about the year
600.

3. **St. Ermenilda**, abbess of Ely, in England, was the daughter of King
Ercombert of Kent and of his wife St. Sexburga. In due course of time, she
became the wife of King Wulfer of Mercia, whom she induced to apply himself
to the extinction of the last vestiges of paganism in the country. After the
death of her husband in 675, she entered the monastery of Ely, where her
daughter Werburga was already a nun and her mother ruled as abbess. Upon
the latter's death, Ermenilda was called upon to govern Ely and guided the
nuns with love and zeal to the day of her death in 703.

4. **SS. Haimon and Veremund** were two brothers and members of
the wealthy family of the Cori in northern Italy. While engaged in the chase,
their lives were imperilled and they made a vow to build a monastery in honor
of St. Victor if they escaped unhurt. Their prayer was heard; they built a
monastery for women at Meda, between Como and Milan, and lived in a separate dwelling near by devoting themselves to penitential exercises. They died
about 790. Cardinal Frederic Borromeo, archbishop of Milan, raised their
remains in 1626.

5. **Ven. Mary de Azevedo**, a nun at Semide near Coimbra in Portugal
found her highest delight in meditating on the Passion of Our Lord, and was
an admirable model of patience. She is said to have been a stigmatic but to
have concealed the fact to the hour of her death in 1610.

14

1. **St. Antonine**, abbot, was a professed monk in a monastery in Italy
under the Rule of St. Benedict, but was driven out with the other brethren
during an incursion by Sico of Beneventum. He found asylum with Bishop
Catellus at Castellamare near Naples, who placed such confidence in the
ability and virtue of the monk, that he committed the diocese to his charge
and withdrew into a retired spot to serve God in contemplation. Antonine
soon followed, and together they built a church in honor of St. Michael, which
in course of time became a popular pilgrimage. Catellus was discovered and
summoned to Rome to explain why he had left his see. In the meantime a
deputation from Sorrento approached Antonine requesting him to settle in
their city. He complied and entered the monastery of St. Agrippinus, of
which he was afterwards elected abbot. His paternal solicitude was unequalled; his patience invincible; he shunned slanderers and backbiters as so many

Stephen: Greg. the Great, Lib. Dial. IV. 19., But.
Ermenilda: Capgrave, Bede, Stan., Stad.
Haimon: Ferrari, Bugatti, Stad. Other forms of Haimon: Aymo, Aymund.
Mary: Schindele.

pestilences. He shared the labors of the brethren in the field and left behind him proof of his skill as a sculptor on the portals of a chapel of St. Martin. He died in the year 830.

2. **St. Boniface**, Apostle of the Russians and martyr, was descended from a noble Saxon family and was born about 970. Having availed himself of the best educational opportunities of the time, he became a priest and was appointed one of the court chaplains to Emperor Otto III. While in Rome for the coronation of that emperor in 996, he visited the church of St. Boniface on the Aventine. As he entered he exlaimed under the impulse of a sudden emotion: "Am I not also called Boniface? Why should I not be a martyr as well as he that is invoked in this church?" Two years later he made the acquaintance of St. Romuald in the monastery of Pereum near Ravenna and entered the Order of Camaldoli. After ten years spent in the austere life enjoined by this reform he was sent to Germany to preach the Gospel to the Slavs between the Elbe and the Oder. He was consecrated bishop by Tagino, archbishop of Magdeburg, in 1004. War between the emperor and the duke of Poland prevented Bruno from achieving many conversions. Biding better times, he turned his steps towards Hungary, where his efforts were also doomed to failure, and finally in 1007, entered Russia where he had scarcely inaugurated his labors when he was slain by pagans in the year 1009. The Roman Martyrology mentions his name on June 19.

3. **Bl. Conrad**, a son of Duke Henry III of Bavaria, abandoned a brilliant career to bury himself in the retirement of a monastery. He entered Clairvaux shortly after its foundation by St. Bernard; made a pilgrimage to the Holy Land and died near Bari in Italy 1149. His veneration was approved April 7, 1832.

4. **Bl. Angelus ab Aquapagana**, a Camaldolese lay-brother of the monastery of St. Benedict at Valido in Umbria, served God in simplicity and humility, delighted in meditating upon Christ crucified, and was a model of obedience and mortification. He died kneeling in prayer in 1324. The province of Umbria venerates him as one of its patron saints and ascribes several favors, such as preservation from fires and pestilence, to his intercession.

15

1. **St. Faustus**, monk of Monte Cassino, had been confided to the tender care of our Holy Father St. Benedict at the age of seven years and was a religious of approved virtue. He was one of the companions of St. Maurus when the latter was sent to the diocese of Le Mans in 542, and remained faithfully by his side, sharing his burdens and trials. St. Maurus on his death-

Antonine: A. Carracioli, Stad., Chev.
Boniface: Sigebert of Gemblours, Baluze, Cath. Enc. (Bruno). Also called Bruno of Querfurt, Chev.
Conrad: Stad., Cist. Suppl. to Rom. Mart. Not in Lechner.
Angelus: Jacobillus, Razzi, Camaldolese Suppl. to Rom. Mart. He is also called A. a Gualdo. In Lechner on August 19.

bed requested Faustus to return to Italy. Two years passed before Bertulph, Maurus' successor, succeeded in persuading him to comply with the Saint's request. In 585 he went back to Rome and joined the monks of Cassino who had been established in a monastery at the Lateran since the devastation of their abbey. Yielding to repeated suggestions, he wrote a life of St. Maurus, which met the approval of Pope Boniface III. Faustus died in 607.

2. St. Walafrid, founder and first abbot of the monastery of Palazzuolo on Monteverde in Tuscany, was a noble of Pisa and a vassal of the Lombard King Aistulph. After spending a number of years in a happy wedded life, he resolved, with his wife and several friends, to ensure the salvation of his soul by embracing the counsels of perfection and entering the religious state. On a site pointed out to him by the bishop on Monteverde, he built a church and monastery in honor of St. Peter and ruled a society of monks as their abbot. At some distance from this house he established another, called S. Salvator, for his wife and the wives of his companions. He soon found himself at the head of a community of sixty members. While gratified by the evident eagerness of all to attain perfection, he experienced the pangs of disappointment at the conduct of his son Gimfrid who, succumbing to the tempter's wiles, left the monastery, bearing with him papers and other property of the house. Walafrid sought refuge in prayer and was shortly rejoiced to see his misguided son return and by a devout, penitential life make atonement for his error. He governed the monastery for ten years and died in the year 764, being succeeded as abbot by his son Gimfrid.

16

1. St. Tanco, bishop of Werden in ancient Saxony, is said to have been an abbot at Amarbary in Scotland, and to have come to the continent to shed his blood for the faith of Christ. The year of his death is 800.

2. Ven. Jaspard de Winck, abbot of St. Denis de Brocheroie near Mons in Hainault, founder of the Congregation of St. Placidus in the Netherlands, met much opposition to his devoted efforts, was driven from his monastery and died at the abbey of Afflighem in 1630.

3. John, abbot of St. Peter and bishop of Salzburg, was appointed to that see by St. Boniface and died a holy death after a holy life in 754.

4. John, Cistercian abbot of Casamare in Italy, was a disciple of St. Bernard of Clairvaux, was favored with many visions and foretold the death of his saintly master. A letter in which he consoles St. Bernard in his distress at the issue of the Crusade preached by that Saint, is extant in the collection of St. Bernard's letters.

Faustus: Petrus Diaconus, Leo Ostiensis.
Walafrid: Andrew of Palazzuolo, Stad. Other forms: Walefrid, Waltfrid. Chev.(Walfrid).
Tanco: Krantz, O'Hanlon, Gropp: Mille Annorum mon. de Amorbach, 1736; But. Other forms: Tenco, Tatta.
Jaspard: Calmet, Stad.
John: Chron. of Salzburg.
John: Barnabas of Montalbo. See letter in Migne P. L. 182. 590.

17

1. **St. Benedict**, a monk of Monte Cassino, was sent by Pope Urban II to be bishop of Cagliari in Sardinia and ruled that diocese with apostolic solicitude and as a model of Christian holiness. He died in 1100.

2. **St. Constabilis**, abbot of Cava, near Naples, was born in the province of Lucania about 1060, was educated in that abbey under abbot Leo and attained a high degree of perfection under his successor Peter. He was a pattern for all by the purity of his life, his conscientious observance of the Holy Rule, his affability and charitable disposition. Abbot Peter, when no longer able to bear the burdens of his office alone, chose Constabilis as his assistant and, with the consent of the brethren, committed the administration of the abbey to him. After Peter's death in 1123, Constabilis was sole abbot but held the office for only one year. The measure of his merit was full and he was summoned to receive his reward in 1124.

3. **Ven. Manegold** was abbot of St. George at Isny in Wuerttemberg. His firmness in maintaining discipline was so distasteful to the monks, that one of them inflicted upon him such severe wounds that he died of them in the year 1100.

4. **Galdric**, monk of Clairvaux and an uncle of St. Bernard, was the first to heed the invitation of the latter to renounce all things and serve God in the retirement of the cloister. Once a soldier of an earthly prince, he now fought the battles of the spirit with equal valor, and struggled manfully to conquer the world, the flesh and Satan. Having been sent from Citeaux to Clairvaux he died in this monastery and after his death appeared to St. Bernard, assuring him that he had entered into bliss. (Twelfth century).

18

1. **St. Helladius**, archbishop of Toledo in Spain, at one time a courtier, preserved his heart free from all improper earthly affection and strove to love God with his whole soul. It was his wont to escape from the distractions of court life and to associate with the monks of Agali, a monastery in the suburbs of Toledo, taking part in their devotions as well as in their humble labor. About the year 600 he severed his connections with the court, and became a monk at Agali. Five years later he was elected abbot. He was already sixty years of age, when he was raised to the archiepiscopal see of Toledo, of which he was one of the most brilliant ornaments. He was distinguished for his charity to the poor, who were among the principal objects of his solicitude. He left no written works; his example was more powerful than books. He ruled the see of Toledo for eighteen years and slept in peace in 632.

Benedict: Peter Diaconus, A. Wion. He does not appear to have been bishop of Cagliari, as there is no such bishop in the list in Gams.(Ser. Epp.)
Constabilis: Chronicles of Cava, A. Rudolph. Vite de Patri Cavensi, where he is called Costabile Gentilcore.
Manegold: Ben. Annals, Stad. Also called Maingold.
Galdric: B. Brito, William of St. Thierry.
Helladius: St. Ildephonse, St. Isidore, Rom. Mart.

2. **St. Angilbert**, abbot of St. Riquier, or Centula, in the diocese of Amiens, in his youth enjoyed the confidence of King Pepin and of Charlemagne, whose daughter Bertha he espoused. After his marriage he was appointed governor of Ponthieu on the northern sea-coast. He was about to give battle to a horde of Norman invaders in 789, when he chanced to visit the abbey of St. Riquier. Here he vowed to embrace the religious state, if he came from this peril unscathed. A violent storm defeated the purposes of the enemy, and Angilbert, true to his vow and with the consent of his wife, begged for admission to the abbey of St. Riquier as a monk. Abbot Symphorian was delighted to receive him and found him a docile disciple. Three years later Angilbert was chosen abbot. With assistance from Charlemagne he rebuilt the monastic church, also erected another in honor of the Blessed Virgin and a chapel in honor of St. Benedict. These three sanctuaries were dedicated at the same time, in the presence of twelve archbishops. In 792 he assisted at a council in Regensburg, at which the heresy of Felix of Urgel was condemned, and in 794 he attended the council at Frankfurt. Two years later the emperor dispatched him on an important mission to Rome. In his monastery there were three hundred monks and a hundred boys who assisted at the choir-chant. The Divine Office was sung by three choirs in such succession that the divine praise was almost continually heard throughout the day and the night. At an advanced age he was summoned to the court of Charlemagne to witness the execution of that monarch's last will and testament. Upon his return to St. Riquier, illness befell him and he died three weeks after the death of the emperor in 814. He was probably canonized by Pascal II in 1110, for since that time the day of his death has been observed as a feast.

3. **Two thousand Martyrs** of the Order of knights and monks of Calatrava (Cistercian) who suffered tortures and death under the Moorish chieftain Jukaf on July 19, 1195, are commemorated in Spain to the present day. The church built in honor of Our Lady over their remains was richly endowed with indulgences by Pope Leo X.

19

1. **St. Boniface**, bishop of Lausanne, was born in the year 1188; at the age of seventeen he was sent to the university of Paris, where after completing the course of study he was appointed a public lecturer. As a result of certain misunderstandings, the nature of which is not described, he left Paris in 1237 to resume his profession as a teacher in Cologne. Two years later he was appointed bishop of Lausanne. At the Council of Lyons in 1245 he favored the excommunication of the Emperor Frederic II. This courageous attitude led to his arrest by imperial emissaries, but he contrived to make his escape. Wearied by the incessant persecutions of which he was a victim he journeyed to Rome and resigned his office in 1247 into the hands of Pope Innocent IV, returned to Paris and subsequently went to the Netherlands where he was appointed spiritual director of the Cistercian nuns of Cambre (Camera S. Mariae). Although not a professed monk of any monastery, he

---

Angilbert: Anscher, Hariulf, Alcuin, Eginhard. Other forms: Engilbert, Ingilbert.
Martyrs of Calatrava: F. R. de Andrade.

wore the Cistercian habit and ordered his life according to the maxims of St.
Bernard.   Well tried in the school of tribulation, he was called to his eternal
reward in 1266.

2.   Ven. Frederic, first abbot of Hirschau in Suabia, was of noble family
and well educated.   The grace of God moved him to forego the pleasure and
advantages offered by the world and to enter the monastery of Einsiedeln in
Switzerland.   About this time, countess Wiltrudis of Calw resolved to revive
the monastery of Calw, which had been laid waste by her husband.   For this
purpose she secured twelve monks from Einsiedeln.   Their leader was Frederic,
who was blessed as abbot by Bishop Einhard of Speier.   In the midst of his
zealous and unselfish labor for the restoration of Hirschau, he was accused to
Count Adalbert, the patron of the abbey, as a hypocrite and as being indifferent to the interests of the community.   The count, who had never entertained friendly feelings for the abbot, condemned him without a hearing and
deposed him.   News of this harsh proceeding having reached Abbot Ulric of
Lorsch, that prelate, who had been informed of the strained relations between
the abbot and the monks of Hirschau, hastened to deliver Frederic from the
hands of his revilers.   He prevailed upon him to leave Hirschau and make his
temporary residence at the monastery of St. Michael on the Ebersberg, where
he died on May 8, 1070.   When the corpse was prepared for interment, it
was discovered that he wore an iron chain which had left deep marks in his
flesh.

3.   Commemoration of the Victory in which our Holy Father overcame
the tempter by casting himself into a bush of briars and nettles and thus ex-
tinguishing the fires of lust, as Pope Gregory relates in the Second Book of
Dialogues (chap. 2).   The day was known as *S. Benedicti in Spinis.*

20

1.   St. Eucherius, bishop of Orleans, at an early age was placed in a
school in which he was prepared for the holy priesthood.   It was his pious
mother's wish and prayer from his very infancy to see him some day ministering in the sanctuary.   In 714 he entered the abbey of Jumieges and seven
years later was elected bishop of Orleans.   So reluctant was he to abandon the
silent halls of Jumieges that he requested the brethren to oppose forcible resistance to any attempt made to carry him off against his will.   Remonstrances were of no avail; he was obliged to accept and in 721 received episcopal
consecration.   The lessons in virtue received at Jumieges fitted him for the
heavy duties of his office.   He was not spared a severe test.   Charles Martel
confiscated some churches to pay his soldiery; the zealous bishop entered a
protest, for which he was banished, in 737, first to Cologne and later to the
castle of Hasbein near Liege. Robert, the governor of the province, appointed
him distributor of his alms and finally allowed him to retire to the monastery

---

Boniface: Le Mire, MS. of Cambre S. Marie.   According to Gams (Ser. Ep.) he resigned in
      1239 and died in 1258.   Stad.
Frederic: Trithemius, Annales Hirsaug.
Benedict: Greg. the Great: Lib. Dial. cap. 2.

of St. Trond, where he employed all his time in prayer and meditation, till the year 743, when he was deemed fit to receive the crown of justice.

2. The devout **Isembard**, monk of Hemmenrode, filled the office of sacristan with the zeal and purity of heart becoming to every one of the "servants of the Lord who stand in the house of the Lord." After thirty years of faithful observance of the Rule, his soul fled from its prison-house of clay to enter its heavenly mansion. On his deathbed he seemed to have a foretaste of the glory and beauty of Heaven, for he is said to have exclaimed: "Oh, how sweet is the Lord to those that taste of Him! What a flood of sweetness! My words cannot describe it. How happy are those who will forever enjoy the sweetness of the Lord."

3. Establishment of the Camaldolese Congregation of **Monte Corona** by Paul Giustiniani (†1528) in 1522, in which year he organized hermitages at Pasci-Lupo in the Apennines and at Masaccio in the Papal States. The Congregation took its name from the hermitage on Monte Corona near Perugia, established by Giustiniani's second successor.

21

1. **Ss. Germanus** and **Randoald** suffered death at the hands of marauders at Granfel near Basle, in Switzerland, in 666. The former was the son of a senator in Trier, had been carefully educated by Modoald and at the age of seventeen had, after distributing his possessions among the poor, become a solitary under the direction of Arnulph, former bishop of Metz, who lived in seclusion near Remiremont. After receiving clerical tonsure, he entered the monastery of Remiremont, where he was joined by his brother Numerian. Later he removed to Luxeuil where the lives of the monks were more severe. Here he lived under the guidance of Abbot Walbert who had him ordained a priest. When Duke Gondon had founded the monastery of Granfel, Germanus was designated its first abbot, and also commissioned to govern the monasteries of St. Ursitius and of St. Paul at Woerth. Gondon's successor Cathicus was a tyrannical lord and oppressed his subjects, harassed the poor and despoiled churches and religious houses. Accompanied by his prior, Randoald, he approached Cathicus and upbraided him for his behavior. His words made no impression and he returned to the monastery. On the way he encountered a band of the duke's servants, whom he begged to desist from their work of destruction. The ruffians slew both and robbed them. The bodies were found by the brethren three days later and were carried first to the church of St. Ursitius; later the remains were taken to Granfel (Grandvilliers), where they were always held in high veneration.

2. **St. Gumbert**, archbishop of Sens, resigned his office, and following a heavenly inspiration founded the abbey of Senones in the Vosges Mountains,

Eucherius: Mab., Stad., But.
Isembard: Caesarius of Heisterbach, Manrique.
Monte Corona: Wion, Heimbucher.
Germanus: Bobolenus in Mab., But., Acta S. Sedis XXI. 693.

which existed down to the time of the French Revolution. He died a holy death in 675.

3. **Guntildis**, abbess of Biblisheim near Hagenau in Alsace, was the daughter of the count of Montbeliard, who founded that monastery. She died with the reputation of sanctity in 1131.

4. **Peter of Toulouse**, monk of Clairvaux, restrained the desires of the flesh by fasts and mortifications to such a degree that the onslaughts of the evil one left him undisturbed. He died in the twelfth century.

22

1. **St. John**, surnamde *Apulus*, abbot of Lucca in Italy, had been a monk and dean at Monte Cassino, and was known for the power of his intercessory prayer, although he made no vain display of his gift lest pride turn him away from the central object of his thoughts. On one occasion a demoniac was brought to the monastery. John assembled the brethren in the oratory, united with them in prayer and sent the woman away freed from her tormentor. When the church of St. George with an adjoining garden was offered to Monte Cassino, John was sent to govern the house as its abbot. He died in 1055.

2. **Bl. Joanna Mary Bonomo**, abbess at S. Girolamo in Bassano, in northern Italy, was born at Asiago, in the diocese of Vicenza August 5, 1606, and placed with the Clares at Trent to be educated. She expressed a wish to become a nun; her father consented upon condition that she enter some religious house nearer to her home. Accordingly at the age of fifteen she became a nun at Bassano, where she received the veil and the religious name of Joanna. Her eminent virtue was a source of delight to the entire community. Having filled several positions, she was finally chosen abbess. Her tender conscience drew tears from her whenever she heard that God had been ever so slightly offended. Even as gold is tried by fire, her constancy was tested by persecutions; malicious tongues belittled her piety, and charged her with hypocrisy. In the midst of trials she preserved her peace of soul, and when some suggested that she complain against her enemies, she replied: "These trials are priceless treasures; tell me rather how to offer them at the foot of the Cross than to resent them." During the last years of her life, she suffered much from sickness. She died in the year 1670, and was beatified by Pius VI on June 2, 1783.

3. **Henry**, monk of Hemmenrode, in the diocese of Trier, experienced unusual spiritual consolations while celebrating Holy Mass, and maintained

Gumbert: Peter Damian, Robert of Auxerre. Also called Gundelbert.
Guntildis: Trithemius, Menard.
Peter: Manrique.
John: Abbot Desiderius of Monte Cassino, Leo Marsicanus.
Joanna: Decree of Beatification in Acts of Pius VI. Buchberger. Her Life was written in Italian by Leo Bracco, O.S.B. in 2 vols. in 1883 of which an English (abbreviated) translation was published in Rome, 1896. Dom Du Bourg, O.S.B.: La bienheur. Jeanne Marie Bonomo, Paris, Perrin, 1910.

the mastery of the spirit over the flesh by the practice of austerities. He lived in the twelfth or thirteenth century.

23

1. **St. Peter Damiani**, Doctor of the Church, Cardinal, monk of the Order of Fontavellana, was born at Ravenna in 1007 of noble but poor parents whose names are not known, and after whose death he was left in the hands of a heartless brother who ill-treated and starved him, and compelled him to be a swineherd. Another brother, called Damian, who was archpriest of Ravenna, took pity on the boy and gave him an education. He progressed so rapidly in his studies that at the age of twenty-five he was already regarded as an able public teacher at Parma and Ravenna. Taking offence, however, at the loose morals of the students, he planned leaving the world to lead a holy life in a religious order. One day he met two hermits of Fontavellana whom he accompanied to their hermitage and joined in their simple and retired life. He was appointed to lecture on Holy Scripture to his fellow-monks at Fontavellana, and later at Pomposa and Perugia. Being recalled some time later, he was commanded by the abbot with the consent of the hermits to govern the community after the abbot's death. In 1041 Peter took upon himself the responsibilities of the office of abbot, and displayed consummate sanctity and wisdom in directing the brethren. Five other hermitages were founded by him and placed under the government of priors. During all this time he was deeply concerned also with the affairs of the universal Church, and was particularly active in combatting evils among the clergy. In 1057 Pope Stephen X appointed him cardinal-bishop of Ostia, a promotion which Peter Damian accepted only after considerable pressure had been brought to bear upon him. It was due largely to his efforts that the unlawful Pope Benedict X renounced his claims and Nicholas II was elected. The latter sent Cardinal Peter to investigate charges of simony lodged against the clergy of Milan. He also vigorously opposed the aggressions of Henry IV, who caused the election of the antipope Cadalous. After achieving these successes, Peter returned to his solitude, but continued to inveigh against prevalent scandals both with word and pen. In 1063 the Pope sent him as legate to France to settle a dispute between the abbot of Cluny and the bishop of Macon at a council held at Chalons-sur-Saone. Once more he returned to Fontavellana, but in 1071 was again called out to reconcile the people of Ravenna, who had been excommunicated for supporting their archbishop, an adherent of Cadalous. Then he yearned to dwell in seclusion to the end of his days. On his return from Ravenna, he was taken ill at the monastery of St. Mary in Faenza, where he died on February 22, at the age of eighty-three years. He never was formally canonized, but has been venerated as a saint ever since his death. Pope Leo XII in 1823 ordained that his feast be celebrated on the 23d day of February and declared him a Doctor of the Church.

2. **St. Boisil**, prior of Melrose in the ancient kingdom of Northumberland, was gifted with the spirit of prophecy. His sanctity attracted St. Cuth-

Henry: Caesarius of Heisterbach, Henr.
Peter Damian: John of Lodi, But., Cath. Enc., Kir. Lex.

bert to become a monk at that monastery. He had often on his lips the holy names of the adorable Trinity and of Jesus, which he pronounced with such evident devotion and with such an abundance of tears that others were moved to weep with him. Not only did he constantly exhort his brethren with word and deed, but also made frequent excursions to preach to the poor in the villages. He fell ill with a disease and died while reading the Gospel of St. John with his disciple Cuthbert, in the year 664.

3. St. Earkongota, nun at Faremoutier, in the diocese of Meaux, in France, was the daughter of King Ercombert of Mercia and his wife Sexburgis, and had consecrated herself early in life to God at Faremoutier. After spending her days in gathering merits for the kingdom of Heaven, she had a presentiment of her approaching end. Commending her soul to the prayers of the sisters, she died a happy death in 660.

4. Nicholas of Prussia, prior of St. Nicholas de Boschetto near Genoa, both as sacristan and as prior was a perfect model of humility, silence and zeal in the divine service. So profoundly was he convinced of his inability to lead others, that he did not desist from asking to be relieved of his office till his request was granted. He died in 1456.

<h2 style="text-align:center">24</h2>

1. Bl. Bartholomew, abbot of Marmoutier near Tours, in France, was elected abbot of that monastery in 1063, and was confronted with discouraging difficulties from the very outset. Count Goffrid assumed sovereign rights over the house and demanded that the abbot receive investiture at his hands. In spite of respectful remonstrances by the monks, who sought to convince the oppressor that they owed allegiance to no one but the King and the Pope, Count Goffrid proceeded to employ force. At this critical moment, the religious, together with the sick and the poor who were supported by the monastery, went in procession to the altar of St. Martin and implored the intercession of that Saint. Their prayer was not in vain, for it so happened that Falko, the count's own brother, seized him and prevented the execution of his wicked design. Peace and security reigned once more and Bartholomew was at liberty to take possession of his office. With wonderful prudence and moderation he brought about an adjustment of certain controversies between the monastery, the bishops and certain landlords with whom the monastery was in litigation. Still greater was his solicitude for the advancement of the brethren in piety and learning. Marmoutier became an important ecclesiastical centre, and its religious were invited by many bishops to establish or conduct monasteries. The abbot's fame for holiness of life grew after he had effected the wonderful cure of two brothers, Haymo and Gautier. He died in the year 1084.

Boisil: Bede, But.
Earkongota: Bede, Fleming(July 7). Also called Ercongota.
Nicholas: Armellini, Pez.
Bartholomew: Mab., Stad.(according to whom he was abbot from 1004-1024).

2. **Bl. Simon,** a Cistercian laybrother of Aune, in the diocese of Liege, enjoyed numerous heavenly consolations. His peculiar gift was the power to read the hearts of men and discover their hidden failings. It is said that Pope Innocent III authorized all priests to absolve from reserved sins all penitents sent to them by this humble religious. He was also present at the fourth Council of the Lateran in 1215, and died about 1220.

3. **Bartholomew,** Cistercian abbot of Poblete, in Catalonia, was distinguished for his learning, his piety and zeal and is said to have restored life to a dead man. He died in the reputation of sanctity in 1445.

25

1. **St. Walburga,** abbess at Eichstaett in Bavaria, was the daughter of an English prince, and the sister of Ss. Wunibald and Willibald. She consecrated herself to God in the monastery of Winburn in England, and upon the invitation of St. Boniface came to Germany with St. Lioba and several other nuns in 748. Having spent two years at Bischofsheim under the direction of St. Lioba, she was appointed abbess of Heidenheim, where her virtues shone with renewed lustre, and she attained to intimate communion with Our Lord through contemplation and the exercises of active life. After her brother Willibald had been consecrated bishop of Eichstaett, he summoned Wunibald to assist him in planting the faith in those parts. Recognizing the importance of monastic institutions in the development of a Christian people, Wunibald established a monastery at Heidenheim for monks who were to educate boys. Near by, both brothers some time after built a house for nuns, and appointed Walburga its superior. She governed both institutions after Wunibald's death. In 777 she witnessed the solemn translation of his remains to Eichstaett, and on February 25, 779 followed him into the region of endless happiness. In 870 her remains were carried to Eichstaett, where they rest in a monastery of Benedictine nuns. A liquid known as St. Walburga's Oil oozes from a rock in which she is buried, and has afforded relief to many who used it devoutly. She is titular saint of many churches in Germany, Brabant, Flanders and France.

2. **St. Adelelm,** at one time prior of St. Blasien in the Black Forest, was abbot of Engelberg in Switzerland, had the gift of prophecy and foretold some of the destinies of his monastery. He was honored as a saint after his death in 1131.

3. **St. Aldetrudis,** abbess of Maubeuge in Hainault, was the daughter of noble parents, Vincent and Waldetrudis. In her early youth, her parents placed her in the care of St. Aldegundis, abbess of Maubeuge. She walked in the footsteps of the saintly abbess in humility and obedience, and received some reward for her virtues even during this life. After the death of Aldegundis,

Simon: Caesarius of Heisterbach, Molanus, Miraeus(according to whom he died 1229).
Bartholomew: Alvarez, Barnabas de Montalbo.
Walburg: Mab., Stad., A. Schneider, O.S.B., But.
Adelelm: C. Hartmann, H. Murer.

Aldetrudis was chosen to succeed her and governed the monastery for the space of twelve years to the day of her death in 696.

4. **St. Valerius,** abbot of St. Peter de Montibus in the Spanish province of Gallicia, was a native of Asturia. Wishing to become a monk at Alcala, his application was rejected, and he withdrew into a solitude near Ebronante, where he suffered much annoyance. He spent twenty-four years in solitary life, then took up his abode near an oratory built by St. Fructuosus of Braga, where he edified the people by the holiness of his life. The place soon became the resort of the pious faithful, some of whom remained and formed a religious community which Valerius governed to the year 695, when he died peacefully in the Lord.

5. **Ven. Mary Adeodata** (Pisani), born at Naples of parents of some distinction in 1806, was brought up religiously both at home and in an institution in her native city. When she was nineteen years of age, the family removed to the Island of Malta, where three years later she entered the convent of St. Peter at Notabile. During the twenty-five years of her life in the convent it was her chief aim to devote all the powers of her body and soul to the worthy service of God. In 1851 she was elected abbess, but choosing to obey rather than to command, she resigned the office after two years and spent the remaining days of her life in patient suffering of bodily infirmity till the Lord called her unto Himself on this day in the year 1855.

26

1. **St. Betto,** bishop of Auxerre, was born in Burgundy, the son of one Alberic and of his wife Angela, and professed as a monk in the monastery of St. Columba at Sens. On account of his piety and learning he was elected abbot of the monastery of St. Heraclius at Auxerre, and some time after prior of St. Columba, over which the prince-abbot Richard presided. With the consent of the latter, he extended the buildings of the monastery, adorned the shrines of Ss. Lupus and Columba and built a strong wall against the Norman invaders. He was raised to the see of Auxerre after the death of Bishop Gerannus, and even as bishop observed the practices of monastic life. He shared his meals with twelve poor persons, whom he daily admitted to his table, and had some edifying book read during the repast to debar useless and trivial conversation. After ruling the church of Auxerre for three or four years he died on the 24th of February 918 and was buried in the church of St. Germain in his episcopal city.

2. **St. Mechtildis,** a recluse at the monastery of Spanheim, in the diocese of Mainz, was a sister of Bernhelm, the first abbot of Spanheim. For seven years she was a recluse near St. Alban's in Mainz, and for twenty-two years at Spanheim. She died in 1154, having passed her days and a great

Aldetrudis: MS. of Rubea Valle, Breviary of Montes.
Valerius: St. Gennadius, Tamayo, Stad.
Adeodata: Acta S. Sedis XXX. 739, Seeboeck: Herrlichk. d. Kath. Kirche.
Betto: Mab.

part of her nights in reading Holy Scripture and in manual labor. Several other holy women, struck by her holy life, placed themselves under her guidance; they all followed the Benedictine Rule.

3. Bl. Leopardus, founder and first abbot of Marmoutier (Maurus-Muenster) in Alsace, won the gratitude of his countrymen by his zealous efforts to christianize and civilize the region about his monastery and died about 615.

4. Andrew, who had been archdeacon at Verdun, became a humble monk at Clairvaux. He visited Clairvaux and while there he was so powerfully moved by the devotion of the monks that he begged Abbot Robert to receive him among the brethren. Some time after, he felt an inclination to enter an Order with a less austere rule, but the prayers of the brethren induced him to abide with them. From this time his resolution was unshaken and he persevered to the end of his days. He lived and died in the twelfth century.

27

1. St. Leander, archbishop of Seville, in Spain, was born at Cartagena in 534. His parents, Severian and Theodora, ware nobles of that country. His brothers were St. Fulgentius, bishop of Ecija, and St. Isidore, who succeeded him in the see of Seville. When that see became vacant by the death of Bishop Stephen, Leander was chosen his successor and by his fervent prayer invoked the blessing of Heaven upon his diocese. One of the difficulties with which he was compelled to contend was Arianism, the religion of the Visigoths. His energetic defence of the Catholic faith was rewarded by the conversion of many Arians, which incensed King Leovigild, pariticularly after his son, Prince Hermengild, had adjured the heresy and become a Catholic. Leander and many others were sent into exile. While in banishment he wrote a monastic rule for his sister Florentine. Leovigild soon felt remorse for having ordered the execution of his son Hermenegild and recalled Leander, whom he even requested to instruct his son Recared in the truths of the faith of Peter. Recared, after his father's death, succeeded to the throne, openly declared himself a Catholic and persuaded the Arian bishops to make their peace with the Church. A council was held at Toledo at which the Visigoths of Spain submitted their profession of faith,—a change of heart which afforded genuine pleasure to Leander, who presided at the gathering. Towards the end of his life he suffered much from the gout, which St. Gregory the Great, who was similarly afflicted, writing to him, calls a mercy and a favor of Heaven. He consoled himself by saying: "By these sufferings of the flesh we can atone for the sins of the flesh." He died in 601. He is considered on of the apostles of Spain and the monastic Breviary styles him a Doctor.

2. St. Marquart, abbot of Pruem in the diosese of Trier, was a monk of Ferrieres before his elevation to the abbatial dignity. In 834 he was com-

Mechtild: Trithemius, Steele: Anchoresses.
Leopardus: Mab. Other forms of the name: Leobardus, Leobaldus, Leonard.
Andrew: Barnabas de Montalbo.
Leander: St. Isidore, Greg. the Great, Mab., But.

missioned with the delicate task of recalling Prince Lothair, son of the Emperor Louis, to a sense of filial duty. Some years later he ordered the deacon Wandelbert to write a treatise on the life and miracles of St. Goar. While visiting Rome, Pope Sergius II. presented him with relics of SS. Chrysanthus and Daria. According to some authorities he was the founder of the monastery of Muenster-Eifel in the duchy of Juelich. He died in 853.

3. Bl. John, abbot of Gorze in Lorraine, was born at Vandiere near Metz towards the end of the ninth century and received his education chiefly at St. Michael's in Verdun. After his father's death, John administered the estate and acquitted himself of this task so ably that he elicited universal approval, even that of the bishop. Being charged with new commissions requiring unusual ability and prudence, John resolved to continue his studies. One day he was profoundly touched at the sight of a person wearing a hairshirt. He at once left everything and placed himself under the direction of the hermit Humbert. After having several times changed his abode, he returned to Humbert's hermitage. His example induced the archdeacon Einhold to distribute his possessions among the poor. John and Einhold later became monks at Gorze and by their edifying conduct breathed new life into the community. The abbot often found it necessary to check John's austerities. After the abbot's death, Einhold was chosen abbot and John procurator. John was sent on an embassy to the Moorish king Abderrhaman III by Emperor Otto I. On his return, Einhold was no longer alive, and John was elected his successor. He died in 973.

28

1. St. Herbert was a disciple of Venerable Bede and succeeded St. Ceolfrid as abbot of Wearmouth and Jarrow. He had been educated at Jarrow and also at Rome. Bede was wont to call him Eusebius and addressed to him the introduction to his commentary on the Apocalypse. The date of his death is not known, but it certainly was before 754, in which year his remains were transferred to Glastonbury.

2 Ven. Victor, a monk of St. Gall's in Switzerland, was at one time filled with a spirit of unrest that drove him to create disturbances even within the walls of the monastery of which he was a member and finally to leave the community. Convinced of the error of his ways by a relative Erchinbald, bishop of Strassburg, he returned to St. Gall's and expiated his youthful follies by a penitential life. He died in the odor of sanctity in 960.

3. Violanza de Sousa, abbess of St. Benedict de Castris at Evora in Portugal, was of noble parentage and in her childhood was offered to the convent at Olivelas near Lisbon. She governed the house at Evora for twenty-eight years, and was remarkable for the angelic sweetness of her life. God

Marquart: Abbot Lupus, Mab.
John: His disciple John of Metz, Mab., Stad. gives date of death 962. Chev., Boll. call him "Beatus".
Herbert: Stocker, Stad. (Huvetbertus). Other forms: Juetbert, Hetbert.
Victor: H. Murer.

visited her with blindness which she bore with amazing patience, till she was blessed with the vision of God in His Kingdom about the year 1400.

4. Establishment of the **Swiss Congregation of the Immaculate Conception** in 1602, chiefly through the efforts of dean Joachim Beroldinger of Einsiedeln. Pope Urban VIII in 1622 endowed it with all the privileges of religious Orders, even those of the Mendicants. It consisted of nine monasteries, and in the nineteenth century took root in the United States, the first monastery being that of St. Meinrad in Indiana.

29

1. **St. Oswald**, bishop of Worcester and archbishop of York in England, was a nephew of St. Odo, archbishop of Canterbury, by whom he was educated and appointed dean of the cathedral chapter of Winchester. Preferring the humble service of Christ to honors and wealth, he left his native land and became a monk at Fleury (S. Benoit sur-Loire) in France. The gratifying reports that reached Odo of his nephew's progress in spiritual life prompted him to invite Oswald, with the consent of his abbot, to support him in the government of his see. In the meantime, before Oswald arrived in England, Archbishop Odo died, and Oswald was summoned to York by another uncle who was archbishop of that city and who shortly after recommended him for the see of Worcester. His administration was marked by many noteworthy events and deeds, among them being the foundation of the monasteries of Westberry and Ramsey. In 794 he was made archbishop of York, but without being required to reside in that city. He was very charitable to the poor, fed twelve of them daily and washed their feet, mindful of those words of the Lord: "Let him that would be the first among you, be the least." He took great delight in visiting the monks at Worcester, and lost no opportunity to exhort them unto fidelity and perseverance. While he was leaving the church on the third Sunday in Lent in the year 992, he turned his eyes towards Heaven and prayed fervently. Some one inquired what he saw, and the Saint replied: "I see whither I am going; tomorrow I shall know the truth." Then he returned to the church, and received Extreme Unction and the Holy Viaticum. During the night he attended Matins with the monks, and spent the remaining hours till dawn in prayer. In the morning, he washed the feet of the poor, as was his wont, and expired while saying the words: "Glory be to the Father and to the Son and to the Holy Ghost," on the 29th of February of the year above mentioned. "St. Oswald made quick progress in the path of perfect virtue, because he studied with the utmost earnestness to deny himself and his own will, listening attentively to that fundamental maxim of the Eternal Truth, which St. Benedict, of whose holy order he became a bright light, repeats with great energy. This holy founder declares in the close of his Rule that he who desires to give himself up to God, must trample all earthly things under his feet, renounce everything that is not God, and die to all earthly affections, so as to attain a perfect disengagement of heart. that God may fill and entirely possess it, in order to establish therein the Kingdom of His grace and pure love for ever." (Butler).

Violanza: B. Brito.
Swiss Congregation: Calmet, Biner, Annales O.S.B. 1909, S. & M.
Oswald: Mab., But., Stan.

March

1

1. **St. Rudesind,** bishop of Duma in Portugal and Compostella in Spain, was of royal blood, his father being the prince Gutierrez Mendes de Arias and his mother St. Ilduara. Born in 907, he was from childhood devoted to practices of piety and displayed such eminent virtue that at an early age he was made bishop of Duma. Though unwilling, he was compelled to yield to the unanimous wish of clergy and people. A lover of the contemplative life, he founded several monasteries, to which he retired at times to renew his spirit by taking part in the spiritual exercises. King Sanchez deposed bishop Sisenand of Compostella for good reasons and found no one better fitted to fill the vacant see than Rudesind, who struggled against the appointment, but found himself compelled to yield and governed both sees. With the support of armed forces he succeeded in driving the Normans out of Gallicia and the Moors out of Portugal. Compostella hailed him as its preserver, but his peace was disturbed for a second time. Bishop Sisenand escaped from prison and forced him to abandon Compostella in 935. Rudesind retired to the monastery of S. Juan de Cabero, where he often spent the nights in prayer. Subsequently he founded the monastery of Cella Nueva and organized a community with abbot Franquilla as its first superior. To the edification of all, the founder himself did not disdain to become a monk in this monastery, thus concealing his high ecclesiastical and civil dignity beneath the poor robes of a religious. After the abbot's death, the brethren insisted that Rudesind be their abbot, and from that day nobles, bishops and abbots might be seen humbly knocking at the gate and begging for admission to the ranks of the monks. After ruling Cella Nueva with much success and with evident tokens of divine pleasure for a number of years, the hour of his death drew nigh. Summoning the brethren to his bedside, he delivered a touching exhortation and, by their request, appointed his successor, after which he closed his eyes and rested from his faithful and noble toil in the year 977. Senorina, abbess of S. Juan de Venaria, who had always entertained the highest veneration for St. Rudesind, heard many voices chanting the words "Te Deum laudamus" at the time of his death. He was canonized by Pope Celestine III in 1195. He is also commemorated in the martyrologies of the Camaldolese and Vallombrosans.

2. **St. Siviard,** abbot of Anisle or St. Carilef, in the province of Maine, in France, was the son of the noble Sigirannus and of his wife Adda, who were inhabitants of Maine. He differed from other youths of his age by his piety and exemplary conduct. Having become a monk at Anisle, he was after some years elected abbot. One of his peculiar gifts was the power of cheering the despondent. After his death in 728 he is said to have appeared to one of the brethren and to have said : "Brother, I give thanks to Christ who has deigned to receive me into the abode of eternal rest."

Rudesind: Stephen, monk of Cella Nueva, Mab., Stad.,Others attribute his canonization to Callixtus III (Battandier).
Siviard: Mab., Chev.

3. Establishment of the **Order of the Knights of Calatrava** in Spain. It owes its beginnings to Abbot Raymond of Fitero in Navarre, who permitted the laybrothers of the monastery to take up arms against the Moors (1157). The Rule adopted by the Knights was that of the Cistercians. The Order was approved by Pope Gregory VIII. With the final subjugation of the Moors in 1492, the purpose for which the Order was established no longer existed and it began to languish. Its possessions and revenues were confiscated by several Spanish kings in the 18th and 19th century and were finally dissipated in the general secularization of 1838.

2

1. **St. Suitbert**, bishop and Apostle of Frisia, a native of England, was educated by St. Egbert, whom he accompanied to Ireland to live as a monk in that country. Egbert himself desired to pass over to Germany and preach the Gospel, but was prevented from doing so; in 690, however, he sent twelve missionaries under the leadership of St. Willibrord to Frisia. Among these apostolic men was Suitbert (Swibert) who planted the faith in Frisia, Geldria and Cleves. When Willibrord was consecrated archbishop of Utrecht by Pope Sergius I in 696, Suitbert was also urged by his flock of converts and by his fellow laborers to receive episcopal consecration. He returned to England in 697 or 698 and was consecrated by St. Wilfrid, archbishop of York, but no definite see was assigned to him, since he was to be merely an auxiliary to the archbishop of Utrecht. Having returned to the continent, he resumed his labors with increased energy and devotion. After providing for order in the churches which he had founded, he left them in the care of Willibrord and his associates and penetrated further into the country later known as Berg and Mark, on the right bank of the Rhine, but saw his hopes blighted by an invasion of the Saxons, who laid waste the country. He now resolved to prepare himself to render an account of his own soul if it pleased the Lord of life and death to call him hence. Withdrawing to the island of Woerth in the Rhine, he founded a monastery there, in which he died on March 1, 713.

2. **Aunofledis**, a nun of Faremoutier, was led to extraordinary heights of sanctity by St. Burgundofara and died 650.

3. **Stephen**, first archbishop of Upsala, in Sweden, had previously been a monk of the Cistercian monastery of Alvastra in Ostergotland, where he was so conspicuous by his sanctity and learning that he was made archbishop in 1162. He died in the year 1185, having ruled his diocese for twenty-three years. His remains are at Alvastra.

3

1. **St. Cunegundis**, empress and virgin, was the wife of Emperor St. Henry II. Having recovered from a dangerous illness, she founded a monastery

---

Knights of Calatrava: Biedenfeld, Heimbucher, C. E.
Suitbert: Bede, Batavia Sacra, But. Other forms of the name: Suitbert, Suidbert, Swidbert, Swibert.
Aunofledis: Bede in the Vita of St. Burgundofara. Also called Annofledis, Lanofledis, Nofledis & c. (Dunbar).
Stephen: J. Magnus, Seguin, Stad.

for Benedictine nuns at Kauffungen, then in the diocese of Paderborn.   While the buildings were approaching their completion, Henry II died in 1024.   Cunegundis now followed the dearest desire of her heart, to join the virgins whose life was spent in the retirement of the cloister.   On the anniversary of Henry's death, in 1025, she invited a number of prelates to attend the dedication of the church.   After the Gospel was sung at the Mass, she laid aside her imperial robes, and put on the habit of a nun; her hair was cut off and she received the veil and the ring, the tokens of her espousal to the Lord.   She lived with the nuns as humbly as the least of them and, before she died in 1039, requested her sisters to bury her in her religious habit.   She was buried at Bamberg, beside her husband Henry, and was canonized by Pope Innocent III in 1200.

2.   **St. Anselm**, abbot of Nonantula, in the former duchy of Modena, was at one time duke of Friuli in Italy, but scorned wealth and honors and preferred to serve God in obscurity and humility.   With the assistance of his brother-in-law, King Aistulph, he founded the monastery of Fanano in 750, and two years later that of Nonantula, where he labored with his own hands clearing the land for the erection of the buildings.   He also founded monasteries at Vicenza and Susonia, in each instance providing a separate house for guests.   While his communities were flourishing and the membership is said to have exceeded a thousand, he experienced a severe trial.   The Lombard King Desiderius banished him, and Anselm spent several years with monks of Monte Cassino.   It was probably after that king had been defeated by Charlemagne (774), that Anselm returned to Nonantula, where he died in 803.   Many devout persons were relieved of sufferings through the intercession of this Saint.

3.   **St. Gervinus**, abbot of Centula (S. Riquier) in Ponthieu, was born at Rheims of respected parents and received an excellent liberal education.   Incautious reading of pagan classics nearly led to his spiritual ruin.   Recognizing the peril from which the grace of God had delivered him, he became a canon of the cathedral of Rheims.   When the bonds which connected him with the world were severed by the death of his parents, he applied for admission to the abbey at Verdun.   Here he lived a most edifying life as a monk, gained the full confidence of his abbot and accompanied him on a pilgrimage to the Holy Land.   Shortly after, he was chosen abbot of Centula, where he exerted a wholesome influence by his fervent prayers and by his constant readiness to receive the confessions of sinners who came to the monastery from distant parts.   Towards the end of his holy career he was visited with sickness, which he bore without complaint to the hour of his death in 1075.

4

1.   **St. Peter**, bishop of Policastro and abbot of Cava near Naples in Italy, was born of the family of Pappacarbone at Salerno, and owed his education to his uncle St. Alferius, founder and first abbot of Cava.   He professed as a monk in that monastery under abbot Leo and became the successor of the latter in 1075.   The eight years preceding Leo's death had been spent by Peter

---

Cunegundis: Mab., But., K. L. Acc. to Battandier she was canonized April 3, 1200.
Anselm: Ughelli, Ferrari.
Gervinus: Hariulf of Centula.

at the celebrated monastery of Cluny studying the discipline, system and spirit of that reform. When he attempted to introduce the practices of Cluny at Cava, he met resistance from the monks and for some time withdrew to another house together with a few that supported his endeavors. The monks of Cava soon regretted their stubbornness and begged him to return. From this time dates the Congregation of Cava which at one time consisted of 333 houses, this number comprising monasteries and parishes. For thirty years he was bishop of Policastro, but could not resist the attraction of monastic life and resigned in 1109, returned to Cava and died at the age of eighty-five years in 1118.

2. **Ven. Burkard**, abbot of St. Gall in Switzerland, ruled that illustrious abbey from 1007-1023. Much of his time was devoted to a reconstruction of the house, which had suffered a sad decline under his immediate predecessor. His efforts and prayer accomplished marvelous results; St. Gall's became one of the most exemplary monasteries. In 1022 he was summoned to accompany the imperial armies to Italy; on the return, a sickness broke out among the troops and carried away abbot Burkard in 1023. He was interred at Frankenmuenster.

3. **Rupert**, abbot of Deutz near Cologne, was educated in the monastery of St. Lawrence at Liege and professed under its abbot Berengarius (1076-1115). One of his teachers, Heribrand, advised him to cherish a special devotion to Our Lady whom we invoke as "Seat of Wisdom," for Rupert was by no means brilliantly gifted. Envious brethren caused him so much annoyance that he left Liege, entered the monastery of Sigeburg and later that of Deutz where he was made abbot in 1117. He was a copious writer, chiefly on scriptural subjects. His death occurred in 1135.

4. **John Gradenicus**, was a Venetian by birth and became a disciple of St. Romuald, the founder of Camaldoli. He is said to have set out, contrary to the holy abbot's wishes, on a pilgrimage to the Holy Land, but to have suffered so severely from a fall that he repented his rashness and after his recovery lived for thirty years in a hermitage near Monte Cassino. He was an enemy of all sins of the tongue, particularly of detraction. The year of his death is 1012. His memory is honored both at Camaldoli and at Monte Cassino, but he receives no mention in the martyrologies of either house.

5

1. **Bl. Peter of Chateauneuf**, a Cistercian monk of Fontfroid and martyr, was sent as papal legate to check the Albigensian heresy in southern France. When he saw that the efforts of the Catholic missionaries were rewarded with little success, he said: "The cause of Christ will never progress till one of us sheds his blood in defence of the truth; would that I were the first to fall." He repeatedly rebuked the crafty duke Raymond of Toulouse for

Peter: Ughelli; Vite de'S. Abbati Cavensi; Gams, according to whom he was bishop of Policastro from 1079-1109 and died 1123.
Burkard: Goldast, Stad., Burgener (Burkard II).
Rupert: Mab., Stad., K. L.

his duplicity and for cherishing the Albigensian error. Raymond feigned willingness to make reparation and arranged a meeting with the legate at the villa of S. Gilles. Here Peter spoke to him in such plain terms that the Count threatened to kill him. Peter was led away by his friends, accompanied by two of the Count's minions, to the banks of the Rhone, where the party spent the night. On the following morning Peter, after celebrating Holy Mass, was on the point of crossing the river when one of the Count's men pierced him with a lance. Dying he said to his slayer: "May God forgive you as I forgive you," and received the martyr's crown in 1208. When his body was exhumed a year later it was found incorrupt.

2. **Ven. Hincmar**, abbot of St. Remigius at Rheims, professed as a monk at a time when discipline was on the wane, but was one of the religious whose prayers wrought a change of heart in the lukewarm and revived the former splendor of the house. Bishop Hugo of Rheims commissioned Erchinbold, abbot of Fleury, to reform the abbey of S. Remigius in 945. His ablest assistant was the monk Hincmar, who was appointed abbot. His success and reputation induced other monasteries, such as Homblieres and Basole, which also stood in need of revival, to have recourse to him. He died in 967, having governed his community during twenty-two years.

6

1. **St. Cadroe**, abbot, was born of Irish parents and was sent to Armagh by his uncle Beanus to be educated in the excellent schools of that city. For some time he also conducted a school in his native land, but in the year 945, when he had already reached the fortieth year of his age, he resolved to leave Ireland and, following the example of so many of his countrymen, to embrace the religious life on the continent. After landing at Boulogne, Cadroe and his twelve companions proceeded to Perronne to visit the tomb of St. Fursey. Near by lived a devout lady, by name Hersindis, who directed them to a chapel and cell in the forest of Thierache. They here formed a religious community of which Cadroe was to be the head; he declined to accept the honor and succeeded in persuading his friends to choose Machalanus, another of their number. For some time they lived together without binding themselves to any of the recognized rules. Feeling the need of more perfect organization and discipline, Machalanus went to Gorze and Cadroe to Fleury, where they took the habit of the Order. Upon the expiration of their novitiate, they were recalled by Hersindis, who furnished them means to establish two monasteries, one at Thierache and another at Vasour. It was only at the instance of Emperor Otto that Cadroe was prevailed upon to assume the office of abbot at the latter place. The fame of his sanctity attracted many to his community. While visiting Metz, the bishop invited him urgently to settle in that city. After appointing a successor at Vasour, he took up his abode at Metz. The people were delighted to have so holy a man in their midst and never grew tired of seeing and hearing him. When the Empress Adelheid sailed up the Rhine on her way to Italy in 975, she expressed a desire to meet all persons standing in high repute for their

---

Peter of Chateauneuf: Peter of Vaux de Cernay, K. L. (Castelnau).
Hincmar: Marlot, Frodoard in Mab.

sanctity.   Cadroe was invited to meet her at Neristein on the Rhine, where she was deeply touched by his edifying conversation.   He had already spent four days at Neristein and was about to return to his monastery, when the empress begged him to prolong his stay for two days.   They were to be his last, for when he was on the point of taking his departure he was seized with a violent fever and died in the seventy-fifth year of his age.   His remains were interred at Metz.

2.   SS. Kyneburga, Kyneswida, Kynedrida, and Tibba were holy nuns in England.   The three first named were the daughters of King Penda of Mercia, and St. Tibba was a relative.   Kyneburga had been the wife of Alcfrid, king of Bernicia, and after his death had become abbess of Dermundcastre. Her two sisters and Tibba had consecrated themselves to God at an early age and lived lives of singular holiness.   Their remains were removed to the monastery of Peterborough where the feast of the three princesses has always been observed on the present day.   St. Tibba died on the 13th of December.   They lived in the 7th century.

3.   Bl. Theodore, third abbot of the monastery at the Lateran in Rome, induced St. Faustus to write the life of St. Maurus, the disciple of our Holy Father St. Benedict.   Abbot Theodore died in 629.

4.   Ven. Gradulph, abbot of Fontenelle in France, was elected coadjutor to the unworthy archbishop Malgerius of Rouen, but died before the burden of that office was actually laid upon his shoulders in the year 1047.

7

1.   St. Esterwin, abbot of Wearmouth in England, was a relative of St. Benedict Biscop, and, like him, was at one time a prominent official at the court of King Egfrid of Northumberland.   In 673 he bade farewell to all prospects of earthly greatness and exchanged his court dress for the cowl of a monk at St. Peter's, Wearmouth.   On account of his learning and virtue he received the order of priesthood; yet he did not disdain the humblest manual labor of his brethren, such as work in the kitchen, in the fields, mill and stables.   When Benedict Biscop undertook his last pilgrimage to Rome, he appointed Esterwin abbot of St. Peter's, in which capacity he was more humble and affable than ever.   Conscious that he must one day render an account of his stewardship and fearing lest he might suffer for being too indulgent, he sought every occasion to prevent misconduct by kindly exhortations and warnings.   Love for the brethren was his distinguishing trait; he even slept in the general dormitory. An illness that befell him towards the end of his life compelled him to occupy a separate cell.   When the hour of his dissolution drew nigh, he called the brethren to his side, bade them a touching farewell and died, in the year 685.

Cadroe: Mab., Stad., O'Hanlon, But.
Kyneburga: Ingulph, William of Malmesbury, Capgrave, But.   According to the Bollandists
    she is identical with Kynedrida.
Theodore: Mab.
Gradulph: Mab., Stad.
Esterwin: Bede, Matthew of Westminster, Flem., Stan. (Easterwine).

2. **St. Ardo**, surnamed Smaragdus, in the days of Charlemagne and of his son Louis, was a saintly monk in the monastery of Aniane in Languedoc. He is the author of a life of St. Benedict of Aniane, and died in the year 843, at the age of sixty years.

3. **John**, second abbot of Mont Blandin at Ghent, in Flanders, was the worthy successor of St. Amandus. He was endowed with unusual gifts of grace, prudence and eloquence, and died in 685.

8

1. **St. Veremund**, abbot of Gerace, was a native of Arellano or of Villa-tuerta in Navarre. At an early age he was clad with the religious habit by his uncle, the abbot Munius of Gerace, and in the course of years made such rapid strides in perfection that he was elected abbot after his uncle's death. He was distinguished for his charity to the poor and his childlike devotion to the Blessed Virgin. Once during a famine, he betook himself to prayer and procured relief for three thousand sufferers who came to his monastery in their distress. Pope Gregory VII spoke of him in terms of praise. St. Veremund died in 1092.

2. **St. Hunfrid**, previously a monk at Pruem, was elected bishop of Terrouane in 856. In 860 he assisted at the Council of Tusey, and in the following year was driven from his see by the Normans, who ravaged the country. Pope Nicholas I consoled him in a letter and encouraged him to return to Terrouane and gather the dispersed sheep of his flock. Hunfrid continued to labor for nine years in his apostolic field. The monks of St. Bertin at Sithiu now chose him as their abbot. He governed that monastery for two years, at the same time discharging the duties of the episcopal office. Charles the Bald arbitrarily deposed him from the abbatial office and substituted the monk Hilduin. In 667 Terrouane was again devastated by the Normans. Hunfrid survived this disaster four years, and died in 871. He was honored at Boulogne and Sithiu.

3. **St. Stephen**, Cistercian abbot of Obazine, in France, was born near Limoges, received an excellent Christian education and was ordained a priest. Following an interior impulse to serve God in retirement from the world, he distributed his possessions among the poor and withdrew to a lonely spot in the forest of Obazine. Here Stephen and his companion Peter, who was also a priest, began to lead an eremitical life not unlike that of the early Egyptian solitaries. Shortly other devout persons joined them, so that it was deemed advisable to establish a regular community. A house and a church were built, and the bishop of Limoges approved the enterprise. Stephen himself was the superior, and while firmly insisting upon observance of the rule which all had agreed to follow, he was the most conscientious of all. He punished even the slightest violation of the rule, every mistake made in chanting the Psalms, every improper posture, laughter and sleepiness, and frequently had others

Ardo: Breviary of Aniane, L. K. (Smaragdus).
John: Sigebert, Sander, Stad.
Veremund: Boll.
Hunfrid: Iperius, Frodoard. Chev. (Honfroy).

administer the discipline to him that he might feel what others were made to suffer. Fearing lest the rule introduced into this monastery and the one he had founded for women at Correze would not be observed after his death, he visited the Carthusians at Grenoble and the monastery of Citeaux for the purpose of acquainting himself with the details of government and observance. He took the Cistercian habit in 1152 and was made abbot of Obazine by the bishop of Limoges. From that time the house observed the rule of Citeaux. Stephen founded two other houses, one at Cahors and one at Santon. While visiting a sick monk he was prostrated by a fever and died in 1159.

4. **Gundulf,** bishop of Rochester in England, had been a monk of Bec in Normandy and was in frequent correspondence with St. Anselm and Lanfranc. He sanctified his labors by incessant prayer and loved to meditate on the Sacred Passion of Our Lord. Gundulf received his heavenly crown in the year 1108.

5. **Ven. Bruno,** bishop of Verden, was born towards the end of the ninth century and was a relative of the Saxon duke, Herman. He embraced the monastic life and in 962 was made bishop of Verden, where he built the cathedral church. He was a staunch defender of the laws of the Church, as is shown by his refusal of Christian burial to the duke, who died in excommunication. When Bruno felt the approach of death, he had himself carried to the church where he publicly asked pardon of all for having served God so poorly. He died in 975.

9

1. **St. Frances of Rome** (Francesca Romana), widow and founder of the Oblates of Tor' di Specchi in Rome with the rule of St. Benedict, was born in the capital of the Catholic world in 1384, her parents being Paul Buxa and his wife Jacobella de Roffredeschi. At the age of eleven years she entreated her parents to permit her to embrace religious life as a nun. This wish was not fulfilled; her parents were of high rank, and preferred her to shine in social circles by the side of Lawrence de Ponziani, to whom she was married in 1396. Without neglecting the duties of her state of life, she shunned feastings and public meetings, delighted in prayer, meditation and visits to churches. If she was interrupted in her devout exercises by her husband or any other member of her family, she would at once obey, saying: "A married woman must, when called upon, quit her devotions to God at the altar, and find Him in her household affairs." In company with several other noble Roman women she placed herself under the spiritual direction of the Olivetan Benedictines. They led a religious life in their homes without making vows or wearing a special religious habit. During the invasion of Rome by King Ladislaus of Naples in 1413, her husband was banished from Rome and her eldest son taken as a hostage. In the midst of these trials, she said: "God hath given and God hath taken away. I rejoice in these losses, because they are God's will." After her

---

Stephen: Boll.
Gundulf: Mab.
Bruno: Stad.

husband's return from banishment he allowed her more liberty to devote herself to her devotions, and permitted her, in 1425, to found a monastery of women under the direction of nuns of Oliveto. The foundation of her Order dates from 1433 when the community, which had rapidly grown, moved into its new quarters. In 1437 Pope Eugene IV approved the statutes which she had added to the Rule of St. Benedict. The members of the institution were styled Oblates; they did not vow but merely promised obedience to the superior. Frances was not a member of the Order herself as long as her husband lived, but after his death in 1437 applied for admission. The superioress, Agnes de Lelli, received her on the feast of St. Benedict, but at once assembled the community and resigned her office into the hands of the saintly foundress, who with extreme reluctance consented to assume such a burdensome and responsible charge. Francesca's holy example was to guide the Oblates for only a short time, for three years after her entrance into the community she died in 1440. She was canonized by Paul V in 1608, and her remains lie in the church which at present bears her name in the Roman Forum and which was formerly called S. Maria nuova.

2. Felix, monk of Fleury, abbot of Ruiz in Brittany, was a zealous and successful champion of reform in the Breton monasteries and rested from his arduous day's work in 1038.

3. Reinhard, first abbot of Reinhausen in Saxony, had previously conducted the schools at the monastery of Stablo, and was raised to the abbatial dignity on account of his ability and virtues. He died about the year 1100. His intercession was frequently invoked for the cure of epileptics.

4. Windric was abbot of St. Aper at Toul, in Lorraine, and of two dependencies, Moyenmoutier and Senones. These houses flourished both in numbers and virtue under his rule. He died in 1061. His epitaph proclaims to the world that he was a "jewel among monks, a pattern of monastic life, a great light of his native land."

5. The Congregation of the **Primitive Observance**, which was founded by Abbot Francis Casaretto, was originally known as the Sublacensian Province of the Cassinese Congregation. It was recognized as a distinct body by Pope Pius IX in 1851, but on March 9, 1872 was made a separate Congregation.

10

1. **St. Attala**, second abbot of Bobbio in Italy, was a Burgundian by birth and professed as a monk in Lerins, where he was little edified by the lives of some religious, so that he decided to join St. Columban at Luxeuil. He ac-

Frances: Mattiotti, But., C. E., C. Stelzer, O.S.B.: Leben der h. Franziska Romana (1888), Lady G. Fullerton: Life of St. F. of Rome.
Felix: Aymon of Fleury
Reinhard: Trithemius.
Windric: Ferr., Saussay, Chev. (Widric de St. Evre), Guerin, in the Mart. of France, calls him S. Vaudrice.

companied Columban when the latter was sent into exile in Italy, and became his successor at Bobbio in the year 614. In the administration of his office, he seems to have copied the severity of his master. The result was that a number of the monks rebelled and were permitted to leave. Some of them perished miserably, others, regretting their insubordination, returned and were affectionately received like the prodigal son in the Gospels. Abbot Attala was gifted with wonderful prudence and cheerfulness, while his love for the poor knew no bounds; he was moderate in prosperity, and strong in adversity. When his days drew to a close, it was revealed to him that he must prepare himself for a journey. He prepared himself both for eternity and for a journey to some earthly destination, ordered repairs in the buildings and surroundings of his monastery, and subjected his body to mortifications by fasts and watching by night. To Jonas, a monk who had never been permitted to visit his parents, he said: "Hasten, my son; visit your mother and your brother, and return without delay." Despite the inclemency of the season, Jonas visited his relations, but during the first night of his sojourn at home he experienced so much unrest, that he returned to Bobbio the next day. When he arrived at the monastery, he found Attala at the point of death. Supported by the brethren, the dying abbot was carried to the foot of a Cross outside of his cell, and lovingly saluted the sign of our Redemption. He bade the brethren leave him and conversed with God alone, while the priest Blidemund stood close at hand, unseen by the abbot. He spent the night in prayer, on the following day exhorted the brethren, bade them farewell and set out on the journey to his heavenly home in the year 627.

2. **St. Aemilian**, abbot of Lagny near Paris, was a native of Ireland and had received instruction in the elements of spiritual life under the guidance of St. Furseus. When the latter had crossed over to France and the fame of his sanctity had reached his native shores, Aemilian decided to join him. He was received among the monks of Lagny, where he excelled all his brethren by his prudence and virtue, so that Furseus appointed him abbot. He ruled the community with great wisdom and piety to the year 676, when he was awarded the crown of life.

3. **Bl. Andrew de Strumis**, a native of Parma, was a disciple of St. Ariald, who died a martyr while battling against simony, and whose body Andrew rescued at the risk of his own life. After he had entered the Order of Vallombrosa, the General, Rusticus, appointed him abbot of St. Andrew de Strumis. He acted as a successful peacemaker between the cities of Arezzo and Florence, and founded several churches and priories. Among his writings are lives of St. John Gualbertus and of St. Ariald. He died in 1097.

4. **Wirnto**, abbot of Formbach in Lower Bavaria, was at first a monk at St. Blasius in the Black Forest, but accompanied the monk Hartmann, who had been appointed first abbot of the newly founded monastery of Goettweig, in Lower Austria, to that house and assisted him in organizing the community-life

Attala: His disciple Jonas of Bobbio.
Aemilian: Saussay, O'Hanlon.
Andrew: Boll.

there. Shortly after, he was sent on a similar mission to Garsten, and in 1108 was elected abbot of Formbach. He was a zealous promoter of discipline and studies. His charity and piety endeared him to princes and people. When the hour of his departure from this vale of tears drew nigh, he consoled his sorrowful brethren with the words: "Do not weep for me, for I am only perishable clay; rather pray, that God may have mercy on me." He died in 1127.

11

1. **St. Vincent,** abbot of St. Claudius in a suburb of Leon in Spain, and martyr, lived while the Visigoths ruled that country and the Arian heresy was devastating the Catholic fold. The king heard of his staunch loyalty to the Catholic faith and summoned him to appear before a council of Arian bishops. When he boldly confessed that he had rather suffer death than renounce the Nicene Creed, the King ordered him to be scourged and to be cast into prison. While suffering from the wounds inflicted upon him, he was visited and healed by an angel, and sang the praises of God in a loud and cheerful voice. Summoned before his persecutors for a second time he repeated the Creed of Nice, whereupon the King commanded him to be executed at the gate of his monastery. Vincent offered his life to God, saying: "Father, forgive them, for they know not what they do." He shed his blood in defense of the faith in 584. The remains were first interred in the church of his monastery, but were later carried to the cathedral at Oviedo, where they repose.

2. **St. Firmanus,** abbot of St. Savinus at Fermo in the March of Ancona, Italy, was illustrious for his virtue. On account of the numerous miracles which glorified his tomb, he was venerated as a Saint. His life was written by the monk Theodoric of Monte Cassino, but was unfortunately lost. Firmanus died in the year 1020.

3. **St. Guitmar,** an abbot of Gournay in Isle de France, died after a holy and meritorious life in 770.

4. **St. Aurea,** a nun of St. Milan de Cogolla in Spain, was born at Villa Velayo and displayed unusual piety in her childhood. Having joined the nuns of St. Milan, her fervor grew with her progress in spiritual life to such a degree that she might in truth have said of herself: "No longer do I live, but Christ liveth in me." Once she beheld in a vision the virgin Saints Agatha, Cecilia and Eulalia, and, on another occasion, the Blessed Mother of God, who counseled her to be more moderate in her mortifications, at the same time informing her of the approach of her death. She died about the year 1100, radiant with joy at the entrance of her pure soul into eternal bliss.

5. Commemoration of all the **saintly and blessed monks** of the monastery of Reinhardsbrunn in Sachsen-Gotha.

Wirnto: Gerhoh of Reichersperg.
Vincent: Brev., of Valladolid, and several MSS.
Firmanus: Mab., Vita by Diederich of Amorbach in Analecta Boll. XVII (1899).
Guitmar: Ben. Annals.
Aurea: Prudentius, Sandoval.
Saints of Reinhardsbrunn: Calendar of R.

12

1. **Pope St. Gregory I,** called the Great, was born in Rome in 540, his father being the senator Gordian and his mother Sylvia. In his youth he applied himself to the studies of grammar, rhetoric and philosophy, and later to the study of the civil law. At the age of thirty-four he was made praetor, or governor, of Rome by the emperor Justin; yet the splendor and honors connected with this dignity did not make him blind to the beauty of a life hidden in God, and he was never more delighted than when he had an opportunity to converse with the monks or to ponder upon heavenly things either in a retired cell or in some church. When his father died, Gregory applied a part of his inheritance to the foundation of six monasteries in Sicily, and of a seventh in his own house on the Coelian hill in Rome. The latter was known as the monastery of St. Andrew. Under the second abbot, Valentine, Gregory himself took the religious habit in 575, devoting himself to such rigorous fasts that he contracted a great weakness of the stomach. So eager was he to fast on the eve of Easter, that he begged the monk Eleutherius to unite with him in prayer that he might have this grace. He found himself so wonderfully restored that he not only fasted on that day, but quite forgot his illness.

Even before he became a monk he had planned the conversion of England; One day he saw a number of youths exposed for sale in the slave market at Rome. Informed that they were from Britain, and that the inhabitants of that island were pagans, he pitied their forlorn condition. He requested Pope Benedict I to provide missionaries for the unforunate dwellers in the gloom of heathenism, but when no one could be found willing to undertake the work, he set out secretly with the blessing of the Pope. As soon as the Romans heard of his departure, they clamored for his immediate return, and prevailed upon the Pope to dispatch messengers who overtook him and brought him back to the city. Not long after, Gregory was created one of the seven deacons of Rome, and Pope Pelagius II sent him as apocrisiarius, or nuncio, to the emperor Tiberius II at Constantinople, where he formed an intimate friendship with bishop Leander of Seville. He was recalled from this honorable post five years later (584) and chosen abbot of St. Andrew's. While he was ever a kind father to his religious, he would suffer no violation of good discipline. He refused Christian burial to the monk Justus, who had appropriated money for his private use.

After the death of Pope Pelagius, Gregory was unanimously elected as his successor. In spite of his attempts to induce the emperor not to approve his election, the approval was given. Gregory dreaded the dignity to which he had been raised and sought to escape it by flight from Rome. He was discovered, brought back and crowned notwithstanding all his prayers and protests in 590 and ruled the Church for fourteen years. While this illustrious pontiff sat in the chair of St. Peter, the disturbances caused by the Nestorian and Eutychian heresies came to an end in the East; Spain was purified of Arianism; simony was checked in Gaul; Rome was saved from the Lombards. Gregory carried out, in 596, one of his earlier projects, by sending St. Augustine and other monks of St. Andrew's to convert England. In the midst of his many duties both while nuncio and as Pope, he found time to write numerous works of an edifying and instructive character, commentaries on parts of Holy Scripture and lives of saintly men and women, particularly in his books of Dialogues. He died in the year 604. He enjoys veneration in both the East and the West and is considered one of the great Doctors of the Church.

2. **St. Elphege,** bishop of Winchester, was formerly a monk and by his excellent qualities won the esteem of all classes. It was due to his efforts that St. Dunstan became a monk and drew down such plentiful heavenly blessings upon his native land. Elphege governed the see of Winchester from 935-951, in which year he rested from his labors. His feast was celebrated on September 1.

3. Bl. **Justina,** a nun of S. Croce at Arezzo, in Italy, was stricken with blindness but bore the affliction with amazing patience, and was a model of religious observance. She died in 1319.

4. Bl. **Rusticus,** third General of the Order of Vallombrosa and a disciple of St. John Gualbertus, followed faithfully in the footsteps of the eminent founder and died in the repute of sanctity in 1092.

5. Institution of the **Perpetual Adoration of the Blessed Sacrament** by Mother Mechtildis of the Blessed Sacrament at Paris in 1654. Hers was the first Benedictine community devoted to Perpetual Adoration. During the conventual Mass one of the community kneels in the middle of the choir, with a rope around her neck, and holding a lighted torch as a reparation for the many insults offered the Holy Eucharist. The statutes of this institute were approved by Pope Clement XI, in 1705.

13

1. The feast of **St. Leander** of Seville who died on this day, is celebrated on February 27.

2. **SS. Ramirus and 12 companions** were monks of S. Claudius at Leon in Spain and martyrs. After the abbot of this monastery had been executed for his steadfastness in adhering to the true faith, Ramirus, the prior, and his brethren were also commanded to abjure their faith, but preferred to shed their blood rather than prove renegades. They were executed in the same year as their abbot, 584. The remains of St. Ramirus were placed above the altar in a chapel of the monastery of St. Claudius in 1596.

3. **St. Heldradus,** abbot of Novalese in Piedmont, northern Italy, was a native of Provence and was born about the year 800. Unceasingly striving to please God by good works, he applied his temporal possessions to the foundation of churches and of hospices for the shelter of the poor and of travelers.

Gregory: Bede, Paul the Deacon, But., K. L., C. E., Abbot T. B. Snow: St. G. the Great (London 1892), Chev.

Elphege: William of Malmesbury, Osbert of Westminster, Flem., Stam. (Elphege the Elder).

Justina: Boll.

Rusticus: Boll.

Perpetual Adoration: K. L. (Anbetung), bibliography in Heimbucher.

Ramirus: Yepez, Sandoval.

He journeyed through France, Spain and Italy in quest of a monastery in which he might permanently bind himself to the exclusive service of God, and finally chose Novalese, where he was clothed with the religious habit by abbot Ambulf. Seven years later, Heldrad was elected abbot. He governed the community from 835-875 and died in the peace of the Lord, remembered both for his virtues and his benefactions.

4. **St. Mactefledis,** first abbess of Habende (Remiremont) in the Vosges Mountains, and a disciple of St. Amatus, was appointed abbess by him, but died after ruling the community two years in 620.

5. **Bl. Sancia,** foundress and nun of Cella S. Mariae in Portugal, was the daughter of King Sancho I. With the riches at her disposal she founded a Franciscan and a Cistercian monastery. The latter was Cella S. Mariae of which she became a member. Here she died, reputed as endowed with the gift of prophecy in 1229, in the presence of her sister St. Tarasia.

14

1. **Two holy monks,** who lived in a monastery near Lake Celano in Italy under the abbot St. Valentine, suffered death for the faith at the hands of the Lombards in 575.

2. **Bl. Mathildis,** wife of Emperor Henry I, was a generous benefactress of our holy Order. She founded five monasteries, among them that of Quedlinburg, in the former diocese of Halberstadt, to which she was wont to repair for edification and spiritual renewal. She died in 968.

3. **John II,** abbot of Monte Cassino, a man of singular humility, reluctantly consented to be abbot of that celebrated monastery, but resigned the office in favor of John III, son of the duke of Benevento. Together with five brethren desirous of living a secluded life, he settled in the forest of Pireto, where he died in 1020. A certain monk John, of the monastery of St. Lawrence at Capua, having beheld in a vision the soul of the saintly abbot ascending heavenward, sent a messenger with the tidings to Monte Cassino; at the same time one of the brethren of Pireto arrived with the same report. It was found that the actual time of his death corresponded with that of the vision.

4. **Paulina** was a recluse in Thuringia and died with the reputation of having wrought miracles, in 1107. She was the daughter of the Knight Udalric and was enclosed after his death in a cell called Paulina's cell (Paulinzelle) near the church of a Benedictine convent founded by her in 1106.

Heldradus: Boll.
Mactefledis: Life of St. Amatus, Stad., Also called Madefledis.
Sancia: Boll., Stad. gives her the title of Saint.
Two martyrs: Gregory the Great.
Mathildis: Boll., But. (Maud).
John II: Chronicles of Monte Cassino, Leo of Ostia.
Paulina: Trithemius, Steele: Anchoresses of the West.

15

1. **St. Sisebutus**, abbot of St. Peter at Cardegna in Spain, lived in the reign of Ferdinand I and died in 1082. So great and widespread was the fame of his sanctity, that his remains were enshrined in a marble tomb in a chapel dedicated to St. James and were venerated by the faithful. A noble lady by the name of Franca was cured of a sickness through the intercession of the Saint and in token of gratitude built a hospice near the chapel. Later, the remains were removed to the high altar. Both before and after this removal it was customary for the community to visit the shrine after Vespers on Saturdays and to chant the antiphon and oration of the Saint.

2. **St. Speciosus**, a monk at Terracina in Italy and a disciple of our Holy Father St. Benedict, was sent to establish a monastery at Terracina. One day, while Speciosus was making a journey, his brother Gregory saw his soul leave its body. Having informed his brethren of the vision, he set out for Capua himself, and learned that Speciosus had died the very hour in which he had the vision. The year of his death in the sixth century is not known. From the entry in the Roman Martyrology it may be inferred that he was a Roman.

3. Pope **St. Zachary**, though not a Benedictine, was a benefactor of our Order, seconded abbot Petronax in his efforts to restore Monte Cassino, granted exemption to the monasteries of Monte Cassino and Fulda, translated the life of St. Benedict into Greek and encouraged St. Boniface in his apostolic labors for the conversion of Germany. He died in 752.

4. **St. Raymond**, founder and abbot of Fitero in Navarra, Spain, was a native of Tarragona and, after completing his studies, betook himself to a solitude. Being attracted by the holy lives of the Cistercians in his country, he became a monk at Scala Dei and subsequently founded the monastery of Fitero. He organized the Order of Knights of Calatrava and governed it for the space of six years, during which time he wrested several castles and cities from the power of the Moors. After a life of meritorious service for Church and country, he died in 1163. With the approval of Pope Paul II his remains were removed from their original resting place to the monastery of Sion near Toledo.

5. **Aldebertus**, abbot of Tarouca in Portugal, was sent by St. Bernard to assist in the establishment of that monastery and succeeded the first abbot Boemund. King Alphonse attributed a rout of the Moors to the pious prayers of this abbot, who died in the year 1125, and was venerated by the faithful who flocked in great numbers to visit his tomb.

Sisebutus: Yepez, Sandoval.
Speciosus: Gregory the Great (Dial. IV, 8).
Zachary: Anastasius Biblioth., But.
Raymond: Henriquez.
Aldebertus: Bernard de Brito.

16

1. **St. Eusebia**, abbess of Hamay, in the diocese of Arras, was the daughter of the noble Adalbald and his wife Rictrudis. After the violent death of Adalbald, Rictrudis with her daughters Clotsindis, Adalsindis and Eusebia entered the monastery of Marchiennes, of which she became abbess. She placed Eusebia in Hamay under the care of St. Gertrude, the abbess, and grandmother of her deceased husband. At the death of Gertrude, Eusebia, though only a maiden of twelve, was chosen abbess of Hamay, but was sent to her mother to receive instruction in the principles of monastic life. When she was deemed fit to rule her monastery, she was sent back to Hamay, and presided over her community as a model of innocence and of religious observance for twenty three years. She died in 680 and her remains were later removed to Marchiennes.

2. **Bl. John de Surdis** was born of a noble family in Cremona, Italy, in 1124. Even as a child he evinced signs of his future sanctity, gave alms and observed a fast three times a week. At the age of sixteen years he entered the monastery of St. Lawrence at Cremona, where his virtue was so conspicuous that he was appointed prior of St. Victor's at the early age of twenty-four. A year later he was elected abbot of St. Lawrence. In 1162 Frederic Barbarossa nominated an antipope in opposition to Pope Alexander III, a proceeding against which John made eloquent and fearless protest. He was banished, and betook himself to a cell in the diocese of Mantua, where he lived in retirement for several years. The see of Mantua became vacant about this time, and John was elected bishop in 1167. Several years later he was transferred to the see of Vicenza, where he endeared himself to the faithful by his generosity to the poor. Full of kindness towards all, he treated his own body with the greatest severity. For the improvement of his clergy he established a seminary, and procured lectors in the various branches of ecclesiastical learning. A certain Peter, who was an unlawful tenant of church property, and refused to deliver it up, was repeatedly warned and finally excommunicated by the bishop. Angered by this punishment, Peter met the bishop while the latter was returning from the lecture hall of his seminary and slew him in the year 1181. The body was at first interred in the cathedral, but was raised in the year 1444 and exposed for public veneration in the chapel of Our Lady.

3. **Bl. Megingoz**, bishop of Wuerzburg, had previously been abbot of Fritzlar, an office to which he had been appointed by St. Boniface. He succeeded St. Burkard in the see of Wuerzburg in 754. After faithfully governing that church for thirty years, he resigned and withdrew to Rorlach (Neustadt), where a religious community soon gathered about him and chose him as their abbot. He encouraged studies in his monastery and lived a life of complete detachment from all concerns of the world. His death occurred in 795; according to some in 794.

Eusebia: But., Stad., Migne-Petin (Eusebie ou Ysoie).
John de Surdis: Boll., Chev. (Jean Sordi-Cacciafronte).
Megingoz: Ben. Annals (Megingaudus).

4. **Bl. Torelli**, a Camaldolese monk and hermit at Poppi in Tuscany, led a very worldly life as a youth but expiated his follies by entering the monastery of St. Felix, and dwelt for sixty years in a hermitage. He died, after a life spent in prayer and penitential exercises, in 1283.

17

1. **St. Gertrude**, abbess of Nivelle in Brabant, was the daughter of Pepin of Landen and his wife Itta, and was born 626. The pious principles instilled in her heart at home were developed under the tuition of St. Amandus. At an early age she consecrated her virginity to God. In the presence of King Dagobert she said to some one who suggested marriage to her: "I have chosen as my bridegroom one whose immortal beauty is the source of all beauty in creatures, whose riches are infinite and before whose countenance the Angels fall down and adore." When she was permitted to have a free choice, she resolved to follow her earlier inclination and became a nun in the monastery recently founded by her mother at Nivelle. At the age of twenty she was elected abbess, and, although she had been reared in the house of wealthy parents lived in poverty and practiced austerities. Her own mother Itta lived as a nun at Nivelle for five years to the time of her death in 652. At the age of thirty-two, Gertrude's health was so seriously affected by her fasts and abstinence from sleep that she decided to resign her office. Having appointed her niece Wilfetrudis to succeed her, she withdrew in 658 and spent the remainder of her days in preparing for death. St. Ultan, of the abbey of Fosse, is said to have foretold the day and hour of her death, which occurred in the year 659.

2. **St. Witburga** was a nun and foundress of the monastery of Derham in England. After the death of her father, Anna, king of East Anglia in 654, Witburga together with her three sisters Ethelreda, Ethelburga, and Sexburga embraced the religious life; she lived for a short time as a recluse at Holkham, and finally founded the house at Derham, but died before it was finished, in 743. In the spot where she was first buried in the churchyard at East Derham, a well of clear water, formerly very famous for cures, still exists and is called St. Withburge's well.

18

1. **St. Anselm**, bishop of Lucca, in Italy, was the nephew of another Anselm of Lucca who governed the Church as Pope Alexander II from 1061-1073, and appointed him bishop in 1071. He was sent to Germany to receive investiture from Henry IV, but could not reconcile such a proceeding with his conscience and returned to Italy without the ring and crozier conferred on such occasions. After the death of Alexander and the accession of Gregory VII he was consecrated bishop but was cautioned against submitting to investiture. For some unknown reason, however, he accepted investiture, but immediately after felt such remorse that he entered the monastery of Polirone in the diocese

Torelli: Armellini: Bibl. Cassinensis.
Gertrude: Boll., Mab., Stad., But., C. E.
Witburga: Boll., Mab., Steele.

of Mantua.   Pope Gregory commanded him to return to his see, where Anselm
sought to improve the clergy by encouraging them to live a community life.
His efforts in this direction were taken amiss; the canons of the cathedral
raised a disturbance and Anselm was driven out of Lucca in 1079 or 1081.   He
lived in retirement in the castle of Canossa and was spiritual adviser to the
celebrated Countess Matilda.   Pope Gregory's successor summoned him once
more to take a share in public life and sent him in the quality of a papal legate
to govern the churches of Lombardy that were not ruled by lawful bishops.
He was well versed in Sacred Scripture and is the author of several exegetical
and ascetical works.   The pleasures of the senses had so little attraction for
him that he appeared to be a spirit rather than a man; he partook of little food,
shunned wine and seldom slept on a couch.   He died in 1086 at Mantua, which
city honors him as its patron saint.

2.   **St. Tetricus**, bishop of Auxerre, had been abbot of St. Germain in
the same city and was elected bishop by popular acclaim.   He was a zealous
preacher of the word of God and ordained that the canons and monks of the
several monasteries alternately sing the Divine Office in his cathedral.   For
fifteen years he had ruled his see, when his life was cut short by the dagger of an
assassin in 707.

3.   **Bl. Gordian**, a disciple of our Holy Father St. Benedict, was one of
the companions of St. Placidus when the latter was sent to Sicily.   He escaped
the massacre of St. Placidus and of his associates; a merchant vessel bore him
to Constantinople where he wrote, in Greek, an account of the martyrdom of
that Saint.   Returning to Sicily, he died at Syracuse in 560.

4.   **Ven. John III**, abbot of Monte Cassino, was a descendant of the
princes of Capua, had been archdeacon of Benevento, but, obedient to an interior
impulse of grace, had renounced all things to become a monk at the cradle of
the Order.   In 997 he was elected abbot and inaugurated what historians of
Monte Cassino regard as the Golden Age of that monastery.   He suffered much
annoyance from rapacious counts in the vicinity, was obliged to seek safety in
flight, but was finally permitted to live in peace.   He died in 1010.

19

1.   **St. Huna**, priest and monk of Thorney in England, whom St. Ediltrudis (Etheldreda) abbess of Ely frequently consulted in matters pertaining
to the things of the soul, lived, after attending the burial of that saintly abbess,
on the island of Huney, wholly devoted to prayer and self-denial.   He died
about 690.   In later times his relics were translated to Thorney where he was
venerated by the faithful.

Anselm: Boll., Mab., But., K. L., C. E.
Tetricus: Mab., Chev., Gallia Christiana.
Gordian: His life of St. Placidus.
John III: Victor, Leo Marsicanus.
Huna: Thomas of Ely in the Life of St. Edildritha; Stan.

2. **Abundus**, Cistercian monk at Villers in Brabant, spent his youth in the practice of Christian virtue and was notable for his innocence and simplicity. As a boy of twelve, he was often seen in churches, kissing the Savior's wounds on the crucifix or engaged in affectionate conversation with Him. On his return from school, he was wont to visit the church and to remain till the hour of Compline or longer. While a Cistercian monk he was favored with many visions, particularly of the Blessed Virgin, for whom he had a special devotion. He died in 1234. His name may be found in the Calendar of Liege for 1618.

3. The **Congregation of St. Joseph** established in the diocese of Constance in 1568 and approved by Clement VIII in 1603, celebrated its titular feast on this day. It no longer exists, the houses having disappeared during the secularization in the 19th century.

20

1. **St. Martin**, archbishop of Braga, by some supposed to have been a native of Pannonia, was a man of unusually brilliant gifts of mind and labored as a missionary at the conversion of the Arian Suevi in Gallicia, Spain. In order to ensure the growth of the new churches, he founded twelve monasteries, one of them being Duma in Portugal, over which he presided as abbot. It was in recognition of his merit and great virtue that Duma was created an episcopal see. Martin was made its first bishop in 570, but continued to live the austere life of a monk and retained the government of his monastery. Later he was promoted to the metropolitan see of Braga, where he died in 580. In 1606 his remains were removed from Duma to Braga. The poet Venantius Fortunatus sings his praise in a poem which is still preserved.

2. **St. Cuthbert**, bishop of Lindisfarne in England, in his youth was a shepherd. One night while absorbed in prayer, he saw the soul of abbot Aidan winging its flight towards heaven. At once he applied for admission to Mailros abbey, of which Aidan had been abbot, and proved such an exemplary religious that the abbot appointed him master of the guest-house at Ripon. Having returned in 663 he succeeded St. Boisil as prior of Mailros. Possessed of unusual eloquence and well versed in Holy Scripture, he preached to the faithful of the vicinity and won many souls for Heaven. After his appointment to the office of prior at Lindisfarne, he often spent whole nights in prayer, imploring the divine mercy for himself and for all men. With permission of his abbot he settled on the island of Farne, where, in his hermitage, he was sought by many in need of spiritual counsel and consolation. The synod of Twiford recommended him for the see of Lindisfarne but Cuthbert opposed vigorous resistance till King Egfrid and bishop Trumwin prevailed upon him to accept the office. Weeping tears of regret, he left his solitude and was consecrated at York on Easter day by St. Theodore. Two years after assuming this burden he had a presentiment that his course was run, resigned his office and withdrew

---

Abundus: Arnold de Raisse, Rosweid.
Cong. of St. Joseph: Calmet.
Martin: Isidore of Seville, Gregory of Tours, Fortunatus in Migne P. L. 88. p 181.

to his beloved solitude where he died in 687. His remains were interred in the abbey of St. Peter at Lindisfarne; later they were removed to Durham.

3. **St. Wulfram**, archbishop of Sens in Champagne, was born of noble parents at Milly in Gatinois and in 690 was appointed to the episcopal see of Sens. Not content with laboring in this part of the Lord's vineyard, he selected several monks of Fontenelle and set out to convert the Frisians. Although his zealous labors were blessed with numerous spiritual conquests, he failed to secure the good will of the Frisian prince Radbod, whereupon he returned to Fontanelle, became a monk of that monastery and closed his days in 720 or 741.

4. **Hugh Lantenas**, a monk and priest of Vendome in France, shone so brightly by his love of God and men, that he was called a saint even during his life-time. When he became aware that the day of his death was at hand, he received Holy Communion as the Viaticum during his last Holy Mass and died shortly after, in 1701.

21

1. **Saint Benedict**, Patriarch of Western Monks, was born at Nursia in Umbria, Italy, about the year 480. His parents were Eutropius and Abundantia, and St. Scholastica was his twin sister. The earliest biography of our Holy Founder was written by St. Gregory the Great and may be found in his Second Book of Dialogues. According to this eminent writer, Benedict "blessed both in grace and name" was sent to Rome to receive a liberal education, but was filled with such disgust by the licentious lives of some youthful Romans that he left the city and, like another John the Baptist, took up his abode in the mountains about Subjaco, where he lived unseen by the world, in converse with God alone for the space of three years. He had received the religious habit from a certain monk Roman, who in his charity supplied him with bread that was let down from the rocks above in a basket. Soon the cavern in which he had chosen to dwell was no longer a place of concealment; neighboring shepherds discovered him and spread the report of his sanctity. The monks of a neighboring monastery—said to have been Vicovaro—visited him, and, notwithstanding his youth, prevailed upon him to be their abbot. Ere long he regretted having left his cavern, for he found the Vicovaro monks to be religious in name only and not disposed to submit to the guidance of an abbot. After they had made an attempt to remove him by poisoning his wine, he took his departure and returned to Subjaco, where in the course of time he established twelve small monasteries, each for a community of twelve monks with an abbot. These houses, the chief government of which was in the hands of St. Benedict, grew rapidly both in renown and membership. St. Benedict's fame attracted many aspirants to the religious life, and induced some of the Roman nobility to place their sons in his care. Thus, Equitius brought his son Maurus, and Tertullus his son Placidus to be instructed in the practices of the Christian life by the Saint.

Cuthbert: Bede; But., Stan., C. Eyre, The History of St. Cuthbert, London, 1887.
Wulfram: Jonas of Fontenelle, But.
Lantenas: Tassin: Hist. litt. de la Cong. de S. Maur.

His success was envied by a certain priest in the vicinity, who endeavored to destroy his good work by accomplishing the spiritual ruin of the monks. St. Benedict, fearing for the souls of his youthful disciples, now resolved to quit Subjaco. Some friend, probably Tertullus, made him a grant of land on Monte Cassino (about 75 miles southeast of Rome and about the same distance from Subjaco) and here Benedict in the year 529 laid the foundations of the celebrated house that was to be the source of the many blessings lavished upon all the countries of the civilized world through the activity of his countless spiritual children down to this day. At the time of his arrival, the people still worshipped pagan deities in the temples and groves on the mountain. St. Benedict cut down the groves and replaced the heathen temples by churches in honor of St. John the Baptist and of St. Martin. For his monks, he wrote a Rule that has been read and admired as a work of consummate widsom not only by ascetics but also by pontiffs and princes of later ages. His claim to the title of Patriarch of Western Monks is based on the fact that he perfected the cenobitic system and that his Rule eventually replaced the other monastic rules, with exception of that of St. Augustine.

In the last year of his life he sent his two beloved disciples St. Maurus into France and St. Placidus to Sicily; the former founded the monastery of Glanfeuil, the latter died as a martyr. The last incident in the Saint's life is the memorable meeting with his sister St. Scholastica; it was their last conversation on earth. Not long after her death, he was seized with a fever; on the sixth day he had himself carried to the oratory, there received the body and blood of Jesus Christ and "standing erect and supporting his weak and languishing body on the arms of his disciples, he raised his hands to heaven, and whilst in that attitude of prayer, gave up his soul to God," in the year 543, the fourteenth of his abode on Monte Cassino. His remains were carried to Fleury in France in 653. Monte Cassino also claims to possess them.

2. **St. Robert,** founder of the Order of Citeaux, died on the feast of St. Benedict in the year 1108. He is commemorated on April 29.

3. **Bl. Santuccia** (de Terrebottis), was a native of Gubbio in Umbria. After the death of her only child, she consecrated herself, with her husband's consent, to God's exclusive service. For some time she presided over a convent at Gubbio, but later founded a house in Rome near the church of St. Anne. She was a zealous promoter of devotion to the Blessed Virgin. After her death in 1305, the houses which she had founded were affiliated to the congregation established by Bl. Sperandeus.

4. **Ven. Christian,** first abbot of St. Pantaleon in Cologne, died in the odor of sanctity towards the end of the tenth century.

5. Establishment of the **Cistercian Order**— or Order of Citeaux—by SS. Robert, Alberic and Stephen who, with eighteen other monks on Palm

Benedict: Gregory the Great, L. II. Dialog.; Tosti: St. Benedict; L'Huillier: S. Benoit; Lechner: Leben des hl. Benedict; But. Chev.
Santuccia: Jacobilli, Stocker, Stadler, Dunbar.
Christian: Mab.

Sunday 1098 vowed observance of the Rule of St. Benedict in all its primitive rigor. . The Order was approved by Pope Pascal II in 1100 and was one of the most active and effective agencies in the reform of ecclesiastical and monastic life.

22

1. Commemoration of all the sainted **monks** and **nuns** of Remiremont in Alsace.

2. **Ven. Conrad,** abbot of Mondsee, diocese of Salzburg, died in defense of the rights of his monastery. He was slain by peasants in 1145.

8. On this day the **Congregation of Our Lady of Calvary**—or Daughters of the Crucifixion—founded by Antoinette of Orleans-Longueville, was erected by Pope Gregory XV in 1622. The first convent was at Poitiers and became the cradle of the Congregation. The final approval was not given before January 17, 1827. The nuns wear a brown habit and a black scapular.

23

1. **St. Ethelwald** was for some time a hermit on the island of Farne from which St. Cuthbert had been summoned to be bishop of Lindisfarne. One day he was visited by three monks from the mainland; while they were returning in a boat a violent storm arose, but Ethelwald's powerful prayer calmed the angry waters till the boat reached the shore, when the storm burst forth anew. After spending twelve years in prayer, tears and penitential exercises, he died about 700, was buried at Lindisfarne but was removed to Durham together with the relics of St. Cuthbert.

2. **Bl. Felix,** a monk at Chieti in Italy, was intrusted with the supervision of the shepherds and flocks of the monastery and attained such a high degree of perfection in virtue that after his death in the ninth century, many visited his tomb and had recourse to his intercession.

8. **Bl. Merbodo,** a count of Bregenz, was a monk at Mehrerau but with leave of his abbot dwelt in a hermitage in the mountains and ministered to the people in the vicinity. He was found dead one morning about the year 1120, having, as is supposed, been slain by some who took offence at the boldness with which he preached against certain prevailing abuses. He was always honored as a martyr.

4. **Ven. Bruno,** at one time a canon of the church of Speyer, became a monk at Hirschau in Wuertemberg. He trained a great number of excellent

Cist. Order: C. E., K. L. Heimbucher.
Remiremont: Bucelin.
Conrad: Wigul. Hund.
Cong. of Calvary: C. E., Heimbucher.
Ethelwald: Bede.
Felix: Peter the Deacon.

religious, many of whom were selected to be abbots of other houses. He died in 1121. In 1460 a blind man is reported to have recovered his sight through the intercession of Ven. Bruno.

24

1. **St. Aldemar**, surnamed the Wise, abbot of Bocchianico near Chieti, Italy, was a native of Capua and became a monk at Monte Cassino. While still a deacon, he was selected as prior for the monastery of St. Lawrence, founded by the princess Aloara of Capua, where he won the love of the poor by his unselfish efforts to relieve their distress. An attempt to recall him to his mother-house resulted in a dispute between the abbot and the princess Aloara. Anxious to put an end to the contention, Aldemar secretly left Capua and joined three brethren who were leading a canonical life near a church at Bojano. One of them attempted to take Aldemar's life, but only injured himself in doing so. Having been ordained priest, he repaired to the monastery of St. Liberator at the foot of Monte Majella, where he instructed the monks in sacred chant and music. To the regret of all, he left this monastery and, at the request of a certain Adam, built a monastery at St. Euphemia, of which he became abbot. Later he built other monasteries, among them that of Bocchianico, where he edified the monks by his affability and humility. While visiting one of his foundations, he was stricken with a fever and died in 1087. His remains were conveyed to Bocchianico.

2. **St. Hildelita**, second abbess of Barking in England and successor to St. Ethelburga, made such rapid strides in holiness that in 685 she was elected abbess. She received St. Cuthburga into religion and was highly esteemed by the holy bishops Aldhelm and Boniface. Her death occurred about 717.

3. **Bl. Bertha**, Vallumbrosan abbess of Cauriglia, in Tuscany, was of noble family and became a nun in the convent of St. Felix. Her abbess sent her to Cauriglia, to restore a convent. After governing this house with success during ten years, she died, as she had lived, in the peace of God in the year 1163.

4. **Ven. Mary Jacobina de Blemur**, descended from a distinguished family in Normandy, was a nun of the Perpetual Adoration first in a convent at Caen and later at Chastellon d'Empurias in southern France. Even after reaching the age of sixty years, she was one of the most regular sisters in the community. She died at the age of seventy-eight in 1696, leaving behind her the memory of her virtues.

5. The monastery of Barking on this day commemorated the suffering of the Nuns who were cruelly put to death by the Danes in 870.

Bruno: Trithem.
Aldemar: Peter the Deacon.
Hildelita: Bede, William of Malmesbury, Stanton. Also called Hildelid.
Bertha: Boll.
Mary de Blemur: Tassin, Zieglbauer, who also mentions her writings.
Nuns of Barking: Ben. Annals.

1. **St. Hermeland**, abbot of Aindre in Brittany, was a native of Noyon, and early in life came to the court of King Clothaire II. While preparations were made for his wedding, he left the palace and entered the monastery of Fontenelle. At the close of the period of probation, he professed and was ordained priest by archbishop Audoenus of Rouen. During the daily celebration of Holy Mass he never forgot to renew the offering of himself to God's exclusive service. St. Pascarius, bishop of Nantes, approached the abbot with a request for monks to organize a monastery on the island of Aindre. St. Hermeland and twelve other brethren were selected to form the first community which under his direction soon prospered in discipline and numbers, so that monks of this house were sought to found or revive other houses. Every year he left his monastery to pass the Lenten season on a neighboring island, called Aindrinette, where he spent days and nights in prayer and mortifications, imploring Heaven's blessing upon his monks and the entire Church of God. The growing infirmities of age bade him lay down the burden of his office. By his request, another abbot was elected, whose severity was, however, so intolerable that the monks complained. As Hermeland had foretold, this abbot died shortly after, and, yielding to the entreaties of the brethren, Hermeland appointed the monk Donatus to succeed him. Having edified his brethren and the people of the surrounding country by his virtue and his retired life, he died in 720. In Brittany his feast was celebrated on November 25.

2. **St. Alfwold**, a monk of Winchester and bishop of Sherburne in England, was a devout admirer of St. Cuthbert, whose tomb he caused to be opened that he might venerate the relics of that Saint. The simplicity of his life was an eloquent protest against the luxury and excess of his age; he lived in poverty, ate from wooden dishes and was content with plain food. He died in 1058.

3. **SS. Barontus** and **Desiderius** were two hermits at Pistoja in Tuscany. The former had been married, but had entered the monastery of Lonrey in the province of Berry, and had been permitted to go to Italy where he was joined by Desiderius and several other devout men. They established themselves in hermitages near Pistoja and labored at the sanctification of their souls by prayer and penance. Barontus is said to have had a vision in which he beheld the glories of Heaven and the sufferings of the damned. He died in 685, and was shortly followed by Desiderius. In 1018 a monastery was built, in the church of which their remains were interred.

4. **Bl. Thomas** (Tomasso). a Camaldolese hermit, had taken the habit of that Order at Sitria, but subsequently lived for sixty-five years in a solitude near Costacciario in Umbria, where he subsisted on herbs found in the forest. Although many came to him for spiritual guidance, he founded no community. All the food offered to him by his visitors he gave to the poor. He died in 1337; miracles wrought both before and after his death witnessed the holiness of his life.

Hermeland: Boll., Mab.
Alfwold: William of Malmes., Stant. (Mar. 26).
Barontus and Desiderius: Boll., Mab.
Thomas: Razzi.

1. **St. Ludger,** bishop of Muenster and apostle of ancient Saxony, now Westphalia, was of noble extraction and born in 743. After some years spent in study in a monastery under the direction of St. Gregory, bishop of Utrecht, he crossed over to England to hear the lectures of Alcuin at York. Four years later he returned to the continent and after the death of St. Gregory was ordained priest by his successor Alberic, who sent Ludger to preach the faith to the Frisians. His zealous activity was marked by many conversions and by the foundation of churches and monasteries. His labors were interrupted by incursions of the Saxons, and he withdrew for a time, to report the progress of his work to the Holy See. He spent four years at Monte Cassino, wearing the habit of the Order but not taking the vows. When Charlemagne had succeeded in subjugating the Saxons in 787, Ludger returned to preach the Gospel to the conquered people and founded the monastery of Werden in Westphalia. In 802 the diocese of Muenster, originally known as Mimigardeford, was established, with Ludger as its first bishop. While ruling that diocese he also attended to the spiritual needs of five cantons in Frisia, in which he had served as a missionary. In the territory of Braunschweig he founded the monastery of Helmstaett, which was later called St. Ludger's. He never grew tired of preaching and of expounding Holy Scripture; in his private life he was mortified, rarely ate meat, and gave generous alms. Certain spiteful persons charged him with neglect of his duties; Charlemagne ordered him to meet the charge. The monarch's messengers found him engaged in prayer and were refused a hearing until he had finished. When the emperor rebuked him for discourtesy, the Saint said: "When your Majesty nominated me a bishop, you told me to prefer the service of God to that of men." These words convinced Charlemagne of the good bishop's innocence. Although ailing he performed his episcopal duties without intermission. On Passion Sunday of the year 809 he preached at an early service, and also delivered a discourse in the evening, in which he stated that he was to die the next night and expressed a desire to be buried at Werden. He died at midnight, as he had foretold.

2. **St. Bertilo,** chorepiscopus and abbot at Dijon, died after a saintly life in 878.

3. **St. Pontius,** abbot of St. Andrew's at Avignon, not only was a model of religious observance within his monastery, but also led others unto God by his fervent eloquence. He taught his monks to sanctify their lives by diligent reading of Holy Scripture, silence and manual labor, and received his heavenly reward in the year 1078.

4. **Bl. Melior,** a Vallombrosan hermit, is said to have fasted so rigorously and to have been so much exposed to the heat of the sun that his countenance had almost turned black. Yet his soul was as clean and bright as that of a child. He was found dead, kneeling in prayer, in 1158.

Ludger: Mab., Boll., Boeser: Am Grabe des hl. Ludger (1909).
Bertilo: Mab.
Pontius: Boll., Mab.
Melior: Monum. of Vallombrosa; Marchesi; Stadler: "Melior a Valiana."

27

1. **St. Rupert**, bishop of Salzburg and Apostle of Bavaria, was of royal Frankish blood, but still more illustrious for his learning and the extraordinary virtues he practiced from his youth. These notable qualities led to his appointment to the episcopal see of Worms, where his zeal was rewarded with harsh treatment. Duke Theodo of Bavaria, hearing of his abilities and virtues, invited him to preach the Gospel to the pagan inhabitants of Bavaria. Bishop Rupert rekindled the torch that had been lighted by St. Severin two centuries earlier and succeeded in converting the Duke, many of his courtiers and a great number of the people. From Regensburg, where Rupert had made this spriritual conquest, he is said to have extended his apostolic labors as far as Pannonia or Hungary. On his return he rested for some time in the city of Lorch where he brought relief to many sick persons through his prayer, and finally established himself at Salzburg about 582, where he founded the abbey of St. Peter, for which he invited twelve monks from France. On the neighboring Nonnberg he established a house for religious women, converted a heathen temple at Altoetting into a chapel which in later times became a celebrated pilgrimage, and is said to have founded the Benedictine monastery of Weltenburg. He died in 623.

2. **St. Bercharius**, abbot of Moutier-en-Der in the diocese of Chalons, was descended from a noble family in Aquitaine and was born in 636. After receiving his education under the direction of St. Nivard, archbishop of Rheims, he entered the monastery of Luxeuil, then ruled by abbot Walbert, who later employed him in the foundation of the monastery of Hautvillers (662). Bercharius was such an ardent promoter of religious life that he in his turn, after Archbishop Nivard's death, founded two monasteries, Moutier-en-Der for men and Pellemoutier for women, both of which he enriched with relics which he brought with him on his return from a pilgrimage to the Holy Land and Rome. On Holy Thursday of the year 685 he foretold the approach of his death, and found it necessary to punish one Dagin, his god-son. The latter conceived an intense hatred of the Saint and plunged a knife into him during the night. When the brethren rushed to the couch of their dying abbot, he was covered with blood but conscious. He pardoned his unfortunate god-child, ordered him to make a pilgrimage to Rome to obtain absolution and died two days later on the present day in the year 685.

3. **Bl. Frowin**, abbot of Engelberg in Switzerland, had been a monk at St. Blasius in the Black Forest. He was a learned and saintly religious, under whose rule the monastery enjoyed prosperity and was noted for the excellence of its discipline. Like St. Benedict, he was an enemy of leisure, and occupied his monks with copying of books and manuscripts, while he himself wrote several treatises of an ascetical character. He had ruled his monastery for thirty-five years, when he was called to render an account of his stewardship, in the year 1178.

Rupert: H. Canisius; Metzger; Butler. All the dates are uncertain. According to Lindner (Monast. Salzb.) he was bishop 696–718.
Bercharius: Adso in Mab.
Frowin: Annals of Einsiedeln; Burgener, Stadler. Also called Frobenius.

4. **Haymo**, bishop of Halberstadt, Saxony, was a monk of Fulda and a pupil of the celebrated Alcuin of Tours. After his return from the latter city he was appointed to teach at Fulda. Subsequently he was appointed abbot of Hirsfeld and finally bishop of Halberstadt. He devoted his time chiefly to the interests of his diocese and avoided entangling himself in affairs of state. The labors of his pen are still extant. He died in 853.

28

1. **Octave** of the feast of our Holy Father St. Benedict, and anniversary of the discovery of his tomb in the church of Monte Cassino in 1066, under Abbot Desiderius.

2. **St. Stephen** Harding, third abbot of Citeaux and one of the founders of the Cistercian Order, was born in England, received his early training at the monastery of Sherburne in Dorsetshire, and afterwards studied at Paris and Rome. On his return to the North, he enjoyed the hospitality of the monks of Molesme, whose mortified lives made such an impression upon him that he remained and joined that community. In the course of time the monks grew remiss in their strict observance; in consequence, the abbot Robert, and the monks Alberic and Stephen left to establish a new monastery. Robert was recalled to Molesme, but did not succeed in reforming the monks; whereupon he left for a second time with his two companions and eighteen other brethren and settled in the marshy district of Citeaux about 20 miles from Dijon, where Duke Eudo had made them a grant of land and had built a chapel in honor of Our Lady. Here the monks cut down trees with their own hands and built cells. On March 20, 1098 they bound themselves by a vow to observe the Rule of St. Benedict in its pristine rigor, and from that day dates the Order of Citeaux. Duke Eudo frequently visited them, was edified by their recollection and expressed a desire to be buried in their church. His son Henry renounced the world and joined the holy community. After Robert had directed the community for a year, he was ordered to return to Molesme and Alberic was made abbot of Citeaux. This abbot secured the approval of the new foundation by Pope Pascal II in 1100. After Alberic's death in 1109, Stephen was elected to succeed him. During his administration he insisted upon the observance of poverty: removed crosses of silver and gold, as well as vestments of silk from the church, restricted visits from the outside and kept his monks busy transcribing books, such as Bibles and missals. The abbot having for some reason incurred the displeasure of Eudo, the resources of the house began to dwindle, and he went about from door to door begging for the support of the monks. Nor was this the only misfortune that befell Citeaux; an epidemic in 1111-1112 carried off a great number of its religious. All signs seemed to point to the extinction of the house, and the blame was laid to the severity of the abbot. Stephen, however, trusted in the help of God and found his reward, for in 1113 thirty-one young men applied for admission, among them the future St. Bernard. Within a short time there was such a great number of monks that Stephen was in position to found four new houses, La Ferte, Pontigny, Bonnevaux,

Haymo: Trithem. C. E.
Benedict: Ben. Annal.

and Clairvaux. In order to preserve unity and uniformity in the body, the first General Chapter—the first of the kind—was held in 1116; the second Chapter, in 1119, adopted a set of statutes, the so-called *Charta Caritatis*, which was approved by Pope Calixtus II in 1120. After attending a Council at Troyes, and effecting a reconciliation between the king and the bishops of Paris and Sens, he resigned his office in 1133 and spent the last year of his life in retirement. He died in 1134. The Roman Martyrology commemorates him on April 17, the date of his canonization, but the Cistercians observe his feast on July 15.

3. **Mary**, or **Mlada**, first abbess of St. George's at Prague in Bohemia, was the sister of the pious Boleslaus, duke of Bohemia, and was appointed abbess by Pope John XIII during a visit to Rome. She was influential in procuring the creation of the see of Prague, the first bishop of which was Dietmar, a learned monk of the monastery of St. John at Magdeburg. She died in the odor of sanctity in 995.

4. At Villers in Brabant, commemoration of all the sainted members of that Cistercian community.

29

1. **St. Simplicius**, third abbot of Monte Cassino, was a disciple of St. Benedict and one of the sources from which Pope Gregory drew information for his sketches of the life of our Holy Father in the Second Book of his Dialogues. After the death of abbot Constantine, the immediate successor of St. Benedict, Simplicius was chosen to be his successor. To him is ascribed the introduction of the custom of publicly reading the Holy Rule. He died in 570. His remains, together with those of St. Constantine and of Bl. Carlmann, were discovered by Abbot Desiderius in 1071.

2. **St. Eustasius**, abbot of Luxeuil, was the child of noble parents in Burgundy and was carefully educated by his uncle Migetus, bishop of Langres. Blind to the allurements of wealth and station, he entered Luxeuil, then governed by St. Columban, and in 611 succeeded that celebrated master of the monastic life. Six hundred monks owned him as their kind father and judicious guide in the path of salvation. Saints Burgundofara and Salaberga attributed their cure from ailments to the prayers of abbot Eustasius. Not content with laboring within his monastery, he went out to preach the Gospel, and even extended his missionary journeys as far as Bavaria. One of his monks, Agrestius, headed a movement to abolish the rule of St. Columban, the founder of Luxeuil. The discussion became so bitter that a synod was held at Macon (between 617 and 627) to consider the matter, and decided in favor of Eustasius. His reputation for sanctity was so great that even bishops sought admission to his monastery. He died on April 29, 625, on the day which he had foretold. His remains were enshrined in the monastery of Vergaville in Lorraine.

Stephen: Boll., C.E., Life by Father Dalgairns.
Mlada: Pontanus, Aeneas Sylvius; Frind: Geschichte der Bischoefe von Prag.
Cistercian: Henriquez.
Simplicius: Peter the Deacon.
Eustasius: Jonas, monk of Bobbio.

3. **Stephen X** (or IX), Pope, was the son of duke Gozilo of Lower Lorraine, and in baptism received the name of Frederic. So conspicuous were his intellectual endowments and virtue, that while he was a deacon at Liege, Pope Leo IX appointed him chancellor and librarian of the Roman Church in 1051. He accompanied Pope Leo on his journey through Europe and was sent as legate to Constantinople to labor for the reunion of the Eastern and Western churches. His efforts proved ineffectual. On his way back he was robbed by the Count of Teate, and to avoid falling into the hands of emperor Henry III, he became a monk at Monte Cassino, of which he was elected abbot two years later. While visiting Pope Victor II in Tuscany to obtain approval of his election, that Pope, mindful of his former services to the Church, created him cardinal. Shortly after, Victor II died and Stephen was chosen his successor (1057). Retaining the office of abbot of Monte Cassino, he ruled the Church for less than one year. He issued a number of important disciplinary ordinances, resisted the aggression of emperor Henry IV, created St. Peter Damian a cardinal and wrote several treatises. While preparing to resume negotiations with the Greek church, he died in the tenth month of his pontificate in 1058 at the age of fifty years and was buried in the church of St. Reparata.

4. **Diemudis**, surnamed the "elegant scribe" on account of her beautiful handwriting, was of noble descent and a native of Bavaria or Suabia. She was born in 1060 and while quite young entered a convent at Wessobrunn. After a long and severe probation, she had herself enclosed in a cell by the church and there lived many years as a strict recluse. Although she devoted many hours of day and night to prayer and contemplation, she copied a number of homilies and ascetical works, of which fifty volumes were still extant at the time of the secularization of monasteries in the 19th century. Her correspondence with Herluka of Epfach was destroyed by the Swedes during the Thirty Years' War. She died in 1130 and was buried at Wessobrunn. When the church in which she was interred was pulled down in 1707, her remains were found, marked by a slab of lead, near the bones of seven martyrs.

30

1. **St. Zosimus**, abbot of St. Lucy at Syracuse, in Sicily, and bishop of that city, was the son of pious parents, who gave all their earthly possessions and their son Zosimus, the fruit of their prayers, to the monastery of St. Lucy, then under the rule of the holy abbot Faustus. Yielding to a natural desire, he once left the monastery to see his parents, but was prevailed upon by them to return and continue his studies, He had already served the Lord faithfully and in all submissiveness and humility, when abbot Faustus died. All the brethren, Zosimus excepted, waited upon the venerable bishop of the city, begging him to appoint a successor to their deceased abbot. Guided by an internal light, the bishop. to the surprise of all, appointed Zosimus and ordained him priest. The saint ruled his community for many years with wonderful prudence, love and energy. At an advanced age he was chosen to succeed the bishop,

Stephen X.: Leo of Ostia, Ughelli.—Lives of Popes.
Diaemudis: Leutner: Gesch. von Wessobrunn; Steele. Also called Diemoth, Demuth.

but reluctantly accepted the distinction.   After governing the church of Syracuse for thirteen years, he died in 660.

2. **St. Clinius,** prior of St. Peter della Foresta at Aquino, in Italy, was a
Greek by birth.   While a monk at Monte Cassino, he distinguished himself
by his eminent virtue, which was attested by miracles.   Since the manuscript
containing an account of his life and miracles has been lost, it is not possible
to ascertain definitely the time when he lived.

3. **Blithildis,** nun of Marmoutier and disciple of St. Burgundofara,
served God faithfully in religion.   Towards the end of her life she was confined
to her cell by illness.   One of the sisters was appointed to read for her during
the hours of the night.   It so happened that the reader was overwhelmed by
drowsiness, and the patient Blithildis was compelled to spend the wearisome
hours without her usual comfort.   To the astonishment of all who came to see
her at dawn, the oil in the lamp had not only not decreased, but began to over-
flow.   This singular phenomenon was witnessed by her brother, Faro, bishop
of Meaux, and abbot Waldebert of Luxeuil,   Blithildis died in 650, and a
delicious odor was diffused throughout her cell.

31

1. **St. Guido,** abbot of Pomposa in Italy, was born at Casamare near
Ravenna in 970.   Ignoring a suggestion of his father to marry, he declared his
preference for the clerical state, left for Rome and was received among the clergy
of that city.   Here he resolved to make a pilgrimage to the Holy Land and
actually set out on the journey, but in a vision was directed to join a saintly
recluse, named Martin, on the banks of the Po, opposite the abbey of Pomposa.
Under Martin's direction he lived a hermit's life for three years, then was advised by him to enter as a monk in the monastery of St. Severus near Ravenna.
In the mean time the abbot William had gone into a solitude and his successor
Angelus had died.   Guido was now elected abbot of Pomposa, but accepted the
office only at the advice of the hermit Martin.   While he was abbot, the number
of religious grew surprisingly.   He rebuilt the monastery, and recognized the
hand of God in all that befell the community.   His mortified life was a source
of wonder to his brethren; he ate as if he were not eating; and possessed the
things of this earth as if he possessed them not.   Having ruled the monastery of
Pomposa for fourty-eight years, he was taken ill on a journey and died at Burgo
in 1046.   His remains were at first interred at Parma; emperor Henry III had
them carried to Verona and thence to Speier, where they found a resting place
in the church of St. John the Evangelist till the time of the French Revolution,
when they were taken to the church of S. Magdalen.   ·

2. **St. Renovatus,** bishop of Merida in Spain, was a descendant of the
Goths, a man equipped with the most enviable qualities of mind and body, and

---

Zosimus: Boll., Mab.
Clinius: Ferrari, Rom. Martyrol.
Blithildis: Mab. in life of St. Burgundofara.
Guido: Boll., Mab., Stad. Not in the Roman Martyrol. He must not be confounded with
   Guido of Arezzo, monk of Pomposa.

had previous to his elevation to the episcopal dignity been abbot of the monastery of Cauliana near Merida. It is related that while he was abbot, all the brethren, with the exception of one whom he could not induce to persevere in the path of virtue, led most exemplary lives. Finally, the Saint suffered the erring brother to go his own way. One day a number of school children rebuked him so earnestly for his excesses that he repented and amended his life. Abbot Renovatus succeeded Innocent as bishop of Merida, and governed that diocese with much fruit to the day of his holy death in 633.

3. **Ven. John I**, abbot of Monte Cassino, had been archdeacon of Capua, and is called by Peter the Deacon a very religious and saintly man. He died in 934 and was buried in the monastery he had founded at Capua.

4. **Bl. Daniel**, a Camaldolese monk of St. Michael de Murano at Venice, was at one time a merchant in Hungary, but left all things behind him to follow Christ in poverty. Thieves suspecting him to have concealed money in his hermitage, entered in the night and slew him in the year 1411. The body was interred in the chapterhouse and was found well preserved when it was raised many years later.

Renovatus: Paul of Merida in Boll.
John I.: Peter the Deacon, Leo of Ostia.
Daniel: Fortunio.

April

1

1. **St. Hugo**, bishop of Grenoble in France, was born in 1053 at Chateauneuf in Dauphine. Fitted out with an excellent education, he was appointed a canon at Valence, and at the council held at Avignon in 1080 was elected bishop of Grenoble, a dignity which he accepted only when he had been commanded under obedience to do so. He was consecrated by Pope Gregory VII, and Countess Mathilda of Canossa presented him costly pontifical ornaments and valuable books. At the time of his accession, the churches of the country were suffering from neglect and the scandalous lives of the clergy. By his unceasing prayer, tears and mortifications he accomplished a remarkable change for the better. He had occupied the see of Grenoble only two years, when he yielded to an inspiration and took the Benedictine habit at Chaise-Dieu. A year later Pope Gregory VII ordered him to return to Grenoble, and he appeared among his people like Moses coming down from the mountain. In 1084 he directed St. Bruno, the founder of the Carthusian Order, to the wilderness of Chartreuse, which became the cradle of that Order. Hugo was exceedingly charitable towards sinners and towards the poor, patiently bore the infirmities which at times caused him great pain, and incessantly yearned for union with God. He died in 1132, and was canonized by Pope Innocent II two years later.

2. **St. Procopius**, abbot at Prague, was born at Chotum in Bohemia, excelled his fellow students both by his progress in studies and in virtue, and was ordained priest. One day he met a Benedictine monk, conversed with him and resolved to devote himself to the monastic life. For some time he lived as a hermit in a cave near Curm, where he was discovered by duke Ulric. The latter is said to have built a monastery in the forest of Sazawa. When the buildings were completed in 1009, Brzetislav, duke Ulric's son, appointed Procopius the first abbot of the community, which was composed of Benedictine monks. Procopius presided over this house, which was dedicated to St. John, for the space of ten years as a loving and prudent father and rested from his toil in 1053. He was canonized July 4, 1204, by Pope Innocent II and was the first Bohemian saint to receive that honor from a Roman Pontiff.

3. Another **St. Hugo**, a Cistercian abbot of Bonnevaux in Dauphine, France, was often tempted to leave during the novitiate, but found strength to persevere in his devotion to the Blessed Virgin Mary. As abbot he was noted for his sanctity, and the gift of miracles and prophecy. He vigorously opposed the pretensions of the anti-pope Octavian, effected an understanding between Pope Adrian IV and Frederic Barbarossa and promoted the observance of the feast of the Crown of Thorns. He died in 1194.

Hugo of Grenoble: Guigo the Carthusian; Butler.
Prokopius: Surius, Stad., Buchb.
Hugo of Bonnevaux: Vincent of Beauvais, Stad., Buchb., Cist. Chronik.

4. **Ven. Lanzo,** prior of St. Pancras in the diocese of Chichester, England, was afflicted with a painful illness, which he bore with admirable patience and without breaking silence by night. He died in the year 1120.

5. The Translation of the remains of the monk **Nicholas de Arcu,** a Cistercian at Neti in Sicily took place on this day in the year 1230. He died about 1220.

2

1. **St. Ebba,** abbess of Coldingham, in Scotland, and her companions, presented a heroic example of virtue during an incursion of the Danes in 870. When these invaders attacked the monastery, Ebba assembled all her nuns in the chapterhouse, and exhorted them to dread no sacrifice in order to protect their virginity. She is said to have set the example by cutting off her nose and her upper lip, whereupon the other nuns resorted to the same expedient. The Danes forced their entrance into the monastery and, shocked by the disfigured faces of these defenceless women, set fire to the buildings. Ebba and all her nuns perished in the flames.

2. The feast of **St. Guido** is celebrated on this day at Pomposa and Ravenna; the day of his death is March 31.

3. **Ven. Bernard,** archbishop of Toledo, in Spain, was a nobleman of Aquitaine. For some time he was a soldier, but obeying the call of divine grace, he entered the monastery of Cluny. Abbot Hugo of that monastery, who esteemed him highly for his worth and services, commissioned him to compile the ' Customs of Cluny ' (*Consuetudines Cluniacenses*). When King Alphonse VI of Castile invited religious of Cluny into his kingdom, abbot Hugo appointed Bernard to lead the first colony of monks. Bernard was made first abbot of the monastery at Sahagun. After Toledo had been taken from the Moors, he was elected archbishop of that see and confirmed by Pope Urban II, who made him primate of all Spain. He was noted for his devotion to the Blessed Virgin and instituted the festival of ' Our Lady of Peace.' With edifying zeal and patience he bore the burdens of his important episcopal charge for forty-four years. For the regeneration of religious life and piety in his see, he installed monks as canons in his cathedral. Not the least of his distinguished services to the country was the reconstruction of Braga which had suffered seriously during the wars. He died in 1128.

3

1. **St. Attalus** was an abbot at Taormina in Sicily and lived about the year 800.

Lanzo: William of Malmesbury.
Nicholas: Buc., Stad.
Ebba: Matthew of Westminster: Stanton: Butler: Dunbar, Stadler.
Bernard of Toledo: Roderic of Toledo: Yepez; Ben. Annals. The year of his death is uncertain.
    Chev. gives his full name as Bernard de Sedirac (1122).
Attalus: Octav. Cajetan; Martyrol. of Sicily.

2.   **Bl. Thiento**, abbot of Wessobrunn, in Bavaria, was a contemporary of St. Ulric and was appointed at a time when the monastery had much to suffer in consequence of incursions of the Huns and oppression from the mighty ones of the country.   When Bavaria was invaded in 955, Thiento permitted the brethren to choose between safety in flight and death.   Six monks determined to remain at his side, prepared to shed their blood for their faith.   At the approach of the enemy they proceeded to a hill near by, where they prepared themselves for death.   The invaders, failing to find the monks within the building, began to make search for them and finally found them on the hill.   Here the bloodthirsty violators of the sanctuary cruelly butchered the blessed abbot and his six devoted monks.   The people of the vicinity buried them on the spot where they had been slain and marked the place with a cross— hence the name of the hill, ' Kreuzberg.'   Shortly afterwards a small chapel of wood was built over the remains .   In 1713 the bodies were disinterred and placed in the abbey church.

3.   **Herman**, a Cistercian lay brother of Villers in Brabant, although not highly gifted by nature and by no means learned, nevertheless acquired an unusually high degree of virtue.   He was a friend of the poor, severe towards himself, abstained from meat and wine, and was favored with ecstasies. After spending fifty years in the monastery in faithful performance of his religious duties he was called to his eternal reward in the 12th century.

4

1.   **Ven. Maurus Xavier Herbst**, abbot of Plankstetten, was born at Pleinfeld in Bavaria on September 14, 1701, and early in life gave promise of a saintly career.   He studied at Neuburg and Ingolstadt, at the age of eighteen entered Plankstetten, and on November 20, 1720 made solemn profession, on which occasion he received the name of Maurus.   For his course in theology he was sent to the abbey of Michelfeld and in 1726 was ordained a priest.   For the next sixteen years he was vicar, or assistant, to the parish priest of Plankstetten.   After the death of abbot Dominic von Eisenberg, he was elected abbot on September 24, 1742.   He was thunderstruck at the result of the election, for he was far from being the oldest member of the community; yet he accepted in deference to the presiding officer.   According to a custom of the day he assumed a new name (his baptismal names were John Florian Frederic)—that of Xavier, and adopted a coat-of-arms representing a pelican opening its breast to feed its young.   To his monks he proved to be a good father; he relieved the poor, assiduously frequented the confessional to lead sinners back to God, and cherished a childlike devotion to Our Lady. Among the exceptional graces which Heaven bestowed upon him was that of prophecy.   On one occasion he is said to have had a vision and to have exclaimed: ' Is it possible that in fifty years there will not be a single monastery in this country?'   He died after an illness of three days at Marienburg on

Thiento: Leutner: Historia Mon. Wessof.
Herman: Raisse.

April 4, 1757, and was buried at Plankstetten. At his tomb many sick recovered through his intercession.

2. **Gunzelin,** Cistercian abbot of Morerola in Spain, shone among men by his pure life, meekness and patience in suffering. He recovered his health after invoking St. Bernard's intercession, and died in the odor of sanctity in 1188.

3. Anniversary of the foundation of the **Portuguese Congregation** in 1566. With the help of several monks from Spain, a reform had been inaugurated in the monastery of S. Thirso, which became the nucleus of a congregation. Portuguese monks were sent to Brazil in 1581.

5

1. **St. Gerald,** founder and abbot of Sauve-majeure. (Silva major) in Aquitaine, was born at Corbie and educated in the famous monastery of the same name. Abbot Fulco in course of time received him among the monks, and even made him his adviser. For a great part of his life, Gerald suffered from severe headaches as a result of excessive fasting. In 1049 he accompanied his abbot on a pilgrimage to Rome and to Monte Cassino; while in Rome both were ordained priests and Gerald after his return to Corbie was appointed sacristan. It was due to his unceasing prayer that he was freed from his suffering through the intercession of St. Adalard. After his return from a pilgrimage to the Holy Land, he was elected abbot of a monastery at Laon, but soon discovered that the views of the monks did not harmonize with his. He consulted a saintly recluse what course he should pursue. It so happened that several noblemen had just confessed their sins to this recluse and were on the point of becoming hermits. Gerald joined them and they set out together to found a new monastery. After several pilgrimages to holy places, they arrived at Poitiers, where count Guido permitted them to establish a monastery at any place of their choice. They selected Sauve majeure and, with the help of the people living about, built a house which stood finished in 1081. Gerald and his monks lived such edifying lives that the community grew rapidly, founded new houses and formed the Congregation of Sauve Majeure. Lamented by his brethren and all the people, Gerald passed to his eternal reward in 1095. He was canonized by Pope Celestine II in 1197.

2. **St. Ethelburga,** daughter of king Ethelbert and wife of king Edwin of Northumbria, after the death of her royal spouse resolved to embrace the religious state and, with the help of her brother, king Eadbald, founded the monastery of Lyming, where, at the head of a pious community, she served God in holiness of life and patient perseverance to the day of her death in 647.

Maurus: MS of Fr. Erhard Richter of Plankstetten, Pastoral. Blatt des Bisthums Eichstaett. 1857 Nos. 4–15. The monastery of Plankstetten was suppressed in 1806, but reopened in 1904.
Gunzelin: Henriquez.
Portuguese Cong.: Calmet; C. E.
Gerald: Boll., Mab., Butler (April 3).
Ethelburga: Stanton, Chev., Dunbar.

3. **Bl. Andrew**, brother of St. Bernard and monk of Clairvaux, followed in the footsteps of his sainted brother. His humble occupation was that of porter. He died in the 12th century—the year is not stated.

4. **Benedict of Sentino**, or Sassoferrato, a Silvestrine monk at Perugia, was a faithful disciple of Silvester, the founder of the Order, and a humble client of Our Lady. He died in 1270.

5. The **Helveto-American Congregation** was established on September 30, 1870, but actually erected by Pope Leo XIII on April 5, 1881. The first house of the congregation was St. Meinrad's Abbey in the State of Indiana.

6

1. **Bl. Notker**, surnamed the Stammerer (*Balbulus*), was a monk of St. Gall's in Switzerland. He was born about the middle of the ninth century at Heiligenau in the canton of St. Gall. In his youth he was offered to that celebrated abbey and received part of his training from the learned monk Iso. After he had received the habit, he devoted all the time not occupied by regular exercises or work, to prayer and meditation. Having been ordained a priest, he devoted himself with great zeal to the instruction and sanctification of the people. He held several responsible positions in the monastery, for some time was librarian and guestmaster, but was principally active as a teacher in the famous schools of St. Gall's. Among his literary labors is a martyrology and a life of the saintly founder of the monastery. One of his chief titles to fame is his devotion to ecclesiastical art, especially music. He introduced the Sequence into the German churches, and composed a number of sacred hymns. One of his biographers, Ekkehard IV, speaks of him as ' delicate of body but not of mind, stuttering of tongue but not of intellect, pushing boldly forward in things divine, a vessel of the Holy Spirit without equal in his time.' Despite his learning and popularity, he was humble and did not disdain to perform the lowliest services in the house. He died in 912 and was buried in the chapel of St. Peter. His beatification took place in 1512 and his feast is celebrated at St. Gall's—which is no longer a Benedictine abbey— on the third Sunday after Easter.

2. **Henry**, Cistercian monk of Villers, in Brabant, was distinguished for his complete detachment from the world, and for his love of silence and recollection. He died in the 13th century.

3. The **Congregation of Vallombrosa** was approved on this day in the year 1090 by Pope Urban II. It was founded by St. John Gualbertus in 1039, the first house being that at Vallombrosa, situated twenty miles from Florence. The habit of the monks originally was gray; while they were, for

Andrew: B. Brito.
Benedict: Jacobilli.
Helv. Am. Cong.: Famil. Confoed.
Notker: Ekkehard; Burgener, C. E., K. L.
Henry: Gall. Martyrology.

a time, united with the Silvestrines, they adopted black, and wear that color at present. The nuns of Vallombrosa were founded by St. Humilitas in 1272.

7

1. **St. Albert,** monk and hermit at Crespin in Hainault, was born about 1060, manifested a great love for prayer in his childhood and even spent entire nights on his knees in prayer. The death of a holy hermit named Theobald prompted him to leave the world and live in solitude. He sought the hermit John a monk of Crespin, and shared his simple life, dispensing with fire in winter, eating uncooked food and regarding even bread as a dainty. For several years he was a monk in the monastery of Crespin, and although he was appointed cellarer and prior, he relaxed in no particular the austerity of his life; he was at all times recollected; slept on the floor and prayed the Psalter before Matins. After twenty years he was permitted to return to his solitude (1118). Here the faithful found him and came in great numbers to benefit by the wisdom of his spiritual counsel. Bishop Burcard of Cambrai ordained him a priest and had a chapel built near his cell, where he received the confessions of many sinners. He died at the age of eighty years in 1140.

2. **St. Eberhard,** monk at Schaffhausen in Switzerland, was the son of Eppo, count of Nellenburg and Hedwig, daughter of King Toxo of Hungary. His father having died, his mother placed Eberhard in the charge of the priest Lupard who trained both his mind and heart. Eberhard married a virtuous lady by name of Itta. After his mother had founded the monastery of Sauer-Schwabenheim and his six sons had come of age, he founded the monastery of Our Holy Redeemer at Schaffhausen in 1050 for monks of Hirschau, and in 1069 entered it as a monk with the consent of his wife, who became a nun at St. Agnes in Schaffhausen and was a devout, conscientious religious. After a pious career of six years, he died in 1075. The town of Schaffhausen owes its growth in large measure to the popularity of this saint, whose holiness was confirmed by numerous miracles wrought at his tomb.

3. **Ven. Bernard,** abbot of Marmoutier near Tours, ruled a number of monasteries. His zeal met opposition, but Pope Urban II encouraged him to remain firm. He was charitable and forgiving; in the monasteries he insisted upon the suppression of all useless conversation. The year of his death is 1100.

4. **Walter,** monk of Cluny died in the year 1040. A number of persons testified to having seen a column of light rising heavenward above the monastery on the night of his death.

8

1. **St. Walter,** first abbot of St. Martin at Pontoise, in France, was a native of Picardy, and early left his home to follow in the footsteps of his

Cong. of Vallombrosa: Bullar., Heimbucher, C. E.
Albert: Archdeacon Robert, Butler.
Eberhard: MSS in Boll. and Mab.
Bernard: Ben. Annals.
Walter: Radulph Glaber.

Redeemer. He was well educated and, in his turn, educated others.
Fearing the snares of conceit, he resolved to become a monk at Rebais, in the
diocese of Meaux, but not before he had tried to live like a monk in the
world. Such was his virtue and ability, that in 1060 he was made the first
abbot of St. Germain—later known as St. Martin—at Pontoise. When
he received investiture from king Philip I he had the boldness to say: ' I
accept the government of this church from God, not from thee, O king! '
The responsibility of his office appalled him after some time; hence, seeking
rest for his troubled soul, he secretly left for Cluny, to live as an ordinary
monk unknown to the world at large. He was discovered and reluctantly
went back to his monastery. Yet he did not venture to occupy the apart-
ments of the abbot, but lived for a number of years in a cabin near by, where
he received his monks and many others who were attracted by his extraordinary
wisdom in spiritual matters. In the course of time these visits, too, proved
to be distracting; hence he settled on an island near Tours. Once more the
brethren, who were unwilling to lose him, joined their entreaties and succeeded
in persuading him to return. Some time later, he journeyed to Rome, where
Pope Gregory was highly edified by his bearing, but at the same time commanded him not to leave his monastery again unless he were urged by a special
divine inspiration. Shortly after his return to France, a council was held at
Paris for the promulgaton of the papal decrees condemning simony and concubinage of the clergy. Walter was one of the prelates who favored the execution of the decrees, but was imprisoned for his boldness. Some friends secured his release, after which he resumed his austere practices. In compliance with two distinct injunctions from the Blessed Virgin, whom he saw in
a vision, he founded a monastery for nuns at Bertulcourt. Convinced that
he had many sins to expiate, he confessed his shortcomings publicly and
ordered all the brethren to give him the discipline. On Palm Sunday of the
year 1099 he informed the brethren that the hour of his departure from this
life was not far distant, received the Holy Viaticum and Extreme Unction
and slept in peace on Good Friday. In 1153 the bishops of Rouen, Paris and
Senlis, who believed that his sanctity was sufficiently attested by the miracles
at his tomb, raised the body and placed it in a better one. Abbot Walter
Montagu removed the remains a second time in 1655.

9

1. **St. Waldetrudis**, nun at Mons in Hainault, was the daughter of
Count Walbert and St. Berthila. Complying with the wishes of her parents
she became the wife of count Maldegar of Hainault, a happy and peaceful
union which was blessed with four children. After the birth of the fourth
child, she prevailed upon her husband to consent to a separation, that both
might devote themselves to God's service exclusively. Her husband entered
the monastery of Hautmont near Maubeuge and received the name of Vincent.
Waldetrudis did not follow his example at once, but remained with her children
and did not take the decisive step till she felt that she was free from all obli-
gations to the world. A relative purchased a parcel of land for her at a place
called Castriloc, and built a house which was to serve as her retreat. To

Walter: MSS in Boall. and Mab. Latin form of his name: Gualterius.

her disappointment it was much larger and better than she desired.   Fortunately, a violent storm swept it away, and it was replaced by a smaller edifice, in which bishop St. Aubert of Cambrai gave her the religious veil.   She was joined by other devout souls who shared the trials and delights of religious life with her.   At first she was beset by many temptations, but she was comforted by Heaven and encouraged to persevere by her sister, St. Aldegundis.   Her saintly life closed in the year 686.   Castriloc in later times was called Mons, and developed into a city of some importance.   St. Waldetrudis is the patron of Mons.

2.   **St. Hugo**, archbishop of Rouen, was a grandson of Pepin of Heristal, and son of Drogo, duke of Champagne and of Adeltrudis, daughter of Waraton, a mayor of the palace.   Educated in sound Christian principles by his grandmother Ansfleda, he led a life so edifying that in 722 he was selected as fittest to rule the see of Rouen; he was also bishop of Paris and Bayeux, and abbot of Fontenelle and Jumieges.   He applied the revenues from his patrimony and other sources to the maintenance of monasteries and embellishment of churches, and died at Jumieges in 730.

3.   **Bl. Gundekar** was one of the associates of St. Boniface in the conversion of the Frisians and suffered death together with that Saint in 754.

4.   **Azo**, dean at Monte Cassino, was taken a prisoner by the Saracens and died in a dungeon in Africa in 1114.

10

1.   **St. Palladius**, bishop of Auxerre in France, had been a monk at the abbey of St. Germain near that city and was elected successor to bishop Desiderius in 633.   He spared no pains to follow strayed sheep of his flock and to lead them back to the fold in which alone they could find salvation. Among his many memorable benefactions it is recorded that he bestowed valuable gifts upon the basilica of St. Stephen and that he founded the monastery of our Blessed Lady.   In the environs of the city he built the church of St. Eusebius, with a monastery.   His name appears among the prelates who assisted at the councils of Rheims and Chalons.   Death removed him from his earthly field of labor in 661.   His remains were buried in the church of St. Eusebius.

2.   **Bl. Paternus**, a recluse of Abdinghofen near Paderborn in Westphalia, foretold the destruction of the city by fire within thirty days unless the people amended their sinful lives.   His prophecy came true; fire broke out in seven distinct places on April 10, 1058 and destroyed most of the houses, including the cathedral and monastery.   Paternus was urged to leave his cell but refused, saying that he preferred to keep his vow never to leave the cell in which he had been voluntarily enclosed.   He perished in the flames. Paderborn has always regarded him as one of its patrons.

Waldetrudis: MS. in Boll. and Mab., O'Hanlon: Butler ("Waltrudis").
Hugo of Rouen: Boll., Mab., Rom. Martyrol.
Gundekar: Ben. Annals.
Azo: Ben. Annals.
Palladius: Labbe, Saussay.
Paternus: Marian. Scotus: Sigebert of Lemblours, Trithemius. O'Hanlon.

11

1. **St. Guthlac**, monk at Croyland, England, and hermit, was of noble birth and is said to have served in the armies of Ethelred, king of Mercia, but to have exchanged the arms of a temporal sovereign for those of the King of Kings. He was twenty-four years of age when he quitted the world to enter the monastery of Rippington. The period of probation having expired, he received permission from his superior to pass over to the island of Croyland. Accompanied by two brethren intent on the same purpose, he reached the island on the feast of St. Bartholomew, for which reason he chose that Saint for his patron. His abode was a cavern, and his food, coarse bread and water of which he partook in the evening only. Although far removed from external occasions to suffer spiritual harm he was molested by violent temptations such as those St. Athanasius relates of St. Antony, but the grace of God made him strong, and heavenly consolation filled his soul whenever he issued triumphant from a trial. Bishop Hedda of Dorchester visited him and ordained him a priest. The Saint who had some foreknowledge of his approaching death sent for his sister Paga, a recluse in another part of the inhospitable island. He was prostrated by a fever on Wednesday of Holy Week, 714, prepared himself for the supreme moment, and expired on April 11 at the age of forty-seven years, of which he had spent fifteeen on the island. According to his last wish, his sister prepared his body for burial; king Ethelbald erected a monument over his resting place.

2. **Bl. Ulric**, first abbot of Kaisersheim near Donauwoerth, Bavaria, in 1135 came at the request of the founder, count Henry of Lechsgemuend, from the Cistercian abbey of Luetzel in Alsace to organize that monastery. Eleven brethren from Luetzel formed the original community which soon began to flourish and attract new members. After presiding over his monastic family with great prudence and as a consummate model of all virtues, he rested in the Lord in 1155.

3. **Father George Gervase**, a native of Sussex, lost his parents when he was twelve years of age, and was soon after kidnapped by pirates and carried off to the West Indies. While revisiting Europe about twelve years later, he entered the English College at Douai and was ordained in 1603. He had labored but two years in the English mission when he was arrested and banished. His zeal urged him to go back; he was seized a second time, and on refusing to take the oath required by James I was condemned to death. He was executed at Tyburn on this day in 1608, exhibiting in his martyrdom the fervor and constancy of the primitive martyrs. A short time before his last return to England he had obtained admission to the Benedictine Order.

12

1. **St. Alferius**, founder and first abbot of the monastery of the Most Holy Trinity at Cava near Salerno, Italy, of the noble family of the Pappa-

---

Guthlac: Felix monk of Jarrow; Bertelin, Guthlac's companion. Butler ("Guthlake").
Ulric: Chronicles of Kaisersheim.
Gervase: Stanton; C. E.; Gillow; Challoner. The name is also written Jervis or Jarvis.

carboni, who claimed descent from the Lombard kings, was born at Salerno. At the court of duke Gisulphus of Salerno he was highly esteemed for his knowledge and exemplary piety. The duke sent him on an embassy to France; on the way he put up at the monastery of St. Michael de Cusa, where he was detained for some time by illness. More than ever he was impressed by the vanity of earthly pursuits and honors, and vowed to devote himself to a contemplative life if Heaven favored him with recovery. He did recover, and accepted an invitation of the abbot of Cluny to join his community. While he was progressing in virtue and perfection, the duke of Salerno commanded him to return. The monks of Cluny assented to his departure with sincere regret. He was commissioned to govern and reform all the monasteries in the principality of Salerno, and found this an occupation that left him little rest or peace. This decided him to lay down his office, and to retire to Mount Fenestra, between Salerno and Amalfi, a locality called *la Cava di Matelliano*. Here he settled and was soon surrounded by a number of devout men who chose him as their spiritual guide. In 980 he established a monastery and built a church in honor of the Blessed Trinity, providing that the number of monks must never exceed twelve. For the remarkably long period of seventy years he presided over this community. Towards the end of his life he foretold that the possessions of the monastery would increase and that a great number of brethren would be admitted. Six days before his death, it was revealed to him that it would occur on the following Holy Thursday. He celebrated Holy Mass on that day, performed the customary washing of the feet, gave bountiful alms to the poor, and remained in his cell while the brethren partook of the noonday-meal. He was found dead shortly after at the age of one hundred and twenty years, in the year 1050. Cava could no longer harbor all the brethren who sought for admission; new houses were founded by princes and other wealthy persons, and the mother house became the centre of the Congregation of Cava, which at one time consisted of 333 establishments in Italy and Sicily. Cava escaped seculariaztion and is still one of the most important houses of the Order; its abbot is an *abbas nullius dioecesis*.

2. **St. Erkenbodo**, bishop of Terrouane in Belgium and abbot of Sithiu, was a disciple of St. Bertin, founder of that monastery and was its fourth abbot. Six years later he was, in addition, made bishop of Terrouane, which see he governed for twenty six years. Renowned both for his virtue and merit he died in 742, and was always venerated as a saint.

3. **Bl. Peter**, Vallombrosan monk and hermit of Montepiano, in the diocese of Pistoja, had been abbot of St. Vigilius in Brescia. He was discovered in his hermitage by several nobles whom he regaled with so much kindness that they founded the monastery of Montepiano.

4. **Bl. Elias**, abbot at Cologne, died about the year 1041. He was a Scot by birth, and received his religious training in Ireland before he crossed

Alferius: Mab., Boll., Vite di Abbati Cavensi.
Erkenbodo: Breviary of Terrouane, Molanus.
Peter: Calendar of Vallombrosa.

over to the Continent. He presided over a number of Irish or Scottish monks in the monasteries of St. Martin and St. Pantaleon in Cologne.

13

1. **Bl. James of Certaldo**, a Camaldolese monk of Volterra, in Italy, was descended from the respectable family of the Guizzi, early displayed a love for prayer and became a monk at the monastery of SS. Justus and Clement at Volterra. Though happy beyond all his expectations in his chosen state, he at times was violently beset by the enemies of salvation, but triumphed over them all by his mortified life. His father Albertinus likewise found rest for his soul in a monastery. For some time James was parish priest. Twice he was chosen abbot and twice his humility bade him to decline the honor, but after the death of the third abbot, both the bishop and his brother plied him so perseveringly with persuasions that he consented to shoulder the burden. Ere long, however, the attraction of his former position grew too strong; he returned to parochial work and influenced many to provide for their salvation by observing the evangelical counsels. Among those whom he induced to embrace the religious state was his brother Ingram, who died shortly after. James survived his brother ten years. In 1292 he was stricken with a fever and brought to death's door; he begged pardon of his abbot and brethren for any injury he had done them, received the Holy Viaticum and died on April 13th of the same year.

2. **Ven. Ida of Louvain**, Cistercian nun of Rosenthal near Malines in Belgium, was born of wealthy and respected parents at Louvain in 1250 and was favored with visions at an early age. At the age of eighteen she experienced a call to a perfect life, but encountered numerous difficulties both from temptations and from unkind treatment at home. She found strength and consolation in pondering upon the sufferings of Our Lord and in Holy Communion. The reward for her fervent love was a flood of spiritual lights and other favors, which were a source of wonder to all who were acquainted with her. In order to escape the danger of growing vain over her privileges, she entered the Cistercian monastery of Rosenthal and there closed her remarkable life in the year 1300, at the age of thirty two.

14

1. **St. Lambert**, bishop of Lyons, was born of a distinguished family in Terrouane, was an official at the court of Clothaire III and despite the opposition of some relations entered the monastery of Fontenelle and received the religious habit from St. Wandregisil. After the abbot's death in 666, the brethren observed a fast of three days, then met and elected Lambert, although he had been in their midst but four years. He consented only after the saintly religious Ansbert had promised to support him in bearing the heavy burden. Both Childeric II and his successor Thierry held him in high esteem and became

---

Elias: Marian. Scot., Trithem., O'Hanlon.
James: Maffei of Volterra.
Ida: Notes of her confessor: Anonymous life written at Rosenthal.

great benefactors of the abbey. On an estate granted by Thierry at Dozere, Lambert founded a monastery. He had ruled Fontenelle for thirteen years when St. Genesius, bishop of Lyons died in 681 and Lambert was selected to be his successor. Adorned with all the virtues of a Christian, a monk and a bishop, he was called to his eternal reward in 690.

2. **St. Bernard**, abbot and founder of the Congregation of Tiron in France, was born of poor parents in 1046. In his youth he was addicted to practices of mortification and at the age of twenty left home to become a monk at St. Cyprian's near Poitiers. Ten years later, his confrere Gervaise was elected abbot of St. Savin and appointed Bernard prior of that monastery. In his efforts to maintain a high standard of discipline, Bernard met with scant sympathy, even from the abbot; hence he returned to St. Cyprian's and lived a secluded life for some time. While on a pilgrimage to the Holy Land the abbot of St. Savin was killed by a lion in 1096. Bernard fearing that the brethren might wish to have him as their abbot, fled but was discovered and persuaded to return to the monastery of his profession, of which he was made prior. Four months later, abbot Raymond died after designating Bernard his successor. He was humble, charitable to all, domestics and guests, strong in faith and an inexorable foe to falsehood and injustice. A dispute with the abbey of Cluny concerning the independence of St. Cyprian's determined him to resign as abbot and to associate himself with Robert of Arbrissel, founder of the order of Fontevrault. He was recalled, however, and sent to Rome to maintain the claims of his monastery against Cluny, and was graciously received by Pope Pascal II, who would have created him a cardinal, had he not declined to accept so great an honor. In 1109 he laid the foundations of the monastery of Tiron on grounds granted by count Rotrou of Perche and Mortagne, introduced the strict observance of the Rule of St. Benedict and thus was the founder of the Congregation of Tiron, which within the course of twenty years counted more than sixty houses, including some in Wales and Scotland. Bernard was endowed with the gift of miracles and prophecy and died after an illness of ten days on April 14, 1117. In 1861 the Holy See authorized the celebration of the Saint's feast in the diocese of Chartres. The Congregation was later incorporated in that of St. Maur.

15

1. **St. Nidgar**, bishop of Augsburg, and second abbot of Ottobeuren, was a pious and zealous prelate, firmly defended the rights of his church and died in the reputation of holiness about 831. Bishop Embrico of Augsburg discovered his remains in 1064 and entombed them with those of St. Adalbero in the church of SS. Ulric and Afra.

2. **Ven. Wolbert**, first abbot of Deutz near Cologne in the Rhineland, was a lover of prayer and silence. In a vision St. Herbert, the deceased bishop of Cologne, informed him that he would die a month later. Wolbert died on the day thus foretold him, in 1021.

Lambert: MS. discovered by D'Achery. The name is also written Lantbert.
Bernard: Gaufrid, monk of Tiron; K. L.; Heimbucher.
Nidgar: Placid. Braun; Feyerabend.
Wolbert: Ben. Annals.

3. **Goswin**, abbot of Anchin in Hainault, although a learned man held in high esteem by the world, deemed it a greater honor to be an humble follower of Christ. He became a monk in the Cluniacensian monastery of Anchin near Douai, on an island in the river Scarpe. As abbot of that monastery he indulged in no vain display of his dignity, but outshone all by his humility and regularity. Some of the brethren reproached him for not proceeding with sufficient energy in asserting the rights of his house in a certain controversy, but soon discovered that he had accomplished more by his calmness and prayers than by excessive worry and excitement. He was honored with the esteem of Pope Eugene III and of St. Bernard of Clairvaux. His death occurred in 1166.

4. On this day the Congregation of Cluny celebrated the feast of all its Saints.

16

1. **St. Fructuosus**, bishop of Duma and Braga in Portugal, was a prince of royal Visigoth blood, early in life recognized the supreme importance of saving his soul, and was more eager to hide his proud descent beneath the cowl of a monk than others are to wear a crown and wield a scepter. After the death of his parents, he received instruction in the sacred sciences under the direction of bishop Conantius of Palentia, sold the greater part of his estate, applied part of the proceeds to relieve the poor, and with the rest built a large monastery in the mountains of Asturia, which he called the monastery of SS. Justus and Pastor. He put on the monastic habit and governed this house as abbot till he saw it settled in good order; whereupon he betook himself into a solitude. The austerity of his life attracted so many pious persons desirous of following his example, that he was enabled to found several other monasteries. So numerous were the applicants, that the King is said to have reserved for himself the right to grant admission. Fructuosus also founded a home for nuns and wrote two rules. He was drawn from his retirement and made bishop of Duma and in 656 archbishop of Braga. Lying on ashes before the altar, he expired in the year 665 and was buried in the monastery of St. Peter at Montella. Later the remains were removed to Compostella.

17

1. **SS. Elias, Paul** and **Isidore**, were monks who suffered martyrdom by hanging at the hands of the Moors in Cordova, Spain, in 856. St. Eulogius was an eye-witness of their suffering.

2. **St. Landric**, bishop of Metz, was one of the sons of the knight Madelgar or Maldegar and of his wife Waldetrudis, and from his childhood showed a predilection for spiritual life. As a priest he cherished every virtue and was distinguished for his love of prayer, fasts and almsgiving. He was made bishop but after the death of his father, who had become a monk and had found-

Goswin: Ben. Annals. The name also appears as Godevin.
Fructuosus: Prudentius; Sandoval; Butler.
Elias: Eulogius.

ed the monasteries of Soignies and Hautmont, he could no longer resist the attraction of the holy place in which his father had died, and resigned the episcopal office to be abbot of both houses, which he governed to the year 700, when he rested from his labors. His remains were interred at Soignies.

3. **St. Robert** of Aurillac, founder and abbot of Chaise-Dieu in France, was the son of Gerald and Raingardis, nobles of Auvergne, was educated at St. Biroude, was canon of the church of St. Julian in that place, and was ordained a priest. Throughout his career he was wholly intent upon promoting the honor of God and the salvation of the souls committed to his care. But his soul yearned for a life of religious perfection and he resolved to enter the abbey of Cluny, a step which he was prevented from taking by the remonstrances of the people. Having returned from a pilgrimage to Rome, he sought for a retired place where he might devote himself and a few companions to a pious life far from the distractions of the world. He was joined by two former soldiers, with whom he began to carry out his design. They had to contend with many difficulties, but persevered manfully in prayer and works of charity, and in 1043 built a monastery, which was approved by the Pope and the King in 1052. Robert, who was made its first abbot, soon had the satisfaction of seeing his foundation the abode of 300 monks. This was the origin of Chaise Dieu and the centre of a Congregation which was united with that of St. Maur by Cardinal Richelieu in 1640. St. Robert died in 1076, famed for his virtues and miracles.

4. **Bl. Wando**, abbot of Fontenelle, son of Baldric of Tallou, became a monk at Fontenelle in 696. In 716 he was chosen its abbot, but six years later was sent into exile to Utrecht. After his recall in 742 he continued to lead his monks on the path of perfection, provided them with many books and displayed remarkable patience while suffering from the gout. In the midst of the excruciating pain he was wont to say: "God loves the child whom he chastises." In 754 he was stricken with blindness, and two years later was called to his reward.

5. **Bl. Gerwinus**, second abbot of Aldenburg in Flanders, was a native of that country, and made two pilgrimages to the Holy Land and to Rome. Since his relatives objected to his manner of life, he entered the monastery of St. Vinoc, where he was ordained a priest. As abbot he is said to have had unusual power over evil spirits, to have been endowed with the gift of prophecy and to have abstained from meat for forty years. After resigning his office he lived retired in the forest of Kosfort, where he died in 1117.

6. The Cistercians on this day celebrate the fesat of **St. Stephen**, third abbot and co-founder of Citeaux, of whom some account is given above on March 28, the day of his death.

18

1. **St. Wicterp**, bishop of Augsburg, and a former monk and abbot at Ellwangen, now in Wuerttemberg, was made bishop in 736 or 738. Above all, he

Landric: Boll.
Robert: Boll., Mab.
Wando: Mab.
Gerwin: Hariulf of Aldenburg.

kept a watchful eye on the lives of his clergy, and was their model in all the virtues that, according to the words of the Apostle, befit a servant in the sanctuary. He died about the year 770 and was buried in the church of St. Lawrence at Epfach, where the remains lay till 980 when they were raised by Bishop Henry. In 1489 they were removed to the church of SS. Ulric and Afra, where they still rest. Bl. Herluka, in the twelfth century, obtained many spiritual favors through his intercession.

2.   **St. Eleutherius,** abbot of St. Mark's at Spoleto, Italy, was renowned for his remarkable simplicity and spirit of compunction. He is said to have freed a child from molestations of the evil spirit. Pope Gregory the Great had recourse to the intercession of this saint and obtained the grace of fasting. Eleutherius died in 586 on this day, but his feast was observed at St. Andrew's in Rome on September 5, the day of his translation.

3.   **Bl. Idesbald,** a Cistercian abbot of Dunes in Flanders, was chosen abbot of that house in 1155 after the resignation of abbot Albero. He was not only pious and prudent, but watchful, just in all his judgments, peaceable, truthful in speech, temperate in punishing infractions of discipline, and patient in trials. Hence he was successful in all his undertakings and beloved by his brethren. He was a zealous promoter of ecclesiastical music. After governing his monastery for twelve years with wisdom, charity and firmness, he died in 1167. His body was found incorrupt in 1239. His veneration was approved by the Holy See July 23, 1894.

19

1.   **St. Elphegus,** archbishop of Canterbury, in England, was born of noble and virtuous parents, who gave him a good education. To escape the fatal allurement of riches, he renounced the world when still very young and first served God in the monastery of Derherste in Gloucestershire. After some years he left that monastery and lived in a cell near the abbey of Bath, of which he was persuaded to assume the direction. St. Ethelwold, bishop of Winchester dying in 984, St. Dunstan prevailed upon Elphegus to accept the appointment to that see. While he was bishop he was wont to rise for prayer at midnight, and gave alms with such liberality that not a single beggar was to be found within the limits of his diocese. In 1006 he reluctantly accepted promotion to the see of Canterbury. He presided at the synod of Exham in 1009 which issued salutary legislation for the reform of the clergy and people. When the Danes invaded the country, he was advised to seek safety in flight, but would not listen to such a suggestion, saying: "By no means; only a hireling will desert his flock when danger threatens." As the peril became imminent, he prepared the people for death, and administered Holy Communion to them. When the invaders had forced their way into the city and were reveling in massacre, the Saint fearlessly stepped among them and endeavored to prevent further disaster. In reply to his protests they seized him and cast him into prison. Seven months later an epidemic broke out among them, and believing this to be a punishment

---

Wiclerp: Stengel, Braun, Paul of Bernried.
Eleutherius: Gregory the Great.
Idesbald: Carl de Visch.   Acta S. Sedis XXVII. 312.

from Heaven for their cruelty, they were inclined to set him free against a ransom which he was unwilling to pay for his release. On Holy Saturday he was brought before the commander of the fleet and again threatened with torture; nevertheless he refused to pay the ransom, upbraided them for their persistence in wicked ways and foretold to them that their stay in England would not last long. Enraged at this language, the barbarians struck him down with the backs of their battle-axes and then stoned him. Like St. Stephen, the Saint prayed God to forgive them. A Dane that had been recently baptized by Elphegus perceiving him in agony, in order to put an end to his pain, clove his head with a battle axe and thus gave the finishing stroke to his martyrdom on this day in 1012. He was first interred in St. Paul's Church, London, but in 1023 the remains were transferred to Canterbury.

2. **St. Ursmar,** abbot of Lobbe in the Netherlands and regionary bishop, was born at Avesnes in Hainault, and even in his youth constantly walked in the presence of God. When St. Landelin had founded the abbey of Lobbe in the diocese of Cambrai, Ursmar entered as a monk and was elected abbot to succeed Landelin in 686. He set his monks an example of mortification by abstaining from wine, meat and fish and is said not to have tasted bread for the space of ten years. He founded several monasteries,—among them Aune and Waslere—and preached the Gospel among the pagans. By virtue of a commission from the Holy See, he, like his predecessor at Lobbe, was authorized to exercise the functions of a bishop. In his old age he resigned his abbatial office to St. Ermin and died in retirement in 713 at the age of sixty-nine years on the 18th of April. He is honored as a patron in Bins, Lobbe and Luxemburg.

3. **St. Gerold,** hermit, and his two sons **Cuno** and **Ulric,** noble Saxons, settled in the wilderness of Fries in Switzerland, where Otto of Jagdberg made them a grant of land for a settlement. Here they built a house and a chapel, both of which they subsequently presented to the monastery of Einsiedeln. They became members of this community and persevered in it to the end; the father died in 980, while the year in which the sons died is unknown. Gerold's remains were transferred from Einsiedeln to the monastery known as Geroldszell in 1663.

20

1. **St. Wolbodo,** bishop of Liege, in Belgium, was born of noble parents in 950, and received an excellent education at Utrecht. Having consecrated himself to the service of God in religious life, he was made master of the school in the city and provost of the cathedral. In 991 he was selected as best qualified both by learning and the virtues of a bishop to succeed bishop Baldric in the see of Liege. Holy and zealous as he was, he did not escape the wicked tongues of men who spread calumnies that finally reached the ear of the emperor. One day while a number of prelates presented themselves at court, and many of them came with gifts, Wolbodo excused himself in the presence of the monarch with the words: "I have nothing to give: I have given to the poor all that I had."

Elphegus: Osbern of Canterbury: Butler; Stanton. Original form of the name: Aelfheah.
Ursmar: Folcuin, Butler.
Gerold: Albert, monk of Einsiedeln.

This candid confession touched the emperor so deeply, that he requested the bishop to be seated by his side. He was commissioned by the same monarch to rebuild and restore the abbey of St. James at Liege, which had been built by his predecessor. After having effected a peace between the emperor and the Frisians, he returned to his see where he died during the week following Easter Sunday in the year 1021. He was interred in the church of the abbey of St. Lawrence at Liege.

2. **St. Hugo,** prior of Anzy-le-duc, in the diocese of Autun, was offered as a boy of seven years to the abbey of St. Savin at Poitiers, where he early gave promise of his future holiness. After his ordination as a priest his virtues shone even more brightly. When Count Badilo of Aquitaine called for monks to restore the monastery of St. Martin at Autun, Hugo was one of the eighteen brethren sent on that mission and proved to be the main support of the abbot Arnulf, under whose rule the monastery flourished both in numbers and discipline. Later Hugo also assisted abbot Berno in the reform of the monastery of Beaume and in the establishment of Cluny. Some years after, he was summoned to govern the newly founded monastery of Anzy-le-duc. The fame of his virtue was so widespread that persons of all stations came to him for counsel or consolation. In 927 he resigned his office, withdrew to a cell and spent three years in tears and prayer awaiting the coming of the Lord. He died in 930. When his relics were brought to the council of Anse, as was customary at the time, in 1025, many miracles were reported to have been wrought through his intercession.

3. **St. Hildegundis,** nun of Schoenau near Heidelberg, was born at Neuss on the Rhine and accompanied her father in disguise on a pilgrimage to the Holy Land. On the way she lost her father who died at sea, and a servant robbed her of the little that she had. After many other curious adventures she was in 1187 directed to enter the Cistercian monastery of Schoenau. She died during the year of novitiate in 1188.

4. **Bl. Dominic** of Vernagolli, a Camaldolese monk of St. Frigidian at Pisa, died in 1218 and was venerated ever since that time.

21

St. Anselm, archbishop of Canterbury, one of the most celebrated prelates of his time, was born at Aosta in Piedmont in 1033. His mother sowed in his heart the seeds of Christian piety which grew into a resolve, in his fifteenth year, to embrace the monastic state. Fearing opposition from Anselm's father, the abbot of the house to which the youth applied, declined to grant him admission. The result was that Anselm became tepid and rather careless in spiritual matters. Unfortunately, too, his mother died and his father treated him so unkindly, that he left his native land, studied at the schools of Burgundy for three years and, attracted by Lanfranc's renown, attended that eminent teacher's lectures at the abbey of Bec in Normandy. News reached him from Piedmont

Wolbodo: Reiner, monk at Liege.
Hugo: Mab., Boll.
Hildegund: Caesar of Heisterbach, Stadler.
Dominic: Silvio Razzi.

that his father had died. He was now his own master, yet was undecided what course he should pursue. Acting upon the advice of Maurilius, archbishop of Rouen, he embraced the religious state, joined the monks of Bec and professed the vows in that abbey in 1060. Scarcely had three years passed when he was appointed prior, while Lanfranc, whom he replaced, was made abbot of St. Stephen's at Caen in Normandy. The many duties of his responsible position as prior did not prevent him from assiduously studying Holy Scripture and theology. Among his many learned writings are the Monologium, the Proslogium, and a treatise on Free Will. Abbot Herluin, into whose hands he had made profession, died in 1078, and Anselm was elected his successor at Bec at the age of forty-five years. He was at that time renowned far beyond the confines of Normandy; all that knew him were filled with admiration of the prelate and were at a loss to decide what charmed them most, his learning, his modesty, or his kindness and charity. The business of his monastery carried him several times to England where the King found boundless delight in his bearing and conversation. In 1092 Count Hugh of Chester urgently invited him to come to England, to assist him in his last illness and advise him regarding a monastery that he intended to found at St. Wereburg's church in Chester. His sojourn in the island lasted about five months, during which time King William Rufus, who was at the point of death, summoned him to his bedside and would not rest until Anselm had accepted the appointment to the see of Canterbury. Anselm was conducted into the metropolitan church on March 6, 1093, but refused to be consecrated unless the king first restored all the possessions of the church and Pope Urban II were recognized as the lawful Head of the Church. A promise to this effect was given, and he received consecration on December 4. The king recovered but instead of redeeming his pledge, began to oppress the Church and to harass his subjects with excessive taxes. He demanded above a thousand pounds of silver from Anselm, confiscated the revenues of vacant abbeys and forbade archbishops to hold synods. Anselm boldly rebuked the monarch for his harshness; in his turn, the king endeavored to procure his deposition from the see of Canterbury. This scheme failing, King William worried the archbishop in every way possible, so that Anselm, to escape molestation, secretly left, accompanied by two monks, in 1097, and journeying over Cluny and Lyons arrived in Rome in March 1098 to offer his resignation to Pope Urban. The pontiff declined to meet his wishes. At a council held in Bari, the King's attitude towards the Church was one of the topics of discussion. It was suggested that William be punished with excommunication, but Anselm earnestly opposed so rigorous a measure and the Pope decided to proceed with greater leniency. Anselm also was present at a council in Rome in 1099, after which he returned northward, making a pause at Lyons. He was at Chaise-Dieu when he learned that King William was dead. The remembrance of all that he had suffered from that inconstant prince did not keep him from shedding tears of sadness over his sudden decease. Being invited to return to England by the new king, Henry I, he crossed the Channel and landed September 23, 1100. Robert, the king's elder brother, returning from the Holy Land laid claim to the crown of England, and might have succeeded, had not Henry, like his predecessor, secured the friendly offices of St. Anselm to effect a compromise. Scarcely had duke Robert left England, when Henry I resumed the policy of William Rufus in order to gain control of the temporalities of the Church. He had already pre-

viously demanded that Anselm receive investiture from him, but the archbishop had refused and referred the matter to the Holy See.   In 1103 he went
to Rome a second time, and was commended for his courageous conduct by
Pope Pascal II.   King Henry refused him permission to re-enter the kingdom;
therefore he stayed at Bec, where he received from the Pope a commission to
judge the cause of the archbishop of Rouen and to receive into communion such
prelates as had accepted investiture from the crown.   The king arrived in Bec
in 1106 and signed articles of agreement between himself and the archbishop.
Anselm then returned to Canterbury, but his health and been undermined.
During the last three years of his life he grew constantly weaker.   He died,
lying on sack-cloth and ashes, in 1109, and was buried in his cathedral.   By
a decree of Clement XI of the year 1720, he is honored as a Doctor of the Church.

22

1.   **St. Opportuna,** abbess of Montreuil near Seez in Normandy, was the
daughter of honorable parents in the district of Hyesmes and sister of St. Chrodegang, bishop of Seez.   She became a nun at Montreuil and was elected abbess.
Her life was extremely mortified; she spent entire nights in prayer, wore no
heavier clothing in winter than in summer, took no food on Wednesdays and
Fridays, and on other days ate only coarse bread and vegetables.   When she
was advised to be less severe towards herself, she said: "Through fasting we return to paradise, from which the immoderate desire for eating has banished us."
She was deeply shocked by the death of her brother Chrodegang who was slain
by his own god-child and ward at the instigation of one Chrodebert.   As the
crime was committed near her monastery, she interred the body in the church
at Montreuil.   From this time forward she yearned without ceasing for her
heavenly home.   On the anniversary of her brother's sad death, she had a premonition that her prayer was about to be heard.   Summoning the nuns to her,
she exhorted and consoled them, and died in 770.

2.   **St. Wolphelm,** abbot of Brauweiler near Cologne, was descended from
a noble Ripuarian family and was born about 1020.   After receiving his education at the cathedral school in Cologne, he went to Trier and became a monk
at the monastery of St. Maximin.   When the people of Cologne learned this,
they prevailed upon archbishop Herimann to recall him.   Wolphelm went back
to Cologne and spent a short time at the monastery of St. Pantaleon, but felt
much annoyance from the demands made upon his time by visitors.   He was
then sent to rule the monastery of Gladbach, and afterwards that of Siegeberg.
Here, too, the temporal interests of the house claimed so much of his time and
attention, that he was permitted to go to Brauweiler, where he led the brethren
in the path of life both by word and example.   Much of his time was devoted to
study and writing.   He addressed a treatise against Berengarius to abbot Meginhard of Gladbach.   Always intent upon doing good, he gave generous alms,
promoted both the active and the contemplative life among his religious, was
gentle and merciful, yet did not overlook offences against discipline; did not
resent personal insults, yet fearlessly maintained the rights of his monastery.

Anselm: Eadmer, Butler, Chev., C. E., K. L.
Opportuna: Adelelm, bishop of Seez; Butler, Chev.

He was active to the age of seventy years, when an angel showed him the heaven ly mansion prepared for him. After receiving Extreme Unction he calmly expired in 1091.

3. **St. Sennorina**, abbess, was of noble descent and became a nun in the monastery of S. Juan de Vieiria in Portugal. As abbess of this house, she decided to remove the community to Basto, wher she was in frequent communication with her relative, St. Rudesind, and in a vision saw his soul leave its habitation of clay. Since her whole life had been a sacrifice on the altar of divine love, she was privileged to hear these words as this world faded from her sight: "Come, thou chosen one, the Lord coveteth thy comeliness." After receiving the Holy Viaticum, she slept in peace in the year 981.

4. The devout **Meingoz**, abbot of Weingarten in Wuerttemberg, was distinguished for his great charity towards all, particularly to the poor, and died reputed as a saint, about the year 1200.

5. Ven. **Antonia of Orleans-Longueville**, foundress of the Congregation of Notre Dame du Calvaire, renounced the prospects of a worldly career to be a nun at the age of eighteen years. She died in the odor of sanctity in 1618.

23

1. **St. Adalbert**, bishop of Prague and martyr, was a native of Bohemia and born in 956, receiving in baptism the name of Wojtiech. In his infancy he was so near death, that his parents made a promise to offer him for the service of God if he recovered. When his health was fully restored, he was sent to Magdeburg to be educated by St. Adalbert, archbishop of that city, who provided him with the ablest masters, and, at confirmation, gave him his own name. All the time not devoted to study, young Adalbert spent in devout exercises or in visiting the sick. After the archbishop's death in 981, he returned to Bohemia and was two years later ordained a priest by Bishop Diethmar of Prague. Diethmar died shortly after; Adalbert was unanimously chosen to succeed him and was consecrated on June 6th of the same year. From that time he was never seen to laugh or smile. He divided his revenues into four equal parts, one for the support of the cathedral, another for the maintenance of the chapter, the third for the poor and the fourth for his personal needs. Disdaining the comforts of a couch, he slept on the floor; he lost no opportunity to preach the word of God, and frequently visited the prisons and the sick. Notwithstanding all his devoted efforts he saw very little fruit in the lives of many of his diocesans, who were still more pagan than Christian. This moved him to journey to Rome in 989, and to resign his see into the hands of Pope John XV. Adalbert and his brother Gaudentius entered the monastery of St. Boniface on the Aventine Hill, and lived like the humblest religious for five years. The archbishop of Mainz urgently requested him to return to Prague; Adalbert was reappointed and went back to his episcopal city where he was received with great

---

Wolphelm: his pupil Conrad.
Sennorina: Salazar; Stadler.
Meingoz: Bucelin; Hess.
Antonia: Chalemot; Bucelin; Stadler: "Antonia de Aurelia."

enthusiasm and promises of respect and submission. The promises were soon
forgotten and Adalbert set out for Rome a second time. He was elected prior
of his monastery and resumed the practices of monastic life. But the archbishop of Mainz once more insisted that Adalbert return to Prague. When the
inhabitants of Prague heard of his re-appointment, they gave vent to their displeasure by maltreating some of the bishop's relatives. Hence Adalbert decided not to go to Prague, but to labor as a missionary in Poland and Prussia.
His toil was not in vain; most of the inhabitants of Danzig are said to have been
converted by the apostolic bishop, who was supported by his two companions,
Benedict and Gaudentius. He met most opposition on a small island in the
Baltic Sea;one of the natives struck him down with an oar,and the saint thanked
God that he was privileged to suffer for the sake of his crucified Redeemer.
In the province of Samland he and his companions were seized and bound. A
pagan priest pierced him with a lance and he expired in the year 997. Duke
Boleslav of Poland had the body conveyed to the abbey of Tremezno; later it
was removed to Gnesen. Adalbert is called the Apostle of Prussia.

2.   Establishment of the Order of **Knights of St. George** of Alfama in
1201 by King Pedro II of Aragon. This Order was united with that of Montesa
in 1369. It had been approved by the Holy See in 1363.

24

1.   **St. Mellitus,** archbishop of Canterbury, was a Roman abbot who in
601 was sent from the monastery of St. Andrew to assist St. Augustine in the
English mission. Augustine three years later consecrated him bishop and assigned as the field of his labors the province of Essex of which London was the
principal town. Mellitus here achieved the conversion of many pagans, among
them King Severt, with whose help he built St. Paul's church in 604, and St.
Peter's, later known as Westminster, in 609. Disaster befell the new Christian
community after the death of King Severt in 616, for his sons had not the piety
of their father and wished to be Christians and pagans at the same time. In the
kingdom of Kent, of which Canterbury was the capital, religion was suffering
in consequence of the scandalous conduct of King Eadbald. Hence Mellitus
and Justus, the bishop of Rochester, passed over to France to await the dawn of
more favorable times. Eadbald repented of his wickedness a year later, St.
Lawrence, the archbishop of Canterbury, died, and Mellitus was invited to return and take possession of that see, which he ruled for five years. He died
in 624.

2.   **St. Wilfrid,** archbishop of York, England, died on this day 709, but
his feast is celebrated on October 12.

3.   **St. Egbert,** monk and priest, was born of illustrious parentage in England about 639, and was at an early age sent to Ireland to receive an education.
Having received the religious habit at Rathmelsig, he nearly fell a victim to a
dreadful sickness that swept the island in 664,and in his anguish regretted that

Adalbert: Canisius; Mab., Boll; Butler.
Knights of Alfama: Bonanni; C. E.
Mellitus: Bede: Wm. of Malmesbury; Stanton; Butler.

he had not served God with more fidelity. Ever after, he led a very mortified life, daily recited not only the Divine Office but also the Psalter, abstained from food one day in every week and made a vow never to return to his native land. After his ordination, he felt a strong desire to preach among the pagans in Germany, but St. Boisil, prior of Mailros, advised him rather to instruct the monks on some of the neighboring islands. Nevertheless Egbert set out for Germany, but the ship was beaten back by a storm, and he concluded to follow Boisil's advice. He settled on the isle of Hy (Iona, or Columbkill), where he induced the monks to observe Easter according to the usage of the Roman Church. After accomplishing this task, he lived thirteen years and died on Easter day of the year 729.

4. **SS. Bova** and **Doda**, abbesses at Rheims, were both of royal blood and relatives of King Dagobert. After Balderic, the founder and abbot of Montfaucon, had founded a monastery in honor of Our Lady near Rheims, his sister Bova became a nun in that house and was conspicuous for her conscientious observance of the Rule. She was made abbess and presided over the community to the day of her death in 673. Her successor was her niece Doda, who followed in the footsteps of her sainted aunt. The year of her death is not known. The remains of these two holy abbesses were removed to the abbey of St. Peter.

25

1. **St. Ermin**, regionary bishop and abbot of Lobbe in Belgium, was of noble Frankish blood and was born at Laon about 660. Abbot St. Ursmar heard of the virtues of Ermin and with the approval of Bishop Madelgar of Laon received him among his monks. Ermin here, too, soon attracted universal attention by his regular and exemplary behavior and won the esteem and respect of all his brethren. When Ursmar's advanced age rendered him incapable of discharging the duties of his office, Ermin was chosen his successor and also received episcopal consecration. Elevated to this high station, he applied himself with even greater zeal to his work, for he was aware that much would be demanded of one to whom much had been entrusted. On several occasions it became clear that he was gifted with a prophetic spirit. One day messengers of Charles Martell announced that their lord was about to visit the abbey; the prior requested Ermin to welcome the eminent guest. Ermin was at his prayers at the time and apparently paid no heed to the request. The prior sent for him a second time, and when Ermin still failed to make his appearance, lost his temper, personally approached him and said: "How can you act in this way? Why do you not come out and tell us what we are to do, since the prince may be here any moment? " Ermin calmly finished his prayers and replied: "Go back to the messengers, give them what they ask for, and tell them to follow their lord, for he is not coming to our monastery." He had spoken truly. His holy career closed in the year 737.

2. **St. Franca**, a Cistercian abbess of Pittoli near Piacenza in Italy, was descended from the counts of Vitalta and was born in Piacenza in 1170. From

Egbert: Bede; Stanton.
Bova: Flodoard; Mabillon: Butler calls her Bona or Beuve.
Ermin: Anso of Lobbe.

her childhood she showed a marked inclination for piety and was exceptionally serious. At the early age of seven she expressed a desire to become a nun; seven years later her fond wish was realized when she took the veil in the convent of St. Syrus. By her scrupulous observance of the rules and her mortifications she was a bright light among her sisters, so that after the death of the abbess, Franca was chosen to preside over the community, which consisted of fifty members. While her community seemed to be prospering with Heaven's blessing under her guidance, she discovered that some of the sisters who had taken advantage of her kindness ill bore the restraint she was compelled to place upon them for violations of discipline. The opposition grew so bitter, that she was at a loss how to proceed. About this time, God sent her another noble young lady by the name of Carentia, to whom she confided her troubles, and whose advice she resolved to follow. Carentia advised her to enter the Cistercian monastery of Rapallo, and after the expiration of her novitiate to found a house of that Order. Eighteen months later a house was established at Montelana for nuns following the rule of Citeaux; Carentia and ten other nuns formed the first community in 1215 under the direction of Abbess Franca. Here they lived for two years, then removed to S. Gabriel de Vallera and finally settled at Pittoli, which became their permanent abode. Franca spent many nights in prayer, was beset by many temptations, but persevered to the end of her days. She died on the feast of St. Mark in 1218. Her remains were raised in 1266.

3. **St. Robert**, abbot, flourished in a monastery in Sicily about the year 800.

26

1. **St. Richarius**, founder and first abbot of Centula in Ponthieu, was born about 570. His life was in no particular remarkable till two Irish priests, Cadoc and Frichorius, came into that country. While they were not bidden welcome by others and were even ridiculed, Richarius extended hospitality to them and was so deeply stirred by their earnest exhortations that he confessed his sins to them and began to lead a new life. After receiving the religious habit from them, he spent days and nights in prayer, ate but twice a week and never ceased striving to grow in perfection. Having been ordained a priest, he went out among the people and preached the Gospel. The faithful brought him many gifts, but he distributed everything among the poor, saying: "Be not solicitous for tomorrow." (Matt. vi. 34). He ministered to the sick with great tenderness, consoled the sorrowful and raised up the dejected, ransomed prisoners and led many sinners back to the path of righteousness. For several years he was a missionary in England, but returned to the continent, where the munificence of King Dagobert enabled him to found the monastery of Centula, of which Richarius was elected the first abbot. At an advanced age and feeling no longer able to rule a numerous community, he resigned his office and withdrew into the forest of Cressy to lead an eremitical life with several companions. Here, too, the offerings of the people were so numerous and rich that he founded the monastery of Foret-Moutier, near which he occupied a cell; and

Franca: MS. of Piacenza.
Robert: Octav., Cajetan.

here he died in 654. His remains were interred at Centula, which later was named for him St. Riquier.

2. **St. Paschasius Radbertus,** abbot of Corbie in France, was born in the territory of Soissons about 786. The death of his mother left him an orphan but the nuns of Our Lady at Soissons placed him under the supervision and tuition of the monks of St. Peter's abbey. After he had received tonsure, he grew lukewarm and even discontinued his studies for a time. The grace of God at last opened his eyes to the perils towards which he was drifting, and he entered the monastery of Corbie which at the time was ruled by St. Adalard, who was pleased to observe the earnestness with which he performed all the duties of a conscientious religious. In 822 he accompanied abbot Adalard to Saxony to assist in organizing the abbey of New Corbie, or Corvey. Since he was conversant with both the Greek and the Hebrew language, he presided with great credit over the monastic school which produced such eminent men as Adalard the Younger, Anschar, Hildeman, Eudo and Warin. Notwithstanding his learning and abilities, he could not be induced to receive the order of holy priesthood and remained a deacon. This did not prevent him from being elected abbot in 844, in which quality he assisted at the synods of Paris 846 and of Chiersy in 849. The distractions and cares of his office interfered with his studies to such an extent that he endeavored to resign, but did not succeed until 851 when he was permitted to retire to Centula, where he finished several of his writings. Having returned to his monastery, he spent his remaining years in studies and practices of piety till the Lord called him unto Himself in 865. In 1073 his remains were removed from the chapel of St. John to the church. In his last sickness he is said to have laid so strict an injunction on all his disciples forbidding any one to write his life that his humility has robbed the world of a biography which would have been a source of edification.

3. **St. John,** bishop of Valence in France and former Cistercian abbot of Bonneval, died in the year 1145. The holiness of his life is attested by numerous miracles wrought by his intercession.

4. **Bl. Alda,** was born at Siena, Italy in 1245 and after the death of her husband became a nun of the Order of Humiliates at St. Thomas' in her native city. She led a very austere life, spent many hours in meditating upon the Passion of Our Lord and expired on her knees before a crucifix in 1309.

27

1. **Bl. Tutelo,** monk of St. Gall's in Switzerland, was of noble descent and was born about 840. Deeming honors and pleasures worthless in comparison with the priceless pearl of eternal life, he became a monk at St. Gall's and shone among his brethren not only by his excellent natural gifts but also by his virtue. His name was known far beyond the walls of the monastery. He was

Richarius: Alcuin; Hariulf; Butler. French form: Riquier.
Paschasius: Engelmod; Sirmond; Butler; C. E.; K. L.
John: Vincent of Beauvais.
Alda: Lombardelli; Razzi. Also called Aldobrandesca. Stadler; Petin.

endowed with a bright intelligence, spirit and wit, had an attractive exterior and a dignified bearing, was cheerful and affable, was a painter, sculptor, architect and goldsmith. At the same time he was very devout, often shed tears while at prayer and was a mirror of humility and condescension. St. Gall's mourned his loss in the year 909.

2. **Bl. Raynald**, first abbot of the Cistercian monastery of Foigny in Picardy, was a disciple of St. Bernard and highly esteemed by that Saint, who extols him for his humility, obedience, industry, self-control and patience. He died towards the end of the 12th century.

3. **Ven. Theobald**, archbishop of Canterbury and former abbot of Bec in Normandy, was made archbishop in 1138. Not heeding the king's prohibition, he attended the council of Rheims in 1148. He seconded the efforts of King Henry II to put an end to partisan strife in England, but withdrew when he saw a new storm gathering and commended his archdeacon Thomas a Becket for the see of Canterbury. He died 1161.

28

1. **Ven. John de la Barriere**, abbot of Notre Dame des Feuillants and founder of the Congregation of the same name (*Fuliensis*), was born at Cahors in France in 1544, and in his youth was appointed commendatory abbot of Rieux near Toulouse. One day he chanced to find a copy of the Rule of St. Benedict; he read the second chapter, which treats of the Abbot, and blushed at the thought of his unworthiness to bear that title. He at once resolved to be an abbot according to the spirit of St. Benedict, renounced all his worldly prospects, put on the monastic habit, and set about reforming his house. When the religious resisted his endeavors, he dismissed them, and admitted a number of others willing to follow his guidance. Their observance was strict:—they abstained from flesh-meat, eggs, milk and even fish, took but one meal a day and slept on the floor. Some were so mortified that they fasted three or four days in succession, although they performed manual labor. Some that were qualified to do so, were sent out to preach in neighboring places, occasionally in two places on the same day, and returned home fasting. The venerable abbot's efforts were recognized by ecclesiastical and civil authorities. Unfortunately he sided with the king, his benefactor, against the League, while many of the monks of his monastery at Paris sympathized with the latter. For this attitude he was accused of disloyalty to the Church and suspended from his office. The matter was appealed to Rome, where a commission of cardinals, among them Cardinal Baronius, acquitted him of the charge shortly before his death in Rome on April 25, 1600. The Congregation had houses both in France and Italy, but disappeared during the French Revolution and the Napoleonic wars.

2. The devout **Bernard**, fourth abbot of Tarouca in Portugal and a disciple of St. Bernard of Clairvaux, was selected by the latter to assist St. Boe-

Tutelo: Eckart, Canisius, Goldast.
Raynald: Montalbo, Miracus.
Theobald: Harpsfield; Dic. Nat. Biog.
John de la B.: Louis de S. Malachia, Malabayla, Heimbucher.

mund in transplanting the Cistercian Order to Portugal and in founding the abbey of Tarouca where he was first prior, then abbot. He died about 1170.

29

1. **St. Robert,** first abbot of Molesme in France and founder of the Cistercian Order, was born of noble parentage in Champagne in 1024. At the age of fifteen, he left his home and became a monk at Moutier-la-Celle near Troyes, of which he was made prior a few years later. Several years after, he was elected abbot of St. Michael's at Tonnerre, but encountered unexpected difficulties when he endeavored to restore the declining discipline of his house. About this time seven hermits near Colan prevailed upon him to be their spiritual guide. He consented, but finding that the health of the brethren suffered from the unhealthful condition of the locality, induced them to remove to the forest of Molesme where they built rude huts of logs, also a chapel which was dedicated in honor of the Blessed Trinity in 1075. The brethren were extremely poor and led such austere lives, that the faithful had pity upon them and supplied them with means of subsistence in abundance. Thus put beyond the reach of need, the brethren were no longer willing to maintain themselves by manual labor. Discouraged, Robert left them and joined some religious at Hauz, who were struck by his virtues and requested him to be their superior. In the mean time the monks of Molesme regretted his departure, and induced the Pope to order him back to his monastery. Robert returned, but saw his efforts frustrated; the monks were divided into two factions, one of which insisted upon introduction of the Rule of St. Benedict in all its severity, the other favoring the observance that had hitherto prevailed. The former humbly submitted a request to be permitted to depart and to establish themselves in some wilderness. Robert not only readily assented but, with the approval of archbishop Hugo of Grenoble, even joined them. Twenty-one in number, they left Molesme, settled in the forest of Citeaux, and founded the Order of that name. Robert was supported in his endeavors particularly by the monks Alberic and Stephen. On March 21, 1098 they all professed strict observance of the Rule of St. Benedict. They devoted but four hours to sleep and lived on vegetable food. A year later, Pope Pascal II commanded Robert to return to Molesme, which he continued to rule peacefully to the year 1110 when he was called to his heavenly reward in the 86th year of his life. He was canonized by Pope Honorius III in 1222.

2. **St. Hugo,** abbot of Cluny, was descended from the dukes of Burgundy and was born at Semur, in the diocese of Autun, in France, in 1024. Although destined for a military career, he had an inclination for higher things, and after receiving an education under the supervision of a grand-uncle, bishop Hugo of Auxerre, he entered the monastery of Cluny at the age of fifteen years, while St. Odilo presided over that famous institution. After Odilo's death he was elected abbot, although only twenty-five years of age. He assisted at the council of Rheims at which Pope Leo IX presided and accompanied that pontiff to Rome. The Pope employed him on several important missions, in the discharge of which Hugo proved to be not only influential but also unusually gifted. He

---

Bernard: B. Brito.
Robert: Guido, his successor; Butler.

possessed all the virtues of an exemplary religious, observed every detail of the
Holy Rule even when he was laboring under the infirmities of old age, and insisted upon conscientious observance on the part of his brethren, whom he encouraged to study, pray and work with their hands.   Under his rule, Cluny
enjoyed unparalleled prosperity and grew in numbers as well as importance.
Even Duke Hugo of Burgundy laid aside his dignity to serve God as a humble
monk in this celebrated monastery.   Hugo had ruled Cluny for nearly sixty
years when during the Lent of 1109 he received a revelation that the end was
not far distant.   During Holy Week he washed the feet of the brethren on Holy
Thursday, officiated on Easter Sunday and died two days later, bidding his
brethren farewell with the word *Benedicite*.   Pope Calixtus II canonized him
in 1121.

3. **Bl. Theogerus**, bishop-elect of Metz, and former abbot of St. George's
in the Black Forest, was as learned as he was pious and humble.   Since circumstances prevented him from taking possession of his see, he remained at Cluny
where he died in the odor of sanctity in the year 1120.

30

1. **St. Erconwald**, bishop of London, in England, was of noble descent
and born about 620.   Preferring to disengage himself from all earthly ties, he
left his home and went into the country of the East-Saxons, or Essex, and
founded two great monasteries, one at Chertsey, in Surrey, the other, for nuns,
at Barking in Essex.   He governed Chertsey for several years till King Sebba
in 675 procured his appointment to the see of London.   He received consecration from St. Theodore of Canterbury and governed the see of London for eleven
years, enlarged St. Paul's church and increased its revenues.   Rich in merit and
famed for miracles, he died in 690.

2. **St. Forannan**, bishop, and abbot of Vasour in Belgium, was born in
Ireland about 810.   That he was bishop or archbishop of Armagh, as some suppose, is not likely.   Since he had dreaded, rather than aspired to, the episcopal
dignity, he, together with twelve companions, passed over to the mainland to
be a monk at Vasour, where he was shortly elected abbot.   Fearing there was
some irregularity in this proceeding, he journeyed to Rome, and offered his resignation to Pope John XIII, who approved of his election as abbot.   By the
express request of this pontiff, Forannan for some time lived with the monks of
Gorze in order to acquaint himself with the discipline of Benedictine monasteries.   He shared all the prayers and labors of the monks with the ardor of a novice
and returned to Vasour, where he achieved a complete renovation of the discipline of that house.   After twelve years of devoted and unremitting toil, he
slept in peace in the year 982.

3. **St. Adjutor**, a hermit at Vernon on the Seine in France, was the son
of the wealthy John of Vernon, the owner of vast estates in that country, and
of his wife Rosamond of Blaru.   At the head of two hundred men he took part

Hugo: Hildebert of Mans; Butler.
Theoger: Ben. Annals.
Erconwald: Bede; Wm. of Malmesbury; Stanton.
Forannan: Robert of Vasour; O'Hanlon; Butler.

in a Crusade, was taken prisoner and suffered much at the hands of the Saracens. Having been released from captivity, he returned to his native land, offered his possessions to the abbey of Tiron, received the religious habit and lived as a hermit near Vernon to the year 1131 when he died a holy death. His remains repose in the chapel of St. Mary Magdalen at Vernon and his feast was annually celebrated in the dioceses of Rouen, Evreux and Chartres.

4. **St. Suitbert** the Younger, first bishop of Werden in ancient Saxony, had been a monk in England and was led by his zeal for souls to preach the Gospel in Germany. His labors covered the countries conquered by Charlemagne. He died as bishop of Werden in 807. His feast is also celebrated annually at Osnabrueck.

Adjutor: Breviary of Evreux; Butler, who gives the French forms of the name: Ajutre, or Adjoutr.
Suitbert: Kranz.

May

1

1. **St. Ultan,** abbot of Perrone on the Somme, was a native of Ireland, where he was born about 610. After his brother Fursey had embraced the religious state, Ultan and another brother by the name of Foilan followed his example, supporting him in the establishment of Knobbersbury abbey in England. Later Ultan and Foilan crossed over to the continent, where abbess St. Gertrude of Nivelle had founded two monasteries, one for men and one for women. The two brothers were sent to the former to instruct the religious in psalmody and monastic practices. After some time, Foilan was made abbot of Perrone succeeding his brother Fursey, while Ultan, with means furnished by St. Gertrude after the death of her nother im 652, founded the monastery of Fosse, west of Namur and between the Meuse and the Sambre. Sustained and strengthened by God's grace, Ultan accomplished much good and was rewarded with the gift of prophecy; among other things he foretold the day of St. Gertrude's death. Ultan died in 680 and was venerated both at Fosse, where he was buried, and at Perrone.

2. **Bl. Margaret,** abbess of St. Catherine's at Amelia, in Italy, was a marvel of piety throughout her life. Heaven had favored her with the gift of prayer and with numerous visions in which the Lord instructed her how to direct her sisters. After serving God faithfully for ninety years in religion she died smiling and with eyes turned heavenward on April 6, 1666.

3. On this day is celebrated at Eichstaett in Bavaria the translation of the remains of **St. Walburga,** from Heidenheim to Eichstaett in 870; and at Aldenburg in Flanders the elevation of the remains of St. Arnulf, whose feast is celebrated on August 15.

2

1. **St. Waldebert,** third abbot of Luxeuil in France, while still only an ordinary monk was so conspicuous for his virtue and ability that his abbot Eustasius employed him in the discharge of important business of the monastery. He took an active and prominent part in the establishment of Grandval and of the convents of Langres, Laon and Faremoutier. As abbot of Luxeuil from 625–665, he was eminently successful in maintaining order and discipline. He died in 665 and was buried in the church of St. Martin.

2. **St. Wiborada,** recluse at St. Magnus near St. Gall's in Switzerland, even in her childhood led the life of a recluse in her home. She had a brother named Hilton, after whose ordination she went to live with him partly in order to lead a stricter and more retired life and partly to provide for his temporal needs. Both made a pilgrimage to Rome; on their return Wiborada induced

Ultan: Bede; Mab.; O'Hanlon; Stanton (May 2).
Margaret: Armellini.
Walburga: Ben. Annals.
Waldebert: Bobolen; Jonas; Chifflet.

her brother to become a monk of St. Gall's while she remained in the world for a few years longer. In the year 887 she visited St. Gall's and settled in a cell near the church of St. George, but was so much annoyed by visitors that she determined to become a regular recluse. The cell chosen was within the territory of St. Gall's and near the church of St. Magnus; here she was solemnly enclosed by Bishop Solomon of Constance. She was famous for the gift of prophecy and of working miracles; thus, by her prayers she healed St. Rachildis of an incurable disease. When the Huns overran the country, she refused to leave her cell. Suspecting her of keeping a treasure concealed in it, they slew her in the year 925. Her remains were buried in the church of St. Magnus. She was canonized by Pope Clement II ; 1047, while the latter was visiting Germany.

3. Bl. **Rachildis**, virgin and disciple of the holy recluse Wiborada, was of distinguished birth, her parents belonging to a noble family near St. Gall in Switzerland. She was afflicted with a malady that was deemed incurable, but was healed through Wiborada's prayers, and in token of gratitude also became a recluse. She was not molested when Wiborada was slain in 925, but continued the practices of penitential life down to the year 946 when she died, and was buried by the side of her friend and benefactress in the church of St. Magnus.

4. Bl. **Conrad**, laybrother and founder of the monastery of Engelberg in Switzerland, was born in the castle of Seldenburen. Following the example of Reginbert, one of his ancestors, he devoted his patrimony to the foundation of a monastery after the death of his parents. The place selected by him was in the canton of Unterwalden. On April 1, 1120 Bishop Ulric of Constance dedicated the church, and the first monks under their abbot Adelelm from St. Blasien were installed by the founder, who joined the community as a laybrother. Five years later the title of the monastery to the lands which it occupied was disputed; Conrad went out to confer with the contestants but was treacherously slain by them in 1123. He always received veneration.

5. Bl. **Malfalda** (Mafalda), queen of Henry I of Castile and Cistercian nun, having learned that her marriage was null on account of the impediment of consanguinity, restored the convent of Aruca in Portugal, introduced Cistercian nuns and became one of their number. Her life was one of rigorous penance; she subsisted on bread and water three days in the week, and spent many hours of the night in prayer. She died in 1252. When her tomb was opened in 1617, the body was found in a fair state of preservation.

3

1. Bl. **Ansfried**, or Aufrid, bishop of Utrecht, was descended from a distinguished family in Brabant and loved God from his tender childhood. He delighted in reading the Holy Scriptures, with which he grew so familiar that he quoted them readily in conversation. On account of his prudence and knowledge he stood in high favor with Otto III, who after the death of bishop Baldwin of

Wiborada: Ekkehard: Hartmann; Steele. Other forms of the name Guiborat, Viborata.
Rachildis: Life of Wiborada; Steele; Dunbar.
Conrad: Murer; Stadler.
Malfalda: Brito; Vasconcelli.

Utrecht nominated Ansfried to succeed that prelate. Ansfried dreaded the promotion, but was induced to yield. He had hitherto been a mailed knight whose bravery several battle-fields had witnessed; now he laid his arms upon the altar of Our Lady, and said: "Hitherto I have fought for earthly honor and warded off the oppressors of widows and of the poor; now I commit myself to the protection of Our Lady that I may save my soul." He ruled his diocese with praiseworthy zeal and promoted the growth of the kindgom of Heaven in many ways; thus, he founded the monastery of Hohorst (Heiligenberg, Marienberg) near Utrecht for monks from Gladbach under the direction of the pious abbot Weringer. His charity was remarkable; on one occasion he is said to have washed with his own hands the sores of a leper, whom he laid in his own bed and sent away newly clad. Towards the end of his life he was afflicted with blindness which he bore with the patience of Job. Shortly before his death he received the habit of St. Benedict at Hohorst and spent the remainder of his days in the practices of the monastic virtues. He was called to his reward in 1008, or 1010.

2. **Bl. Alexander,** a Cistercian laybrother at Foigny in the diocese of Laon, France, is said to have been the son of a Scottish king. He was about to ascend the throne when his sister Mathilda persuaded him to renounce his claim and to join her in leading a religious life in France. He applied for admission at Foigny, where he performed the lowliest services in the dairy before he received the religious habit. His sister, who had in the mean time lived near him, now removed to a place called Lapion and became a recluse at the Cistercian monastery of Thierache, where she died in 1205. Alexander served God in humility for many years without revealing his rank. One day he saved the life of a noble hunter who was attacked by a wild boar; the skill with which he accomplished the feat aroused a suspicion that he had the training of a nobleman. It was only on his deathbed and in response to pressing inquiries that he confessed that he was the brother of Mathilda of Lapion and of Scottish royal blood. He died in 1217 or 1227 and was venerated from time immemorial.

3. **Bl. Sperandeus** (Sperandus), after consenting to his wife's entrance into a religious community, professed as a monk at St. Peter's in Gubbio. He was elected abbot and founded a new congregation, which is known by his name. He died regarded as a Saint about 1261.

4

1. **St. Godhard,** bishop of Hildesheim, was born at Reichersdorf in Bavaria about 960, received his early training in the monastery of Niederaltaich, and under the auspices of archbishop Frederic of Salzburg attended schools, in which he was fitted for service in the Church. Three years later he was ordained a subdeacon, sent back to Niederaltaich and became a member of that community. At the age of thirty he was promoted to the holy priesthood and appointed prior by abbot Erchambert. After the death of the latter, in 995, the

---

Ansfried: Monk of Utrecht. Also called Aufrid.
Alexander: Thomas Cantipratanus; Barrett; Steele calls his sister Mechtild.
Sperandeus: Stadler; Armellini: Bibliotheca Cassinensis, calls the Congregation "de Speraindeo."

brethren elected Godhard abbot, but he resolutely declined for the space of two years to accept the dignity, till the bishops of the province prevailed upon him to yield to their wishes. In 1005 he was invited to restore the discipline of the monastery of Hersfeld, and seven years later that of Kremsmuenster. Having provided these two houses and that of Tegernsee with new abbots in 1021 he returned to Niederaltaich where he saw in a dream an uprooted olive-tree, the branches of which were set in the ground and produced other olive trees. This he interpreted as a forewarning of his approaching death. About this time (1021) the see of Hildesheim became vacant in consequence of the death of St. Bernward. The emperor nominated Godhard to succeed him, and he was consecrated by the archbishop of Mainz on the first Sunday of Advent, 1022. The relief of the poor, both spiritual and temporal, was everywhere the first object of his attention. He also endeavored to improve the lives of his clergy, encouraged the foundation of schools, the building and embellishment of churches, and built a hospice for the poor and infirm. On his way to the national council of Mainz in 1023, he performed a successful exorcism, which served to increase the reputation which he already enjoyed. He ruled the church of Hildesheim for sixteen years and slept in peace in the year 1038. Pope Innocent II canonized him at the Council of Rheims in 1131.

2. St. Ada, abbess of St. Julian at Mans, had previously been a nun at St. Mary's in Soissons. She was a generous benefactress of other religious houses; among others of that of St. Maximin which she presented with a book of the Gospels written in letters of gold and bound in covers of gold studded with precious stones. She died in 690, and her remains were raised in 836.

3. On Mount Tabor in Palestine, a number of Cluniacensian monks suffered death for the faith at the hands of the Saracens in the year 1114. They lived in a monastery on the mountain hallowed by the Transfiguration of Our Lord. The number of monks is not known.

4. The devout Paulinus, Silvestrine monk at Perugia in Italy, was descended from the noble families of the Bigazzini and Collaltini and enrolled himself under the standard of St. Benedict in the monastery of SS. Mark and Lucy. He was a faithful disciple of the founder of his Order, St. Silvester Gozzolini, whose holy death he beheld in a vision. Paulinus died in the year 1280.

5

1. St. Maurontius, abbot of Breuil in the diocese of Terrouane, was the first child of his saintly parents Adalbald and Rictrudis, and was born in 634. The years of his youth were spent at the court of Clovis II and St. Bathildis. The death of his father left at his disposal considerable material resources and the title of Count of Douai. On his way back to Flanders, he had resolved to enter the matrimonial state, but God disposed otherwise, employing Bishop St.

Godhard: Wolpher; Butler calls him Godard.
Ada: Ben. Annals. Also called Adrehild.
Clun. Martyrs.: Baronius.
Paulinus: Jacobillus.

Amandus, then at the monastery of Elnon, to turn the young man's thoughts in another direction. So eloquently did that Saint, while entertaining him, discourse upon the transitory character of all the world has to offer, that Maurontius determined to consecrate himself without reserve to God as a humble religious. Having arranged his affairs and severed the bonds that bound him to creatures, he went to the monastery of Marchiennes, which his mother had founded, and received the religious habit from the hands of St. Amandus. Several years after, he was ordained a deacon, and appointed superior of the monastery of Hamai on the Scarpe, about two miles from Marchiennes. To meet the wishes of the numerous candidates, he established the monastery of Breuil on his estate at Merville and governed it as abbot. When Bishop Amatus of Sens had been driven from his see by Thierry III, Maurontius received him with open arms and even requested him to rule the monastery during his sojourn. After the death of Amatus in 690, Abbot Maurontius continued to govern his home for another decade and died in 701. In the ninth century his remains were transferred to Douai, and placed in a shrine in the church of St. Amatus. Douai ascribed its delivery from a siege in 1556 to the intercession of St. Maurontius and honored him since that time as its patron.

2. **The Congregation of Notre Dame des Feuillants** was approved on this day in the year 1586 by Pope Sixtus V. It was founded by the Ven. John de la Barriere (see April 28), and had two establishments in Rome, at St. Pudenziana and at St. Bernardo, the members of which had the privilege of making the waxen "Agnus Deis" that are blessed by the Popes every seven years.

6

1. **St. Petronax**, abbot of Monte Cassino, is said to have visited Rome as a pilgrim coming from Brescia about 720 and to have become a monk in one of the Roman monasteries. Pope Gregory II selected him to be the second founder of the abbey of Monte Cassino, which had been in ruins and uninhabited, save by a few hermits, ever since it had been ravaged by the Lombards under duke Zoto of Beneventum. Petronax gathered the hermits about him and set about the restoration of the monastery. In his efforts he was seconded by the three brothers Paldo, Taso and Tato, who several years earlier had founded the monastery of St. Vincent on the Voltorno in the same province as Monte Cassino. Assistance came from the Pope in the shape of material resources and of zealous candidates, so that two years later Petronax was officially installed as abbot. He walked faithfully in the footsteps of St. Benedict and soon the report of his virtue and success was spread abroad. Monks from distant parts came to familiarize themselves with the discipline of the monastery and to transplant its traditions to the utmost bounds of the earth. St. Willibald arrived in 728 and remained ten years; Carlmann, once King of the Franks, spent the last eight years of his life there as a lay-brother. Sturmius, abbot of Fulda, came to study the observance of the Rule; queen Tasia and her daughter Ratruda, who had at their own expense rebuilt St. Scholastica's monastery at Plumbariola, placed themselves under his spiritual direction. From that time Monte Cas-

---

Maurontius: MS. of Douai; Stadler (Maurontus); Butler.
Feuillants: Biedenfeld; Heimbucher.

sino's fame was continually on the increase and rare flowers of learning and holiness bloomed within its inclosure.   Pope Zachary sent Petronax the manuscript of the Holy Rule written by St. Benedict himself, also the measure of bread and wine daily allowed the monks.   The manuscript is said to have perished in a fire at Trani.   After presiding wisely over St. Benedict's venerable foundation thirty-two years Petronax was laid to rest near the tomb of the holy founder in the year 750.

2.   St. Eadbert, bishop of Lindisfarne in England, was the successor of St. Cuthbert in that see and governed it for eleven years.   It was his custom twice a year, in Lent and forty days before Christmas, to retire into a solitary place and to spend the time in abstinence, prayers and tears.   When the body of St. Cuthbert was found intact and even the garments were still fresh and well preserved, the brethren brought some of the vestments to Eadbert who devoutly kissed them, exclaiming: "The tomb that has been glorified by such a miracle, will not remain empty for a long time."   Eadbert fell dangerously sick a short time after and died on May 6, 698.   His remains were laid in St. Cuthbert's tomb, while the remains of the latter were placed in a shrine above it.

3.   Ven. Remigius, bishop of Lincoln in England, was a native of Normandy and a monk of Fecamp.   His biographers say that he was small of stature, but great of mind.   His abbot sent him to accompany the troops who followed William the Conquerer into England, where he was made bishop of Dorchester.   He was distinguished for his liberal charities, built a hospital, fed thirteen beggars at his table daily, once a week performed the ceremonial washing of their feet and withheld his alms from no sufferer.   He effected the transfer of his see to Lincoln, where he preached with the fiery zeal of an apostle against the prevailing vices, particularly adultery and perjury, and the barbarous custom of selling children as slaves.   He was about to consecrate his new cathedral, when he died on the feast of the Ascension in the year 1092.

4.   Ven. Aldulf, bishop of Worcester and archbishop of York, was previously abbot of Medeshamstede and died in the reputation of sanctity in 1002. His remains were interred in St. Mary's Church at Worcester.

7

1.   St. John of Beverley, archbishop of York in England, was a native of Harpham and was educated under the supervision of SS. Theodore and Abbot Adrian at Canterbury.   Following the religious bent of his mind, he entered the monastery of Whitby, but was summoned to the episcopal see of Hexham in 688. He was not only zealous in preaching the word of God and in the discharge of his other episcopal functions, but much given to prayer and meditation.   During Lent it was his custom to dwell in spiritual retreat in a cell near the church of St. Michael.   With touching tenderness he ministered to the wants of the poor.   A poor mute who suffered from a loathsome disease found lodging in the bishop's

---

Petronax: Paul Warnefrid; Leo Marsicanus.
Eadbert: Bede; Butler; Rom. Martyrol.   Also called Edbert.
Remigius: Giraldus Cambrensis; Wm. of Malmesbury; Barrett, who gives 1091 as the year of his
    death and calls him Saint.
Aldulf: Mabillon.

house and was nursed by the holy prelate himself, under whose hands he completely recovered from his malady.   John is also said to have restored the poor man's speech by signing his tongue with the sign of the Cross.   When St. Wilfrid returned from banishment in 704, John voluntarily withdrew from the see of Hexham, which he had temporarily administered, and was promoted to the see of York, which he maintained to the year 718, when he retired in favor of Wilfrid the Younger.   He died in the monastery which he had founded at Inderawood, later known as Beverley, in 721 and was canonized in 1037 by Benedict IX.

2.   **St. Serenicus**, abbot in the diocese of Seez in Normandy, was born at Spoleto, in Italy, about the year 600.   He found his greatest delight in reading Holy Scripture and the writings of the Fathers, from which he learned the noble destiny of man and the importance of treading in the footsteps of Jesus.   Since his brother Sarenedus was of a similar disposition, both made a pilgrimage to Rome to pray for light at the tomb of the Apostles, where Pope Vitalian ordained Serenicus a deacon.   Fearing the snares of unworthy ambition the brothers travelled to France and made their abode at a place called Saulge in the diocese of Mans.   It was not God's will, however, that both should live in one place; hence Serenicus, accompanied by a boy, his godchild, settled in the territory of Hyesmes on the banks of the Sarthe, where he intended to live unknown to the world.   His place of concealment was soon discovered; people flocked from all sides to receive consolation and spiritual strength from his lips.   Some remained with him and lived a monastic life under his direction.   The offerings of the faithful were so plentiful that he built a church in honor of St. Martin.   His humility forbade him to receive the order of holy priesthood.   All the time not occupied by the care of souls and singing of the divine offices, he devoted to the study of Holy Scripture and to meditation.   So great was his charity, that he regarded his enemies as his best friends; in adversity he always said with Job: "The Lord gave, the Lord hath taken away; blessed be the name of the Lord."   On his deathbed he consoled his weeping brethren and departed to receive his reward about the year 668.   His brother, Sarenedus, remained at Saulge and is said to have had the gift of miracles.

3.   **Ven. Gisela**, sister of Emperor St. Henry II, disciple of bishop St. Wolfgang, wife of King St. Stephen of Hungary, and mother of St. Emmeric, after the death of her husband took the veil as a nun in the convent of Niedernburg at Passau, in Bavaria and set the sisters an example in humility by observing the Holy Rule most scrupulously.   Enjoying the reputation of a Saint, she died in 1095.

8

1.   **Bl. Itta**, wife of Pepin of Heristal, foundress and nun of Nivelle, devoted herself and her daughter Gertrude to the service of God after the death of her husband in 640.   Both turned to Heaven in fervent prayer, meditation and devout reading to find the path to perfection.   In 642 they met the holy bishop Amandus of whom they sought spiritual counsel.   He advised Itta to

John: Folcard of Canterbury; Butler; Stant.
Serenicus: Boll.; Mab.   Stadler gives the form Cerenicus.
Gisela: Rader; Arthur de Moutier; Petin (in Appendix.)

build a monastery, a suggestion upon which she acted without delay. To the surprise and dismay of the world, she was the first to receive the sacred veil. Her enemies, not content with reviling her with their tongues, molested her in various other ways while the construction of the monastery at Nivelle was in progress, and even sought to shake the purpose of her daughter Gertrude by placing tempting offers in her way. She had no misgiving as to her daughter's constancy, yet in order to put an end to persecution, cut off Gertrude's hair, gave her the veil and made her abbess of Nivelle. Itta died in the year 652.

2. **St. Peter,** archbishop of Tarantasia in Savoy, was a native of Dauphine in France. A strong inclination to learning, coupled with exceptional mental gifts, carried him successfully through his studies. At the age of twenty years he took the Cistercian habit at Bonnevaux in the diocese of Vienne, where he shone above all the rest by his obedience, meekness, humility and modesty. It may have been owing to Peter's prayers that his father and mother also embraced the religious state. The year after Peter had taken the habit, his example was followed by Amadeus, nearly related to emperor Conrad III. Amadeus built four monasteries: among which was that of Tamies in the diocese of Tarantasia, of which he designated his friend Peter the first abbot. Peter was only thirty years of age, yet presided over his monks with such happy success that Tamies seemed an abode of angels. With assistance from count Amadeus III of Savoy he founded a hospice to shelter the sick and strangers. In 1124 he was elected archbishop of Tarantasia but would not accept till St. Bernard and the General Chapter of the Order compelled him to submit. The diocese stood in sad need of repair, for his predecessor has squandered the revenues; parish churches and tithes were wrongfully held by laymen, and the clergy disedified rather than improved the faithful by their bad example. This deplorable state of affairs profoundly affected the archbishop, who prayed and wept by day and night, mortified his body, and preached penance throughout the territory over which his jurisdiction extended. Thirteen years after taking possession of his see he disappeared and made his way to a Cistercian monastery in Germany where he was not known. He was discovered after some time and compelled to return to his see. During the schism in the time of Frederic Barbarossa he declared in favor of the rightful Pope Alexander III and in 1170 he was sent by the Pope to affect a reconciliation between Louis VII of France and Henry II of England. Returning from a second embassy of the same nature, he died in the Cistercian abbey of Bellevaux in 1174, and was canonized in 1191 by Pope Celestine III.

3. **Bl. Wulfhildis,** nun at Wessobrunn in Bavaria was the daughter of duke Henry IX of Bavaria. At the suggestion of her parents she married Count Rudolf of Bregenz, after whose death she became a nun at Wessobrunn. In her new surroundings she strove to forget what she had abandoned for Christ's sake, and discovered a source of endless delight in meditating upon the sufferings of our Lord. Occasionally she was called from her solitude to perform the office of peacemaker between her relatives. She died towards the end of the eighth century and was always venerated at Wessobrunn.

Itta: Life of St. Gertrude in Mab. Also called Iduberga.
Peter: Godfrey, abbot of Hautcombe; Butler.
Wulfhildis: Leutner; Braun.

9

1. **St. Gregory**, cardinal and bishop of Ostia, was abbot of SS. Cosmas and Damian in Rome, when Pope Benedict IX promoted him to the episcopal dignity. Later he is said to have been sent as legate to Spain, where a plague of locusts was suppressed through his prayers. He died in 1044 and was buried in the monastery of S. Salvador de Pinnava in the kingdom of Navarre.

2. **Bl. Fortis**, hermit and monk of the Congregation of Fontavellana, was a scion of the Gabrielli family. His epitaph in the cathedral of Gubbio in Italy praises his splendid candor, constancy and piety. The year of his death is 1040.

3. **Bl. Peter**, a Cistercian monk, was a brother of king Alphonse of Portugal, and was converted by St. Bernard from being a servant of the world into a servant of Christ. Whereas he had hitherto found his chief pleasure in seeking the favor of men, he now strove with all his heart to please God alone, spent nights in prayer, ate very frugally but once a day, wore a hairshirt and in the hour of temptation never failed to have recourse to the Blessed Mother of God. His humble life closed in the year 1160.

4. In Portugal the **Order** of the **Knights of Christ** was established by King Dionysius in 1317 to replace the Knights Templars who had been suppressed several years before. The Order was approved by Pope John XXII on March 14, 1319; its rule was that of the Order of Calatrava and its purpose to repress the Saracens. Later it was placed under the jurisdiction of the Cistercian abbot of Alcobaza and endowed with the estates of the suppressed Templars.

10

1. **Bl. Beatrice** of Este, abbess of Gemmula in the diocese of Padua, abandoned the delights of high and choice society to serve God in the obscurity and holy calm of the cloister. After the death of her parents, Azo and Eleonora of Este, she begged her brother Azolinus to permit her to leave his court and take the veil. Being refused, she left home secretly for the convent of Salarola, after instructing some friends to soothe the wrath of her brother. For eighteen months she devoted herself to the exercises of religious perfection; then, desirous of settling in some place farther removed from contact with the noisy world, she obtained leave of her abbess and of the bishop of Padua to establish herself with some congenial associates in the monastery of Gemmula which had been vacated by a community of monks. In the practice of the virtue of poverty she was the brightest example to her sisters. One day a silver coin was found on the altar; Beatrice would not use it to supply the needs of the house but gave it in alms to the poor. Five years after organizing her community at Gemmula, she slept in the peace of God at the age of only twenty years in the year 1226.

Gregory: Ughelli; Marietta; Stadler.
Fortis: Jacobillus; Ferrarius.
Peter: Brito; Vasconcello.
Knights of Christ: Bonanni.
Beatrice: Boll.

2.   **Bl. Garinus,** bishop of Toul in Lorraine, previously abbot of St. Aper, led a devout life from the days of his youth and was illustrious for his piety and zeal as a bishop.   He resigned his office after two years and died in 1230.

3.   **Ven. Alberic,** cardinal of the title of Quatuor Coronatorum, was a monk of Monte Cassino, whose rare powers of intuition, prudence and other remarkable gifts led to his promotion to the cardinalate.   He was one of the prominent figures in a Council convoked by Pope Gregory VII to combat the teachings of Berengarius, against whom he also wrote a treatise.   Alberic died about 1085.

4.   **Bl. James,** monk of the Congregation of Fontavellana in the monastery of St. Stephen at Parano, was most conscientious in observing the Holy Rule, and was especially known for his love of prayer and mortification.   He died about the year 1300.

5.   **Frodoin,** abbot of Novalese in Piedmont, died in the odor of sanctity in 816.

11

1.   **St. Majolus,** abbot of Cluny, was born of wealthy parents at Avignon, in France.   During a Saracen invasion he withdrew to Macon, and became a canon at the cathedral of that city.   Having completed his studies in philosophy at Lyons, he returned to Macon to hear lectures in theology and was appointed archdeacon.   In 941 he was considered eligible for the archiepiscopal see of Besancon, but entered the monastery of Cluny to escape the appointment. Shortly after his profession, he was appointed librarian and treasurer by Abbot Aymard, and when the latter resigned in 948 on account of old age and blindness was elected as his successor.   During his administration he laid the foundations for the greatness and influence of Cluny and was one of the most notable figures in the Church of his day.   Through his vigilant efforts, discipline was restored in a number of houses and the monks were encouraged to devote themselves to studies.   So great was his popularity that emperor Otto II recommended him as a worthy successor of Pope Benedict VI, but Majolus declined for he was as unassuming as a child.   On his return from a journey to Rome, he fell into the hands of the Saracens.   He prayed for deliverance and had the happiness of celebrating the feast of the Assumption of Our Blessed Lady, to whom he ascribed his escape, with the brethren of his monastery.   In all his doings he observed moderation and would rather be a Saint than appear to be one.   In 991 he chose St. Odilo as his assistant and from this time devoted himself exclusively to penitential practices, prayer and meditation.   At the request of Hugh Capet he set out for Paris to reform the abbey of St. Denis, but was taken sick on the way and expired at the monastery of Souvigny near Moulins on this day in the year 994.

2.   Saints **Lambert** and **Bellerius,** monks of St. Gislen in the Netherlands, were holy disciples of St. Gislenus and died in the reputation of sanctity

Garinus: Gallic. Martyrol.
Alberic: Ben. Annals.
James: Boll.
Frodoin: Chronicles of Novalese.
Majolus: Syrus, monk of Cluny; Chev.; Butler.   French form of the name: Majeul.

about 690.   Their bodies repose in the church of St. Guillain in Hainaut.   Little
is known of their lives or deeds.   According to one account they were Greeks
by birth, and accompanied St. Gislen from Rome to Belgium, where they received the names by which they are known.

3.   **Ven. Joachim,** priest and monk of Maria-Zell in Lower Austria, was
curate of Inzersdorf and preached with great zeal and fervor against the Protestants who were beginning to disseminate their teachings in those parts.   Some
adherents of the new sect were angered by his opposition, fell upon him and inflicted twenty five wounds upon him of which thirteen were fatal.   He died
praising God for the privilege of laying down his life for his faith.   His body lay
in state in the church for two weeks without showing signs of decomposition.
Many Catholics and Protestants who were present, averred that they saw a
luminous sphere rising heavenward at the time of his death in the year 1617.

12

1.   **St. Rictrudis,** abbess of Marchiennes in Flanders, was born of noble
parents in Gascony in 614.   She became the wife of Count Adelbald, a noble of
the court of Clovis II, and was the mother of four children—Maurontius, Clotsendis, Eusebia and Adalsendis, all of whom are venerated as Saints.   After
the death of her husband, king Dagobert sued for her hand, but she preferred to
pass her widowhood in religious exercises under the guidance of St. Amandus.
Near the monastery founded by her late husband and herself for monks at Marchiennes, she established a convent, in which she took the veil together with her
three daughters.   Of this house she was chosen abbess, in which capacity she
set the example of a life hidden in God by wearing a hairshirt, observing long
fasts and spending many hours in prayer.   She was not spared trials and afflictions, but suffered meekly for forty years.   In order to have more time for prayer
and recollection she resigned her office a short time before her death and passed
to her reward in 688.   Her remains were preserved in a costly shrine in the monastery of Marchiennes.   At one time many churches and altars in Flanders
were dedicated to her memory.

2.   **Bl. John,** abbot and second general of the Order of Monte Vergine in
Italy, was one of the bright lights in the Church of Italy in his day and closed his
meritorious career in the year 1189.   He was venerated as Blessed in his monastery.

3.   **Ven. Engelbert,** abbot of Admont, possessed the grace of meditation
in an eminent degree and had the spirit of prophecy.   He suffered with the
patience of a Job, and was a devout client of Our Lady, to whose intercession he
ascribed numerous spiritual favors.   His death occurred in the year 1331.

Lambert: Life fo St. Gislen.
Joachim: Pez; Stadler who calls him J. Tabernicius.
Rictrudis: Hucbald of St. Amand; Butler.
John: Arnold of Douai.
Engelbert: Pez; Ziegelbauer; Brunner: Ein Benediktinerbuch (1880) gives 1327 as the year of his
     death.

13

1. **St. Merwina**, abbess of Ramsey in Huntingdonshire, England, governed her monastery ably in the early days of its existence. She had been appointed abbess by king Edgar about 967 to govern the monastery which was founded by his grandfather, Edward the Elder. Beyond this, little is known of her life which closed about 985 (or 976).

2. On this day St. Oswald discovered the bodies of the Ven. abbots **Botwin, Tilbert, Sigred** and **Wilden**, who had governed the monastery of Ripon in the course of the 8th and 9th century.

3. Ven. **Alawic**, abbot of Reichenau near Constance, was elected successor to abbot Liuthard in 934. He was visited by St. Ulric, who presented the monastery with many relics. St. Wolfgang and Henry, who subsequently was bishop of Trier, pursued their studies at Reichenau while Alawic was its abbot. In 945 he renewed a fraternal pact with St. Gall's to recite the Vigils and celebrate a Holy Mass at the death of a monk of either house. During this Mass all the brethren were to lie prostrate upon the floor from the *Sanctus* to the *Pax Domini*, and a monk's daily ration was given to the poor for the space of thirty seven days. Alawic died in 958.

4. **Ellinger**, abbot of Tegernsee in Bavaria, presided over that monastery in troublesome times, but proved to be a firm champion of order and discipline. Being elected abbot about 1016, he laid his hands to the spiritual improvement of those entrusted to his care, but encountered such persistent opposition, that he was compelled to withdraw for a time to the monastery of Niederaltaich. During his absence the obstinate monks realized their wrong and entreated him to return. Their change of heart appears to have been sincere, for Ellinger dwelt among them in peace for forty years to the day of his death in 1056.

5. **Thomas**, Cistercian monk of Dunes in Flanders, was sent to England in the days of King Henry to rule a monastery on the island of Shepey, and was hanged and quartered by the enemies of the Church in 1544.

14

1. **St. Paschal I**, Pope, was a Roman by birth, and while quite young was taken to the Lateran palace to be educated for the Church. His integrity of life and his charity induced Pope Leo III to appoint him abbot of the restored monastery of St. Stephen near the Vatican. Here he also conducted a hospice for the poor and the pilgrims. On January 24, 817 he was elected Pope to succeed Leo III and was consecrated and enthroned on the following day. During a new outbreak of the Iconoclast controversy under emperor Leo the Isaurian, Pope Paschal sided with Theodore of Studium against Theodosius, the unlawful

Merwina: Matthew of Westminster; Wm. of Malmesbury; Boll., Dunbar; Butler: Mervema.
Botwin: E. Mayhew.
Alawic: Hepidan.
Ellinger: Pez.
Thomas: Henriquez; B. de Montalbo.

patriarch of Constantinople, but met with no success in striving to convert the emperor from the Iconoclastic heresy. He also encouraged missionary enterprises; thus, in 822 he dispatched Ebbo, archbishop of Rheims, as papal legate to the far North. Much of his activity was devoted to building, restoring or beautifying churches and monasteries. It was in his pontificate that the remains of St. Cecilia were discovered and transferred to the church bearing her name in the Trastevere district of Rome. Pope Paschal died in 824 and was always honored as a Saint.

2. **St. Erembert,** bishop of Toulouse, born in the territory of Poissy, in France, left the world in his youth to seek guidance in the path of salvation at the monastery of Fontenelle. Clothed with the sacred garb by abbot St. Wandregisil, he seemed to be living in Heaven rather than upon earth, and his only concern was to avoid sin and practice virtue. But he was not to enjoy peace and quiet long, for at the suggestion of King Clothaire III he was chosen for the episcopal see of Toulouse about 656. One day while visiting his brother Gamardus, a fire broke out that threatened to destroy the town. Erembert hurried into the church to pray; then coming forth in response to the entreaties of the people he lifted up his staff, whereupon the wind that had been fanning the flames changed its direction and the peril ceased. He had ruled his flock for twelve years when the increasing infirmities of old age induced him to resign his see and return to Fontenelle where he died a few years later, about 670.

3. **Bl. Tuto,** bishop of Regensburg, was at one time private secretary to Emperor Arnulph, became a monk at St. Emmeram in Regensburg and was appointed bishop of that city in 895. Although the friend of monarchs, he maintained the rights of his church against unwarranted aggressions. Emperor Conrad I once ordered him to deliver a costly book of the Gospels to the public treasury in order to cover a financial deficiency, but Tuto refused and laid the book upon the altar with the words: "May St. Emmeram at the last judgment be the accuser of him that dares to remove this book from the church dedicated in his honor." He also built a splendid altar in honor of St. Emmeram, for the adornment of which the gold and precious stones of the crowns presented by Charlemagne, Carlmann and Arnulph to that church, were used. Towards the end of his life Tuto was afflicted with blindness, and he spent all his time in prayer and meditation to the day of his departure from this life in 930.

4. **Iso,** monk of St. Gall's, was chosen on account of his extensive learning by duke Rudolph of Burgundy to establish and direct the schools of the monastery of Grandval in the diocese of Basel. God bestowed upon him not only wonderful intellectual gifts together with eminent skill in imparting knowledge to his pupils, but also the grace of prayer with which he cured sick, blind and lame persons. He died in the year 871.

15

1. **St. Brithunus,** abbot of Beverley in Yorkshire, England, had been a deacon of the cathedral of York and enjoyed the esteem and confidence of his

Paschal: Liber Pontificalis; C. E., K. L.
Erembert: Mab. Gams calls him Arembertus.
Tuto: Arnulph of St. Emmeram; Hundius.
Iso: Ben. Annals. Also called Yso and Uso.

bishop, St. John of Beverley.   When the latter founded the monastery of Beverley, he appointed Brithun as its first abbot and with the consent of the latter spent the last four years of his life within its walls.   Brithun was truly an abbot according to the mind of St. Benedict, irreproachable in his conduct, a lover of prayer, liberal in his alms to the poor, invariably meek and charitable, just in his judgments and a cherisher of exact observance,   He received the crown of eternal life in 733.

2.   Ven. Adelgar, archbishop of the united sees of Bremen and Hamburg, was the faithful companion of St. Rembert in converting the Danes.   After enduring many hardships and suffering persecutions and insults in return for his devoted labors, he was summoned to receive his eternal reward in 909.

3.   Ven. Richard, abbot of Fountains in Yorkshire, England, became a monk in the monastery of St. Mary's at York and for some time was its prior.   Being attracted by the success of St. Bernard's reform, he left the monastery with twelve brethren and entered the Cistercian Order.   St. Bernard commended him in glowing terms for his resolve and encouraged him to persevere.   In 1132 archbishop Trustin granted him grounds at Ripon for a monastery; here Richard and his associates dwelt for some time in the open air and subsisted on herbs gathered in the hills.   The monastery which they built received so many offerings and endowments that it grew to be wealthy.   Richard died in Rome whither he had gone on business of the Order, in 1140.

16

1.   St. Herchantrudis, nun of Faremoutier in France, was born of noble parents and took the veil in that monastery at the time when it was governed by St. Burgundofara.   For many years she was severely tried by sufferings, but bore them all with the holy resignation of Job of old.   While still a youthful religious she was forbidden to receive Holy Communion for some unintentional violation of the Holy Rule.   She wept bitterly, particularly because she could not approach the holy table on the feast of St. Martin, which was near at hand. While praying for deliverance from her fault, she heard a voice in the night saying: "Go and make thy peace with Christ, for thy offence is forgiven; tell the abbess what I have said."   She did so and was permitted to receive Holy Communion with the rest.   As the hour of her death was close at hand, she suddenly cried out: "One of your number is dead, hasten and expel her from the community, for it is not meet that those who are crucified to the world and live not for themselves, should harbor a dead member in their midst."   When her sisters asked for the meaning of these words, one of the nuns fell prostrate in shame to the floor, confessed her fault and promised amendment.   Shortly before she died, she asked the sisters to extinguish the light and said: "Do you not see the bright light coming? do you not hear the choir of heavenly voices? "   When the sisters asked her to what light she referred, she replied: "Praise the Lord, for He is good and His mercy endureth forever."   With these words she expired about the year 650.

Brithunus: Bede; Folcard; John of Tinmouth; Stan.
Adelgar: Albert of Stade; Adam of Bremen.
Richard: Seguin; B. de Montalbo.
Herchantrudis: Life of St. Burgundofara.

2. The **Order of Monte Olliveto** was founded in Italy under the invoca-
tion of the Blessed Virgin Mary, by St. Bernard Tolomei in 1319, and was approved by Pope John XXII. It was named for the locality in which its first
house was situated near Siena. The purpose of the founder was to inaugurate
a return to the austerity of the early monks. From the church to which one of
the communities was attached the monks were also known as *Fratres Sanctae
Mariae novae.* St. Frances of Rome placed her Oblates under the spiritual direction of priests of this Order.

17

1. **Bl. Rasso,** monk, was a descendant of the counts of Andechs and Diessen in Bavaria. He was a man of stalwart frame and was chosen by duke Henry
I to combat the Hungarian invaders whom he defeated in two battles. To
thank God for his success in arms, he made a pilgrimage to the Holy Land and
after his return resolved to found a monastery in which he might spend the remainder of his days. With the approval of the secular and ecclesiastical authorities, he built a monastery and a church in honor of our Blessed Redeemer and
of the holy Apostles Philip and James on the island of Woerth in the Ammer
river. St. Ulric of Augsburg dedicated the church and installed thirteen monks,
who were shortly joined by the founder himself. He wore the religious habit
and lived like the humblest of his brethren to the day of his death in 954. Later
the church and the monastery were destroyed by invading armies, but three
of the monks rescued his relics and transferred them to Andechs, whence they
were removed to Grafrath, or Woerth, which became a popular pilgrimage.

2. **Walter,** abbot of Mondsee in Austria, died in the odor of sanctity in
1158 and was buried in the chapel of St. Peter.

3. **Paul,** a deacon of Monte Cassino, was a Lombard by birth and historian to the Lombard king Desiderius. He was ordained a deacon at Aquileja,
and accompanied his monarch into exile in France, where he was held on a suspicion of harboring treacherous plans against Charlemagne. For this he was
banished, but he escaped several years later and after spending two years at the
court of duke Arichi at Salerno he became a monk at Monte Cassino. In addition to a number of historical works, he is also said to have written the hymn
Ut queant laxis, which is still sung on the feast of St. John the Baptist. He died
about 799.

18

1. Abbot **Peter Monoculus,** of Clairvaux, was of illustrious descent, but
spurned the advantages of his rank to become an humble follower of the Redeemer. His candor and piety endeared him to all men. He was abbot first of
Villerri, then of Igny and finally of Clairvaux. Once when he was asked how
he contrived to maintain equanimity under all circumstances, he replied: "When
I was still a novice, it seemed to me, that a spirit entered within me, leading and

Olivetans: Bullar., Heimbucher; C.E.
Rasso: Hundt. The name also appears as Ratho or Grafrath.
Walter: Hundt.
Paul: Yepez; Arnold of Douai; C.E., K.L.

directing me like the sheep of Joseph; it enables me to be recollected despite distractions, urges me to prayer when I would attend to other things, and causes me not to notice what I see or hear." He was privileged to see the Blessed Virgin in visions. Once while he was praying in the cathedral of Speier for the remission of faults committed during the journey, she appeared to him and recited the prayer of the Itinerarium: "Almighty, eternal God, have mercy on this Thy servant, and in Thy ineffable goodness forgive what he may have sinned by hearing or seeing any evil thing, through Christ Our Lord." Sickness deprived him of one eye, but he consoled himself with the reflection that he had one enemy less to fear. He died in the year 1186.

2. The **Gregorian College** in Rome was founded in 1621 by Constantine Cajetan, abbot of St. Barontius in the diocese of Pistoja, with the approval of Pope Gregory XV, for Benedictine monks coming to Rome from various parts of the world either to study or to visit its sanctuaries. Eleven years later it was united with the Propaganda. The idea was revived by Pope Pius IX and carried into effect by Pope Leo XIII in establishing the International College of San Anselmo on the Aventine in 1893.

19

1. **St. Peter Celestine**, Pope, was born of virtuous parents at Isernia in Apulia about the year 1221, early in life lost his father and with the consent of his mother prepared himself for the clerical state. The hidden life had such a powerful attraction for him, that after completing his studies, he made his way to a distant hill and dwelt in a narrow cavern. Here he was discovered and induced to take holy orders in 1245. A year later he returned to Abruzzo and lived for five years in a cave on Monte Morone, where he suffered so much spiritual anguish that he felt himself unworthy to celebrate Holy Mass. His peace of mind was restored by his confessor. When in 1251 the woods about his hiding place were cut down, he withdrew to Monte Majella, where he was joined by two hermits and several other pious souls, with whom he led an extremely austere life. Here he was too much molested by visitors; hence he went farther up the mountain, where again he found no rest. Returning to Monte Morone, he founded a monastery in which the Rule of St. Benedict was to be observed in all its rigor. This was the nucleus of the Order of Celestine Benedictines which was approved by Pope Gregory X in 1274. Within a few years it counted thirty-six houses. After the death of Pope Nicholas IV in 1292 the Holy See was vacant for twenty seven months and Peter was elected at Aquila on August 29, 1294, taking the name of Celestine V. By request of the king of Naples he resided in that city for a while. His unfamiliarity with ecclesiastical business and the fact that he appointed several unpopular cardinals, led to a series of misunderstandings that culminated in his abdication after four months. He had intended to return to Monte Morone and govern his monastery as abbot, but was seized by his successor, Boniface VIII, who feared intrigues on the part of Celestine's friends. Celestine was detained in the castle of Fumone for the space of nine months, during which he devoted himself entirely to prayer. On the feast of Pentecost 1296 he foretold that he would die

Peter: Vincent of Beauvais; Peter Equilin.
Gregorian College: Bullarium; Ziegelbauer.

before the end of that week.   It happened as he had said, and he passed to his
reward on May 19 of the year mentioned.   Pope Boniface celebrated a Solemn
Requiem for the repose of his soul; the remains were interred at first at Fer-
rento, but were later removed to Aquila.   St. Peter Celestine was canonized by
Pope Clement V in 1313.

2.   **St. Dunstan,** archbishop of Canterbury, was born of a distinguished
family at Glastonbury in 924.   In his youth he made such remarkable progress
in human learning that at the instance of his uncle Athelm, archbishop of Canterbury, he was sent to the court of King Athelstan, from which he was driven
by the envy of certain men who could not bear to see his popularity.   Bidding
a heartfelt adieu to the glitter of earthly fame, he became a monk and was ordained priest a by Elphegus, bishop of Winchester.   While serving the church
of Glastonbury, he dwelt as a hermit near by.   Having upbraided King Edwy
for his dissolute life, that monarch sent him into exile.   A year later he was recalled by Edwy's successor, and made bishop of Worcester in 957.   In 958 he
was also appointed bishop of London, and in 961 he was transferred to the archiepiscopal see of Canterbury.   His chief concern was the regulation of the lives
of the clergy and of the monks, for which purpose he issued a number of canons
and compiled a "Concordance of Rules."   Married priests were deprived of
their churches without mercy, and public sinners were subjected to canonical
punishments.   A penance of seven years was imposed upon King Edgar for a
sin that could not but scandalize his subjects.   Dunstan assiduously visited the
churches and religious houses in his archdiocese, preached most eloquent and
touching sermons and devoted his income to the relief of the poor.   On the feast
of the Ascension he preached three times; bade his people a last farewell; designated the place of his burial and prepared for the end.   He died after receiving the Holy Viaticum on May 19 of the year 988.

3.   **Bl. Alcuin,** abbot of St. Martin at Tours, was born at York, in 735,
received as good an education as could be had in his day and was appointed
master of the cathedral school and library by archbishop Aelbert in 767.   Alcuin
visited Rome in 781 to obtain the pallium for archbishop Eanbald, and, while on
his way back to the North, at Parma met Charlemagne, on whose invitation he
organized and conducted the Palace School of that monarch.   Five years later
and again in 790 he was in England, on missions of either an ecclesiasical or political character.   At the synods of Frankfurt 794 and Aachen 799 he was one of
the most vigorous opponents of the Adoptianist heretics Felix and Elipandus.
He was already sixty years of age, when Charlemagne appointed him abbot of
St. Martin's of Tours, where Alcuin is said to have introduced the reform to St.
Benedict of Aniane.   Although an abbot, he appears to have been only a deacon,
for he frequently signs his letters *Albinus, humilis levita.*   Having resigned his
office some years before his death, he spent the remainder of his mortal career in
the monastery and died on Pentecost Sunday 804.

4.   **St. Hadulphus,** bishop of Arras in Artois, and a former abbot of St.
Vaast, was known for the holiness of his life and for miracles that confirmed it
after his death in 728.

Peter Celestine: James de Alliaco; Maffeus Vegius; Butler; C.E., K.L.
Dunstan: Osbern of Canterbury; Eadmer; Stanton; Butler.
Alcuin: MS. of Rheims; C.E., Buchb., Chev.   Other forms of the name: Alcvin, Albinus, Albuinus.
Hadulph: Mab.

20

1.   **St. Basilissa,** abbess of the convent of Ohren in Trier, died a happy death after a holy life, in the year 780.

2.   **Bl. Albert,** abbot of a Vallombrosan monastery in Bologna, died in the year 1245, reputed a Saint.   The monastery later was known by his name, and his tomb was visited by the faithful, particularly by peasants who there implored Heaven's blessing for their seed grain.

3.   **Bl. Orlandus,** a Vallombrosan laybrother in Tuscany, devoted all the time not occupied by duties to fervent prayer.   He was kind to everyone and cheerful.   He is said to have forgotten the needs of his body in anticipation of the delights of Heaven.   He died in 1242.

4.   **Ven. Gomez,** abbot at Florence, was born at Lisbon in Portugal and was one of the first companions of Abbot Luigi Barbo, the founder of the Congregation of St. Justina of Padua, now called the Cassinese Congregation.   His monks were pointed out as models of piety and holiness.   To the poor and needy he was generous; where discord estranged hearts, he was at hand as a peacemaker.   His efforts as a restorer of monastic discipline were so successful that he was invited to perform a similar service in Portugal.   Pope Eugene IV also appointed him general of the Camaldolensians, which position he held for two years.   He died in his monastery at Florence in 1442.

21

1.   **St. Godric,** hermit, was born at Walpole, in England, about 1080, and in his youth made his living by selling wares from village to village.   He also set up a booth at public fairs and even made several voyages to Scotland.   In the course of one of these voyages he put up at the island of Lindisfarne, where he was so wonderfully moved by an account of the life of St. Cuthbert and by the holy lives of the monks, that he prayed God might grant him the grace to follow in the footsteps of that Saint.   He at once severed his connections with the world, and commenced his new career by making pilgrimages to Jerusalem, Compostella and several other sanctuaries, after which he lived for a short time with the monk and hermit Godevin of Durham, who dwelt in a solitude at Carlisle.   After Godevin's death he visited the Holy Land for a second time, and, upon his return, settled first near Whitby and finally in the solitude of Finchal near Durham, to which monastery he appears to have been attached, for it is related that on certain days he received visitors with the permission of the prior of Durham.   A priest from the monastery celebrated Mass in a chapel near his cell and was his confessor.   Godric spent sixty-three years in this seclusion and died in 1170.

Basilissa: Trithemius; Arnold of Douai.
Albert: Wion.
Orlandus: B. Locatelli; Jerome of Vallombrosa.
Gomez: Armellini.
Godric: Wm. of Newbridge; Matt. of Paris; Butler; Stanton.

2. Seven monks of Besue, in the diocese of Langres, France, Ansuin, Aiman, Genesius, Gerard, Sifard, Rodio and Adalric, were slain by the Normans in the year 888.

22

1. **St. Romanus,** abbot of Fontrouge in the diocese of Auxerre, is said to be identical with the Romanus who gave St. Benedict the religious habit at Subjaco and supplied him with food. He lived under the direction of a certain abbot Theodatus, but during the invasion of Italy by the Goths went to France, where he established a religious community at Fontrouge. Here he received St. Maurus, who was on his way to Le Mans, and heard of St. Benedict's glorious death. Romanus died about 545; his relics are preserved in the church dedicated to his name at Sens.

2. **St. Atto,** born at Paz in Spain about the year 1070, made a journey to Italy and was so powerfully attracted by the lives of the monks of Vallombrosa that he became a member of that Order about 1100. Five years later he was elected abbot and general of the Order and in 1134 was appointed bishop of Pistoja. He died in the odor of sanctity in 1155. His body was found incorrupt when the Order tomb was opened nearly two centuries later.

3. **St. John,** abbot of St. John's at Parma in Italy, was born about 915 and at an early age received among the clergy of his native city. The religious life attracted him so powerfully that while on a pilgrimage in Jerusalem he received the monastic habit. Upon his return, Bishop Sigefredus appointed him abbot of the monastery of St. John close to the city walls. Abbot John's saintly life, as well as his liberality, drew many to the monastery either to find temporal relief or to receive spiritual advice. He died in the year 982, and so great was the sorrow of his fellow citizens that every house is said to have been in mourning. He was canonized by Gregory VII.

4. **St. Humilitas,** Vallombrosan abbess of St. John's at Florence, was born at Faenza in Italy in 1226 and desired above all things to be permitted to serve God in some religious house. In 1241 she was married to a young nobleman by the name of Ugolotto, but nine years later both agreed to embrace the religious life, the wife entering the convent of St. Perpetua at Faenza. Longing for greater seclusion, she left this house, for a short time was in a convent of Clares; dwelt for twelve years in a cell near the church of S. Apollinaris at Faenza, but at the request of the Vallombrosan General founded, near that city, the convent known as *S. Maria alla Malta* about 1265, and was its abbess to the time of her death in 1310. She was adorned not only with the virtues of a perfect religious, but was favored with other unusual gifts which enabled her to search the human heart and guide souls along the difficult path that leads to perfection.

Ansuin: Mab.
Romanus: Greg. the Great; Mab., Boll.
Atto: Monuments of Vallombrosa.
John: Anon. monk of his monastery.
Humilitas: Contemporary monk of Vallombrosa.

5. **Bl. Benedict,** prior or provost at Capua, became a monk at Monte Cassino under abbot Desiderius and shone by his eminent virtues to the day of his death in 1055.

6. The **Congregation of the Holy Cross,** consisting of houses in Poland and Lithuania, was approved by Pope Clement XI in 1709.   Its statutes resembled those of the Bavarian Congregation.

<h2 style="text-align:center">23</h2>

1. **St. Siagrius,** bishop of Nice in Piedmont, was a relative of Charlemagne and was abbot in a monastery founded by that prince in honor of St. Pontius at Cimeille near Nice.   He governed his abbey with such success, that he was made bishop of Nice and ruled that see for ten years.   He died in 787 and was interred in his monastery.

2. **St. Guibert,** founder and monk of Gemblours in Brabant, was born of wealthy parents about 900, and led a devout life even in the army.   He would frequently ponder how he might serve God more perfectly.   One day while meditating upon the words spoken by Our Lord to the rich young man, he felt an impulse to follow the same sublime counsel.   With the advice and under the direction of the monk Erluin of Gorze he founded a monastery on his patrimonial estate of Gemblours.   Far from coveting the position of abbot, he entered Gorze as a novice and caused Erluin to be made first abbot of Gemblours, while the founder remained a plain monk at Gorze.   Several attempts to involve Guibert in lawsuits failed, to the disappointment of his enemies.   When the country was overrun by foreign invaders, he went among them as a missionary and led many of them to embrace the faith.   He died in the year 962.   With the permission of the abbot of Gorze, and despite the protests of the inhabitants of that place, the remains of the Saint were carried to Gemblours.

<h2 style="text-align:center">24</h2>

1. **Bl. William,** a Cistercian monk of Villers in Brabant, scorned the nobility of his descent and perferred to serve God as a monk in poverty and humility.   He never sought to be privileged above others, and was always willing to take the last place.   He died in 1249.

2. **Bl. John of Montfort,** a Knight Templar following the rule of St. Bernard, gave evidence of sanctity during life, and died at Nicosia on the island of Cyprus in the 12th or 13th century.

3. **Ven. Hildebert,** archbishop of Mainz, was born at Fulda and educated in the famous monastery of that place, of which he also became a member.

Benedict: Peter the Deacon.
Cong. of Holy Cross: Bullarium.
Siagrius: Barrali; Saussay; Menard. Lechner calls him Siacrius.   Gams gives 777 as the date of death.
Guibert: Sigebert of Gemblours.
William: A. de Raisse; Le Mire.
John: B. de Montalbo; A. de Aranda.

For his learning and virtue he was chosen to rule the see of Mainz.   He crowned
emperor Otto I at Aachen.   On the day of his death in 936 he thanked God that
he had never squandered the possessions of his church, nor enriched it with property unjustly acquired.

4.   The monks, SS. Worard and Winewald, priests, and Gerwald and
Raynard, deacons, were slain at the monastery of Sithiu by the Normans for
refusing to deliver the treasure of their church to the invaders in 861.

5.   The English Congregation was established in 1603 by English monks
in Spain for the conversion of England.   In addition to the usual vows, they
made the vow of the mission, obliging themselves to go to England at the peril
of their lives to propagate the faith that had been suppressed in the sixteenth
century.

25

1.   St. Gregory VII, Pope, was born at Saona in Tuscany about 1020.   In
baptism received the name of Hildebrand, and was educated in the monastery
of Our Lady on the Aventine in Rome, where he also became a monk.   As a
cleric in minor orders, he studied under the direction of John Gratian, and when
the latter was elected Pope as Gregory VI, Hildebrand served him as a chaplain.   When that Pope was forced to abdicate, Hildebrand accompanied him to
Cluny, where he soon grew so popular that Abbot Odilo appointed him prior.
Both Odilo and Hildebrand accompanied Pope Leo IX to Rome in 1049, where
Hildebrand was made a cardinal and abbot of St. Paul's outside the walls of the
city.   In 1054 he was sent to Germany to conduct Gebhard, bishop of Eich-
staett, now Pope Victor II, to Rome.   This Pope sent him to France to suppress
the simoniacal practices connected with the collation of ecclesiastical benefices.
For this purpose he presided at a council held at Lyons; also at another held at
Tours in which Berengarius retracted his heretical views regarding the Real
Presence.   In the pontificate of Stephen IX, Hildebrand was sent on an embassy to Germany .   The Pope on his deathbed ordered the cardinals to wait for
Hildebrand's return before proceeding to the election of a successor.   Both
Popes Nicholas and Alexander II were elected chiefly through the influence of
Cardinal Hildebrand, then archdeacon of the Roman Church.   When Alexander II died on March 24, 1073, the Roman clergy and people as with one voice
clamored for Hildebrand's elevation to the chair of Peter.   He was unwilling
to take the burden upon his shoulders. but could accomplish nothing by his protests nor by his appeal to Henry IV.   During his pontificate he was intent upon
carrying out two noble projects: that of ridding the Church of the stigma of
simony and of enforcing the law of celibacy among the clergy.   The question of investitures involved him in a bitter struggle with emperor Henry IV, who presumed to depose the Pope in a council held at Worms.   Gregory replied by ex-
communicating the emperor.   The latter promised amendment and was absolved at Canossa in 1077, but resumed his wayward course, which provoked
Gregory to declare that Henry had forfeited the crown and that duke Rudolph

Hildebert: Trithemius.
Worard: Ben. Annals.
Eng. Cong.: Rainer; Ziegelbauer; Weldon: Chronological Notes (1881)., E. Taunton: The Eng.
    Black Monks of St. Benedict.

of Suabia, whom some of the princes had elected, was rightful claimant of the empire.   Henry inaugurated a new schism by appointing the anti-pope Clement III (Guibert of Ravenna), in 1084 entered Rome with an army, and besieged Gregory who had taken refuge within the Castle of Sant Angelo.   Robert Guiscard, duke of Calabria, forced the imperial troops to retire, rescued Gregory from danger, conducted him for greater safety first to Monte Cassino and then to Salerno, where the heroic sufferer was to rest from his toil.   Three days before his death he withdrew all the excommunications which he had pronounced— except those against the two principal offenders, the emperor and the antipope. On his deathbed he said to the cardinals present: "I will not boast of any of my deeds, but I am confident that I have always loved justice and detested iniquity: therefore I die in exile."   He died on this day of the year 1085, and was buried at Salerno.   He was beatified by Gregory XIII in 1584, and canonized by Benedict XIII in 1728.

2.   St. Gennadius, bishop of Astorga in Spain, was at first a monk in the monastery of Agen under the direction of abbot Arandisellus.   Moved by a desire to revive the monastery of S. Pedro de Montes, which had been established by St. Fructuosus, he undertook the task with the permission of his abbot and supported by twelve of his brethren who elected him their abbot in 898.   So bright was the light of his sanctity that after the death of Bishop Ranulfus of Astorga, clergy and people demanded Gennadius as their bishop.   He founded a number of monasteries in his diocese, among others St. Andrew's, St. James of Pennalva, and St. Thomas, all of which he liberally endowed.   He resigned his episcopal charge in 920 and returned to the monastery of S. Pedro where he dwelt in loving communion with the God of his heart to the day of his blessed death in 921.   His remains first rested in the monastery of St. James at Pennalva, but were transferred to Vallodolid.

3.   St. Aldhelm, bishop of Sherburne in England, was born in Wessex, and is said to have been a relative of King Ina.   For his excellent education he was chiefly indebted to abbot Adrian of Canterbury, under whose intelligent tuition he became familiar not only with the branches of learning cultivated by students of his day, but even with the Greek and Hebrew languages.   An Irish monk named Maidulf had recently established a monastery at Malmesbury; here Aldhelm took the religious habit in 661 and succeeded Maidulf as abbot in 675.   He not only raised the reputation of the house by his virtue and great learning, but also increased its revenues and enlarged its buildings.   His biographers describe him as an enemy to gluttony, avarice, vain glory and all idle amusements.   Literary history assigns a prominent place to him as one of the first Englishmen to cultivate the art of Latin poetry.   He also wrote a treatise "On the praise of Virginity" and one on the Easter controversy.   After the death of Bishop Hedda of Winchester, that diocese was divided into two—Winchester and Sherburne, and Aldhelm, who had been abbot for thirty years, was taken out of his cell by force and consecrated first bishop of the new see, which he governed with the zeal of an apostle for the space of five years.   During a tour of visitation of his diocese he died at Dulling, in Somersetshire, in 709. William of Malmesbury relates several miracles wrought by St. Aldhelm.

Gregory: P. of Bernried; Lampert of Aschaffenburg; Butler.
Gennadius: P. Sandoval; T. Salazar.
Aldhelm: Wm. of Malmesbury; Wharton; Butler; Stanton; C.E.

26

1. **St. Augustine**, first bishop of Canterbury and apostle of England, was prior of St. Andrew's in Rome when Pope Gregory the Great entered upon his project of sending missionaries to convert the heathen inhabitants of England. Augustine was selected to lead the band of missionaries to their destination, furnished with recommendations to such bishops as he should meet on the way. When the party arrived in Provence, they were given such an exaggerated account of the fierceness of the people living farther north, that the missionaries lost courage and sent Augustine back to Rome to explain the situation to the Pope. The latter would not hear of their turning back, wrote them a letter of encouragement and dispatched Augustine northward as quickly as possible. The monks and their guides pursued their journey accordingly, crossed the Channel and arrived in the island of Thanet in the kingdom of Kent in 596. At once Augustine sent word to King Ethelbert, asking for a conference. The king was not a complete stranger to the truths of the Christian religion, for his wife Bertha was the daughter of the Frankish prince Charibert. He met Augustine and his companions on the island of Thanet, and listened attentively to their leader as he explained the principal truths of the Christian faith. Although admitting that what he had heard, might be true, he did not embrace the true faith, pleading that it was all so new to him and that he must take time to consider; yet he permitted the missionaries to preach to his subjects and to reside at Canterbury, which was his capital. Heaven's blessing rested upon the work of the monks; they succeeded in converting and baptizing great numbers. Augustine was consecrated a bishop by Virgilius bishop of Arles in 597, and in the same year is said to have baptized ten thousand converts on Christmas-day. Additional help was necessary to minister to the growing Christian communities; the monks Peter and Lawrence were sent to Rome, and brought back with them Mellitus, Justus, Paulinus and Rufinian and a supply of vestments and sacred vessels. Ethelbert recognized the service of the monks to his people by building Christ church and the abbey of SS. Peter and Paul at Canterbury. In the year 600 Augustine was empowered to consecrate twelve suffragan bishops, also to establish the province of York with an equal number of suffragan sees. He consecrated Mellitus bishop of the East Saxons in London, and Justus bishop of Rochester, and then in his quality as metropolitan and papal legate began to make a general visitation of his province. On the confines of the Wiccians and West-Saxons he invited the British bishops and priests to confer with him regarding the celebration of Easter and the manner of administering Baptism, but did not win them over to his cause even by a miracle wrought in their presence. A second meeting of the same kind was equally unsuccessful; the British prelates would not yield, whereupon Augustine told them "that if they would not preach to the English the way of life, they would fall by their hands under the judgment of death." This prediction was verified after Augustine's death, when Ethelfrid, king of northern England, overthrew the Britons at Caerleon. After appointing St. Lawrence as his successor in the see of Canterbury, St. Augustine died on this day in the year 607 and has ever since been venerated as a Saint.

Augustine: Bede; Goscelin; Lingard; Butler.

2. **St. Lambert,** bishop of Vence in southern France, was a monk at Lerins and was singled out for his eminent virtue to be bishop. He governed his see during forty years. When asked on his deathbed how he was faring, he said: "All is well; I hope to see the good things of the Lord in the land of the living," and thus he died in the year 1154.

3. **St. Berengarius,** monk of St. Papoul in Languedoc, was distinguished for the virtues of a good religious, but also for unusual spiritual gifts. He is said never to have slept in a bed, to have been extremely frugal in his meals and never to have used a horse or wagon when he travelled. For some time he taught the boys at the monastery; later he was appointed almoner and finally administrator of the temporalities of the house. His holy life was crowned by a holy death in 1093.

4. **St. Guinizo,** monk and hermit, came from Spain and became a monk at Monte Cassino, shortly before that house was threatened with extinction for a second time. Prince Pandulph of Capua seized the possessions of the monastery and reduced its resources to such an extent that no more than twelve monks could maintain themselves. Guinizo and his disciple **St. Januarius** fled into a solitude and prayed that God might avert the scourge. The emperor Conrad crossed the Alps, checked the ravages of Pandulph and restored Monte Cassino. Guinizo died about 1050, and was followed several years after by his disciple Januarius.

5. **Bl. Probus,** priest and monk of St. Alban's at Mainz was as pious as he was learned and died in the odor of sanctity in 858.

27

1. **St. Bede,** called the Venerable, priest and Doctor of the Church, was born in England about 673, and educated at the abbeys of Wearmouth and Jarrow. He pursued a course of higher studies under archbishop Theodore and abbot Adrian at Canterbury and was exceptionally proficient in the Greek language, a rare distinction in those days. Having been ordained a deacon by St. John of Beverley, he studied Sacred Scripture to the year 702, when he was ordained a priest. Although he shared even the menial labors of the brethren, such as working in the garden, he devoted much time to study, presided over a large school, and instructed his six hundred brethren. At the same time he was an indefatigable writer; his writings cover a wide range of subjects—commentaries on Holy Scripture, philosophy, astronomy, mathematics and history. His brethren wished to make him their abbot, but in his humility he declined that honor. The report of his learning drew many distinguished visitors, including King Ceolwulf, to Jarrow. At the request of bishop Egbert of York, he repaired to that city to organize a cathedral school, of which the celebrated Alcuin was one of the principal luminaries. Bede had already reached the age of sixty-two years when he began to ail shortly before Easter, yet he continued to work and to teach with his wonted cheerfulness, and even undertook to trans-

Lambert: Barrali.
Berengarius: Boll.
Guinizo: Paul the Deacon.
Probus: Serrarius.

late the Gospel according to St. John into English.   On the Tuesday preceding
the feast of the Ascension he was dictating to his pupils; he urged them to
greater speed saying: "Go on quickly: I know not how long I shall hold out, and
whether my Maker will soon take me away."   On the following day he received
the last sacraments and at three o'clock in the afternoon bade the priests attend
him in his cell.   He distributed some trifling keepsakes among them and begged
them to remember him during the Holy Sacrifice.   All wept, while he was speaking cheerfully of the approach of his departure.   After he had dictated the last
sentence of the work he had in hand to his pupil Wilbert, he sat down upon the
floor of his cell, faced the oratory and uttering the words "Glory be to the Father
and to the Son and to the Holy Ghost" expired on the Vigil of the Ascension in
the year 735.   His remains rested for some time at Jarrow, but were afterwards
removed to Durham.   The second council of Aachen in 836 spoke of him as
"the venerable and wonderful teacher of recent times."   Pope Leo XIII on
November 13, 1899 declared him a Doctor of the Church and ordered the celebration of his feast on May 27.

28

1. **St. William,** founder and monk of Valgellon in Languedoc, was of
illustrious birth and at an early age came to the court of Charlemagne, where he
enjoyed such esteem and popularity that he was envied by not a few of his fellow
courtiers.   Charlemagne conferred upon him the title of Duke of Aquitaine
and sent him against the Saracens, whom he defeated in several battels.   Neither
this triumph, nor the esteem in which he was held by his monarch, contented
him; it was his ambition to please, above all, the King of Kings, to serve whom
is truly to reign.   For this purpose he founded a monastery in the valley of
Gellone in Languedoc, gathered a number of exemplary religious from other
houses and placed at their head St. Benedict of Aniane, the zealous reformer.
From this time William felt an irresistible desire to cut loose from the world and
all that it has to offer, and to join these devout and happy men.   When he approached Charlemagne with a request to be permitted to follow the yearnings
of his soul, that prince consented with much reluctance and in earnest of his
esteem and good will presented William with a particle of the true Cross.   In
800 William recived the habit as a monk at Valgellon, and from that day could
not be distinguished from the humblest of the brethren, whose labors he shared
in the construction of the buildings, in the stables and fields.   With the approval of his abbot he spent the declining years of his life in seclusion and died
in 812.

2. **Bl. Lanfranc,** archbishop of Canterbury, was born at Pavia about
1020 and received an education that fitted him for an honorable career in the
world, but he preferred the pursuit of learning.   After the death of his parents,
he went to France and was for some time connected with a school at Avranches.
As the years went by he realized more and more that but one thing is necessary
and therefore decided to devote himself to the service of God alone.   While
journeying towards Rouen, he was attacked by highwaymen who robbed him
and bound him to a tree.   In his plight he prayed that God might deliver him
and enable him to carry out the pious resolve he had taken.   At dawn he was

Bede: Cuthbert., Wm. of Malmesbury; Butler.
William: MS. of Valgellon.

rescued by two other travelers, from whom he also learned the way to Bec, where abbot Herluin was at the time organizing a monastic body. Lanfranc without delay offered to join him in his holy undertaking and was received with great joy. He had been a monk at Bec three years, when he was directed to open a school to which young nobles from all parts of France were sent for an education. In addition he was appointed prior of Bec and was adviser to many distinguished personages, including Duke William of Normandy. Misconstruction of certain passages in his letters laid him under the suspicion of entertaining Berengarius' heretical views concerning the Real Presence, but he cleared himself of this charge while visiting Rome in 1050. In 1066, he was appointed abbot of St. Stephen's at Caen, which had been founded by Duke William, and four years later was, at the instance of the same prince, now king of England, promoted to the see of Canterbury, an honor which he accepted only after the bishops and abbots of the realm had joined their voices with that of the monarch. Even as primate, Lanfranc was as humble as he had been as as simple monk, knelt to kiss the hand of abbot Herluin when the latter came to visit him, and reserved the place of honor for him. He championed the rights of the Church on numerous occasions, strove to better the lives of the clergy, built churches and hospices, held several synods, annually distributed 500 pounds in alms to the poor and supported the king in the administration of the government. After ruling his see for nineteen. years he died in 1089.

3. **St. Thietland**, abbot of Einsiedeln in Switzerland, was a brother of duke Burkard of Suabia, and was elected to succeed abbot Eberhard, although already advanced in age. He wrote commentaries on the Epistles of St. Paul and edified his community by his rare virtues and exemplary observance. He died in the year 963 and was buried in the church of the abbey near the chapel of Our Lady.

29

1. **St. Gerard**, bishop of Macon, in France, was such a lover of the contemplative life that he resigned his see, and lived as a hermit near Brou, which eventually developed into a monastery. He died in 930 and was venerated as a Saint in his diocese.

2. **Bl. Joachim**, abbot of S. Giovanni di Fiore in Calabria, and founder of the Congregation of Fiore, was born about 1132 near Cosenza in Italy. At the age of fourteen he was a page at the royal court, but on attaining the age of manhood felt a longing to lead a retired life and went to Palestine where he passed the season of Lent in prayer and recollection on Mount Tabor. On his return to Italy, he sojourned for a time at the monastery of Sambucina without taking the religious habit. Feeling an inclination to preach to the people, he entered the Cistercian monastery of Corace and took holy orders. After the abbot's death he was elected his successor, fled to escape the honor, but was found and compelled to yield to the wishes of the brethren. The duties of an abbot prevented him from pursuing his favorite study of Holy Scripture; hence he turned to Pope Lucius III for relief. That pontiff commended his work, relieved him

Lanfranc: Milo Crispin; Eadmer; C.E.
Thietland: Chron. of Einsiedeln.
Gerard: Breviary of Macon.

of the temporal administration of his abbey and authorized him to continue his pursuit in any monastery of his choice. After spending a year and a half at the monastery of Casamari, he entered a solitude at Fiore, where he founded an abbey which became the centre of a congregation with an observance even stricter than that of the Cistercian Order. It received the approval of Pope Celestine III in 1196. Joachim was a powerful preacher, exceedingly charitable to the poor, wore garments of the poorest quality that he might bestow better ones upon the poor, and was indifferent to the claims of blood. He died in 1200 on Holy Saturday "on which *Sitivit* is sung, attaining the true Sabbath, even as the hart panteth after the fountains of waters." He had submitted his writings to the Holy See, but died before he learned the result. Although some of his teachings were condemned, it was admitted that the holiness of his life was unquestionable, and although never formally beatified, he has always been honored as Blessed.

3. **Ven. Egil**, archbishop of Sens, in France, had been abbot of Pruem, where emperor Lothair was clothed as a monk during his administration in 855. Having resigned the office of abbot, Egil lived for some time as a solitary, till he was chosen abbot of Flavigny, whence he was called in 866 to govern the church of Sens. Even as an archbishop he led the humble, penitential life of a monk. He founded the monastery of Corbigny and died in the year 870.

30

1. **St. Hugbert**, priest and monk of Bretigny, in the diocese of Soissons, entered that monastery as a boy of twelve years, and was deemed worthy to receive the honor of holy priesthood. Three bishops are said to have assisted at his first Holy Mass. At the meal following the celebration, he touched no food, but gave his portion to a beggar, in whose person he gave food to a celestial visitor. Throughout his life he was wont to fast on Mondays, Wednesdays and Fridays. He died about 753.

2. **St. Madelgisil**, monk and hermit at St. Riquier in Picardy, was a faithful companion of St. Furseus, and after the death of the latter attached himself to the community of St. Riquier. After some time he secured the permission of the abbot for himself and a companion, **St. Vulgan**, to live as hermits near Monstrelet, where he died about 685. Later his remains were carried to St. Riquier.

3. The Order of the **Humiliati** was approved by Pope Innocent III in 1199. The Humiliati were founded in the early years of the twelfth century by Lombard nobles whom Henry V had led as captives into Germany. Making a virtue of necessity, they adopted a penitential garb and devoted themselves to works of charity and mortification. Having been permitted to return to Italy, they were induced by St. John of Meda to embrace the Rule of St. Benedict. The Order also had a female branch. The male branch was suppressed in 1571.

Egil: Necrol. Flavigny.
Joachim: James, a monk of Fiore; C.E.
Hugbert: Breviary. Also called Hucbert.
Madelgisil: Hariulph of St. Riquier.
Humiliati: Heimbucher; Biedenfeld; C.E.

1.   **St. Benedict,** abbot of St. Michael at Chiusa, in the diocese of Turin, was born at Toulouse in 1033 and was placed with the monks of St. Hilaire at Carcassonne to be educated.   Later he entered the monastery at Chiusa, where he was ordained a priest.   After the abbot's death, Benedict was elected to succeed him, but encountered opposition from bishop Cunibert of Turin, who claimed the right to appoint the abbots of Chiusa.   Benedict would gladly have stepped back, but his brethren pressed him to assert the rights of the chapter. Benedict accordingly went to Rome and presented his case with so much spirit and candor, that the Holy See ratified his election.   On his return he began to abolish abuses both in church service and in discipline, dismissed recalcitrant brethren into priories and trained novices who aspired to genuine perfection. Like the great St. Benedict, whose name he so worthily bore, he set his brethren an example of what a true religious ought to be.   He often joined penitent monks in their retirement, and subsisted, as they did, on water and bread.   He never tasted either meat or wine, eggs or cheese, and prayed many hours of the night.   Guests were received by him with unbounded charity; he waited upon them in person and enjoined upon the brethren to supply them with all they might need.   Bishop Cunibert, who had not forgotten how the abbot had scored a victory over him at the outset of his career, gave him no rest and succeeded in expelling him from the monastery.   Benedict was seized by order of Henry IV on the way to Monte Cassino, but succeeded in making his escape, and returned to Chiusa, where he died in 1091.

2.   **St. Gislemar,** a monk of Corbie and associate of St. Anschar in the missions of Denmark, died after a holy and meritorious life in 870.

3.   **Commemoration of the Miracles** by which God deigned to honor Our Holy Father St. Benedict, whose life and teachings have shone like a bright light throughout the ages.

Benedict: Mab.
Gislemar: Ben. Annals.

June

1

1. **St. Eneco,** abbot of S. Salvador de Onna in Old Castile, for a long time was a hermit. By the death of abbot Garcias, Onna had been left without a head, and King Sancho could find few men better qualified than Eneco to continue the work of the deceased abbot. He dispatched messengers to Eneco to inform him of his appointment, but the hermit was not moved to consent till the king came in person and begged him to accept the office. In his new capacity, Eneco strove to be an abbot according to the spirit of the Holy Rule, never relaxing his vigilance, always cherishing order, benevolent, and patient in adversity. In 1057 he was suddenly taken ill at Solduego and was at onec conveyed to his monastery where he died shortly after, in the same year. He was canonized by Pope Alexander II.

2. **St. Theobald,** Camaldolese abbot of Vangadizza near Vicenza, was the son of a nobleman in the diocese of Troyes in France, but left his native country to become a religious in Italy. His life bore an unmistakable stamp of sanctity, which was also confirmed by remarkable heavenly favors. He died in 1050.

3. **Bl. Rupert,** abbot of Tegernsee in Bavaria, was so well known for his charity to the poor and other virtues that Pope Alexander III granted him the use of the mitre,—a privilege which not all abbots formerly enjoyed. Abbot Rupert died in 1186.

2

1. **St. Adalgisus,** monk and priest of St. Michael's in Picardy, was one of the companions of St. Fursues and for a time lived in the monastery of Lagny. After he had been ordained a priest, he entered a solitude and also made a pilgrimage to Rome. He died about 670 and was always venerated as a Saint.

2. **Ven. Louis de Estrada,** Cistercian abbot of Huerto de Maria in the Spanish diocese of Siguenza, was rector of the college at Alcala de Henares and was distinguished for his irreproachable conduct and piety. He was a friend and protector of the Society of Jesus which was still in its infancy and was not popular with some of the faculty of Alcala. Royal personages, such as Don Juan of Austria and King Philip II respected him and sought his counsel. While abbot of Huerto he was exceedingly charitable to the poor, to whom he was wont to carry food in the winter when it was impossible for them to leave their shelter. Marvelous multiplications of bread are said to have taken place several times when crowds of poor people flocked to the monastery for food. Ven. Louis died in 1581.

Eneco: Mab.; Roman Martyrol. Another form of the name is Inigo.
Theobald: Ferrari.
Rupert: Phoenix of Tegernsee.
Adalgisus: Boll.
Louis: Calzolari; Manrique.

3

1. **St. Isaac,** monk and martyr at Cordova, Spain, was thoroughly educated in his youth and on account of his familiarity with the Arabic language was appointed to a lucrative civil post, from which he withdrew, however, to become a monk at Tabanos. Three years after receiving the habit, the spirit of God impelled him to make public profession of his faith before the Mohammedan authorities. He boldly stepped into the public court room and asked the judge for information regarding the religion of Mohammed. The judge complied but was refuted by Isasac at every step. Isaac was then cast into prison and beheaded in 851.

2. **St. Morandus,** prior at Altkirch in the diocese of Strassburg, was descended from respectable ancestry and was born near Worms, where he received his education. Returning from a pilgrimage to Compostella, he was fascinated by the discourse of abbot Hugo of Cluny and became a member of that community. The abbot sent him to Auvergne for the purpose of reforming several dependencies of Cluny and finally appointed him prior of Altkirch which had been recently founded. The peace, love and joy which filled his soul, radiated from his features. He was favored with the gift of miracles even in this life and exercised wonderful power over the spirits of darkness. He died in 1115.

3. **St. Conus,** monk, was born at Diano in the former kingdom of Naples. Even in tender childhood he practiced severe mortifications. Without waiting to obtain the consent of his parents he entered the abbey of S. Maria de Cardosse, whose abbot, having discovered the rare worth of the brother, appointed him to several important positions, including that of prior. He loathed contact with the world which he had abandoned, and is said to have hidden himself in a heated oven one day when his parents came to visit him. He died about 1200. His remains were carried to Diano in 1261.

4. **Bl. Peregrinus,** a hermit at Camaldoli, while filling the office of sacristan, was favored with a number of visions which he communicated to his spiritual director, the priest Simon. He was distinguished for his simplicity, candor and innocence, and died in the year 1288.

5. **Ven. Hildeburg,** widow and nun of St. Martin's at Pontoise, was born of noble parentage at Chartres and became the wife of Robert of Ivrey. When her husband at an advanced age had become a monk at Bec and had died shortly after, she was on the point of yielding to suggestions to enter upon a second marriage, but an accident turned her mind heavenward. She went about on pilgrimages to several holy places, but finally settled in a cell adjoining the abbey of St. Martin at Pontoise, and wore the religious habit, but did not take the vows. Here she died in 1115.

Isaac: Eulogius of Cordova.
Morandus: A monk of St. Morand.
Conus: Boll.
Peregrinus: Fortunius Florentin.
Hildeburg: Ancient document at Pontoise; Steele; Stadler.

6. **Ven. Berneredus** (Bernard), abbot at Soissons, and later cardinal bishop of Palestrina, died in the reputation of sanctity in 1181.

4

1. On this day Monte Cassino celebrates the feast of all the Saints whom that celebrated monastery has produced.

2. **St. Peter de Bono,** monk of Cluny, had previously been a merchant and married, but embraced the clerical state after the death of his wife. Shortly after his ordination he apparently died, but returned to life during the funeral services. This experience made such a profound impression upon him, that he resolved to devote the rest of his life to preparation for death. For this purpose he became a monk of Cluny, where he died on the feast of Pentecost 1441.

3. **Ven. Werner,** first abbot of Wiblingen near Ulm in Wuerttemberg, had been a monk of St. Blasien in the Black Forest, and both as monk and abbot was an ornament to the religious state. He died in 1126.

4. **Bl. Margaret,** abbess of the Cistercian monastery of Valdeduc in Brabant, was a daughter of duke Henry II of Brabant and of his wife Mary, the daughter of emperor Philip of Suabia. Although sought in marriage by several princes, she chose the veil by which she consecrated herself to the celestial bridegroom. Revered for her humility, abnegation and zeal, she died about 1230.

5

1. **St. Boniface,** archbishop of Mainz and apostle of Germany, was born at Kirton, in England, about 675. Before he became a bishop he was known as Winfrid. Early in life he became a monk at Exeter, where he also received his education. Thirteen years later he was sent to the monastery of Nutcelle, diocese of Winchester, where he studied and taught for a few years. At the age of thirty he was ordained a priest and began to devote himself to preaching and the care of souls. In 716 his abbot permitted him to pass over to Frisia to preach the Gospel to the pagan inhabitants of that region. He succeeded in reaching Utrecht, where he received so little encouragement from prince Radbod that he returned to England. Shortly after he was elected to succeed abbot Winbert of Nutcelle, but could not be prevailed upon to accept. Uppermost in his mind was a burning desire to be an apostolic missionary; hence he journeyed to Rome in 718 and received canonical authorization to preach from Pope Gregory II. Returning to Germany, he labored successfully in Bavaria and Thuringia, joined St. Willibrord in his missionary labors among the Frisians, and extended his activity to the Hessians and the Saxons. In 722 he came as far as Amoeneburg, in Hessia, where he laid the foundations of a monastery. The favorable reports which Winfrid sent to the Holy See induced the

Berneredus: Ben. Annals. Mabillon had promised to treat of the virtues of this saintly monk in the seventh volume of his Acta Sanctorum O.S.B. but did not live to publish that volume.
Peter: Chron. of Cluny.
Werner: Schindele.
Margaret: Seguin.

Pope to invite him to Rome in 723. On November 30 of that year the Pope consecrated him bishop without assigning him to a special see, and gave him the name of Boniface. Returning to his northern field of labor, he cut down the famous oak at Geismar, built several churches and established the monastery of Ohrdruf. In 732 Pope Gregory III made Boniface archbishop and primate of Germany. Boniface next built a monastery at Fritzlar, in 736 at the request of duke Hugibert visited Bavaria and in 738, in his quality as papal legate, defined the boundaries of the sees of Salzburg, Regensburg, Passau and Freising, for all of which he also appointed worthy bishops. Shortly after, he established the sees of Eichstaett, Erfurt and Buraburg, regulated the affairs of the see of Wuerzburg and in 746 founded the abbey of Fulda. Since 751 Mainz was his archiepiscopal see. After all these achievements he might have rested, but his missionary fervor had not died out. Having resigned the see of Mainz in favor of Lullus, whom he had consecrated bishop in 752, he set out to labor once more among the Frisians in 754. But his noble day's work was done; as he was proceeding to confirm a number of neophytes on the vigil of Pentecost, he was slain together with a number of other Christians on this day in the year 755. His remains were first interred at Utrecht, but were later transferred to Fulda. On June 11, 1874 Pope Pius IX extended the celebration of his feast to the whole world.

2. St. Felix, a monk of Fritzlar in Hessia, received the palm of martyrdom as a reward for his zeal in preaching the faith to the pagan Saxons.

3. St. Elzearius, monk of St. Sabin in the diocese of Tarbes, in France, lived a saintly life which was crowned by a holy death, probably early in the tenth century.

4. Bl. Ferdinand, Infante of Spain and Grandmaster of the Order of Avis, was sent on a warlike expedition into Africa. The forces under his command were outnumbered by those of the enemy. Rather than hazard a battle in which defeat of the Spanish arms was certain, he entered into negotiations with his adversary and consented to be one of the hostages. He and his companions spent five years in captivity, and were subjected to many humiliations. Ferdinand sustained the spirits of his fellow sufferers by his own admirable patience, but finally fell a victim to the hardships and privations to which his delicate health could oppose only a feeble resistance. His remains were removed to Portugal in 1463 and buried in the monastery of S. Maria de Victoria.

5. Bl. Boniface, Cistercian prior at Villers in Brabant, was noted for his extraordinary self-abnegation and devotion to prayer, He died in 1170 and was buried in the chapel of St. Bernard, where his remains were venerated together with those of the other saintly brethren buried in the same place.

6

1. St. Claudius, bishop and abbot, was born of a distinguished family at Salins in Burgundy about 603, and was the model of the clergy of Besancon,

Boniface(1): Willibald; Othlo; C.E; K.L., Butler.
Felix: Trithemius.
Elzear: Saussay.
Ferdinand: J. Alvarez.
Boniface(5): Henriquez.

when he was chosen to succeed archbishop Gervaise who died about 685. Dreading the responsibilities of such a charge, he tried to escape it by hiding himself, but was discovered and compelled against his inclination to assume the burden. Seven years passed before he found a suitable opportunity to resign; he retired to the monastery of St. Eugend, or Condat, on Mount Jura, and took the religious habit about 693. The monks chose him as the successor of their deceased abbot. He governed them with the zeal and sanctity of an Anthony to the time of his death about 693. In 1243 the body was still incorrupt. At one time his shrine was visited by numerous pilgrims from all parts of France.

   2. **Ven. Joseph of S. Germanus,** monk of the Congregation of the Feuillants, was a native of Sicily, and was distinguished for his erudition and virtuous life even while living surrounded by the distractions of the world. As a monk in one of the houses of the Feuillants in Rome, he was not only conscientious in observing the strict rule of his Order but also enjoyed the grace of contemplation, so that his life seemed to be a continuous ecstasy. He died a few years after his profession in 1608, and was immediately venerated as one of God's elect.

   3. **Falco,** sixth abbot of Cava, closed his saintly and meritorious life in 1146.

7

   1. **SS. Peter, Walabonsus, Sabinian, Wistremund, Habentius** and **Jeremias,** monks at Cordova in Spain, following the example of the monk Isaac, boldly appeared in the presence of the Mohammedan judge and professed their faith, for which they were at once condemmned to die. The venerable Jermias, the first to be executed, was scourged to death. On their way to the place of execution the holy confessors of the faith encouraged one another and were as cheerful as if they were going to a feast. The priest Peter, the deacon Walabonsus and the others were strangled; their bodies were then bound to stakes and exposed to public view for several days. Afterwards they were burned and the ashes thrown into the river in 851.

   2. **St. Deocarus,** first abbot of Herrieden in the diocese of Eichstaett, was at first a hermit in that place, which was still a wilderness at the time. He enjoyed the good will of Charlemagne, who built a small church for him in honor of the Blessed Virgin, and also a monastery of which Deocarus was made the first abbot. Deocarus was well versed in the Holy Scriptures and died in the odor of sanctity about 850. In 1316 the body was raised by the bishop of Eichstaett and enshrined in a more conspicuous place.

   3. **Bl. Landulph,** bishop of Asti in Piedmont, was born about 1070, and educated in the monastery of Cielo-aureo at Pavia, where he also took the religious habit. His exceptional abilities were recognized by archbishop Anselm of

Claudius: Chifflet; Butler.
Falco: Chron. of Cava.
Joseph: Carol .de S. Maria.
Peter etc.: Eulogius of Cordova.
Deocarus: Gretser; Trithemius; Bavaria Sancta. The name is a translation of Gottlieb.

of Milan, who appointed him dean of the collegiate church of St. Nazarius, and chose him as his companion on a Crusade.   The archbishop having died at Constantinople, Landulph returned and successfully adjusted a dispute regarding the validity of the election of the new archbishop.   He was elected bishop of Asti in 1103, courageously maintained the rights of his church, and opposed Henry V and the antipope Anacletus II.   How highly he was esteemed by Pope Innocent II appears from the fact that this Pontiff, on his journey from France to Rome, spent Easter week at Asti as guest of the saintly bishop.   His holy and active life closed in 1130.   In 1450 the remains were raised and placed beneath an altar.

4.   St. Robert, Cistercian abbot of Newminster, England, was a native of Yorkshire, and even in his childhood indifferent to the amusements in which children are wont to delight.   After his ordination he was made rector of a parish in the diocese of York; but after discharging that office some time with great assiduity and zeal, he resigned and took the Benedictine habit in York.   About this time, Richard, the prior of this house, desirous of living according to the letter of the Rule of St. Benedict, left the monastery with twelve brethren, by the leave of the abbot, and founded the abbey of Fountains.   Robert was one of the first monks of this house and seemed to excel the rest by the lustre of his piety so far that they all had their eyes on him in their religious duties.   Ranulph of Merley, baron of Morpeth, paying a visit to the monastery of Fountains five years after its foundation, was so struck with the edifying deportment of the monks, that he obtained a certain number of them and built for them Newminster, near Morpeth in Northumberland, in 1137.   Of this foundation Robert was appointed the first abbot.   He founded a monsatery at Rivebelle in Northamptonshire and lived in a union of holy friendship with St. Bernard and St. Godric.   A holy death crowned his devoted active career in 1159.

8

1.   St. Sabinian, abbot of St. Chaffre at Carmeri in Languedoc, was the successor of St. Theofrid in the government of that monastery and received the reward of the just, about 740.

2.   Bl. John Rainuzzi, monk of St. Margaret's at Todi in Italy, was so generous to the poor that he was popularly known as the "Almoner."   He died in the odor of sanctity in 1330.

3.   Ven. John Chianones, priest and monk at Montserrat in Catalonia, was a native of France and was vicar general of the diocese of Mirepoix before he took the monastic habit.   Under his guidance, St. Ignatius Loyola is said to have spent some time in spiritual retreat after his conversion.   He was respected and esteemed by his contemporaries for his holiness of life, his prudence and other remarkable gifts.   In his old age he was stricken with blindness so that it was impossible for him to read Holy Mass, but he did not suffer a day to pass

Landulph: Phil. Malabayla.
Robert: Capgrave; Dugdale; Le Nain; Roman Martyrol.
Sabinian: Mab. Lechner notes that the French Martyrology does not mention abbot Sabinian.
John Rainuzzi: Boll.

without receiving Holy Communion.   On the eve of the feast of Corpus Christi his soul left its earthly tenement to be united with the God of his love in the year 1569.

9

1.   **St. Maximian,** bishop of Syracuse, was a native of Sicily, and a friend of Pope Gregory the Great.   He succeeded abbot Valentine in the government of the monastery of St. Andrew, which Gregory had established in Rome about 583, and visited Gregory while the latter was papal nuncio at Constantinople. On his return voyage, a storm almost completely disabled the ship that bore him but he succeeded in reaching Crotona, where it sank after he had left it.   When Gregory had been elected Pope, Maximian and the deacon Peter were his most intimate friends and counsellors.   In 591 the Pope appointed him bishop of Syracuse, thus sacrificing a trusted friend to the needs of a portion of his flock. At the same time Maximian was appointed papal legate for Sicily.   He was so zealous in his episcopal labors and so watchful over the conduct of the clergy that Pope Gregory confessed that he could find no equal to this holy bishop, whom he styled "a most holy servant of God."   He was on the point of setting out for Rome, when he died in 594.

2.   **St. Cumian,** of whose early life little is known, was an Irish bishop— of what see, is unknown—who resigned at the age of seventy five years, left Ireland and became a monk at Bobbio, where he spent the last twenty years of his life as a humble and devout monk.   He died about 720 and was buried near his illustrious countryman, St. Columban, the founder of Bobbio.   The Lombard King Luitprand built a handsome monument over his tomb.

3.   **St. George,** priest and monk at Vabres in France, was the son of noble parents, was educated at Conques and, after his ordination, entered that monastery.   His constant endeavor was to progress daily in perfection through assiduous prayer, watches and fasting.   From Conques he was sent to Vabres where he spent the remainder of his days and died about 880.

4.   **Bl. Silvester,** Camaldolese laybrother of S. Maria degli Angeli at Florence, had been a merchant, but was so deeply touched by the sermons of a certain Jordano that he decided to quit all things in order to save his immortal soul.   He followed Jordano into a solitude near Castaneo, and lived a strict eremitical life, but realizing his inability to struggle single-handed against the enemy of souls, he entered the monastery at Florence in the fortieth year of his life, in 1318.   His duties as cook so fully occupied his time that he found less leisure to pray than he desired; hence he resolved to go back to his hermitage. As he was about to step out of the gate of the monastery, he met a laybrother who had been a brave soldier and who reproached him with the words: "What are you doing, Brother Silvester?   For God's sake, do not abandon yourself!" Filled with shame, Silvester within himself said: "Oh, what a wretched creature I am: a soldier has converted and humbled me."   He remained and was never more content than after receiving this lesson.   Although unable to read, he was

John Chianones: C. Cajetan; Yepez; Stadler.
Maximian: Oct. Cajetan.
Cumian: Ughelli.
George: Boll.

very familiar with Holy Scripture. After serving four years in the kitchen, he was made servitor in the refectory; in this occupation he found more leisure for prayer and meditation in his cell. His humility was touching; he would accuse himself of the most trifling offences, detested the vice of murmuring and enjoyed intimate communion with God. He died in the year 1348.

10

1. **St. Bardo**, archbishop of Mainz, was born at Opershofen, in Hessia, in the year 980, and educated at Fulda, where he also took the monastic habit. He was beloved by all on account of his cheerfulness and readiness to befriend every one who stood in need. After his ordination, his abbot sent him to rule the newly founded abbey of St. Andrew. Having been successiveley abbot of Kaiserswoerth and Hersfeld, he was appointed archbishop of Mainz in 1031. A simple sermon delivered on Christmas day at Goslar was seized upon by his personal enemies to disparage him in the eyes of emperor Conrad as an unfit and unlettered prelate. The emperor regretted having nominated him, particularly when bishop Dietrich of Metz pronounced an eloquent discourse on the day following. Things took a turn more favorable, when Bardo mounted the pulpit on the feast of St. John and spoke with such unction that his audience was spell-bound and the emperor felt reconciled to the choice he had made. From this day forward Bardo was called a second Chrysostom. Nothwithanding his dignity and prerogatives, he remained humble, spent nights in prayer, and did not eat meat until Pope Leo IX advised him to moderate his austerity in this particular. He finished the cathedral begun by St. Willigis and consecrated it in honor of St. Martin; endowed the church of St. John and founded the monastery of St. James. At the synod of Mainz in 1049 Pope Leo IX appointed him papal legate. He seems to have been gifted with the spirit of prophecy, for he foretold that Gebhard of Eichstaett would be Pope. The prophecy was fulfilled in 1055 when Gebhard was enthroned as Pope Victor II. While celebrating Pentecost at Paderborn in 1051 he foretold his own approaching death. On his journey back to Mainz, he had a fall at Dornhagen and realized that the end was near. He summoned his auxiliary bishop, Abellinus, who administered the last sacraments and assisted him in preparing for death. Lying on sackcloth he died on June 10, 1051, after uttering these words of the Psalmist: "Let thy mercy be upon us, O Lord, as I have always hoped in thee."

2. **St. Ebremund**, abbot of Montmaire, was formerly a courtier in the service of King Theodoric III and lived in happy wedlock with a virtuous wife. By mutual consent, they separated and resolved to strive for higher perfection by observing the evangelical counsels. Ebremund founded several monasteries, among which was that of Fontenay, which he ruled for some time as abbot. At the request of St. Aunobert (or Alnobert) of Seez, he became abbot of Montmaire in Normandy, which he governed to the time of his death in 720. His remains were transferred to Creil in the diocese of Beauvais during the Norman invasion, but were burnt by the Huguenots in 1567.

Silvester: The monk Zenobius.
Bardo: Lambert of Aschaffenburg; Trithemius.
Ebremund: Baillet; Saussay; Trithemius. Another form of the name is Evremond.

3. St. Bogumilus, bishop and afterwards a Camaldolese monk and hermit, was descended from the Polish counts of Libycz and studied at Paris with his brother Boguphal. Returning to Poland, Bogumil built a church at Dobrew and provided it with revenues for a pastor. His uncle, John, archbishop of Gnesen, delighted with his nephew's progress in virtue, made him chancellor and ordained him a priest. It was Bogumil's dearest ambition to save souls of others as well as his own; hence he begged for leave to serve the church at Dobrew. While discharging the duties of an humble parish priest, he was appointed to succeed his deceased uncle in the metropolitan see of Gnesen in 1167. He had been archbishop three years when the disedifying lives of the clergy and an irresistible desire to lead a contemplative life moved him to resign his see and to enter the Camaldolese Order. He passed the novitiate in Hungary, then returned and dwelt in retirement at Dobrew, at times sharing in the labors of the pastor. He was venerated as a Saint even during his life time and died in 1182.

11

1. St. Spinolus, a disciple of St. Hildulf and prior of a small house founded by one Bego in the Vosges mountains, applied himself with his whole soul to the work of self-sanctification and died in 671.

2. St. Hugo, abbot of Marchiennes, a former monk of St. Martin's at Tournai, by his edifying example wrought a marvellous change for the better in the community in which he had professed. He was chosen abbot of Marchiennes and continued to set such attractive examples of charity, zeal and benevolence that he was universally regarded as a Saint. The Lord deemed him fit for his eternal reward in 1148.

3. St. Parisius, a Camaldolese priest and monk, was born at Bologna in 1151 and in his childhood was noted for his inclination to prayer and practices of mortification. At the age of twelve he was sent to the Camaldolese monastery of St. Damian, and after his ordination at the age of thirty years was appointed chaplain to the convent of St. Christina at Treviso. Many other devout souls chose him as their spiritual adviser and confessor, even bishop Albert of Treviso. Unusually favored with spiritual light and the gift of prophecy, he died in 1267. His veneration has been authorized.

4. Bl. Aleidis, Cistercian nun of Cambre St. Marie near Scarbeke in Brabant, was offered to that monastery at the tender age of seven years and early gave promise of her future holiness. In order to test the fidelity of this favored soul, God sent her an affliction that cut her off from the companionship of her sisters. At first she was disconsolate in her loneliness; but in response to her prayer, cheerfulness re-entered her heart and she gloried in the privilege of suffering with her Redeemer. In the summer of 1249, when the last sacraments

---

Bogumilus: Damalewiez. According to another account, he resigned the see of Gnesen and retired into a solitude at Uniesovia in northeastern Poland where he lived twelve years to the time of his death. Stadler. According to Gams (Ser. Ep.) he resigned in 1172.
Spinolus: Ben. Annals; Greven. Also called Spinulus.
Hugo: Ben. Annals.
Parisiis: MS. in Florence; Stadler.

were administered to her, as she was believed to be on the point of death, she received a premonition that she was to live another year. It was a year of great bodily suffering; there appeared to be not a sound spot on her body, yet she ceased not to praise God for all mercies till He changed her sufferings into joy on the feast of St. Barnabas in 1250.

12

1. **SS. Marinus, Zimius**, priests and **Vimius**, a laybrother, were Scottish hermits near Griesstetten in the diocese of Regensburg in the 11th century. Zimius and Vimius are said to have come from Scotland (or Ireland) while Christian was abbot of the Scots monastery in Regensburg, and to have established themselves as hermits at the place above mentioned. Here they were joined by Marinus, prior of the Scots in Regensburg, and lived according to the rule of St. Benedict. After their death they were venerated as Saints. Abbot Christian interred their bodies on a spot some distance from their hermitage and built a church in honor of St. Martin, which became a favorite pilgrimage. In 1680 the remains were raised and placed in new tombs behind the altar of the choir. The present day being the anniversary of this raising, is for that reason observed as their feast. On July 2, 1862 the body of St. Marinus was placed beneath the mensa of the high altar and the bodies of the other two Saints under the side altars at Griesstetten.

2. **St. Placidus**, founder of the Cistercian monastery of S. Spirito at Pretula in the diocese of Aquila, Italy, was the child of virtuous parents in the former kingdom of Naples. After returning from a pilgrimage to Compostella, he was prostrated by sickness for the space of five years. Although he could scarcely move a limb of his body, he was always cheerful. Having recovered, he received the religious habit from a hermit on Monte Corno and was instructed by him in the principles of Christian perfection. A year later he entered the monastery of St. Nicholas and subsequently that of S. Salvatore, which he left in order to escape certain dangers threatening his spiritual welfare. After several other changes of his abode, he finally settled at Pretula, where he lived an extremely austere life for thirty-seven years. Upon the invitation of Count Bernard of Ocri he established the monastery of S. Spirito and governed it according to the Rule of St. Benedict. When death drew nigh, he entrusted the care of his monastery to the Cistercians of Casanova and died shortly after Pentecost in the year 1248 amid the tears and laments of the inhabitants of the surrounding country.

3. **Bl. Sigo**, abbot of Glonne and Saumur, successor of blessed Frederic, was an able scholar, possessed of fine artistic taste, and a model of true holiness. Among his accomplishments was a thorough knowledge of Greek and Hebrew; he was an excellent organist, and provided in every way for the intellectual and spiritual advancement of the brethren, at the same time not forgetting the temporalities of the houses committed to his charge. He died in 1070.

Aleidis: Boll. Other forms of the name are Adelaide, Alizon, Alizette.
Marinus: Report of the Translation in Boll.; Stadler. These three Saints have been known for centuries as the "elenden" (i.e. foreign) Saints.
Placidus: Paul of Celano.
Sigo: Ben. Annals.

13

1. **St. Fandila**, priest and monk, was a native of Cadiz in Spain and received his early training in Cordova. Desiring to strive for perfection, he put on the religious garb without binding himself permanently to any house. After visiting several monasteries, he finally selected that of Tabanos and made rapid progress in spiritual growth under the guidance of its holy abbot Martin. After his ordination he was sent to the monastery of San Salvador at Cordova, which at the time was in the hands of the Mohammedans. Caliph Mohammed I treated the Christians with exceeding harshness, destroyed their churches and impoverished the people by excessive levies of taxes. Fandila publicly denounced the teachings of Islam and proclaimed the faith of Christ, for which he was thrown into prison and executed in 853.

2. **Bl. Gerard**, Cistercian monk and brother of St. Bernard of Clairvaux, was endowed with enviable gifts of mind and body. One day after vain attempts to induce Gerard to become a religious, St. Bernard spoke these prophetic words: "You will not listen to the voice of God till He lays His hand upon you." Gerard received a wound in a conflict, was taken prisoner and in these straits resolved to follow his brothers. Immediately after recovering his liberty, he entered Citeaux and was received by Abbot Stephen. In 1115 he joined St. Bernard, who had been appointed abbot of Clairvaux, and was made cellarer of that house, because he was familiar with the arrangement of domestic affairs. In 1137 he accompanied St. Bernard on a journey to Italy, but was taken seriously ill at Viterbo. He ascribed his recovery to the prayers of his saintly brother. Having returned from this journey, he fell ill a second time and died with these words: "Father, into thy hands I commend my spirit" on this day in 1138. St. Bernard pronounced a touching eulogy at his funeral.

14

1. **SS. Anastasius, Felix and Digna**, martyrs, were religious at Cordova in Spain. After St. Fandila's glorious martyrdom, Anastasius, a monk and priest, fearlessly stepped before the Mohammedan judge, professed his faith and was executed. At the same time, the monk Felix, a native of Alcala, shed his blood for the same noble cause. In the afternoon of the same day, Digna, a nun in a monastery at Tabanos, appeared before, the judge at Cordova and upbraided him in these words: "Why do you slay our brethren? It is because we worship the true God, profess the Holy Trinity, Father, Son and Holy Ghost, and detest whatever is contrary to our belief." She, too, was awarded the palm of martyrdom and the lilies of virginity on this day in the year 853.

2. **Bl. Villanus**, bishop of Gubbio, had been a monk of the Congregation of Fontavellana, and was selected for the see of Gubbio on account of his many excellent qualities. He was a father to the poor and to orphans, for whom he

Fandila: Eulogius; Surius; Florez: Espana Sagrada.
Gerard: Conrad of Clairvaux.
Anastasius: Eulogius.

established a refuge, and also founded two monasteries.   Rich in virtue and merits he rested from his labors about 1230.

3. Bl. Richard, surnamed *Gratia Dei*, abbot of St. Vannes at Verdun, was born of noble parents at the villa of Banton in the territory of Montfaucon about 980, received his education at Rheims and was made dean of the chapter of the church of Notre Dame in that city.   In company with count Frederic of Rheims, who was also inclined to a life devoted to the service of God, he entered St. Vannes and received the monastic habit.   Disappointed by the laxness of discipline prevailing in the house, both friends repaired to Cluny to ask the advice of abbot St. Odilo.   The latter counselled them to return to St. Vannes, but they found conditions so little to their taste that they decided to enter the monastery of St. Paul near by.   They were on the point of leaving when a pious recluse, acting under an inspiration from above, advised the abbot of St. Vannes, Fingenius, to admit the novices Frederic and Richard to profession, lest the Church suffer the loss of two such excellent religious.   The abbot persuaded them to remain, and received their vows.   Three years later, the abbot died and Richard was elected his successor.   He was blessed and duly installed, and from that day labored with the zeal and self-sacrifice of an Apostle at the spiritual improvement of the souls confided to his charge.   He renovated the monastery and wrought such a pronounced change in the spirit of his brethren that he was invited to reform a score of other monasteries.   During the famine prevailing from 1028–1030 he fairly exhausted the resources of his house and even sold the altar plate, in order to relieve the distress of the poor.   He died in 1046; a great concourse of bishops and nobles attended the burial.

15

1. St. Landelin, abbot of Crespin in Hainaut, was of noble descent and was born at Vaux-en-Artois, in the territory of Cambrai.   For his excellent education he was chiefly indebted to his god-father, St. Autbert, bishop of Cambrai. The latter was about to confer clerical tonsure upon Landelin, when some relatives persuaded the youth to seek for happiness in a wordly career.   So completely did he break with the past, that he fell into evil ways and became a robber.   One night as he was about to rob a house, one of his companions in crime was suddenly stricken by death.   This sad occurrence was such a shock to Landelin, that he abondaned his wicked pursuit, and returned to Cambrai, where Autbert received him with great kindness and compassion.   Shortly after, satisfied that Landelin's conversion was sincere, Autbert gave him tonsure and sent him on a pilgrimage to Rome; on his return from Rome ordained him a deacon, and after a second pilgrimage to Rome, elevated him to the dignity of the priesthood.   After a third pilgrimage, he established himself and two friends, Adelenus and Domitianus, in hermitages, which subsequently developed into the famous abbey of Lobbe.   Somewhat later he founded the monasteries of Aune on the Sambre, and Waslere in the forest of Faigne.   Not content with founding these houses and endowing them with revenues, he entered the forest

---

Villanus: Monum. of Gubbio.
Richard: Hugh of Flavigny.

between Mons and Valenciennes and founded the monastery of Crespin, which he ruled as abbot and in which he closed his eyes in the sleep of death in 686.

2. **Ven. Adelwin,** abbot of Mont Blandin at Ghent, in Flanders, was a man of rare holiness and prudence, who prepared his own tomb and promoted virtue among his brethren by the light of his example. He died in 995.

16

1. **St. Benno,** bishop of Meissen and patron saint of Bavaria, was the son of the Saxon count Frederic of Bullenburg and his wife Bezela and was born at Hildesheim in 1010. At the age of five years he was placed by his relatives in the care of bishop Bernward and educated under the supervision of Prior Wiger of the abbey of St. Michael until he was eighteen years old, when he received the religious habit and entered upon the study of Holy Scripture. By order of his abbot Adelbert, he was ordained a priest and is said to have wept copious tears whenever he offered the Holy Sacrifice. After Adelbert's death, Benno was elected abbot, but after holding this office for three months, retired in favor of the monk Sigebert, that he might serve God without being disturbed. While evading one honor, he was forced to accept another, for in 1049 emperor Henry III appointed him a canon of the imperial chapel at Goslar. Sixteen years later, he was made bishop of Meissen. In this capacity he made a visitation of the churches of his diocese every year, preached unceasingly, was ever ready to give alms, watched over the discipline of his clergy and left nothing undone to enhance the beauty and splendor of divine worship. At the same time he lived personally as poor as a monk. Benno was among the Saxon nobles who incurred the displeasure of Henry IV and were banished from the country. During the struggle between Pope Gregory VII and the emperor, he never wavered in his loyalty to the sovereign Pontiff and even journeyed to Rome to pledge his support. When this season of storms and trials had passed, Benno not only ruled his church in peace, but despite his advanced age set out to evangelize the Slavs beyond the Elbe, among whom he labored with great success. He rested from his long and faithful toil in 1106 at the age of ninety-six years. His remains were raised in 1270 and he was canonized by Pope Adrian VI on May 31, 1523. At the instance of the Elector Albert V of Bavaria his remains were transferred to Bavaria in 1576 and enshrined in the Liebfrauenkirche at Munich. Since that time he has been regarded as the patron saint of Bavaria.

2. **St. Lutgardis,** Cistercian nun of Aviers in Brabant, entered the convent of St. Catherine in the diocese of Liege at the age of twelve years in 1194 and subsequently, although young in years and profession, was made abbess of the community, which she left twelve years later by the advice of her spiritual director John of Lyra to enter the Cistercian convent at Aviers. She was an ecstatic and enjoyed many other singular heavenly favors. Her piety was by no means selfish, for she fasted seven years to save the sountry from the Albigensian heresy, seven years for the conversion of sinners in general, and seven

---

Landelin: Mab.; Boll.; Stadler. The date of death is variously given.
Adelwin: Sander.
Benno: Jerome Emser; Stadler; Chev.

years to avert a great peril threatening Christendom.   Eleven years before her death she became blind.   She died at the age of sixty-four in 1246.

17

1.   **St. Ramuold**, abbot of St. Emmeram in Regensburg, was born in 901 in Franconia and was educated in Trier, where he also entered the monastery of St. Maximin.   The report of his sanctity and eminent abilities reached the ears of St. Wolfgang, bishop of Regensburg, who invited him to preside over the monastery of St. Emmeram in his episcopal city.   Ramuold was noted for his charity; he built two hospitals for the sick and the poor and ministered to their needs with his own hands.   He delighted in discoursing on spiritual topics, but wasted few words over concerns of a purely temporal nature.   For two years he suffered from blindness and after bishop Wolfgang's death also had the misfortune to incur the ill will of the emperor.   After recovering his eyesight and regaining the favor of the prince, he died a centenarian in the year 1001.

2.   **St. Botulph**, abbot, was born in England about 570.   Together with his brother Adulph he crossed over to Belgic Gaul to find some religious house in which they might be schooled in Christian virtue.   They made such rapid progress that Adulph was shortly chosen bishop.   Botulph returned to England and begged King Ethelmund to grant him a place for a monastery.   The king gave him the wilderness of Ikanhor, where he founded an abbey and taught the brethren whom he assembled there the rules of Christian perfection and the institutes of the holy Fathers.   He was beloved by every one, being humble, mild and affable.   When he was oppressed with any sickness, he never ceased thanking and praising God with holy Job.   He was purified by a long illness before his happy death which happened in the year 655.   The monastery having been destroyed by the Danes, his remains were conveyed to Ely, and, later, parts of them to Thorney and Westminster.

3.   St. **Tarasia**, queen of Portugal and Cistercian nun at Lorvan, was the daughter of King Sancho I of Portugal and was married to her cousin, king Alphonse of Leon, at the age of sixteen years.   This marriage having been declared null by Pope Celestine III in 1196, Tarasia resolved to quit the world and in 1212 founded the monastery of Lorvan in which she and her sister Blanche took the veil.   Oblivious of her former rank, she obeyed her abbess with the simplicity of a child, and mortified her flesh by wearnig a hairshirt.   After having prepared her tomb, she seemed to be in continual communication with Heaven in prayer.   Shortly after burying her sister, she died on the present day in 1250.

4.   **Bl. Euphemia**, abbess of Altomuenster in Bavaria, was the daughter of Count Berthold of Andechs and the sister of Bl. Mechtildis of Diessen.   Unconquered by the allurements of wealth and honor, she made an oblation of herself to God by taking the vows of religion at Altomuenster, became abbess of

---

Lutgardis: Thomas Cantipratanus; Stadler.   Her name is mentioned in the Roman Martyrology although she was never formally canonized.   Also called Luitgard or Ludgard.
Ramuold: Arnulf monk of St. Emmeram.   Other forms: Ramwuold. Rambold.
Botulph: Butler; Stanton; Capgrave.
Tarasia: F. Macedo.   Another form of the name is Theresa or Teresa.

that house and died after a holy life in the year 1180. Her remains were interred in the vault of her family at Diessen by the side of her sister Mechtildis.

18

1. **St. Elizabeth,** prioress of Schoenau near Bingen, was offered to the convent of Schoenau at the age of twelve years, and spent her youth in the exercises of monastic virtue. Her perseverance was tried by long and painful suffering. At the age of twenty-three she was favored with extraordinary visions, the contents of which she dictated to her brother Egbert, a priest and monk at Schoenau. The trials sent her by God were manifold; at times she felt so desolate, disconsolate and harrassed by doubts that life almost became a burden to her. Yet she bore all her afflictions, physical and mental, being strengthened by the conviction that with God's grace one can do all things. She died in the thirty-sixth year of her age in 1165. Although she has never been formally canonized, her name is mentioned in the Roman Martyrology.

2. **Bl. Cincuinus,** was a monk of St. Peter's, Lindisfarne, whose sanctity was attested by numerous signs at the time of his death. His life was written in verse about 870 by Ethelwulf, a monk of the same monastery.

19

1. **St. Deodatus,** bishop of Nevers and founder of the monastery of St. Die, was descended from a distinguished French family and received a careful training and education. He was elected bishop of Nevers in 665, but resigned in 668, yielding to an inclination for a contemplative life. For some time he lived in a secluded spot in the forest of Hagenau where he was associated with St. Arbogast, but later removed to Ebersheim near Schlettstadt. Here he found a number of hermits who welcomed him with great joy and requested him to rule them. With assistance from King Childeric II, Deodatus built a church and thus laid the foundation to the monastery of Ebersheimmuenster. Longing for retirement that he might devote himself entirely to contemplation, he left this place and passed into the Vosges mountains, where he settled in a valley called Galilee, and built a cell and a chapel in honor of St. Martin. Again disciples flocked around him, for whom he built, on a neighboring hill, a monastery in which at first the rule of St. Columban but afterwards that of St. Benedict was observed. This house later became known as the monastery of St. Die, or Jointure, because it was situated at the junction of two streams, the Meurthe and the Rothbach. After this monastery had been well established, he withdrew to his cell of St. Martin and died in the arms of St. Hidulphus on this day in the year 680. St. Die (Diez) formed the nucleus of a settlement that grew into a city and was made an episcopal see by Pius VI in 1777.

2. **St. Hildegrim,** bishop of Werden on the Ruhr, was a brother of St. Ludger and a grandson of the Frisian Wissurg, who had been converted by St.

Euphemia: Raderus.
Elizabeth: Egbert, her brother; Butler; Stadler; C.E.
Cincuinus: Harpsfield.
Deodatus: Mab.; Butler; Stadler; Chev.

Willibrord. Accompanied by his brother, he went to Monte Cassino, took the religious habit and in 785 founded the monastery of Werden. From 804–809 he was bishop of Chalons-sur-Marne, but was promoted to the see of Halberstadt, at the same time governing the monastery of Werden as abbot, and died in the year 827.

3. Bl. Odo, bishop of Cambrai, was a cleric of the city of Orleans, and was called in 1087 to preside over the school of Tournai, where his abilities won for him a reputation that passed far beyond the limits of the province. Learning and the praises of men were far from satisfying the cravings of his soul; hence he resolved to leave the world and embrace religious life with five of his pupils. No sooner had this determination become known to the people, than they requested bishop Radbod to induce Odo to carry out his resolve without leaving the city. The bishop consented, persuaded Odo to remain and gave him the church of St. Martin, where Odo and his companions lived a community life accordig to the rule of St. Augustine. At first they lived in pitiful poverty, from which they were relieved by the charitable donations of the people. The resources of the house were soon so abundant, that in times of need Odo was in position to mitigate the distress of the poor. Unavoidable and frequent contact with the outer world threatened to weaken the religious fervor of the brethren; hence Odo took counsel with abbot Aimeric of Anchin, who advised him to adopt the Rule of St. Benedict, an arrangement to which the brethren unanimously agreed. They put on the black garb of Benedictines and on March 1, 1095 began to live according to the Benedictine Rule. The house visibly prospered from this time; within a few years the community counted seventy members and its revenues had surprisingly grown. After governing his house as abbot for ten years, he was chosen bishop of Cambrai, but difficulties of a political character prevented him from taking possession of his see. Hence he established his residence at Anchin and from that point occasionally visited his diocese, till he was permitted to take formal possession in 1106. Seven years later, when he felt the approach of his last hour, he had himself carried to Anchin where he died June 19, 1113.

20

1. St. Adalbert, first bishop of Magdeburg, had formerly been a monk at St. Maximin in Trier. In 960 he was sent as a missionary to Russia, where he was consecrated a bishop. Despite his devoted labors, the result was discouraging and he returned to Germany three years later. Emperor Otto in 966 appointed him abbot of Weissenburg in the diocese of Speier, and in 970 first archbishop of Magdeburg. Here he resided at the abbey of St. Maurice and founded another monastery in honor of St. John the Baptist. It was his wont to visit these houses by night to see if the brethren attended the night offices. He died reputed a Saint, in 981.

2. St. Bainus, bishop of Terrouane about 660, resigned that see and became a monk at St. Wandrille, or Fontenelle. Being a model religious, pious and humble, he was made abbot, and after the foundation of Fleury by Pepin

---

Hildegrim: Altfrid.
Odo: Amand de Castello.
Adalbert: Ditmar of Merseburg.

of Heristal in 706 was selected to rule that house, in which he died in the odor of sanctity in 711.

3. **St. Adelgundis,** nun at Drongen near Ghent, was the daughter of the king and martyr St. Basinus and a disciple of St. Amandus. She died a holy death about 650, and was always venerated as a Saint.

4. **St. John de Matera,** abbot and founder of the Congregation of Pulsano, was a native of Apulia, left his home early in life and served as a shepherd in the service of a monastery on an island near Tarentum. Even at that time he was given to austerities, which he continued to practice after he had passed over to Sicily. Obeying an interior impulse, he returned to the mainland and dwelt in a locality near the residence of his parents, to whom he did not reveal his identity. Several years after his arrival, he restored a dilapidated church near Genosa and dedicated it to St. Peter. Being suspected of finding a treasure at this place, he was cast into prison, but was acquitted of the charge and set at liberty. At Capua he was directed, in a vision, to return to Apulia where he should win many souls for Heaven. In Apulia he joined St. William of Vercelli, who was at the time dwelling with several disciples on Monte Laceno. A fire destroyed their dwellings and they removed to Monto Cogno, but John left them and went to Bari, where he labored zealously, but again was rewarded with opposition and imprisonment. Having been released, he revisited the church at Genosa, and a year later built a monastery at Pulsano not far from Monte Gargano. Within six months his commuuity numbered sixty members, some of them being of noble birth. He was endowed with the gift of miracles and prophecy, and was regarded as a second Elias or Anthony. He died on June 20, 1139. The statutes framed by St. John for his discalced penitents were adopted by several other houses, thus forming the Congregation of Pulsano, which has ceased to exist.

21

1. **St. Leutfrid,** abbot of Lacroix in Normandy, was a native of the territory of Evreux and was born about 670. From early youth he manifested a desire to serve God in the clerical state, but could not obtain his father's consent to follow his inclination. Upon the pretext of visiting some relatives, he was permitted to leave home, and seized this opportunity to receive instruction from a teacher at the church of St. Taurin. Although found by his parents, he refused to yield to their suggestion that he renounce the idea of becoming a priest. He finished his studies at Chartres and returned to his home where he conducted a school that was frequented by a great number of youths attracted by the report of his learning. But this pursuit did not satisfy him; he desired to sanctify himself by following Christ, and therefore resolved to retire from the distracting life of the children of the workd. Having invited his parents and relatives to a banquet, he distributed gifts among the guests, left during the night and made his way to Cailly where he dwelt in seclusion for some time with the servant of God Bertramnus. Abbot Sidonius, a man of rare sanctity, governed a monas-

Bainus: Chronicle of Fontenelle; Butler.
Adelgundis: A. Sander.
John de Matera: Anon. contemporary; Heimbucher; Stadler.

tery at Caux, in the diocese of Rouen, Leutfrid repaired to this holy religious and received the habit from his hands. Bishop Ansbert of Rouen and abbot Sidonius advised him to return to his own country to labor for the honor of God and the salvation of souls. On a spot about five miles (2 leagues) from Evreux, on the banks of the Eure, where St. Audoenus had erected a cross, Leutfrid built a monastery which he called Lacroix, and which he ruled forty-eight years. He died happily after receiving the holy Viaticum in 738 and was buried in the church of St. Paul. During the Norman invasion in the 9th century, the monks took refuge at the abbey of St. Germain-des-Pres at Paris, carrying with them the relics of St. Leutfrid. His name is mentioned in the Roman Martyrology also on this day.

2. St. Agofred, abbot of Lacroix-St. Ouen, succeeded his brother St. Leutfrid in the government of that monastery, and appears to have died before 851, in which year Bishop Gumbert of Evreux raised the remains of the two saintly brothers and interred them in the church of the monastery.

3. St. Engelmund, abbot of Velsen, in the diocese of Harlem, in the Netherlands, was born in England, in his youth became a monk, and subsequently was made abbot. Inspired by the apostolic enthusiasm of St. Willibrord, he passed over to the continent and preached the Gospel in the vicinity of Kennemar. His unremitting efforts brought a number of pagans into the fold of Christ. Engelmund was stricken with a fever while preaching near Velsen, and died in the 8th century. His remains repose in Harlem.

22

1. St. Eberhard, archbishop of Salzburg, was descended from the counts of Hilpoltstein and Biburg and was born at Nuernberg about 1085. He received his early training and education in the higher branches of learning at the monastery of St. Michael at Bamberg, and was appointed to a canonicate in the cathedral of that city. His soul found no rest, for his heart was fixed upon high things; resigning his canonicate, he became a monk at St. Michael's, but was not to enjoy the quiet of the cloister long, for the provost of the cathedral sent him to Paris to finish his studies. Still his resolve to be a religious was so firmly rooted, that after his return from Paris he was permitted to re-enter the monastery. By request of Bishop Otto of Bamberg, he joined the Benedictine community of Pruefening founded by that holy prelate and here continued the work of self-sanctification. Eberhard's sister founded the abbey of Biburg near Ingolstadt in 1127 and requested Eberhard to be its first abbot. He withheld his consent for five years, till he was appointed at the request of the monks by Pope Innocent II. Much has been written in praise of his charity, prudence and fatherly kindness and solicitude. When the see of Salzburg was vacated in 1146 by the death of archbishop Conrad, Eberhard was by unanimous consent elected his successor and was consecrated on May 13, 1147. His first official act was to effect a reconciliation between the cathedral chapter and the monasteries of Hoegelwerth and St. Peter. The lives of the clergy were the object of his par-

Leutfrid: Mon. of Lacroix; Butler. Other forms: Leufred, Leufroi.
Agofred: Stadler. (not in Lechner.)
Engelmund: Breviary of Harlem; Stanton.

ticular care. He was a most devout client of the Blessed Virgin and denied no favor that was asked in her name. During the controversies between Pope and Emperor, he remained faithful to the Supreme Pontiff and refused to recognize the antipopes intruded by the emperor. Such was Eberhard's firmness and sincerity, that the emperor forbore to molest him on account of his loyalty to the Holy See. In 1164, although eighty years of age, he set out to put an end to a feud that had broken out between the commandant of the castle at Leibnitz and Margrave Ottokar V of Styria. Success crowned this effort, but the hardships of the journey bought on an illness to which he succumbed in the Cistercian abbey of Rein on this day in the year 1164. Oh May 29th his remains were conveyed to Salzburg and entombed in the cathedral.

2. **St. Domitian**, monk of Crespin in Hainaut, and disciple of St. Landelin, died as abbot of Lobbe in the beginning of the eighth century and was always honored as a Saint.

23

1. **St. Ediltrudis**, abbess, was the daughter of the pious King Anna of East Anglia and of his wife Hereswida. Her sisters were SS. Sexburgis, Witburgis and Ethelburgis. She was born at Ermynge in Suffolk, brought up in the fear of God and in compliance with the desire of her friends married Tonbercht, prince of the southern Girvii. Three years after her marriage, she lost her husband with whom she had lived in perpetual continence, and who for her dowry settled upon her the island of Ely, where she dwelt for five years in poverty and prayer. Notwithstanding her earnest desire to save her soul by leading a retired life, she was drawn back into the world when King Egfrid of Northumbria so persistently sued for her hand in marriage that she reluctantly consented, but persuaded the king to allow her the privilege she had enjoyed in her previous union. They lived together like brother and sister for twelve years; after which Ediltrudis obtained her husband's consent to embrace the religious state. After taking the advice of St. Wilfrid and receiving the religious habit from him, she withdrew to the monastery of Coldingham to live under the obedience of the abbess St. Ebba, who is said to have been the aunt of King Egfrid. When she learned that the king was designing to lead her back into the world, she left Coldingham and returned to Ely, where she founded a double monastery in 672. The nunnery she governed herself, and was by her example a living rule of perfection. She ate but once a day, except on great festivals, and never returned to bed after matins, which were sung at midnight. After a lingering illness, she breathed forth her pure soul in profound sentiments of compunction in the year 679. She was buried, according to her direction, in a wooden coffin, but her sister Sexburga, who succeeded her in the government of the monastery, caused the body to be taken up and put into a stone coffin, which was placed in the church.

2. **Bl. Peter**, prior and confessor at St. Juley in the diocese of Langres, was a native of England, but passed over to France about 1095 to lead a religious

---

Eberhard: Anonymous disciple; Stadler. No formal canonization ever took place; nor is the name in the Roman Martyrology, or in the Benedictine Supplement thereof.
Domitian: Life of St. Landelin.
Ediltrudis: V. Bede; Thomas of Ely; Butler. Other forms: Etheldreda (see Stanton) and Audry.

life in some house in that country.   By a happy chance he met his countryman, Stephen Harding, with whom he took the monastic habit at Molesme.   Here he remained even after Stephen departed for Citeaux, and was favored with the gifts of miracles and prophecy in an extraordinary measure.   He was made aware of the state of souls after death, read the hearts of men and by his prayers healed the sick.   He was appointed spiritual director to a community of nuns at Juley and lived in a cell in the churchyard.   When he felt the hour of his dissolution drawing nigh, he received the last sacraments and bade farewell to his spiritual charge in touching words.   He died in the year 1136.

24

1.   The feast of **St. John the Baptist** is celebrated by the entire Order, which imitates the example of its Holy Founder, who built a chapel in honor of St. John on Monte Cassino.

2.   **St. Theodulph**, bishop and abbot of Lobbe in the Netherlands, under whose wise administration the monastery prospered materially and spiritually, died in the odor of sanctity in 776.   His remains are at Binghen in Hainaut.

3.   **St. Erich**, monk of St. Germain at Auxerre, was offered to that monastery at the age of seven years, and made such progress in virtue and learning that all were pleased with the acquisition of such a valuable and devout member. By the request of his abbot Lothair, son of Charles the Bald, he wrote a metrical life of St. Germanus, and a life of St. Alban.   His useful career closed in the year 924.

4.   **St. Bartholomew**, monk and hermit, in his youth wandered about aimlessly from one country to another, till he finally reached Norway, where he made the acquaintance of a priest who procured his ordination.   After struggling manfully and overcoming two severe temptations, he left Norway after three years, went to England and became a monk at Durham.   As he was most anxious to be a good religious, he practiced every virtue of a perfect monk.   Before the year of his probation had expired, he was instructed in a vision to betake himself to Lindisfarne.   Here he suffered much from one Elwin, and found ample occasion to study patience and constancy.   Like a penitent he wore a hairshirt, slept on a hard couch, never ate meat or tasted wine.   God favored him with the grace of counsel.   The last nine years of his life were spent in greater fervor, for he was aware that his end was nigh.   During his final illness he was visited by brethren from Lindisfarne and Coldingham.   Praising God to the last moment, he expired in 1182.

5.   Foundation of the **Knights of St. John** at Jerusalem in the year 1100 by Cassinese monks in their monastery of S. Maria Latina.   The object was to shelter and protect pilgrims to the holy places.   In consequence of differences

Peter: MS. publ. by P. F. Chifflet. S.J.
Theodulph: Mabillon.
Erich: Boll.; also called Erricus.
Bartholomew: Boll.; Butler.

that arose in the course of time, the rule of St. Augustine was adopted and the Knights were affiliated to those of Malta.

25

1. **St. Adelbert,** monk of Echternach, was of the royal blood of the kings of Northumberland, but was not dazzled by the attractions of the world, preferring to serve God by saving the souls of men sunken in the mire of paganism. For this purpose he joined St. Willibrord, became a monk and shared his labors in Frisia and the Netherlands. When Willibrord established his episcopal see at Utrecht, he appointed Adelbert his archdeacon. Adelbert died at Egmont about 740 and his tomb became famous for miracles. A monastery for Benedictine monks was founded in that place by Count Thierry in the beginning of the tenth century.

2. **St. William,** abbot and founder of Monte Vergine in Italy, was born in Piedmont in 1085, early in life lost his parents and was educated by a kind relative. At the age of fifteen he took the religious habit, and made a pilgrimage to Compostella in Spain. Returning in 1106, he resolved to visit the Holy Land, but while enjoying the hospitality of a certain Roger at Melfi, he learned the 119th Psalm, in pondering upon which a new light entered his soul. The next two years he spent in the society of a hermit named Peter on a neighboring hill, where he led a very mortified life. In 1108 he visited St. John of Matera with whom he seemed to be but one heart and one soul. A second attempt to set out for the Holy Lgnd was frustrated by robbers who stripped him of the little he had and maltreated him. He would have preferred to abide with St. John, but an inner impulse moved him to labor for the salvation of men elsewhere. William settled on Monte Vergiliano—since called Monte Vergine—not far from Salerno, where he subsided chiefly on chestnuts and coarse bread. Here he was joined by a fervent disciple, Albert, who was followed by several other devout persons, including a few priests, for whom he built a church in honor of Our Lady. About this time William was ordained a priest, as is generally supposed. As the faithful made liberal offerings to the monastery and William was exceedingly generous in almsgiving, the brethren complained that he was recklessly squandering their substance. William replied by telling them that greater blessing rests on giving than on receiving. After some time he designated one of his most reliable disciples to govern the community and retired to Monte Laceno, where he lived in undisturbed solitude. A fire having destroyed his cabin, he resolved to establish himself elsewhere and in 1129 selected Serra Cognata (Mons Cuneatus), where he was annoyed more than ever. A hunter treated him as if he were a robber. God punished the hunter by sending him an affliction, from which he was freed through the prayers of the Saint. Here, too, William was discovered; many pious persons, even Count Robert of Caserta, visited him, to receive counsel and spiritual guidance. Having founded a monastery and given it a superior, he resumed his wanderings and chose an abode in the vale of Conza, where he dwelt a year in a wilderness. Subsequently he founded two monasteries, one for men, and another for women at Guleto, for

---

Knights of St. John: Ben. Annals.
Adelbert: Mab.; Le Mire; Butler.

which he wrote strict statutes. King Roger at one time harbored an unworthy suspicion against him; but God soon enlightened him, and he gave expression to his esteem for the Saint by granting his monastery complete exemption and building another at Palermo. William was seized with extreme weakness in 1142, had himself carried to the church and there, lying on the floor at the foot of the Cross, he yielded his soul into the hands of his Maker in the morning of June 25. The Congregation of Monte Vergine has ceased to exist, but the monastery of that name survives. The habit of the monks, even to this day, is white.

3. **St. Milburga,** abbess of Wenlock in the diocese of Hereford in England, was the daughter of Merwald, king of Mercia, and of his wife Ermenburga and despised the riches of this world to purchsae the pearl of great price. She became a nun at Wenlock and in recognition of her eminent virtue was elected abbess, which office she filled to the time of her death about 725. Numerous miracles accompanied the discovery of her body in 1101.

26

1. **St. Babolenus,** bishop and abbot, paid a visit to Abbot Remaclus of Stablo and gave such edification to the brethren by his exemplary conduct that Remaclus begged him to remain in the monastery. Babolen became a monk at Stablo and afterwards was appointed abbot of Malmedy. After the death of Remaclus he governed both houses, which since that time always had a common superior. In a letter, King Clovis III calls him an apostolic man and a bishop, from which it may be inferred that some part of his career was devoted to missionary labors. He died about 700.

2. Another **St. Babolenus,** a Columban monk whose country is not known, came to France and was after some time chosen to rule the abbey of St. Maur des Fosses, founded near Paris in 638 by the archdeacon Blidesgisil. By his virtues Babolen rendered it a house of saints, and by the perfect spirit of charity, piety and all virtues which reigned in it, a true image of Paradise on earth. In conjunction with St. Furseus he labored much for the spiritual interests of the diocese of Paris. He founded many churches and hospitals in that diocese, and in his old age resigned his abbacy, that he might pass the remainder of his days in recollection and prayer. He died about 700 and was honored at Paris.

3. **St. Rodulfus,** bishop of Gubbio in Italy, in the year 1056 visited St. Peter Damian and offered him his castle and the adjoining grounds, upon which a monastery of the Congregation of Fontavellana was immediately established. Rodulf and his brother led a most edifying life under that Saint's direction and merited unstinted praise from him for their fervor and constancy. Their food was simple; the bare ground was their couch, coarse bread their food. Rodulf

---

William: John of Nusca; Butler.
Milburga: Wm. of Malmesbury; Dunbar; Stanton (Feb. 22). Also called Winburg.
Babolenus(1): Life of St. Remaclus; Reg. SS. Belg.; Butler (Papolenus).
Babolenus(2): Mab.; Le Comte; Butler.

was chosen bishop of Gubbio, but did not grace that see very long, for he was called to his reward in 1063, at the age of thirty years.

27

1. **St. Adelenus**, abbot of Crespin in the Netherlands, joined St. Landelin in the pursuit of Christian perfection. Like his companion, Domitian, he remained faithful to his spiritual master and shared all the hardships of missionary and monastic life. Beyond the fact that Landelin appointed him abbot of a monastery, little is known of Adelen's deeds, but he appears to have been a fervent disciple of his Redeemer, for after his death, about 700, he was always honored as a Saint at Crespin.

2. **Daniel**, Cistercian abbot of Schoenau near Heidelberg, had previously been a canon at the cathedral of Cologne, but laid aside that dignity to become a Cistercian monk at Hemmenrode where he lived as monk and prior for several years before he was called to rule Schoenau. God blessed him with the gift of contemplation, and filled his heart with extraordinary graces and consolations during the Holy Sacrifice of the Mass. He died in the odor of sanctity about the year 1290.

3. Approval of the Order of **Silvestrines** by Pope Innocent IV in 1247. The Order was founded by St. Sylvester Gozzolini in 1231. The Silvestrine habit is similar in cut to that of the Cassinese, but its color is blue. Since 1855 the Order has been active in the missions of Ceylon. A branch known as the Congregation of Vallisumbrosella was established in France at the instance of King St. Louis IX.

28

1. **St. Argimirus**, monk and martyr at Cordova in Spain, was of a distinguished family and held the office of public censor in that city. Desirous of attaining perfection, he became a monk, probably at Cordova. Being accused of blaspheming the religion of Mohammed and of openly confessing the divinity of Christ, he was arraigned before the judge who endeavored to make him unfaithful to his religion by flattery and seductive offers. Argimirus was proof against all such weapons, and was executed in the year 865. The body was suspended from a gibbet, but was recovered by some monks and given honorable sepulture near the bodies of SS. Ascisclus and Perfectus.

2. **Ven. Notker Labeo**, abbot of St. Gall's in Switzerland, stood so high in the good graces of his abbot that the latter appointed him his successor.

Rodulfus: Peter Damiani. According to Gams he was bishop from about 1061–1066. Stadler says he was made bishop at the age of 27 in 1059 and died Oct. 17, 1061. His name is not in the Roman Martyrology, but an altar was dedicated to his honor in the Camaldolese church of S. Gregory on the Coelian hill in Rome A. D. 1740 (Stad).

Adelenus: Life of St. Landelin. Also called Hadelin. Not identical with St. Hadelin, Feb. 3.

Daniel: Henriquez.

Silvestrines: Bullarium; Gruber; Heimbucher.

Argimirus: Eulogius. The name is written Argymirus in the Rom. Mart.

Notker's familiarity with Holy Scripture, the writings of the Fathers and the classics, and his knowledge of music, poetry, mathematics and astronomy placed him in the first rank of the scholars of his time and country. At the same time he did not neglect the exercises of piety or suffer his brethren to abandon themselves to study at the expense of devotion. At the approach of death, he summoned several poor people to his bedside and there had a meal served them. He died on the present day in 1022, after requesting to be buried in the clothes that he was wearing, that none might see the heavy chain with which he had been in the habit of mortifying his body.

3. Approval of the **Suabian Congregation of the Holy Ghost** by Pope Benedict XIII in 1725. It was granted all the privileges of the Cassinese. Like so many other religious bodies it disappeared during the general suppression of monasteries early in the 19th century.

29

1. **Bl. Salome** was the niece of a king of England, who adopted her as his daughter. Longing to consecrate herself entirely to Christ she left her home with two handmaidens and made a pilgrimage to Jerusalem. On their way home they went through Bavaria to avoid meeting acquaintances and to visit the shrine of St. Aegidius. Her companions died during this journey and she continued her way alone. She was afflicted with blindness and other bodily ailments, but thanked Heaven for escaping so many perils to both soul and body and resolved to live as a recluse. She was sent to the abbot of Niederaltaich, who placed at her disposal a cell attached to the sanctuary of the church. Several years after her arrival she was joined by her coussin **Judith** who had gone in search of her and who now resolved to be a recluse also. The abbot caused a cell to be built for her near Salome's. She was tempted terribly by evil spirits and suffered from fear at night, but persevered in the life she had chosen. Salome died first; they were both buried in their cells. The date of their death is uncertain, differing by as much as three centuries.

30

1. **St. Ehrentrudis**, abbess of Nonnberg near Salzburg, was a niece of St Rupert, bishop of Salzburg, who invited her to that city about 585 and appointed her abbess at the convent he had founded. She labored hand in hand with her saintly relative, a loving mother to her subjects, a skillful teacher of the spiritual life, a devout religious much given to prayer and devotional reading, and an unfailing friend to the poor. She died about 630.

2. **Bl. Clotsendis**, abbess at Marchiennes, was the eldest daughter of St. Rictrudis, and succeeded her mother in the government of that house in 688. Clotsendis received the crown of eternal life about 703.

Notker: Chron. of St. Gall; C.E.; K.L.
Suabian Cong.: Bullar. Mag.
Salome: Chron. of Niederaltaich; Stadler; Steele. Her companion is sometimes called Jutta.
Ehrentrudis: Ranbeck; Esterle: Chronik; Stadler.
Clotsendis: Hucbald of Elnon.

3. **Bl. Arnulph**, a Cistercian laybrother of Villers in Brabant, was born at Brussels about 1189, spent his youth in great indifference to the interests of his soul, but obeying a call of grace cast off the shackles of sin at the age of twenty two and entered the Cistercian monastery at Villers. He treated his body with excessive rigor, yet was ever obedient, humble and charitable and led many back to God by the force of his example. One of his pious practices was to do penance for others; by way of a reward, he is said to have seen the souls of several persons enter Heaven. Greeting death as the friend that was to open the gates of Paradise for him, he departed this life in the presence of his brethren in 1228.

4. **Ven. Mazelin**, abbot of St. Peter's at Salzburg, while assisting at a translation of the remains of St. Ehrentrudis on September 4, 1023, appropriated a relic and by way of punishment was stricken with blindness. Shamed and humbled, he prostrated himself before the shrine of the Saint and promised to live as a hermit if his eye-sight were restored. God granted the favor and Mazelin kept his word, lived a solitary life on the Geisberg at Salzburg and died in the odor of sanctity 1025.

5. **Ven. Marquard**, monk of St. Blasien in the Black Forest, whose cheerful obedience was rewarded in a most striking manner on several occasions, died on the day foretold by himself about the year 1080.

6. **Ven. Philip Powell** (called Morgan), was born at Tralon in Brecknockshire on February 2, 1594. At the age of sixteen he came to London to study law, but four years later passed over to Douay, where he became a Benedictine monk in 1614. Having been ordained in 1618 and sent into the English mission in 1622, he labored for more twenty years under most trying circumstances till he was arrested in 1645 on the charge of having performed priestly functions in England. He was condemned to death and was hanged, drawn and quartered at London on this day in the year 1646.

Arnulph: Goswin of Villers.
Mazelin: New chronicle of Salzburg; Metzger, etc.
Marquard: Monum. of St. Blasien.
Powell: Challoner; Bucelin; Taunton; C.E.; Gillow.

July

1

1. **St. Theobald,** Camaldolese hermit at St. Thibaut-aux-Bois near Auxerre, was descended from the counts of Champagne and was born at Provins about 1030. While reading the lives of the fathers of the desert in his youth, he resolved to walk in their footsteps, and for this purpose took counsel with the solitary Burchard, who lived on an island in the Seine. All efforts of his father to dissuade him from following his pious inclination proved ineffectual and he finally gave his consent. Accompanied by his friend Walter, Theobald journeyed to Rheims, where both exchanged their respectable garb for the ragged raiment of beggars. Then they travelled eastward and settled in a forest in Suabia, toiling by day as servants to peasants in the vicinity and spending the greater part of the night in prayer. After some time they made a pilgrimage to Compostella, whence they intended to go to the Holy Land, had they not learned at Rome that the outbreak of war prevented them from executing this design. They established themselves in a solitude at Salanigo near Vicenza, where Walter died two years later. The death of his friend was interpreted by Theobald as a warning that his own end was not far distant. He increased his austerities, abstained even from bread and nourished himself with herbs and vegetables only; he always wore a penitential garment, a board was his couch. His unusual sanctity attracted the attention of the bishop, who ordained him priest. The renown of his virtues had gone abroad and reached the ears of his parents, who at once set out for Italy to visit him, and were so deeply moved at the sight of him that they also resolved to leave the world. The father returned home to dispose of his temporal concerns, the mother, however, remained and lived in a small cell near that of her son. Seven years had Theobald spent in this solitude, when he was afflicted with a sickness that caused him intense suffering and ended in paralysis. A year before his death he begged Abbot Peter of the neighboring monastery of Vangadizza to vest him with the religious habit. Having suffered with admirable patience and having commended his mother and his spiritual children to Abbot Peter, he received the last sacraments and expired in peace on June 30, 1066. The remains were first entombed in the cathedral at Vicenza; later they were removed to Provins in the diocese of Sens. Theobald was canonized by Alexander II.

2. **Ezzo,** bishop of Salzburg and former abbot of St. Peter's in the same city, labored zealously, and, when physical strength failed him, devoted himself exclusively to contemplation till the Lord invited him to take possession of the heavenly mansion prepared for him, about 790.

2

1. **St. Swithin,** bishop of Winchester, was of distinguished stock in England and was ordained a priest by bishop Helmstan. He became a monk in the

Theobald: Abbot Peter; Stadler; Buchberger; Butler. French form of name: Thibault, Thibaut. *Ezzo*: Hansiz.

old monastery in his native city, and was in the course of time appointed prior. King Egbert appointed Swithin his chaplain, at the same time commissioning him to educate prince Ethelwulf, who not only was a docile pupil and admirer of the Saint but, after his own accession to the throne, made him bishop of Winchester in 852 after the death of Helmstan.   Notwitstanding his learning and dignity, Swithin always was humble and unassuming, frequently made journeys of visitation on foot and delighted in the company of the poor, whom he made happy with alms.   Swithin survived his royal benefactor but five years; he died on this day in 862, and according to his own request was buried in the churchyard.   In 971 the remains were raised by Bishop Ethelwold and removed to the church.

2.   St. Adegrinus, monk and hermit, at first bore arms for a secular prince, but, obeying a call of grace, laid aside his armor, took tonsure and joined St. Odo, who was then living in seclusion at Tours and was not yet a monk.   Together they set out in search of a monastery in which they might serve God undisturbed, but when they failed to find a house that suited them, they resumed their eremitical life.   Subsequently Adegrin, while on a pilgrimage, visited the monks of Beaume, who received him with much kindness.   Adegrin was so favorably impressed by this reception and by the excellent discipline prevailing in this house, that he returned to Tours and told Odo about the discovery he had made.   Both received the habit at Beaume in 909; Odo later became abbot of Cluny, while Adegrin, by leave of the abbot of Beaume, retired to a cell a few miles from the monastery and lived the mortified, quiet life of a hermit for thirty years, till his soul was released from its earthly prison in the year 939.

3.   St. Lidanus, abbot at Sezza, Italy, was born 1026 at Atina in the Abruzzi mountains, and at the age of nine years was placed in the monastery at Monte Cassino.   When he was seventeen years of age, his parents died and left him heir of their possessions, part of which he devoted to the erection of an abbey in honor of St. Cecilia near Sezza.   Lidanus here ruled a community of monks who had to struggle with bitter poverty, yet were contented and never ceased praising God.   This holy abbot guided his brethren in the narrow path that leads to glory for seventy-two years and died in 1118.   Bishop Drusinus removed the remains from the abbey to Sezza, where they were deposited beneath the high altar in the church of St. Mary.

3

1.   John Gersen, reputed author of the "Following of Christ," was abbot of St. Stephen's at Vercelli, and was distinguished for his prudence, piety and learning.   He lived in the thirteenth century; the year of his death seems to be unknown.

2.   The Congregation of St. Vannes— or *Sanctorum Vitonis et Hidulphi* —was founded in the year 1600, chiefly through the efforts to Desiderius de la

Swithin: Wolstan, monk of Winchester; Wm. of Malmesbury; Stanton says he died 863.   Also called Swithun.
Adegrin: Chifflet; Stadler.
Lidanus: Ughelli; Ferrari; Carrara.
John Gersen: Bucelin.

Cour, a monk of Verdun. For many years he had been praying for a renovation of religious fervor in the monasteries of France. With permission of his ecclesiastical superiors he began reconstructing the community at Verdun and with such success that Moyenmoutier shortly accepted the reform and affiliated itself with St. Vannes. One of the monks was sent to Rome to obtain recognition from the Holy See; on April 7, 1604, Pope Clement VIII authorized the establishment of a Congregation similar to that of Cassino and endowed with all the privileges of the latter. This congregation, which comprised about forty monasteries, disappeared during the French Revolution. Abbot Augustine Calmet, the celebrated biblical scholar, was a member of this body.

4

1. **St. Odo the Good**, archbishop of Canterbury, was the son of Danish pagan parents who had settled in England, They disinherited him for his unconcealed attachment to the Christian religion. With support from duke Athelm, Odo was enabled to study and was ordained a priest. The duke appointed him as his chaplain, recited the Hours with him and chose him as a companion on a pilgrimage to Rome. Kings Alfred, Edward and Athelstan on more than one occasion employed the services of the Saint. Athelstan had him promoted to Canterbury in 942. The Saint resisted for a long time, alleging his unworthiness, the harm done by translation and the fact that he was no monk. No attention was paid to the two first considerations, and he was finally prevailed upon to take the habit of a monk from the hands of the abbot of Fleury, or S. Benoit-sur-Loire. Odo anointed King Edwin at Kingstown in 955, but joined St. Dunstan in rebuking this reckless ruler. Even in his old age, Odo displayed a lively and active interest in the education of his clergy and instruction of the people. Rich in merit, he rested from his labors in 961 and was ever since that time honored as a Saint.

2. **St. Aurelian**, archbishop of Lyons, the son of noble parents in the province of Lyons, was appointed archdeacon of Autun when he had reached the years of manhood. At the same time the abbey of Aisnay was conferred upon him, probably *in commendam*. Since the spiritual interests of this house were dearer to him than its revenues, he introduced monks from the flourishing abbey of Bonnevaux near Chartres, taking the religious habit himself and governing the house as its real abbot. Later he also founded the abbey of Sessieu. On account of his eminent virtue and abilities, he was made archbishop of Lyons, which see he governed from 875 to the time of his death in 895.

3. **St. Bertha**, widow, and abbess of Blangy in Artois, was the daughter of Count Rigobert and Ursana, and related to one of the English kings. She was married to Count Sigfrid, by whom she had five daughters, two of whom, Gertrude and Deotila, are Saints. After her husband's death she became a nun at Blangy, and was followed by the two daughters just named, in 682. Count Roger, to whom she had refused the hand of her daughter Gertrude in marriage,

---

Cong. St. Vannes: Bullar. Mag.; Boll.; Heimb.
Odo: Matthew of Westminster; Florence of Worcester; Eadmer; Butler; Stanton (June 2).
Aurelian: Mab.

sought revenge by spreading discreditable reports about her, but Count Thierry, convinced of her innocence, assured her of his protection.   She caused several churches to be built, and after establishing religious observance in her convent, resigned, leaving the house in charge of her daughter Deotila, and shut herself up in a cell, devoting herself exclusively to prayer.   She died about 725.   During the Norman invasion her remains were carried to Erstein in Alsace, but in the eleventh century were taken back to Blangy.

4.   **Bl. William,** abbot of Hirschau, in Wuerttemberg, was born of noble parents in Bavaria and became a monk at St. Emmeram in Regensburg, of which he eventually became prior.   The fame of his holiness and learning spread far beyond the walls of his monastery, so that the monks of Hirschau elected him as their abbot.   Upon his arrival he learned, to his regret, that his predecessor, Frederic, had been compelled to resign without cause and that the monastery was unlawfully interfered with by its patron.   Although at first disinclined to accept the election, he was induced to remain lest the lack of a superior resulted in decay of discipline, but he did not assume the title and rank of an abbot before his predecessor's death in 1070.   On the feast of the Ascension 1071 he was solemnly inducted into office by the bishop of Speier.   During his administration he finished the beautiful church of his abbey, appointed twelve monks to copy books in the *Scriptorium*, and introduced the institute of laybrothers and of oblates.   In his efforts at reform he was warmly seconded by the papal legate, abbot Bernard of Marseilles.   On several occasions he sent monks to Cluny to familiarize themselves with the distinctive features of that reform.   The movement organized by him was blessed with such gratifying success, that for the growing numbers of his community he established the monasteries of Reichenbach, St. George in the Black Forest, Chiemsee and St. Margaret in Bavaria.   Other abbeys, such as Schaffhausen, Petershausen, Camberg, Altdorf and Isny, were completely regenerated under his influence. Abbot William died on July 4, 1091.

5.   **Bl. Hatto,** monk and recluse, was of noble birth and entered the monastery of Ottobeuren in his youth, enriching that house with his patrimony. Desiring to lead a purely contemplative life, he was permitted to live as a recluse.   He is said to have been unduly attached to some trifling objects which he concealed in his cell and regarded as his property.   The abbot regarded him as unworthy to enjoy the privileges of a recluse, and ordered him to take his place once more among the brethren, where he atoned for his fault by many years of tears and penance.   He died in 975 and was buried in the abbey church.

6.   **St. Ulric,** bishop of Augsburg, although not a Benedictine by profession, was educated by Benedictine monks and while bishop wore the Benedictine habit.   Rich in merits for his services to religion and society he departed from this life in 973.   He was the first Saint solemnly canonized.

Bertha: Mab.; Boll;.
William: Haimo, monk of Hirschau; Heimb.
Hatto: Feyerabend; Braun.
Ulric: Gerard of Augsburg; Gebhard; Raffler: Der hl. Ulrich; Fontanini: Codex Canoniz.; Butl.
    Latin form: Udalricus.

5

1. **Bl. Berthold**, bishop, had been a Cistercian abbot at Loccum in Hannover, and died a martyr for the faith while preaching in Livonia, in the year 1200.

2. **Bl. Angelus de Masatio** was a Camaldolese monk whose zeal in preaching against a sect known as the Berlotans in Italy was so great that the sectarians in their fanaticism slew him in the year 1458. His remains lie in the monastery of S. Maria de Serra near Masaccio. His name occurs in the Camaldolese supplement to the Roman Martyrology. The veneration of Bl. Angelus was approved by Gregory XVI on April 16, 1842.

3. **Eberhard**, Cistercian laybrother of Villers in Brabant, was a great lover of silence. One day a soldier, to whom he had given some information, asked him a number of curious questions, to which the brother made no answer. The enraged soldier struck him in the face, whereupon the brother, pursuant to the evangelical injunction, offered the other cheek. Moreover, he humbly held the stirrup for the passionate man, who was so deeply moved that he afterwards became a monk himself. Eberhard's kindness made him the friend not only of men but also of animals. He died about 1390.

4. **Martha**, Cistercian nun of Cambre St. Marie near Brussels, with unflagging diligence and attention waited upon St. Aleidis, who was suffering of a malady that repelled others from her bedside. Aleidis had a vision in which she saw the place prepared in Heaven for her faithful attendant. This humble hero of charity passed away in the 13th century.

5. **Florbert**, monk of Corbie in Saxony and a pupil of St. Anschar, was killed with a writing-tablet by a classmate and died praying for his slayer in 825. St. Anschar saw his soul rising heavenward.

6

1. **St. Sexburgis**, widow and abbess at Ely in England, was the daughter of King Anna of the East Angles and of his wife Hereswida. She was carefully brought up, instructed in the principles and practices of the Christian religion, and married to Ercombert king of Kent, about 620. She never felt content in her new surroundings, and since it was not possible for her to find peace and rest for her soul, she provided an opportunity for others by founding a convent on the island of Shepey. After the death of her husband in 654, she held the regency during the non-age of her son Egbert. When the latter assmumed the reigns of government, Sexburgis assembled seventy-four nuns at Shepey, but hearing of the sanctity of St. Etheldreda at Ely, and wishing to live in greater

Berthold: Manrique; B. de Brito.
Angelus: Stadler; (not in Lechner).
Eberhard: Chron. of Villers.
Martha: Life of St. Aleidis.
Florbert: Rembert.

obscurity, she retired to Ely before 679, in which year she was chosen abbess to succeed Etheldreda. She died as abbess of Ely in 699. Her monastery in Shepey was destroyed by the Danes but rebuilt in 1130 and consecrated by William, archbishop of Canterbury, in honor of the Blessed Virgin Mary and St. Sexburgis; it was in the hands of Benedictine nuns to the time of the general dissolution under Henry VIII.

2. The servant of God, Sister **Mary Rose** (Susan Agatha de Loye), was born at Serignan near Orange in France on February 4, 1741. At the age of twenty she entered the Benedictine convent at Caderousse, where she was admitted to profession in 1762 and remained to the time when that house was suppressed during the French Revolution. She then withdrew to her native place, but was discovered and carried off to Orange. After being detained in prison about two months, she was condemned to death by the revolutionaries and executed on July 6, 1794.

<h2 style="text-align:center">7</h2>

1. **St. Willibald,** bishop of Eichstaett in Bavaria, was a son of the English prince St. Richard and was born in 704. At the age of three years he was seized with a sickness that threatened his life; when natural remedies proved ineffectual, his parents laid him at the foot of a great cross which was erected in a public place near their house and vowed to consecrate him to God's service if his life were spared. God accepted the pious offering and the child was immediately restored to health. At the age of five or six, he was placed under the care of Agbot Egbald in the monastery of Waltham. When he was seventeen years of age (about 721) he accompanied his father and his elder brother Wunibald on a pilgrimage to Rome and the Holy Land. His father died at Lucca, while he and his brother went on to Rome where both received the monastic habit. Two years later Wunibald returned to England, while Willibald set out for the Holy Land in company with two noble countrymen. At Emesa in Syria, Willibald was taken by the Saracens for a spy and imprisoned. He was set free through the intervention of a Spanish merchant, and continued his pious journey as far as Jerusalem. Having spent seven years in the East, he returned to Italy and entered Monte Cassino, which had just been restored by Abbot Petronax. During the first year he served as sacristan, during the second as dean, and for eight years acted as porter, or doorkeeper. Visiting Rome in the company of a Spanish monk in 738, he was informed by the Pope that St. Boniface had asked for his assistance in the German missions. Willibald was ordered to proceed northward without returning to Monte Cassino and was welcomed with great joy by St. Boniface, his cousin, in Thuringia. For several years he preached the Gospel in Franconia and Bavaria. In recognition of his service and virtue, St. Boniface consecrated him bishop and designated Eichstaett as his see (745). In his new station he labored with renewed zeal, confident that God rewards every effort made in behalf of the salvation of souls. He built a cathedral, invited monks to form his chapter and lead a monastic life with him, and built a double monastery at Heidenheim—the monks being governed by his brother

Sexburgis: Bede; Capgrave; Butler; Stanton.
Mary Rose: Acta Apost. Sedis, 1916. p. 230.

Wunibald, and the nuns by his sister Walburga. He died at Eichstaett in 786 or 787 and was buried in the cathedral. Pope Leo VII canonized him in 938.

2. **St. Hedda,** bishop of Dorchester in England, was a Saxon monk of the monastery of St. Hilda and was abbot of that house before his appointment to the see of Dorchester in 676, but resided at Oxford. King Ina frequently sought his advice and employed his services in compiling laws for the country. Hedda governed his church with great sanctity and died in 705.

3. **St. Edelburga,** was the daughter of the East Anglian king Anna. Impelled by a strong desire to strive for Christian perfection, she crossed over to France and became a nun at Faremoutier in Brie. After the death of St. Fara, the foundress of that house, Edelburga was chosen her successor. She died in 655; when her body was raised many years later, it was found incorrupt, as Venerable Bede testifies.

8

1. **St. Grimbald,** abbot at Winchester in England, was a native of St. Omer in Flanders and was a monk at Sithiu at the time when King Alfred the Great visited that monastery on his way to Rome. The king was so favorably impressed by Grimbald's personality that he sent messengers to Sithiu in 835, requesting bishop Fulco to send him to England. Grimbald is said to have taught for some time in a school at Oxford. Upon the death of archbishop Eldred of Canterbury, Alfred pressed Grimbald to accept that dignity, but the Saint preferred to remain a monk and was appointed abbot of Newminster at Winchester. In his last sickness, though he was extremely feeble, he left his bed and lay prostrate upon the ground to receive the Holy Viaticum. After this he desired to be left alone for three days; on the fourth, the community was admitted to his apartment and amidst their prayers he calmly breathed forth his soul in the year 903. His remains were interred in the church but were taken up by St. Elphegus and exposed in a silver shrine.

2. **St. Landrada,** abbess of Muensterbilsen in the Netherlands, was descended from royal stock, esteemed the service of God preferable to earthly glitter and honors, became a nun and died as abbess in 695. Her remains were later removed to Wintershofen, and subsequently to Ghent.

3. **St. Theobald,** Cistercian abbot of Vaux-de-Cernay, in the diocese of Paris, was one of the most illustrious ornaments of the family of Montmorency and was born in the castle of Marly, His father gave him an education suitable to his birth and trained him for the profession of arms. Theobald, however, was inclined towards a life of retirement and was always on his guard against perils to his innocence. He took the Cistercian habit at Vaux-de-Cernay in 1220, and was elected its abbot in 1234. Charity, prudence and zeal charac-

Willibald: Mab.; Boll.; Butler; Stanton; C.E.
Hedda: Bede; Wm. of Malmesbury; Butler; Stanton.
Edelburga: Bede; Butler; Stanton (Ethelburga.)
Grimbald: Boll.; Butler; Stanton.
Landrada: Boll.; Chev. says she died about 700.

terized his rule; among his brethren he lived as if he were the least of them, and excelled all in his love of poverty, silence and prayer. While, on the one hand, he was reprimanded at a General Chapter for exposing his abbatial dignity to contempt by his humility, King St. Louis and the archbishop of Paris treated him with all reverence and esteem. He died on December 8, 1247 but he was always venerated at his monastery on the present day.

4. **St. Albert,** was a Cistercian monk at St. Albert near Sestri de Ponente in the diocese of Genoa. His relics are venerated in the church at that place. It is not known when he lived or when he died.

5. **Bl. Eugene III** (Bernard Paganelli), a native of Pisa and a canon of the cathedral of that city, was attracted to the religious life by St. Bernard of Clairvaux and became a Cistercian monk. While abbot of the monastery of SS. Vincent and Anastasia in Rome he was chosen to succeed Pope Lucius II in 1145. He governed the Church with wisdom, gentleness and courage and passed to the reward of his toil in 1153. His veneration was approved September 28, 1872.

9

1. **St. Auremund,** abbot, was offered as a child to the abbey of Maire l'Evescau near Poitiers, where he was trained under the eyes of Abbot Junian. Such was his progress in knowledge and virtue that Abbot Junian shortly before his death recommended him as his successor. Auremond trod faithfully in the footsteps of his saintly master in the spiritual life and died in the reputation of sanctity about 600.

2. **St. Agilolf,** archbishop and martyr, former abbot of Malmedy and Stablo, was raised to the archiepiscopal see of Cologne in 745. While employed, apparently, in the mission of a peacemaker, he was slain by an assassin about 770. The remains, which were originally buried at Malmedy, were exhumed by Archbishop Anno and interred in the church of St. Mary *ad Gradus* in Cologne, where he has always been venerated as a martyr.

3. **Angelus,** monk of Monte Cassino, atoned for the sins of his youth by taking the habit at Monte Cassino and leading a penitential life to the time of his death in 1010.

10

1. **St. Etto,** an Irish bishop and missionary, came to France with St. Furseus and several other associates and lived a holy life at the abbey of Liessies in

---

Theobald: Le Nain; Butler.
Albert: Boll.; Stadler.
Eugene: Acta S. Sedis, VII; K.L.; C.E.; Mann: Lives of the Popes v. 9.
Auremund: Wulfin. Boethius in the life of this Saint.
Agilolf: Boll. Gams (Ser. Ep.) has no Agilolf among the archbishops of Cologne. The K.L.
    however says (in the article on "Koeln"), Agilolf succeeded Reinfried in 745, when St. Boniface was proposed for the same see.
Angelus: Peter the Deacon.

Hainaut. He died about 670, and was buried at Liessies, where he enjoyed veneration for centuries.

2. **St. Amalberga**, widow and nun at Maubeuge in Belgium, was a relative, perhaps the sister, of Pepin of Landen. She was married, contrary to her inclinations, to Witger, duke of Lorraine, by whom she had three children, all of whom are saints—Emebert, bishop of Cambrai, Reinildis and Gudila. By mutual consent, she separated from her husband, and both embraced the religious state. Amalberga received the veil at the hands of Bishop Autbert at Maubeuge, and lived a holy life to the year 690, when she received her reward. Her remains were carried to Lobbe, and later to Binghen in Hainaut.

3. Another **St. Amalberga**, also of illustrious descent, was sought in marriage by Charles Martell, but declined in order to consecrate herself to God in the religious state. No threats of violence caused her to waver in her resolutions. She took the vows in the convent of Muensterbilsen, of which St. Landrada was abbess. After a godly life, she entered into her rest in 772. Her remains were first interred at Tamise, on one of her estates, and were later carried to Mont Blandin, where they were destroyed during the religious wars.

4. **Bl. Peter**, founder and abbot of Caprario near Perugia, after being ordained a priest, begged Bishop Honestus of Perugia for the church of St. Peter on Monte Caprario, which was in a very dilapidated condition. After some hesitation the bishop gave his consent. A community was organized and gave such splendid promise that the bishop caused Peter to be appointed abbot by Pope John XIII, 967. Peter lived most frugally, fasted three days of the week, never tasted of wine, and was most punctual in his religious duties. When the troops of Otto II during their passage through Perugia harassed the poor inhabitants by pillage, the Saint courageously appeared before the emperor and protested against the lawlessness. The emperor was impressed by his virtue and fearlessness and put an end to the disorders. Peter died after ruling his community for forty years in the year 1007.

11

1. Feast of the **Solemn Commemoration of St. Benedict**, which has been celebrated during more than a thousand years to remind the children of St. Benedict of the triumph and glory of their Holy Father, who prayed and labored that in all things God may be glorified.

2. Fleury (St. Benoit sur Loire) and many other monasteries commemorate on this day the **Translation** of the relics of SS. Benedict and Scholastica about the year 652, in the reign of King Clovis II. During the Norman invasion the remains were hidden in different places and for a long time reposed in the church of St. Anian at Orleans, until they were finally carried back to Fleury.

Etto: Boll.
Amalberga(1) :Ghini.
Amalberga(2): Mab.; Boll.
Peter: MS. of the monastery.

On March 20, 1107 they were placed in an elaborate shrine in the presence of King Louis VI and of bishops John II of Orleans and Humbald of Auxerre. When the commendatory abbot Aventin apostatized in 1561, he appropriated the costly reliquary but left the contents with Prior Foubert. The relics were placed in a silver shrine in 1653. Several other monasteries claim to possess relics of St. Benedict—notably Monte Cassino and Metten. The relics of St. Scholastica were at one time preserved in Mans.

3. **St. Hildulph,** bishop and abbot of Moyenmoutier, was probably born in Bavaria, studied in Regensburg and was ordained in that city. In 666 he was summoned to the see of Trier, but only consented after considerable pressure had been brought to bear upon him. He introduced the Rule of St. Benedict into the celebrated abbey of St. Maximin, increased the revenues of the house and improved its discipline. He resigned his see in 671 and withdrew to St. Maximin's, but was so much annoyed by visits from acquaintances, that he went into the Vosges mountains and founded the monastery of Moyenmoutier, so called because it lay between four other monasteries—Senones, St. Die, Estival and Bon Moutier. The community consisting of three hundred monks flourished under his wise and pious rule. Choosing to obey rather than to command, he resigned his place in favor of Leutbald, upon whose death three years later, he was induced to resume the government of the house and presided over it to the day of his death in 707.

4. **St. Sigbert,** abbot of Dissentis, in the canton of Grisons in Switzerland, was a disciple of St. Columban, and settled in the mountains of that canton on grounds granted him by a wealthy man named Placidus. While the new establishment was flourishing, Placidus was slain by the rapacious count Victor, but Sigbert continued to govern the community to the end of his days about 615, if not later. Both were venerated as Saints and interred in one tomb.—The abbey of Dissentis, (or Disentis), founded about 612, still exists.

5. **Ven. Turketul,** abbot of Croyland in England, was related to the English kings, and was chancellor to Kings Athelstan, Edmund and Edred. When already advanced in years he visited Croyland, where he was entertained by the three only surviving monks of that once flourishing religious centre. Yielding to their pressing entreaties to remain and revive the glories of the past, he requested the king to dismiss him from his service and became a monk. Under his direction, Croyland recovered from its decline and became a model monastery. Abbot Turketul died in 975.

6. The Servant of God, Sister **Magdalen of the Blessed Sacrament** (Magdalen Frances de Justamond), a Cistercian nun at Avignon, born July 26, 1764, fell a victim to the French Terrorists on this day in 1794.

Translation: Paul Warnefrid; Adrewald; Mab.; K.L.
Hildulph: MS. of Moyenmoutier; Butler. Other forms: Hidulph and Hydulph.
Sigbert: Boll; Burgener and Stadler give the year 636 as the year of his death. Other forms of the name: Sigebert, Sigisbert, Sisbert.
Turketul: Mab.
Magdalen: Acta Ap. Sedis 1916. p. 230.

12

1. **St. John Gualbertus**, abbot, founder of the Order of Vallombrosa, was born at Florence, in Italy and was carefully instructed in religion and in various branches of human learning. Influenced by the example of worldly-minded companions, he indulged in the frivolities to which careless youths deliver themselves when they cast off the restraints of religion. His brother, Hugh, was slain by a nobleman and John undertook to avenge his death. On a Good Friday he met his brother's slayer in a narrow passage and was on the point of killing him, when the latter fell upon his knees, entreating him by the passion of our Lord, to spare his life. This appeal touched John so depply that he not only spared the man's life, but even offered him his friendship. Pursuing his way, he arrived at the monastery of San Miniato, where he felt an impulse to spend some time in the church in devout prayer. Shortly after, he called upon the abbot of San Miniato and asked to be admitted among the candidates for the Order. The abbot dreading the wrath of John's father was reluctant to grant his desire. In the mean time, the father came to the monastery and reproached his son bitterly for the step he was about to take, but observing that John was steadfast in his resolution, he blessed him and exhorted him to persevere. As a religious, John subdued his body with much fasting and watching. After the abbot's death, he was elected to succeed him, but he resolutely refused to accept the office, and some time after departed from the monastery to seek a place of solitude. At Vallombrosa he met two hermits who consented to assist him in establishing a Benedictine monastery in that place. The abbess of St. Hilary's near by, furnished the grounds. A monastery and church were built within a short time, and were dedicated by the bishop of Paderborn. John, although but a layman, was elected abbot. In the course of a few years he founded monasteries at St. Salvi, Moschetta, Passignano, Rozzuolo, and Monte Salario which, together with the motherhouse at Vallombrosa, formed a Congregation which was approved by Pope Alexander II in 1070. One of John's leading traits was his great love for the poor, to supply whose needs he would empty all the chests and granaries of his house. Having summoned all the superiors of the dependent houses, he delivered to them his final instructions and exhortations, devoutly received the last sacraments and expired on this day in 1073 at the age of seventy-four years. He was canonized by Pope Celestine III in 1193.

2. **St. Ansbald**, abbot of Pruem in the diocese of Trier, was successor to Abbot Egil, who resigned in 860. Ansbald, who died in 886, was always honored as a Saint.

3. **St. Leo**, abbot of Cava, Italy, was born at Lucca, studied at Salerno, but in order to ensure the salvation of his soul became a monk at Cava shortly after the establishment of that house and during the administration of the first abbot, Alferius. The latter, recognizing his virtue and splendid mental endowment, made him his assistant. After the death of Alferius, Leo was elected abbot in 1050. He taught his monks by deeds rather than by words; shared

---

John Gualbertus: B. Melanisius, Gen. of the Order; Butler.
Ansbald: Regino; Brouwer.

their toil and hardships, cut wood, carried it to the markets, sold it and distributed the money among the poor. Among his monks was his nephew Peter, who subsequently became bishop of Policastro and who succeeded Leo when the latter died in 1079. His veneration was approved by Pope Leo XIII on Dec. 19 and 21, 1893.

4. The Servant of God, Sister **Mary of St. Henry** (Margaret Eleanore de Justamond), born 1746, was a nun in a Cistercian convent at Avignon and fell a victim to the French Revolution on this day in 1794. Her sister was executed on the eleventh day of July.

13

1. **St. Mildred**, abbess, was a daughter of the Mercian king Merwald and of his wife Ermenburga. She was educated in the convent at Chelles near Paris and after her return to England was made abbess of Minstrey, which had recently been founded on the isle of Thanet by her pious mother. Mildred and seventy other maidens received the veil from archbishop Theodore of Canterbury and formed the first community. She ruled her sisters in the spirit of love by her example rather than by words and died about 700. Her relics were carried to St. Augustine's at Canterbury in 1033.

2. **Bl. Olbert**, abbot of St. James at Liege and of Gemblours, was a former monk of Lobbe and had been tutor of Bishop Burchard of Worms. His piety and learning were so conspicuous that he was called a "mirror of abbots and an ornament to the monastic state." He died in the odor of sanctity in 1048.

3. **Ven. Ernest** was the first abbot of Neresheim in Suabia. This monastery was founded in 1095, and Ernest with twelve other monks from Zwiefalten were installed as the first community. Some time after, he accompanied a body of Crusaders to the Holy Land, but fell into the hands of the Saracens and died in captivity in 1096.

14

1. **St. Vincent**, monk of Soignies in Hainaut, was born at Strepy near Binghen in Hainaut and espoused the virtuous Waldetrudis. Both Vincent and his wife, by whom he had four children, decided to enter the religious state. Vincent founded the monastery of Hautmont and there became a monk. When the growth of this house was assured and the community numbered as many as three hundred members, Vincent founded another monastery at Soignies, where he lived with a small community to the day of his death in 677. His remains and those of his son Landeric were buried at Soignies.

Leo: An abbot of Venosa; Acta S. Sedis v. 26. 369.
Mary of St. Henry: Acta Apost. Sedis. 1916. 228–231.
Mildred: Wm. of Malmesbury; Capgrave; Stanton, who gives the year of her death ca. 725.
    Other forms of the name: Mildreda, Mildrandis.
Olbert: Mabillon.
Ernest: Monumenta of Neresheim.
Vincent: Mab.; Boll.; he is also known as Madelgar.

2.   **St. Ulric**, prior of the Cell of SS. Peter and Paul in Breisgau, was descended from an illustrious family of Regensburg and consecrated himself early in life by making a vow of chastity.   The bishop of Freising ordained him deacon and provost of the cathedral.   Ulric filled this position conscientiously, reformed the lives of the clergy and was exceedingly generous in his alms to the poor.   While he was absent from Regensburg on a pilgrimage, a rumor was spread at home that he had died, and another provost was appointed in his place.   Now he resolved to serve God in some religious house far from the former scene of his labors, for which purpose he applied for admission to the monastery of Cluny.   He received the habit in that celebrated monastery and soon was recognized as one of the most zealous among the brethren.   Having been ordained a priest, Abbot Hugo appointed him confessor and master of novices.   The noble Hesso of Breisgau had founded a monastery, and abbot Hugo of Cluny sent Ulric with several other monks to organize the new establishment.   The locality in which the first settlement was made proved unsatisfactory, and Ulric exchanged it for another several miles south of Freiburg, where he built a monastery called *Cella sanctorum Apostolorum Petri el Pauli*, and, after his death, known as Ulrichszell.   At Bollschweil he founded a house for nuns.   Although always active, he was a lover of contemplation.   He possessed, in an eminent degree, the gift of tears.   One day a brother asked him, why he was weeping, and received this reply: "I weep in order to wash away the stains caused by my sins; I weep because so few of us are monks in deed though so many of us bear the name."   At the request of abbot William of Hirschau he compiled the "*Consuetudines Cluniacenses.*"   He died July 10, 1093 and was buried in the cloister of his monastery.

3.   **St. Marchelm**, monk of Deventer in the Netherlands, was born in England and received his early education from St. Gregory, who afterwards became abbot at Utrecht.   He made a journey to Rome, where he finished his theological studies.   Upon his return he was ordained a priest and sent into the Frisian mission, in which he persevered to the time of his death about 800.

15

1.   **St. Ansuerus**, abbot of St. George at Ratzeburg, in the principality of Mecklenburg, was slain together with thirty of his monks by pagan invaders about 1065.   These martyrs for the faith were stoned to death, Ansuerus at his own request being the last to suffer that he might encourage his brethren in their hour of trial.

2.   **St. David**, abbot at Snevingen, or Munktorp in Sweden, was a native of England and entered a monastery of the Congregation of Cluny.   Hearing of the death of several martyrs in Sweden, and burning with a desire to lay down his life for his faith, he departed for that country, where St. Sigfrid advised him to establish himself at Snevingen.   Here David organized a monastic

Ulric: Anonymous monk of St. Ulric.
Marchelm: Boll.; Stadler, who calls him "Marcellinus;" acc. to Stanton he was also called "Marculphus."
Ansuerus: Albert of Stade; Krantz; Ferrari.

community to second him in his missionary enterprises and ruled it for many years.   He died in peace about 1060.

3.   **Ven. Egino.** abbot at Augsburg, was born in that city and educated in the monsatery of SS. Ulric and Afra, of which he became a member in 1080. In consequence of dissensions among the local clergy, occasioned by the suspension of the intruded bishop Heriman in 1096, Egino left the city and went to St. Blasien in the Black Forest, where he made the acquaintance of Gebhard, bishop of Constance, who had been banished by Henry IV.   In 1109 the monks of SS. Ulric and Afra begged Egino to return and be their abbot.   After deliberation with his friend bishop Gebhard, he consented and within a short time repaired the harm wrought in the monastery by several unworthy abbots. Heriman, who had succeeded in persuading Pope Pascal II to reinstate him as bishop, failed to win the friendship of abbot Egino, and vented his wrath by driving the abbot and his monks out of the city.   The dispossessed religious were received at the abbey of Thierhaupten, where they remained a week, after which they returned to Augsburg at the request of the citizens.   A synod held in Mainz, in which complaint was made of the scandalous conduct of Heriman, sent Egino to Rome, where he received a kind reception from Pope Calixtus II. On his homeward journey, he was taken sick and died in a Camaldolese monastery at Pisa, in Italy, in 1122 and was buried in that city.

16

1.   **St. Fulrad,** abbot of St. Denis near Paris, was the son of count Riculf and of his wife Ermengarda and was born in Alsace.   Convinced that no earthly possession is as valuable as a human soul, he entered the abbey of St. Denis, of which he was made abbot.   He founded several monasteries, such as that at St. Hippolyt and that at Leberau in Alsace.   Kings Pepin, Carlmann and Charlemagne conferred upon him the office of grand-almoner and employed him in diplomatic missions.   He died in the year 784 and was interred at St. Denis; later his remains were removed to Leberau.

2.   **Bl. Irmengard,** first abbess of Frauen-Chiemsee, in Bavaria was the daughter of the German King Louis, and died reputed as a Saint in 866.

3.   **Ven. Ansoaldis,** abbess of Maubeuge, in Belgium, instructed her brother, Blessed Theodoric, or Thierry, who later was abbot of St. Hubert, in the rudiments of learning and in the Psalms.   Her life was a series of uninterrupted austerities; she never slept in a bed and ate nothing but bread and vegetables.   Tried and purified by suffering from cancer during seven years, she entered into the joy of her Lord about 1040.

4.   The Cistercians on this day celebrate the solemn commemoration of their founder **St. Stephen.**   Pope Benedict XIII, in 1724, granted a plenary Indulgence for this day.

David: Vastovius; Cl. Castellanus; Stanton.
Egino: Udalschalk; Braun; Stadler calls him Blessed.
Fulrad: Mab.   Leberau is now called Lievre.
Irmengard: Bucelin; Bruschius.
Ansoaldis: Mab.
Stephen: Brev. of Citeaux.

17

1. **St. Leo IV**, Pope, the son of a Roman nobleman, was educated in the monastery of St. Martin without the walls and was made priest of the church of the *Quatuor Coronati* by Pope Sergius II, whom he succeeded in the chair of Peter in 847. He governed the Church for eight years, three months and several days, during which time he repaired the damage wrought by the Saracen invaders. In order to prevent similar desecration of the resting place of the Apostles, he enclosed the whole Vatican hill with a wall and within it built the city quarter since that time called Leonine. Meanwhile the Saracens were preparing for another raid into Italy; the Neapolitans sent a body of troops to support the Romans. Pope Leo met these troops, blessed them and gave them Holy Communion with his own hands. In the battle that ensued the Saracens were defeated and the danger was averted. Pope Leo died in 855.

2. **St. Fredegand**, abbot of Kerkelodor (Deurne) near Antwerp, was a contemporary of St. Willibrord and labored many years for the salvation of souls. He died about 730 and was always honored as a saint in the Low Countries. His remains reposed for a long time in his monastery, but were scattered by the Normans. At Antwerp he was invoked for protection against pestilence.

3. **Bl. Benignus**, abbot and General of the Order of Vallombrosa, was born at Montevalchi about 1136, and after his ordination to the priesthood was appointed pastor of the church at Fighini. He had a tender devotion to the Blessed Virgin and spent much time in prayer. He was repeatedly tempted to sin and was upon the point of yielding, when divine grace saved him from falling. This experience filled him with such shame that he resolved to spend his life in penance in the Order of Vallombrosa. At his earnest request, he was permitted to live as a hermit according to the statutes of the Order. From this retirement he was summoned to visit the monasteries of the Order and restore discipline where remissness had crept in; later was made abbot of St. Salvio and finally General of the Order. When this burden grew too heavy for him in his advanced age, he resigned the office at a General Chapter and withdrew to his hermitage, where he died, after receiving the last sacraments, in the year 1236. He wrote a book entitled "Claustrum animae."

18

1. **St. Bruno**, bishop of Segni, in Italy, was born at Solero in Piedmont about 1048 and received his education in the monastic school of St. Perpetua in the diocese of Asti. Having completed his studies in one of the celebrated schools at Bologna, he was appointed a canon at Siena. At a synod held in Rome in 1079, he defended the doctrine of the Real Presence with such ability that Berengarius was compelled to retract his erroneous views and teachings on this point. For this and other eminent services rendered the Church, Pope Gregory VII suggested Bruno for the episcopal see of Segni; he was elected and

Leo IV: Liber Pontificalis. Lives of Popes.
Fredegand: Boll.; Stad.
Benignus: MS. in Florence.

received with the greatest joy by the clergy and laity of his diocese. In 1095 he accompanied Pope Urban II to France and in the year following assisted at the council of Tours. In 1102 he was permitted to enter Monte Cassino as a monk and five years later was elected abbot. The Pope offered him the dignity of a cardinal, but Bruno was not a friend of high honors and declined. Pope Pascal II had, while in imprisonment, been compelled to make rather large concessions to emperor Henry V in the matter of investitures in the year 1111. Bruno and a number of cardinals and bishops raised their voices in protest against this action of the Pontiff, with the result that the latter, provoked by this opposition, commanded him to resign the abbacy, which he had retained, and return to Segni. Bruno readily obeyed, was received by his diocesans with every possible token of respect and love, and continued to rule them down to the year 1123, when he slept in peace. He has been styled "the brilliant defender of the Church." St. Bruno was the author of several works, chiefly scriptural and dogmatic. He was canonized by Pope Lucius III in 1183.

2. **Bl. Robert of Soleto** (Salentinus), was born at Soleto in the Abruzzi in 1272. His parents Thomas and Benevenuta were plain burghers, who provided their son with an education and kept a watchful eye on the development of his character. At the age of sixteen he joined St. Peter Celestine and received the religious habit from his hands. When Celestine was elected Pope, he invited Robert to follow him to Rome, but Robert was so strongly attached to the new life he was leading that he was permitted to continue his mortifications undisturbed. After his ordination in 1297, he lived for twelve years in a cell of the monastery of St. George on Rocca Moria. In the year 1311 he was permitted to live in seclusion with two brethren on Monte Piano. He received so many gifts and bequests that he was enabled to build fourteen monasteries and seven hospitals. The bishop of Chieti saw with great displeasure how Robert was prospering and laid claim to a part of his income. Robert appears to have had little ready money on hand, for he sold the very chalice of the church in order to be able to meet the bishop's exactions. The bishop called him a hypocrite and even excommunicated him, but Robert did not lose his calmness. His only reply was to beg the bishop for pardon, penance and absolution. Robert died in 1341 and was buried in the Celestine monastery of Monte Morone (or Murrone.)

3. **Alanus**, monk of Sassovivo in Italy, though possessed of much learning and piety, declined to receive the order of priesthood and lived alone in a cavern for a number of years to the day of his death in 1313.

19

1. **St. Ambrose Autpert**, abbot of St. Vincent on the Voltorno in the former kingdom of Naples, left the court of the Frankish kings to serve his Sovereign Lord in the peace of a monastery. He was abbot of the monastery for a little more than a year. As a writer, he is known as the author of a treatise

Bruno: Peter the Deacon; C.E.
Robert: MS. of a contemporary; John a Bosco; Telera. Stadler calls him Saint.
Alanus: Armellini.

on the Apocalypse. He incessantly prayed for wisdom and virtue, and rather for the latter than for the former. Full of years and merit, he rested from his labors in 778 or 779.

2. St. Aurea, nun of Cuteclara, in Spain, for a time yielded to flatteries and intimidations from the Moorish judges, but repenting of her weakness, made public profession of her faith and received the crown of martyrdom and virginity at Cordova in 856. Her remains and those of a number of other martyrs were thrown into the Guadalquivir.

3. Ven. Herman Contractus, monk of Reichenau, was born at Altshausen in Suabia in 1013 and was sent as a boy seven years of age to the abbey of Reichenau, where, although a cripple and unable to move about without assistance, he applied himself to study with so much diligence and success, that he was regarded as a prodigy of erudition. At the age of thirty, he took the monastic vows, and died eleven years later, in 1054. Among his many writings is a chronicle covering the entire Christian era down to his day. His learning did not puff him up with pride: his own physical infirmity constantly reminded him of his dependence upon the Giver of all gifts and this thought preserved him in proper humility.

4. Wibald, abbot of Stablo in the diocese of Liege, devoted himself to the service of God in the abbey of Vassour in Belgium and was so conspicuous for his virtue and ability that he was made abbot of Stablo. In 1137 he accompanied emperor Lothair to Italy and was appointed abbot of Monte Cassino in place of the abbot Raynald, who had been unlawfully elected. Several months later, however, the death of Lothair and the forcible intrusion of Raynald induced him to return to Stablo. He declined the archbishopric of Bremen, content to govern his abbey and to labor for his own salvation. Frederic I sent him on an embassy to Constantinople from which he never returned alive, having died —some say of poison— in Paphlagonia in the year 1158.

20

1. St. Wulmar, abbot of Samer near Boulogne in Picardy, was born in Picardy about 620. He left his affianced bride to take the religious habit at Hautmont, where he made such progress in his studies that he was selected to receive holy Orders. This elevation, far from making him proud, only served to increase his humility. He is said to have cleaned the shoes of the brethren during the night. After spending several years in the monastery as a priest he was, in view of his tried virtue, permitted to become a monastic hermit in a locality north of the monastery, where he found shelter in a hollow tree. Three days after his arrival, he was visited by a man who brought him food and offered him a parcel of ground upon which he might build a cell. Here he dwelt several years edifying the people by his example and miracles. In order to escape

Ambrose: MS. edited by Cajetani. C.E.
Aurea: St. Eulogius.
Herman: Ben. Annals: C.E.; Buchberger.
Wibald: Mabillon; M. Ott in C.E.

the visitors who sought him, he left about 677 and settled in a hut a mile from his native town, where he was discovered by his brother, who brought him food but could not persuade him to visit his home.   Numerous benefactions made it possible for him to found two monasteries, one for men and one for women. These monasteries had to contend with difficulties and privations for a time, but Wulmar spoke words of encouragement that reconciled the brethren with the poverty and want which they suffered.   Wulmar died in 700 or 710 and his settlement was the nucleus of the town of Samer (supposed to be a contraction of St. Wulmer, or Vulmar).

2.   **St. Ansegisus,** abbot of Fontenelle, diocese of Rouen, was born about 770 and received the religious habit from abbot Gerald of the same abbey. Charlemagne placed such reliance upon his learning and other gifts both of mind and heart, that he made him abbot of St. Sixt at Rheims and of St. Memius in the diocese of Chalons-sur-Marne.   The improvement visible in these houses was so gratifying to the monarch, that he appointed Ansegisus abbot of Flay and supervisor of imperial works.   From Flay he was promoted to Luxeuil in 817, and after the death of abbot Eginhard in 823, to Fontenelle, which he reformed with the aid of some zealous monks from Luxeuil.   He encouraged studies in his abbey and enriched its library with the works of the great Doctors of the Church.   His meritorious career was closed in the year 833 or 834.

3.   **St. Severa,** nun at St. Symphorian in Trier, was appointed abbess by the founder St. Modoald, her brother.   She governed the house in wisdom and holiness and died about 660.   In the days of archbishop Ludolph, her remains were removed to the church of St. Matthias at Trier.

21

1.   **SS. John** and **Benignus,** twin brothers, joined St. Hildulph when he laid the foundations to Moyenmoutier in the Vosges Mountains.   They were vested at the same time and strove in brotherly emulation to attain the heights of perfection.   John, the elder brother, was ordained a priest, Benignus, a deacon.   Shortly after the death of their beloved master, in 707, both were seized with a dangerous illness.   On the tenth day, John made inquiry regarding his brother, and when he learned that Benignus had just died, he also closed his eyes in death in the year 707.   They were both buried in one tomb.

2.   **St. Constantine,** abbot of Monte Cassino and disciple of our Holy Father St. Benedict, succeeded the latter in the government of that house in 543.   St. Gregory the Great, who was indebted to him for information about St. Benedict, calls Constantine a "most venerable man".   He died about 560 and was laid to rest near the tomb of the holy Founder.

Wulmar: MS. of Anchin; Stadler gives 697 as the year of his death.
Ansegisus: Chron. of Fontenelle; M. Ott. in CE.   Also called Ansigisus:
Severa: Lectionary of Trier.
John and *Benignus*: Life of St. Hildulph.
Constantine: Greg. Mag.; Mab.

3.   Ven. John Dederoth, of Muenden, (or of Northem), abbot and founder of the Congregation of Bursfeld in Saxony, was a monk of Reinhausen
near Mainz and, while listening to the earnest appeals made at the Council of
Constance in behalf of improvement of monastic discipline, resolved to enlist
his brethren in a movement in that direction.   Meeting with a cold response
from them, he turned to the devout duchess of Braunschweig, who prevailed
upon her husband Otto to grant John the declining abbey of Clauss (Clusa)
about 1430.   In consequence of his endeavors to introduce a radical reform, he
found himself without subjects.   Leaving Clauss, he gathered several novices
with whom he established a new community in the dilapidated monastery of
Bursfeld, of which only one aged monk survived.   He secured several exemplary monks from St. Matthias' in Trier, which had recently been reformed by
abbot John Rode, and thus laid the foundation of the Congregation of Bursfeld,
which was actually organized by his successor.   Abbot John died in 1462.

4.   Higbald, abbot of Barton in the diocese of Lincoln, England, a man
forgetful of self and intent only upon the glory of God and the welfare of the
brethren, lived and died in the 8th century.

22

1.   St. Wandregisilus, founder and first abbot of Fontenelle, was a relative of Pepin of Landen and Erchinwald, two great Austrasian lords.   In his
youth he was made count of the palace by King Dagobert I, yet remained humble
in the midst of honors and applause.   Complying with a wish of his parents, he
took to wife a virtuous lady, but on the day of marriage both consented to embrace the religious state.   Wandregisil took the habit at Montfaucon in Champagne in 629, and afterwards built a monastery on one of his estates called Eli-
sang.   In order to perfect himself in religious observance, he spent five years in
some of the most illustrious monastic houses, especially at Bobbio and in Rome.
After his return into France he spent ten years in the monastery of Romans on
the Isere, where the abbot had received him with great kindness.   With the
consent of the abbot, he was ordained a priest by St. Audoenus, bishop of
Rouen.   In 648 he founded Fontenelle, and within a short time saw himself at
the head of three hundred brethren.   His life was very austere; he slept little,
wore sackcloth, observed the Holy Rule to the minutest detail and labored with
the monks, whose numbers grew to such an amazing extent that several other
monasteries had to be built for them.   He died after an illness of three days at
the age of ninety-six years in 666, and was buried in the church of St. Peter;
after several translations, the relics were lost in the religious wars in 1578.

2.   St. Meneleus, abbot of Menat near Clermont in Auvergne, descended
from illustrious parentage in Anjou and was noted for unusual piety in childhood.   Rather than take the wife selected for him, he left privately a short
time before the day set for the marriage, and accompanied by two friends of
similar disposition, became a monk at Carmery, then governed by St. Theofred.

John Dederoth: Trithemius; Stadler.
Higbald: Bede; Marcellin.
Wandregisil: contemporary monk of Fontenelle; Butler: "Vandrille."

Seven years later he settled at Menat in the valley of Vavere, where he was visited by his mother, sister and bride, for whom he built cells near by. This aroused the anger of Barontus, his bride's father, who raised his arm to do violence to the Saint, but was paralyzed in the act, and did not recover the use of his limb till he had prayed the Saint for forgiveness. From that day Barontus was the friend of Meneleus and liberally supported his foundations. Meneleus, foreseeing the hour of his death, appointed a monk to succeed him as head of the community, and died in the year 720. He is venerated in Auvergne and Anjou, where he is known as S. Menelee.

3. **Bl. Godfrey**, bishop of Langres in France, had been a Cistercian monk at Clairvaux, of which he was appointed prior by St. Bernard. He accepted the mitre of Langres only at the express command of the Pope, and ruled the diocese from 1140–1163, then resigned, returned to Clairvaux, compiled the three last books of the life of St. Bernard, and died a holy death in 1165.

23

1. **St. Offa**, abbess of St. Peter's in Benevento, in Italy, had lived several years in seclusion on a hill near Capua and gained such a high reputation for sanctity that she was called to rule the house above mentioned. She was distinguished for her love of Christ crucified and for her mortification; even in time of sickness she subsisted on vegetable food only. She died in the presence of her sisters in the year 1070.

2. **Ven. Apollinaris**, dean at Monte Cassino, entered that monastery at an early age, and was master of novices for thirty years. His distinguishing traits were regularity, simplicity, amiability; moreover he was well versed in Holy Scripture, the Fathers and theology. In his humility, he declined all other distinctions and offices. He died in 1581.

3. The **Spanish Congregation** of Benedictines was established in 1454 through the efforts of the Ven. Abbot Garcia de Cisneros. From the fact that the central house of the reform was at Valladolid, this body was also known as the Congregation of Valladolid (*Vallisoletana*). Some of its monks were sent to South America and Mexico, but met with scant success.

24

1. **St. Godo**, nephew and disciple of St. Wandregisil, received the habit at Fontenelle from the saintly founder of that house and was later sent by him to Rome, whence he brought many precious relics and a copy of the works of St. Gregory the Great. Having proved by his exemplary obedience that he was qualified to command, he built the monastery of Oye, and ruled a community

---

Meneleus: Mon. of Menat; Butler: "St. Meneve."
Godfrey: C. de Perales; Bernard of Bonnevaux; Stadler; "Godefredus."
Offa: Desiderius of Monte Cassino; Peter Damian. Lechner observes that her name does not occur in church calendars and that the present date is assigned to her arbitrarily.
Apollinaris: Schindele; Ziegelbauer.
Span. Cong.: Ben. Annals.

of three-hundred brethren. He prayed without ceasing and diligently exhorted his monks to persevere in the school of Christ. He died about 690.

2. **Bl. Sigolena**, abbess of Troclar in Languedoc, was descended from a noble family in Aquitaine, and was married in 710 to a noble named Gisluf, after whose death she became a deaconess. Not content with this sacrifice, she desired to leave the country and enter a convent. Her father, yielding to her desire, but preferring to have her abide in the country of her birth, built a convent at Troclar, in which she took up her permanent abode and governed a numerous family of spiritual children. Although mother and superior, she was the servant of all. Her charity knew no bounds; she afflicted her body with penances and kept her heart constantly uplifted to God in prayer. She died about 750 amid the tears and lamentations of all within and without the convent. Her remains were at first buried in a chapel near by, but were later transferred to the cathedral of Albi. The city of Albi chose her for its patron saint.

25

1. **St. Theodemir**, monk of Carmona, in Spain, died as a martyr at Cordova during the Moorish persecution in 851.

2. **St. Clodesindis**, abbess at Metz, was the daughter of Wintro, an Austrasian nobleman, and of his wife Gudila. She had early in life consecrated herself to God by a life of virginity, but was nevertheless urged by her parents to enter the married state. The first bridegroom was carried off a short time before the wedding, tried on certain charges and executed. Her father then arranged another marriage for her, which she sought to escape by taking refuge in the church of St. Stephen at Metz. The church was besieged by her father for a week, after which, when it was evident that her purpose could not be shaken, she was permitted to take the veil. After some time spent in Trier with her cousin Rotlinda, who instructed her in the elements of the monastic life, she returned to Metz and established herself in a locality granted by her parents. Here she built a convent and ruled a community of one hundred sisters with great prudence and piety for the short space of only six years, when the Lord called her unto Himself in the thirtieth year of her age about the year 610. Her remains were buried in the cemetery of St. Arnoul outside of the city, but were later translated to the abbey church of St. Arnulph.

26

1. **St. Simeon**, a Basilian monk, hermit at the Benedictine abbey of Polirone, in Italy, came from Armenia, which country he had left in order to escape compulsion to marry. He became a monk in an eastern monastery, and after taking the order of deaconship, was permitted to live as a hermit in the company of two other brethren. Some years later he made a pilgrimage to Jerusalem

---

Godo: C. Espence in Mab.; Boll.
Sigolena: Mab. Also called Segolina.
Theodemir: St. Eulogius.
Clodesindis: Mab.; Boll. Also called Glodesindis.

and thence to Rome, where his peculiar garb drew upon him the suspicion of being a Manichean. Continuing his peregrinations—through Italy, Spain, France—he finally stopped at Polirone, where abbot Venerandus permitted him to dwell as a hermit under the obedience of the superior of that house. He lived a holy, mortified life in his cell for twenty five years and died in 1016. Pope Benedict VIII canonized him (between 1016–1024).

2. **Ulfo,** a Swedish prince and husband of St. Birgitta, spent the declining years of his life as a Cistercian monk in the monastery of Alvastra in Sweden, and died in the year 1344.

27

1. **St. Berthold,** abbot of Steyergarsten in Upper Austria, was born about 1090 and became a monk at St. Blasien in the Black Forest, where he displayed such ability and piety, that he was first appointed prior in that monastery, subsequently was sent to act in the same capacity at Goettweig, and finally was elected abbot of Garsten in 1131. To his community he was both father and ruler, teaching his monks by his edifying example. He was given to severe austerities and was so emaciated in consequence of fasting that he appeared to be only skin and bones. One of his favorite employments was hearing the confessions of the faithful, who flocked to him in great numbers, especially on feasts, so that he was obliged to celebrate Holy Mass at a late hour, as it was his practice to hear all the penitents who thronged about his confessional. One day he ordered the cellarer to give a beggar a piece of money, but was told there was none at hand. He entered the monastery, opened the chest and found that it contained a number of coins. These he would not touch, but considered them unclean and ordered them to be thrown into the river. In 1124, when he was invited to attend the funeral of Abbot Godfrey of Admont, he said to the bearers of the message: "Return home, your abbot is recovering and will live. But tell him to come at once, if he receives news of me." The abbot of Admont recovered; Berthold was shortly afterwards prostrated by a mortal illness. He heard the confessions of his religious, gave them touching admonitions, recommended his chaplain Eberhard as his successor and died in 1142. The burial was conducted by abbot Godfrey.

2. **Christian,** Cistercian monk of Notre Dame d'Aumone at Chartres, was originally a hermit, but having heard of the newly founded Order of Citeaux, joined its monks and died after a long and bitter struggle with the enemies of salvation in the course of the 12th century.

28

1. **Bl. Salvius,** monk of Monte Cassino, was a native of Campania, and was given charge of the church of St. Clement at Piombata near Cassino. He

Simeon: Anonym. monk of Polirone.
Ulfo: Seguin; Surius.
Berthold: Studien & Mitt. 1880; St. Bened. Stimmen, 1881; Seeboeck: Herrlichkeiten der kath. Kirche.
Christian: Vincent of Beauvais; Barnabas of Montalbo.

was a very virtuous monk and holy priest, and died in the reputation of sanctity in the 9th century.

2. **Bl. Jerome of Prague,** a Camaldolese monk, after spending twenty years in the eremitical life, was sent to preach the Gospel to the heathens in Lithuania, Aeneas Silvius,—who subsequently became Pope Pius II—met him at the Council of Basel and heard from his own lips the story of his hardships, which Heaven had blessed with glorious success. He died at Venice, July 17, 1440.

3. **Guichard,** archbishop of Lyons, entered the Order of Citeaux in the days of St. Bernard and was singled out, for his piety and other good qualities, to rule the abbey of Pontigny. When the see of Lyons became vacant in 1165, he was chosen to preside over that celebrated church. For fifteen years he proved to be an apostolic prelate, assiduous in preaching the word of God, visiting the sick and the poor, and losing no opportunity to improve himself in the company of learned and prudent men. Rich in virtue and merits he died in 1180.

4. The **Austrian Congregation** was approved on this day in 1625 by Pope Urban VIII.

29

1. **Bl. Urban II,** Pope (Otto or Odo de Lagery, or de Chatillon), was born in France about 1036 and was made a canon of Rheims. Following a call of grace, he left the world and all its prospects and entered the monastery of Cluny, which at that time was governed by abbot St. Hugo. The monk Otto's virtue may be inferred from the fact that he was made prior of this famous institution. Pope Gregory VII, his former confrere, created him cardinal and bishop of Ostia, and sought his advice in all important matters. In 1082 he was sent as legate to France and Germany, and on his journey back to Rome was for some time held a prisoner by Henry IV. When Gregory VII lay on his deathbed, he pointed out cardinal Otto as best qualified, next to Desiderius, abbot of Monte Cassino, to fill the chair of Peter. The cardinals accordingly elected Desiderius, who took the name of Victor III, and upon his death in 1088 elevated Otto to the papacy, as Urban II. Among the councils convoked by him, the most notable is that of Clermont in 1095, at which he called upon the Christian princes to rescue the holy places in the East from the hands of the Saracens. He raised his voice in the same cause for the last time in a council held at Rome in April 1099. Three months later the Crusaders captured Jerusalem, but Pope Urban was dead before the news reached him; he died on July 29th of the same year.

2. **Ven. Halinard,** archbishop of Lyons, was born in Burgundy, carefully educated and at an early age made a canon of Langres. Complying with

---

Salvius: Leo Marsicanus. Acc. to Lechner this date is arbitrarily chosen.
Jerome: Boll.; Stadler. This date is also arbitrarily chosen.
Guichard: Barnabas of Montalbo; J. Chenu.
Austrian Cong.: Chron. of Salzburg.
Urban II: Mab.; C.E., K.L. His veneration was approved July 12, 1881. Acta Sanctae Sedis. 1881.

an impulse to aspire to greater perfection, he entered a monastery, from which his parents, with the consent of the bishop, removed him by force. He now was more resolved than ever to devote himself to the monastic state, and to carry out his purpose fled to another country and took the religious habit. When he had been found and brought back to the bishop, who esteemed him highly, the prelate was convinced that Halinard was called to the religious life, and withdrew his objections. Halinard now joined the monks at St. Benigne at Dijon, where he was appointed prior in 1028 and abbot four years later. In the monastery he was distinguished for his prudence, zeal and regularity. Henry III offered him the see of Lyons, but his humility bade him to decline the nomination, and to suggest Odalric for the place. After Odalric's death five years later, Halinard was obliged to accede to the wishes of Pope, prince and people, and became archbishop of Lyons in 1044. He accepted the appointment under obedience, but refused to take the oath of allegiance, saying: "If I should prove disobedient to the laws of my heavenly King and of the Holy Rule, who will believe that I will keep an oath made to the emperor? " The emperor did not press the matter and Halinard was allowed to proceed unmolested. He was trusted and honored by Pope Leo IX, whom he accompanied to Rome and on several other journeys, and died in 1052.

3. **Alexander,** abbot of Citeaux, had previously been a canon at Cologne and had gained an enviable reputation as a teacher. One day while conversing with St. Bernard on religious perfection and the monastic state he remarked: "I think of nothing less than of being a monk." Some time later, a thrice repeated dream prompted him to follow in St. Bernard's footsteps. He received the religious habit, was sent into Gascony to establish the monastery of Grandselve, and was finally chosen abbot of Citeaux and General of the Order in 1164. He died a holy death in 1175.

4. **Ven. Beatrice,** a Cistercian nun of Nazareth, in the diocese of Malines, led an extremely mortified life and was favored with many remarkable graces. She died in 1250.

30

1. **St. Tatwin,** archbishop of Canterbury, was taken from the abbey of Bredon in Mercia to occupy the see of St. Augustine. A controversy with the archbishop of York touching the primacy of Canterbury induced him to visit Rome, where Pope Gregory III gave him the pallium and recognized him as primate of England. After governing his church with zeal and profit to his flock, he was called to his reward in 734, and was always honored as a Saint.

2. **St. Hathebrand,** abbot of Old Kloster, or Feldwerth, was born in Frisia and educated for the priesthood. After his ordination he took the religious habit and lived the life of a monk, although there were no monasteries in

Halinard: Chron. of St. Benigne.
Alexander: Exordium Cist.; B. de Brito.
Beatrice: Gillemann; A. Le Mire.
Tatwin: V. Bede. Other forms: Tatuini, Tadwin.

his country.   He was soon joined by two monks, Frederic of Mariengarten and Tacho, with whom he organized a small monastic community which found ample means of subsistence in the alms of the faithful.   Hathebrand was elected abbot of Old Kloster and was installed by the bishop of Muenster.   He presided over his monks with discretion and holiness, was given to prayer, fasting and watchings and insisted upon regular observance.   It appears that some of the brethren chafed under the yoke, but became submissive, overawed by his charity, firmness and example.   After leading his brethren and many of the faithful in the path of righteousness, he died in 1198.   In 1619 his relics were transferred to the monastery of St. Salvator at Antwerp.

31

1.   St. Neot, abbot, is said to have been related to King Alfred and was born in England.   He was small of stature, yet towered above many of his countrymen by his erudition.   Of his own accord he became a monk at Glastonbury, and was ordained a priest.   Fearing peril to his soul from popularity, he requested leave to depart from the community and established himself as a hermit in Cornwall, where he dwelt in solitude with but one companion.   After seven years he visited Rome, and upon his return founded a monastery which later was known by his name.   Men of all stations of life applied for admission, even nobles of the realm came to be led heavenward by his hand.   Having set his brethren an example of wonderful devotion and charity, he died in 877.   His remains were later carried to Einsbury in Huntingdonshire, where a monastery bearing his name was founded.   A part of his relics was brought to the abbey of Croyland.   Two towns—one in Cornwall and another in Huntingdonshire— preserve his memory in their name.

2.   Godefrid (van Cortebeke), a Cistercian monk at Villers in Brabant, was first a monk at Afflighem, but was so strongly attracted by the reform of Citeaux, that he obtained leave to join the community of Villers.   He attained such a perfection of virtue that all were amazed and regarded him as a model of sanctity.   He died about 1170.

Hathebrand: Saussay; Le Mire.
Neot: Mab.; Boll.
Godefrid: Chron. of Villers.

August

1

1. St. Ethelwold, bishop of Winchester, England, shares with SS. Dunstan and Oswald the merit of having rescued the church in England from its rapid decline in the tenth century. He was a native of Winchester and of distinguished birth, was esteemed by King Athelstan and, on his recommendation, received tonsure from St. Elphege, bishop of that city. Before long he joined St. Dunstan at Glastonbury and was made dean of that abbey. St. Dunstan was favored with a dream, or vision, in which the future greatness of his disciple was revealed to him. Not only did Ethelwold advance in piety while a monk, but at the same time he made progress in learning, so that, when King Edred sought for a worthy superior for the monastery of Abingdon, he could find no fitter person than Ethelwold. When Edgar became king, and Dunstan was primate, Ethelwold was chosen to fill the see of Winchester. His first attention after receiving consecration was devoted to his own cathedral church; finding the clergy hopelessly relaxed and unmindful of their high calling, he removed them and substituted a community of monks. The same was done at the New Monastery, near the cathedral, which had been founded for St. Grimbald in the days of King Alfred. He also founded, or restored, a community of religious women in the city, and provided a sufficient maintenance for these institutions. He became possessor of the abbeys of Ely and Thorney, both in ruins for many years past, and repeopled them with monks about 970. Peterborough abbey, also, in great measure owes its renewal to him, as he was the chief adviser of chancellor Adulph, who undertook to restore that monastery. Ethelwold ruled his diocese for twenty-two years with unwearied zeal and charity, and so numerous were his miracles, that it was doubtful whether he or his holy predecessor Swithin was more powerful in this respect. His devotion to the poor was shown in a season of terrible famine, when, besides other efforts to save the perishing, he caused the sacred vessels to be broken up and sold on their behalf. He died in 984 at the abbey of Abingdon and was interred in the cathedral at Winchester.

2. St. Jonatus. a disciple of St. Amandus, was appointed by the latter as abbot of Marchienne, which had been founded with means supplied by one Adelbald in 645. In 650, Jonatus was also appointed to govern the monastery of Elnon and, two years later, to direct the convent built at Marchienne by Adelbald's wife, St. Rictrudis. His meritorious career closed about the year 690.

3. Ven. Theodoric, abbot of St. Evroul in the diocese of Seez, in France, was at first a monk of Jumiege, where he was noted for his mortification, particularly for his indifference to cold. He was made abbot of St. Evroul, but had to suffer much from malicious men. Every moment of his time was spent in some useful employment, and he encouraged his monks to flee idleness. Partly in order to satisfy his devotion, and partly to withdraw himself from annoyance

Ethelwold: Stanton; Wulstan. Called Athelwold in Gams (Ser. Epp.)
Jonatus: Chron. of Marchienne.

by his enemies, he made a pilgrimage to the Holy Land in the company of a Bavarian bishop. On the island of Cyprus, Theodoric was befallen by illness in a church, and died lying at the foot of the altar in 1058.

4. In 1604 took place the translation and beatification of the **Vallombro-san monks**—six of whom had been Generals of the Order—Rudolph, Rusticus and Erizzo of Florence, Albert, Jerome, Melior of Valiana, Benignus Benizzi of Florence, Orlandus, Thesaurus Beccheria of Pavia and Michael Flammini of Arezzo.

2

1. **St. Peter**, bishop of Osma in Spain, was born in the district of Berry in France, spent several years in military camps, and finally severed his connection with earthly prospects by entering the monastery of Cluny. When archbishop Bernard of Toledo, also a former monk of Cluny, came to secure some of the brethren for Spain, he took with him Peter, who for a short time ruled the monastery at Sahagun, the first Cluniacensian house in Spain, but in 1096 was made archdeacon of Toledo. His wisdom, piety and zeal were so well known that he was appointed bishop of Osma four years later. He rebuilt the cathedral, but was even more solicitous to rear a worthy spiritual edifice. Peter was about to seek for rest after a well-spent, laborious career, when in 1109 he was summoned to the deathbed of King Alphonse at Toledo, whom he assisted in his supreme struggle. He accompanied the funeral escort, but was taken sick at Palencia, where he died in the same year. His remains were entombed at Osma.

2. **St. Etheldrita**, recluse, was the daughter of Offa, king of Mercia, and was born about 770. She was betrothed to the blessed prince Ethelbert, who was cruelly murdered by order of her parents when he came to court to celebrate the marriage. Etheldrita was filled with horror at the perpetration of this crime and without delay resolved to consecrate herself to God in penance and prayer. She withdrew to Croyland, where she lived forty years in a cell adjoining the church and died in 834.

3

1. **St. Peter**, bishop of Anagni, Italy, was descended fom a distinguished family of Salerno and was educated by his uncle, an abbot in that city. Later he took the religious habit and displayed such commendable traits of character, that cardinal Hildebrand brought him to the notice of the Pope, Alexander II, who called him to Rome, appointed him one of his chaplains, and in 1062 bishop of Anagni. Peter devoted himself with great energy to the spiritual and temporal interests of his see. Entertaining some doubt that the relics of the martyr bishop St. Magnus reposed in his cathedral, he was satisfied by a miracle wrought through the intercession of the latter. In a vision Peter was informed by the

Theodoric: Odericus Vitalis.
Rudolph: Boll.
Peter: MS. publ. by Tamayo.
Etheldrita: Boll.; Stanton; Dunbar; Butler. Other forms: Alfreda, Althryda.

same Saint that the Pope was about to send him to Constantinople to liberate emperor Michael from a corporal malady. The vision came true. Notwithstanding the irreproachable character of his life, he suffered much from personal antagonists. He accompanied a Crusade in 1097 and did not return till his patron St. Magnus ordered him to go back to Anagni. Here he died in 1105. His canonization by Pope Pascal II took place in 1109.

2. **St. Walthen**, Cistercian abbot of Melrose in Scotland, was the son of Simon de Liz, Earl of Northampton and Huntingdon, and, when he chose the religious state, abandoned the most brilliant prospects in the world. He entered the institute of the Canons Regular of St. Augustine at York, where he was shortly after ordained a priest, and made prior at Kirkham. While occupying this responsible post, he heard of the reputation which the Cistercian Order was enjoying on the Continent, and felt a desire to embrace the monastic state. Being encouraged by the advice of his friend, St. Aelred, abbot of Rieval, he took the habit at Wardon, a Cistercian house in Bedfordshire, although the Canons endeavorsd to retain him at Kirkham priory. Simon, the Saint's brother, alleging that the practices of the Cistercians were too austere for his brother, employed the secular and ecclesiastical power to force him to leave the Order and threatened to destroy the monastery if he refused. Walthen was sent to Rieval that he might be out of his brother's reach. During the year of probation he suffered more from an interior trial than from the persecutions of his kindred; but his soul reaped plentiful spiritual advantages from the darkness and desolation that a kind Providence had seen fit to visit upon him for a hidden purpose. Four years after his profession, he was chosen abbot of Melrose on the Tweed in Scotland. He founded the monasteries of Kylos in Scotland and that of Holm-Cultram in England. By his liberal alms he supported the poor of the whole country round his abbey. In the famine of 1154, about four thousand poor people came and settled in huts near Melrose, for whom he provided food for several months. In the same year, he was chosen archbishop of St. Andrew's in Scotland, but by his tears and pleadings he persuaded his superior, abbot Aelred, not to oblige him to accept that dignity. After exhorting his brethren to charity and regular discipline, and having received the last sacraments, he calmly yielded up his soul to God on August 3, 1160.

3. **Bl. Gregory**, abbot of Nonantula, ruled that monastery from 914–929, in which year he withdrew and lived in obscurity for a very short time. As soon as his successor Engelbert had been installed, he returned and spent the last years of his life as a plain monk. He died reputed as a Saint in 933.

4. **Bl. Benno**, bishop of Metz, had been a canon of Strassburg, but laid aside that dignity to live as a hermit in the hermitage of St. Meinrad at Einsiedeln in Switzerland about 906. His example was followed by several other devout men; they cut down the forest and laid the foundations of the monastery of Einsiedeln, which was endowed with Benno's possessions on the island of Ufnau in the lake of Zurich and the grant of an estate called Sirenze. Benno's

Peter: Vivianus; Fontanini.
Walten: Boll.; Butler; Stanton (Aug. 9. "Waltheof"). Also Walthen or Walene.
Gregory: Ughelli; Wion.

holiness was known abroad; in 927 the canons of Metz elected him bishop; the emperor consented, and Benno accepted with the greatest reluctance. His fiery zeal provoked the wrath of some of the people, who seized him, put out his eyes and maimed him. Benno bore the affliction with patience, but resigned his see and returned to Einsiedeln, where he died a peaceful death in 940.

4

1. **St. Raynerius,** a monk of Font Avellana, was appointed bishop of Cagli and later promoted to the archiepiscopal see of Spalato in Dalmatia. Some of the temporalities of his see were, at the time of his arrival at Spalato, in the hands of one who had acquired possession of them by fraud or violence. He turned for relief to Manuel Comnenus, the Eastern emperor. The latter assured him that he would be reinstated in all his rights, but on the homeward journey Raynerius was stoned to death at Montecrasso by his enemies in 1180. His remains were entombed in the church of St. Benedict outside the walls of Spalato. He enjoys great veneration in Dalmatia and in the Camaldolese Order.

2. **Thomas Lombard,** Cistercian priest, was born at Waterford, Ireland, entered the Cistercian Order in Spain in 1591 and after ordination was sent on the mission in his afflicted native land in 1602. He labored with wonderful zeal and energy and on one occasion even dared to hold a public procession with the Blessed Sacrament on the feast of Corpus Christi, prepared to die for the faith which he professed. He died in 1604, a martyr to charity, while visiting the people during a pestilence and contracting the sickness which brought on his early death.

5

1. **St. Abel,** archbishop of Rheims, came from England and spent some time at Lobbe, where he also ruled the community in the absence of Abbot Ermino, who devoted much of his time to apostolic labors. He was designated for the see of Rheims in 743 by St. Boniface and the choice was approved by Pepin the Short. During the seven years of his episcopate he was almost continually worried by enemies. Milo, the intruded archbishop of Trier, by his wiles succeeded in deposing him. Abel, welcoming the opportunity to embrace retirement, went back to Lobbe where he died in the odor of sanctity about 752.

2. **St. Sigirada,** widow and abbess of Notre Dame at Soissons, was the mother of bishop St. Leodegar of Autun and of St. Gerinus. She was shut up in the monastery of Notre Dame by Ebroin, who was persecuting all her family; her goods were confiscated and her son Gerinus stoned. Eventually she took the veil and was elected abbess. Her death occurred about 678.

Benno: F. Guillimann; Tschudi.
Raynerius: Boll.; Stocker; Suppl. to Roman Mart.
Thomas Lombard: Henriquez.
Abel: Fulcuin; Flodoard; Saussay.
Sigirada: Ben. Annals; Dunbar; Stadler.   Other forms: Sigrada, Segrete, Sigradiz, Sigrade.

3.   **Ven. John Feckenham,** last abbot of Westminster, was born in Worcestershire about 1515, became a monk at Evesham, studied at Oxford, and taught the junior monks in the monastery of his profession to the time of dissolution in 1540, when he received a pension of fifteen marks.   For some time he was chaplain to Bishop Bell of Worcester, and subsequently to Bishop Bonner of London.   He was sent to the Tower by Cranmer on the charge of defending the faith, but was temporarily released to hold disputations with the Protestants Jewel and bishop Hooper.   Having been discharged from prison after the accession of Queen Mary, the latter appointed him dean of St. Paul's in 1554.   In 1556 he was appointed abbot of the restored abbey of Westminster.   As a member of parliament he defended the privilege of sanctuary.   Elizabeth repaid the generosity he had showed her, by having him imprisoned in the Tower in 1560.   From this time to the end of his life, he was either in prison or in the custody of some Protestant prelate who tried to seduce him to conformity.   The last five years of his life were spent with a number of other confessors of the faith at Wisbeach castle, where he died in 1585.   Even Protestant writers praise his virtues, particularly his kindness of heart, gentleness and charity to the poor.

4.   **Ven. James Gerius,** a Camaldolese monk at Florence, was a man conspicuous for his mortification, self-denial and patience, and was regarded as a second Job by his brethren.   Even in the midst of bodily pains and suffering he would not ask for alleviation, but replied to all the questions of his attendants, saying: "I am doing well; God is too good to me; you are doing too much for me."   His soul took its flight heavenward in 1345.

6

1.   **St. Stephen Sanctius,** abbot of St. Peter's at Cardenna near Burgos in Spain, together with two hundred monks, suffered death at the hands of the Moors in 872.   Pope Clement VIII authorized their veneration in a brief of January 11, 1603.

2.   **Ven. Agibodus,** a monk of Bobbio, was spiritual director to a convent of nuns and is said to have had a glimpse of the splendor of Heaven a short time before he died.   After revealing this privilege to his brethren, he departed this life, in the 7th century.   His body was raised on August 31, 1482, for which reason some Benedictine martyrologies commemorate him on that day.

3.   **Ven. Eigil,** abbot of Fulda, although a prudent and wise prelate, never embarked in any enterprise without first consulting the brethren, and thus secured wonderful harmony and unanimity among them.   He had his tomb prepared during his lifetime and composed the epitaph.   Great was the sorrow of the entire community when he bade them a last farewell and breathed forth his soul in 822.   His memory was always revered at Fulda.

John Feckenham: Camden; Stapleton; Sander; Camm: Lives of Eng. Martyrs; Gillow.
James Gerius: Annals of Florence.
Stephen: Boll.·
Agibodus: Jonas of Bobbio; Mab.
Eigil: Mab.

4.   **Goderannus,** bishop of Saintes in France, was descended from a noble Frankish family and received his earliest training from his aunt.   He left his native city, Rheims, to pursue higher studies at the abbey of Hautvillers, where he was so unfavorably impressed by the discipline there prevailing, that he returned to Rheims to finish his studies at the monastery of St. Remy.   Here, too, he was disappointed for the same reason, and therefore decided to become a monk at Cluny about 1050.   Abbot Hugo was charmed with the virtues and talent of Goderannus and shortly appointed him his chaplain.   In 1060 he was made abbot of Maillezais near Poitiers, and ten years later Bishop of Saintes.   Four years later, in 1074, he was summoned to receive his eternal reward.

7

1.   **St. Donatus,** bishop of Besancon in France was the son of Duke Waldelenus and was the fruit of the prayers of St. Columban.   After receiving a pious training at home, he entered the monastery of Luxeuil.   At the age of thirty years he was made bishop of Besancon, but this elevation by no means changed the simplicity of his private life.   He always wore his religious habit, was generous to the poor, and founded the monastery of St. Paul, where the Rule of St. Benedict was observed together with that of St. Columban.   As his mother Flavia also founded a monastery, in which she and her daughter Sirudis took the veil and which she governed as abbess, he compiled a rule for them from the rule of St. Benedict and that of St. Caesarius.   Donatus died about 660 and was buried in the monastery of St. Paul.

2.   **Bl. Jordan Forzate,** abbot at Padua, was born in 1158 and early in life entered the monastery of S. Benedetto-Novelli at Padua.   As superior of this house, he was so influential that the government of the city was entrusted to him during a period of political dissension.   When Ezzelino entered the city in 1237 and succeeded in winning the senate for his party, the abbot was sent into prison.   After having been detained two years in the fortress of St. Zeno at Treviso, he was set free by emperor Frederic II, whereupon he betook himself to Venice, where he died at an advanced age about 1240.   His remains reposed twenty years in the convent of the Benedictine nuns at Venice, after which they were removed to Padua.   The frequency of miracles wrought at his tomb induced the senate to order an inquiry as to his sanctity.

8

1.   **St. Mummolus** was appointed second abbot of Fleury (S. Benoit-sur-Loire) which had been founded by abbot Leodebodus of Orleans.   Deeply grieved at the lamentable condition of Monte Cassino, which had been desolate for sixty years, he sent one of his monks, Aigulf, to search for the remains of St. Benedict and carry them to France.   Aigulf was successful and Fleury was for a long time in possession of the precious relics.   Mummolus died

---

Goderannus: Peter of Maillezais; Trithemius.
Donatus: Jonas, a disciple of Columban.
Jordan: Tomassinus; Boll.

at Bordeaux about 678 at the age of seventy years and was buried in the monastery of the Holy Cross in that city.

2. **St. Famianus,** Cistercian monk and hermit, was the son of Godschalk and Giumera, inhabitants of Cologne, and was born in 1090. At the age of eighteen, he set out on a pilgrimage to Rome; after which he visited other holy places in western Europe. For many years he dwelt as a recluse near a church of SS. Cosmas and Damian on the banks of the Minho in Spain, but when he heard of the rise of the Cistercians he applied for admission to that Order. It appears, however, that he wished to remain a hermit. About this time he also received ordination. Two years later, being now a well-tried soldier of Christ, he was permitted to make a pilgrimage to the Holy Land. Returning after three years, he was instructed in a vision to settle at Gallese on the banks of the Tiber. He obeyed and took lodgings there with a pious man named Ascarus, in whose house he became ill two weeks later and died on this day of the year 1150. At his own request he was buried in the garden of his host. Pope Adrian IV canonized him in 1154. A decree of the S.R.C. Dec. 3, 1701 authorized the Cistercians to celebrate this feast.

3. **Ven. Hartwich** was abbot of Tegernsee in Bavaria. That monastery had fallen a prey to the avarice of the mighty, who filled its halls with their women, menials and hounds. One day the house was struck by lightning and completely destroyed. Otto II, desirous of restoring it, invited Hartwich, a monk of St. Maximin at Trier, to be its first abbot. He was blessed by Bishop Abraham of Freising in 978 and labored successfully for the material and spiritual prosperity of the abbey, which he ruled for only four years, dying in 982.

9

1. **St. Maurilius,** archbishop of Rouen, the son of noble parents, studied at Rheims and Liege, and afterwards was appointed head master, or *scholasticus*, of the cathedral school at Halberstadt. Resigning this position, he became a Benedictine monk at Fecamp and a few years after obtained leave of his abbot, William, to make a pilgrimage to Italy, where he lived such an edifying life with his associate Gerbert that the Margrave Boniface appointed him abbot of La Badia in Florence. The monks of this house disliked him and appear to have tried to remove him. Like St. Benedict, abbot Maurilius left the misguided men and returned to the abbey of Fecamp. After Bishop Malgerius of Rouen had been deposed in 1055, Maurilius was chosen to succeed him. He held three councils, at one of which Pope Victor II presided in person. At his suggestion the bishops of Normandy defined their attitude towards the teachings of Berengarius by signing a profession of faith in which the doctrine of the Real Presence was formulated in clear terms. It was upon his advice, also, that St. Anselm embraced the religious life and became a monk at Bec in Normandy. Rich in good works, he expired in 1076.

Mummolus: Adrewald; Mab.; Migne-Petin. Other forms: Mommolus, Mommolin, Momble.
Famianus: Pennazzi; Stadler. His original name was Quardus.
Hartwich: Mab.
Maurilius: Orderic. Vitalis; Trithemius.

2. Bl. Harveus, monk of Vendome, with the permission of his abbot retired into solitude at Calonne in Anjou and there pointed out to many the right way to salvation. A devout English woman, named Eve, who lived as a recluse near the same church, seems to have been one of the pious souls under his spiritual direction. He died in 1093.

3. Ven. Hugo Norwold, bishop of Ely, and former abbot of Bury St. Edmund's, was a prelate renowned for his mild and amiable disposition. Matthew Paris calls him "the flower of the Benedictine Order, shining brilliantly as an abbot among abbots, and as a bishop among bishops; profuse in his hospitalility." He died in 1254.

4. Ven. Claudius Martin, monk of the Congregation of St. Maur, was born at Tours April 2, 1619, lost his father in early boyhood, but received a virtuous training from his mother. In 1641 he became a monk at Vendome; after being professed, he continued his studies at Tiron and finished them at Jumiege. His patience was severely tried by long continued headaches. Once while suffering in this way, his General, John Harel, ordered him to preach on the feast of the Assumption of Our Lady. He obeyed and was not troubled with headache from that day. In 1654 he was elected prior of the monastery of Blanc-Manteaux at Paris, and subsequently at Compiegne and Angers. He reformed the monastery of Bonnenouvelle at Rouen and in 1668 was elected assistant to the General, Bernard Audebert. At the General Chapter of 1687 he was president and would doubtless have been elected General, had not the king interposed his veto. In 1690 he was appointed prior of Marmoutier at Tours and died six years later, in 1696. The faithful reverently kissed his remains as if they were those of a Saint.

10

1. St. Hugo, bishop of Auxerre, was a descendant of the Counts of Semur and was educated in the abbey of Cluny under the supervision of his uncle, the Abbot Hugo. In due course of time he was professed in the same monastery, and in 1100 was elected abbot of St. Germain at Auxerre, in which position he preserved the humility that had distinguished him as a simple monk. He ruled his monks by his example rather than by words with such success that in 1115 he was considered eligible for the vacant episcopal see of Auxerre. Some of the canons and the king himself were not favorable to him, but the majority of the canons nevertheless cast their votes in his favor and compelled him to make a journey to Rome and secure the approval of the Holy See. Pope Pascal II received him with great kindness and conferred upon him the episcopal consecration. As bishop he delighted in making visits to monastic houses, and was particularly kind to the Cistercians. Once while visiting St. Bernard, he accompanied that Saint and the brethren into the field and helped them at cutting grain. Three Cistercian monasteries—Rigny, les Roches and Boras—were

Harveus: Mab.
Hugo: Wion. The Dic. of Nat. (Eng.) Biography has a two-page sketch of him under "Northwold, Hugo of."
Claude Martin: Martene.

founded in the diocese during his administration. So completely detached was he from flesh and blood, that he refused to appoint one of his nephews to a canonicate. On the day of his death, he said to the brethren: "Let us say the remaining Hours; after that I shall rest." He passed away after Complin in 1136.

2. **St. Malchus,** bishop of Lismore in Ireland, was a native of that country and entered a monastery at Winchester in England, where he served God with great fidelity. The fame of his virtue re-echoed in his native land and he was chosen bishop of Lismore, where he shone by his piety, prudence and learning. King Comarcus honored him by seeking his instruction and counsel, and Bishop Malachi held him in the highest esteem. Malchus entered into his well-earned rest about 1150.

3. **Ven. Erluin,** abbot of Gemblours in Brabant, was at first a secular priest, but as he always strove after that which is more perfect, he left the world to become a monk. His friend, a pious noble by the name of Guibert, founded the monastery of Gemblours, made Erluin the first abbot and himself took the habit as a religious under his obedience. Erluin was a peace-loving man and even succeeded in curbing the wild temper of Count Rayner of Hainaut, who subsequently entrusted to his care the neglected abbeys of Soignies and Lobbe. The monks, who had lived under the mismanagement of commendatory abbots for a long time, refused to acknowledge him; several conspired against him, laid violent hands upon him, blinded him, and sent him back to Gemblours. Erluin lived twenty eight years longer, edifying all by the patience with which he bore his affliction, and died 986.

11

1. **St. Agilberta,** abbess of Jouarre in the diocese of Meaux, had entered that monastery under the rule of her predecessor Theodechildis and succeeded her in the year 660. Bishop Philip Caspeau in 1627 raised her relics, and exposed them for veneration in a silver shrine.

2. **Daniel,** a Cistercian monk at Hemmenrode, was distinguished for his wonderful self-abnegation. Once in a vision Our Lord said to him: "Daniel, ask of Me what thou wilt, and thou shalt have it," Daniel replied: "Thy grace suffices; grant me the gift of tears when I meditate upon Thy sufferings." And the Lord said: "I grant thee that grace." From that day Daniel could not refrain from shedding copious tears whenever he dwelt upon the Lord's sacred Passion. Praying to the very last breath, he departed from this vale of tears in 1206.

3. **Seraphina Cajetana,** abbess at the convent of Monte Vergine at Syracuse in Sicily, left a comfortable home and wealthy parents to follow the Saviour in a life of renunciation and sacrifice. She lived and died in the 13th century.

Hugo: Labbe; Stadler; Chev.
Malchus: Boll.; St. Bernard; O'Hanlon.
Erluin: Boll.
Agilberta: Saussay; Mab.
Daniel: Barnabas de Montalbo; Caesarius of Heisterbach.
Seraphina: Menard.

12

1. **St. Porcarius,** abbot of Lerins, had been elected on account of his admirable qualities to succeed abbbot Silvanus in the government of that monastery.   In 731 Vandals from Africa appeared off the southern coast of France; Porcarius sent a number of junior monks, and the boys trained in the monastery, for safety to Italy, while he and the elder monks calmly awaited the end.   The cruel invaders slew the abbot and a great number of monks.   It appears that only four or five escaped the massacre; these returned to Lerins and interrred the remains of their brethren in 732.

2. **St. Cecilia,** abbess at Remiremont, was the daughter of St. Romaric, the founder of Remiremont, and with her sister followed the example of her father by embracing the religious state.   She ruled the community to the year 670 when she received her reward.   Her intercession was frequently sought by persons suffering from impaired eyesight.

13

1. **St. Eberhard,** first abbot of Ebersheimmuenster and founder of Murbach in Alsace, was highly respected by King Thierry I of France and by St. Odilia of Hohenburg, whose family he had instructed in the truths of religion. He received the recompense of the faithful servant in 690.

2. **St. Junian,** first abbot of Maire l'Evescau in France was born in the territory of Briou of distinguished parents and had the benefit of a sound education.   An impulse to consecrate himself entirely to Christ drove him into a solitude where he communed with God in prayer and devout reading.   He built a cell for himself at Chaulnay, where he received some charitable aid from Queen Radegundis.   His cell soon was frequented by numbers of devout persons who placed themselves under his spiritual direction.   After he had been ordained a priest, he grew still more popular, so that in the end he resolved to quit that locality.   He next took up his abode in the district of Chastelacher.   Accusations were preferred against him that he had presumed to settle on a royal domain, but Clothair, before whom he was summoned to appear, was so favorably impressed by his demeanor that he permitted the Saint to occupy as much ground as he chose.   Junian selected Maire (Mariacum) and there built a monastery which he ruled.   His love of retirement had not died out; occasionally he would withdraw from the monastery into solitude and finally built a cell at Chaulnay, in which he lived alone for many years.   His most docile and faithful pupil was Auremund, whom he proposed as his successor at Maire.   He died in 587, on the same day as St. Radegundis.   His remains were interred at Maire, but later removed to Noaille.

3. **St. Wigbert,** was a monk of either Glastonbury or Wimborne and was called to Germany by St. Boniface to assist him in his holy undertaking.   Shortly

---

Porcarius: Mab.
Cecilia: Mab.; Boll.   Also called Clara, and Gegoberga.
Eberhard: Mab.
Junian: Mab.; Boll.

after his arrival, he was appointed abbot of Fritzlar and somewhat later at Ordruf. In both places he restored excellent discipline and trained many zealous missionaries. Worn out by his labors, he obtained leave from St. Boniface to return to Fritzlar, where he did in peace in 747. Archbishop Lullus of Mainz translated his remains in 780 to Hersfeld, the celebrity and prosperity of which abbey was in a great measure due to the possession of this treasure.

4. **SS. Ludolph** and **Druthmar** were abbots of Corvey in Westphalia. The former began to rule the abbey in 965 and took great interest in the development of the monastic schools. Sons of the noblest families came to Corvey for their education. The abbey prospered as never before. Rich in merit and beloved by all, Ludolph departed this life in 983. Druthmar, who was installed as abbot in 1013, had been a monk of Lorsch and had been recommended by Bishop Meinwerk of Paderborn. At first the monks were reluctant to receive him, since he was a stranger; however his affability and other amiable traits soon won their respect and admiration. He ruled the abbey for many years and slept in peace on February 15, 1046. In 1662 the remains of both abbots were raised and entombed in a chapel.

14

1. **Bl. Eberhard,** first abbot of Einsiedeln in Switzerland, had been provost of the cathedral chapter at Strassburg and was of noble descent. For the love of God, he resigned his office and in 934 betook himself to the cell of St. Meinrad, which St. Benno had rescued from ruin in 906 and made the nucleus of a religious settlement. Eberhard's holy life attracted a number of fervent souls, for whom he built a monastery out of his own means. Hitherto the religious had lived in separate cabins sacttered about the wild country. Eberhard was truly a father to his monks, and a model of charity to the poor, for whose sustenance he purchased a copious supply of grain during the famine of 942. Many nobles sought the seclusion of Einsiedeln, among others Thietland, brother of Duke Burkard of Alemannia, who was Eberhard's successor as abbot. Eberhard had ruled wisely and faithfully for many years, when he was summoned to his reward in 958. After this time the cell of St. Meinrad was known as Eberhardzelle.

2. **Simeon,** a Vallombrosan monk and hermit, was unusually favored with the gift of contemplation and attained a high degree of perfection. He begged God not to be spared sufferings; his prayer was heard, but at the same time he received the grace to suffer cheerfully and patiently. He died in the odor of sanctity in 1509.

3. **Cassian Spiss,** monk of St. Ottilien in Bavaria, and Vicar Apostolic of Dar-es-Salam in East-Africa, was murdered together with four companions by rebellious natives while he was on a missionary journey to Ungoni in the year 1905. His companions were the laybrothers Gabriel Sonntag and Andrew Scholzen, and Sisters Felicitas Hiltner and Cordula Ebert.

Wigbert: Servatus Lupus of Ferrieres; Stanton; Butler.
Ludolph: Annals of Corbie. Stadler calls Ludolph "Saint" and Druthmar "Blessed."
Eberhard: Hartmann; Guillimann.
Simeon: Annals of Vallombrosa.
Cassian: Studien & Mitt. 1905; Heimbucher; Kath. Missionen.

1. **St. Arnulph,** abbot, and bishop of Soissons, was born about 1010 in Flanders and was known among the youth of his day to be as brave as he was strong. Disgusted with the empty joys of the world, he left his country with two esquires and received the habit at the hands of abbot Raynald in the monastery of St. Medard at Soissons, where he was made dispenser of alms to the poor. After the death of the recluse Grembold, he obtained leave to occupy his cell, in which he dwelt three years in perfect silence, water and coarse bread being his only food. In the meantime abbot Raynald had died, and one Pontius had been simoniacally intruded as his successor. As he displayed none of the traits of a "father and lord," but ruled tyrannically, the monks caused him to be deposed and elected Arnulph in his place. Arnulph, dreading such a responsibility, fled during the following night, but was discovered and was installed to the joy of the monks and of the citizens. Arnulph maintained the rights of his house by recovering several possessions forcibly wrested from it and personally visited all the tenants of the abbey. When King Philip I summoned the abbot to accompany him to war, Arnulph resigned. A prudent monk named Girald was elected in his place. Scarcely had Arnulph left, when Pontius appeared and violently ejected Girald. The latter then founded Sauve-majeur; Arnulph withdrew into solitude where God employed him as an instrument for the salvation of many. An intruder, Ursio, had occupied the see of Soissons for some time but the papal legate Hugo convoked a council at Meaux, which elected Arnulph as rightful bishop. He yielded with extreme reluctance, but was prevented from entering the city by Ursio's brother Gervasius, and was obliged to govern the see from some other place. At the request of Pope Gregory VII, he made peace between Count Robert of Flanders and his subjects, and founded the monastery of Aldenburg. He resigned his see and died at Aldenburg, lying on sack-cloth and ashes, in 1087. Several miracles regarded as genuine by a synod at Beauvais 1121, were wrought at his tomb.

2. **St. Altfried,** who was, as Trithemius says, a monk of Corvey, was made bishop of Hildesheim after the death of bishop Ebbo about 851. He built a cathedral, founded monasteries at Essen, Seligenstadt, and Asuede, and died at the last named place in 875.

3. **Bl. Rupert,** abbot of Ottobeuren in Suabia, had been prior of St. George's in the Black Forest, and was sent to Ottobeuren at the earnest request of the monks of this monastery. He shed many tears at his departure from St. George's and was installed as abbot at his arrival on November 7, 1102. In order to effect a thorough renovation of the house, he secured exemplary religious from other houses. Both the church and the abbey were rebuilt during his administration, and were dedicated on November 1, 1126 by bishops Herimann of Augsburg and Ulric of Constance. The monks observed the Rule of St. Benedict and statutes compiled from those of Cluny and Hirschau. Abbot

---

Arnulph: Hariulf of Aldenburg; Stadler; Butler: "Arnoul." He was canonized at the council of Beauvais, at which the papal legate, the cardinal bishop of Palestrina presided, in 1120. (Battandier, Annuaire Pont. 1903. 412.).

Altfried: Mab.; Wion; Stadler; Ebeling ("Alfried").

Rupert died in 1145. having governed wisely, patiently and in all charity for forty-three years.

16

1.   **St. Arnulph**, bishop of Metz, was born in France in the sixth century and held a position at court second to that of the mayor of the palace.   In the midst of splendor, honors and distractions he cultivated the virtues of a perfect Christian.   His wife Doda bore him two sons, one of whom, Cleodulph, became a Saint, the other, Ansegis, the founder of the Carolingian line of rulers.   Later in life Arnulph appeared at the court of Clothair, and it was about this time that he was elected Bishop of Metz.   He was consecrated in 614, and his wife took the veil at Trier.   Arnulph always wore a penitential garment and subsisted on the plainest of food.   When after the division of the realm, Dagobert I, the son of Clothair II, received the kingdom of Austrasia, Arnulph became the youthful ruler's tutor and chief minister, although bishop of Metz, but he was secretly longing for the day when he might serve God alone.   Life at court and implication in political affairs grew distasteful to him and the responsibilities of the episcopal office seemed greater than he could bear.   Hence he secured the appointment of a successor in the see of Metz, and together with St. Romaric went into the Vosges mountains, where they lived as hermits.   Here Arnulph died in 640 or 641, and was buried by his friend St. Romaric.   His remains were later transferred to Metz.

2.   **Bl. Lawrence**, called *Loricatus*, was born at Fanello in Apulia and lived a virtuous and upright life.   Having by accident killed a man, he was filled with such deep sadness that he voluntarily made a pilgrimage to Compostella, and at his return in 1209 made his abode in a cavern above the grotto once occupied by St. Benedict at Subjaco.   He subjected himself to the abbot of Subjaco and lived an austere penitential life.   When he had lived there sixteen years, Cardinal Hugolinus visited him and found him very ill.   At the prelate's suggestion, he mitigated his austerity.   His solitude was shared by one Amatus. He was at all times kind and hospitable to all that visited him.   He died after a penitential life of thirty-three years in 1243 and was interred in his cavern.   Public veneration of Bl. Lawrence was authorized in 1778.

3.   **Ven. Margaret**, abbess of Val de Grace, was active in the restoration of discipline in a number of French monasteries.   She devoted every leisure hour to the reading of Holy Scripture and other devout books.   Death closed her useful and edifying career on August 26, 1626 at Lizy in Berry, where she had just arrived to reform a convent.

17

1.   **St. John**, first bishop of Monte Marano in the former kingdom of Naples, had been a monk before his elevation to the episcopate in 1074 and had

Rupert: Braun; Feyerabend.
Arnulph: Mab.
Lawrence: Boll.
Margaret: Pez; Bucelin; Stadler (Aug. 26).

only accepted the election by order of Pope Gregory VII. His holy life was crowned by a holy death towards the end of the 11th century.

2. **St. Amor**, first abbot of Amorbach in the Odenwald, was a disciple of St. Pirmin and was so successful in his missionary efforts that Pirmin considered him worthier than any other to rule the brethren who formed a community in the Odenwald. A monastery was built for them by Count Rudhard and Duke Charles, and Amor made its first abbot. One of his friends and patrons was St. Burkard, bishop of Wuerzburg. Since he hoped that the monastery would exercise a benign influence upon the country, he spared no pains to improve its schools; at the same time he had a warm heart and an open purse for the sick and the poor. His tender devotion to the Blessed Virgin doubtless was the cause why his labors were rewarded with such abundant blessings. Amor died about 767 and was buried in the chapel of Our Lady at Amorsbrunn.

3. **Bl. Carlmann**, monk of Monte Cassino, was the eldest son of Charles Martell and of his wife Rotrudis. After his father's death he assumed the government of Austrasia, Suabia and Thuringia. Carlmann and his brother Pepin reigned together and supported one another in war until 747, when the former abdicated in favor of Pepin, made a pilgrimage to Rome, received the religious habit from the hands of Pope Zachary and founded a monastery on Monte Soracte. When the solitude of this spot was invaded by visitors who interfered with his devotions, he retired to Monte Cassino, which was then governed by its second founder, St. Petronax. Carlmann revealed neither his name nor his rank, but only said that he had come to do penance for his sins. One day, after he had professed, he was rather awkward at washing the dishes, for which reason the cook struck him three times. Carlmann's associate, aware of the rank once occupied by the chastised prince, incontinently repaid the cook in kind. The abbot called the avenger to account, and asked him why he had struck the cook. He answered : "Because I saw the most contemptible of men strike the best and most pious man the earth bears." When pressed to explain himself, he said: "He is Carlmann, once ruler of the Franks, who for the love of God has left the world." All the monks craved the prince's forgiveness, but he cast himself at their feet and accused himself as a sinner and a murderer. Like the other monks he performed menial tasks enjoined upon him, even herding the sheep. Having been sent by his abbot to France to negotiate with his brother concerning Lombardy, he died at Vienne in 755. Pepin sent the body in a coffin of gold to Monte Cassino, where it was entombed beneath the high altar.

4. **St. Donatus**, monk of Monte Vergine, in Italy, was born at Ripa Candida near Venosa in 1179, applied for the religious habit at the age of fifteen at the monastery of St. Onuphrius at Petina, and, although the monks were not inclined to receive him, did not desist from his request till it was granted. To the astonishment of all, he not only practiced all the customary austerities, but even excelled all and was a model of obedience, humility and self-denial. He died

---

John: Ughelli; Mab.; Boll.

Amor: Gropp; Eckhard; Mab. The monastery of Amorbach was secularized in 1803. According to O'Hanlon, Amor, or Amator, was a Scot or an Irishman.

Carlmann: Eginhard; Labbe; Mab.

at the early age of nineteen years in 1198. At the request of his parents, his remains were taken to Ripa Candida, a considerable relic being sent to Auleta, where his feast was also observed, as it was throughout the Order.

5. The new **Brazilian** Congregation was organized on this day in 1895 by monks of the Congregation of Beuron, who devote themselves, in part, to missionary labors. The original Congregation of Brazil was established in 1827 by Pope Leo XII.

18

1. **John**, was one of those fervent brethren who accompanied St. Robert of Molesme to Citeaux and was noted for his spirit of mortification. He is said never to have partaken of prepared food, fish or wine, and died about 1120.

2. **Bl. Balderic**, abbot of Montfaucon, while still pursuing a secular career, founded a monastery for nuns at Rheims. So signally was this pious enterprise blessed by Heaven, that Balderic next resolved to found a monastery for monks and chose the hill called Montfaucon, near Verdun, as the site for the new house, in which he governed a devout community. He maintained a spirit of piety and profound seriousness in his monks by frequently reminding them of the last things of man, which were the favorite themes of his meditations. After his holy death in 640 he was interred in the house he had founded at Rheims, but was later translated to Montfaucon.

19

1. **St. Bertulph**, abbot of Bobbio, was of illustrious descent and was closely related to St. Arnulph, bishop of Metz, whose holy life induced him to abandon the world and to take the habit from abbot Eustasius of Luxeuil. Once abbot Attala of Bobbio visited Luxeuil and was so favorably impressed by Bertulph that he invited him to his monastery in Italy. Bertulph went and in 627 was unanimously elected Attala's successor. He not only cherished piety and religious discipline, but manfully defended the monastery against the arbitrary interference of bishop Procus of Tortona. For his zeal in combatting Arianism, he was praised by Pope Honorius I, who spoke almost daily with Bertulph while the latter was visiting Rome. On his return he fell ill of a fever that threatened his life, but recovered miraculously and reached his monastery, in which he died 640.

20

1. **St. Bernard**, abbot of Clairvaux and Doctor of the Church, was born of noble Burgundian parents at the castle of Fontaines, near Dijon, in 1091. His mother Aletha offered him to God in his infancy and placed him with the secular canons at Chatillon-sur-Taine, for his education. Although his success in the

Donatus: Castus; Jordanus; Boll.
Braz. Cong.: Heimbucher; Familiae Confoed.; Acta Leonis XII. July 1. 1827, *"Inter gravissimus curas."*
John: Seguin.
Balderic: Mab.
Bertulph: Jonas of Bobbio.

study of letters won the admiration of his teachers, they were more deeply impressed by his virtue and his devotion to the Blessed Virgin. At the age of nineteen he lost his mother. He might have returned to Fontaines and delivered himself up to the gay life of youth in his day. Temptations were not wanting, but he had ready weapons at hand and never suffered the purity of his body or his soul to be sullied by compliance with the suggestions of the evil spirit. Robert of Molesme had recently founded the monastery of Citeaux. This foundation, aiming at the restoration of primitive Benedictine observance, appealed to Bernard, and one day in 1113 he stood at the gates of Citeaux with thirty other youthful nobles begging for admission. Among his companions were his own brothers Guido, Gerard, Bartholomew and Andrew and his uncle Galdric of Touillon. Abbot Stephen was overjoyed at this accession to his monastic family and found the new brethren to be sincere, enthusiastic religious. So completely had Bernard won the good opinion of abbot Stephen that in 1115 the latter sent him with twelve other monks to found the monastery of Clairvaux in the diocese of Langres. Work and austerities in a short time affected his health, and this experience taught him the expediency of mitigating the severity of the reform, especially with regard to external mortifications. Bernard's enlightened and prudent guidance was so successful that within a short time as many as seven hundred brethren stood under his direction, so that in 1118 he was in position to found the monasteries of Trois Fontaines and Fontenai in France, and of Tarouca in Portugal. Throughout his life he is said to have founded as many as one hundred and sixty monasteries in various parts of Europe. In 1145 he preached the second Crusade and bestowed the cross upon emperor Conrad III, but was disconsolate at the failure of that movement. Towards the end of his life, his infirmities increased, but although his body wasted away his mind was bright and active to the day of his death in 1153. Alexander III canonized him on January 18, 1174 and Pope Pius VIII conferred upon him the title of a Doctor of the Church on August 20, 1830.

2. **SS. Leovigild** and **Christopher** were monks who suffered death for the faith at Cordova, in Spain, at the hands of the Moors, in 852.

3. **St. Philibert**, abbot of Nermoutier in Poitou, was born in Gascony, and early in life came to the court of Clothair II. Here he met St. Audoenus, whose virtues and conversation moved him to become a monk at Rebais in the diocese of Meaux. After the death of Abbot Agil, Philibert ruled the monastery for a short time, but withdrew when he found that he could not prevail against the perverseness of some of the brethren. He visited several monasteries of good repute, and in 654 founded Jumiege, which within a short time was the abode of nine hundred monks. At Pavilly he founded a monastery for women and appointed Austreberta its first abbess. In consequence of having incurred the displeasure of the majordomo Ebroin and of St. Audoenus, he retired to the island of Her and founded Nermoutier (Noiremoutier) which he governed to the time of his death in 684. During the Norman invasion his remains were carried to Tournus in the diocese of Macon.

Bernard: Wm. of St. Thierry; Arnold of Bonnevaux; Life by Ratisbonne. Bibliography in Chevalier.
Leovigild: Mab.; Boll.
Philibert: Chifflet; Mab.

4. **Bl. Gobert**, a Cistercian monk of Villers in Brabant, was a count of Aspremont, born about 1187 and had been a Crusader. Obedient to a call of grace he had laid aside his arms in 1139 and become a monk at Villers. He was a determined enemy of detraction and slander and a model of humility. His death occurred in 1163.

5. **St. Bernard**, a Cistercian monk in the monastery of Val-de-Iglesias in the province of Estremadura, Spain, lived a holy life in the 12th century and was venerated after his death.

21

1. **St. Bernard**, monk and martyr, was the son of Almansur, vice-gerent of a Moorish prince at Valencia, Spain, and occupied a distinguished position at court. Once, being sent to Barcelona to ransom Moorish prisoners, he and his companions lost their way and were obliged to spend the night in the woods. They heard many harmonious voices chanting for two hours and at dawn came upon a group of cells at Poplet. Curious to learn what manner of men might dwell there, he was struck with wonder to see them walking about in white garments and employed in various pursuits. He dismissed his companions, sought instruction in the truths of the Christian religion, was baptized and received the Cistercian habit. His familiarity with the management of affairs proved of valuable service to the settlement, which he served as procurator. He converted his aunt and two sisters but failed to win his brother, at whose hands he suffered death for the faith in 1180. His remains were taken to Alcira, where they were always venerated.

2. **Bl. Bernard Tolomei**, founder of the Congregation of Our Lady of Monte Oliveto, was born at Siena in 1272, received the name of John at baptism and was educated by his uncle, the Dominican Christopher Tolomei. Had he followed his own inclinations, he should have become a Dominican, but his father would not approve of such a step. Therefore he joined a pious lay congregation and at the same time pursued his legal studies, finally graduating as Doctor in both canon and civil law. For some time he was with the armies of emperor Rudolph, and on his return to Siena was elected to some of the highest offices of the commonwealth. If he was in any degree vain of his honors and accomplishments, he fully realized human misery when in 1313 he was suddenly stricken with blindness shortly before he was to take part in a public disputation. In his dismay he prayed to God and to the Blessed Virgin, vowing to devote himself to God's service if his sight were restored. His prayers were heard, and when the day for the disputation arrived, he surprised his hearers by dwelling upon the contempt of the world and the importance of salvation. Thereupon, he bade farewell to his friends and relatives, and with two companions set out for a solitary place. Not far from Siena was a small estate which he had reserved for himself when he had distributed his wealth among the poor. The locality was called Accona, and was excellently suited for his purpose. Here he and his companions lived like the early Egyptian solitaries, meeting only for

Gobert: Life of Gobert.
Bernard(1): Boll.
Bernard(2): Manrique.

prayer in a chapel. They were soon joined by others willing to adopt their manner of life. The evil spirit strove to undo this work by embarrassing Bernard at every step and even by inspiring some one to poison the Saint. He was accused of heresy and was summoned to Avignon by Pope John XXII, who acquitted him of the charge and sent him to Bishop Guido Petramalius of Arezzo, who prescribed the Rule of St. Benedict for his institute and on March 24, 1319, clothed Bernard and his two earliest associates with a white habit. At the same time the bishop authorized them to build a monastery. This house was erected on Montoliveto at Accona and was dedicated to Our Lady; hence the Congregation was known as the "Order of the B.V.M. of Montoliveto." Bernard clothed his other companions in the same manner, but would not consent to be their abbot when the first election was held. The first superior was Patrizi, a former councillor of Siena; three years later, however, the brethren overcame Bernard's reluctance and he ruled the congregation with great wisdom and ability. The Order was spread into other countries and received the approval of Popes John XXII and Clement VI. Bl. Bernard died on August 21, 1348. His public veneration was recognized by a decree of the Congregation of Rites in 1644 and Pope Innocent XII in 1692 approved the Mass and Office for his feast.

3. **Bl. Baldwin,** Cistercian abbot at Rieti in Italy, was a disciple of St. Bernard of Clairvaux and was treated with affectionate regard by that Saint. He died in the odor of sanctity in 1140 and was buried in the cathedral. According to the Cistercian Martyrology, which commemorates him on July 15, he is a Saint, and was abbot of the monastery of St. Pastor.

4. **Bl. Florus,** a disciple of St. Maurus at Glanfeuil, had been a high official at the Frankish court, and founded the monastery of Glanfeuil, in which he became a monk and died a holy death after a holy life in 558.

22

1. **St. Sigfrid,** third abbot of Weremouth in England, was elected abbot to succeed St. Esterwin. He was a saintly, mortified, gentle religious, well versed in the Sacred Scriptures. He was also remarkable for his strict observance of abstinence, but his bodily health did not correspond with the vigor of his soul, as he was suffering from an incurable disease of the lungs. He presided, under the superiorship of St. Benedict Biscop, for only three years. Both he and Benedict were prostrated by their final sickness. Assisted by the brethren, they were enabled to give one another the last embrace, and made the last arrangements for the government of the house. Sigfrid survived this meeting two months and then exchanged a life of suffering for one of eternal rest in 689. He was buried at the entrance of the church, but afterwards his relics were translated and placed beside those of abbot Benedict before the altar of St. Peter.

2. **Bl. Witmer,** monk of Weremouth in England, had been wealthy and respected in the world and was reputed to be a learned man. Late in life, he re-

Bernard: Boll.; Roman Martyrol.
Baldwin: Barnabas de Montalbo; Martyrol. Cist.
Florus: Mab.
Sigfrid: Bede; Mab.; Stanton; Book of Saints (†688).

solved to strive for Christian perfection, disposed of his riches, took the religious habit at Weremouth and lived as an exemplary monk under abbots Esterwin, Sigfrid and Ceolfrid to the year 716, when he died, and was buried beside these holy abbots.

23

1. **SS. Altigianus** and **Hilary,** monks of Sestre, or St. Seine, in the diocese of Langres, in France, were slain by Saracens for their constancy in confessing their faith, in 731.

2. **St. Ascelina,** Cistercian nun at Boulencourt in Champagne, was a relative of St. Bernard and was piously brought up by her mother, her father having died when she was five years old. Even at that time she experienced a longing for the exclusive service of God and was favored with extraordinary spiritual gifts. For several years, mother and daughter led a religious life at home so far as was possible under the circumstances, but in 1149 both took the veil at Polongey, where Ascelina was appointed to the office of sacristan. Her life was spent in great part in prayer, and the ardor of her love of God was so great that she yearned for the grace of martyrdom. After leading a life of exemplary holiness for many years, she received a premonition that she was to die in a year. It so happened; she died on the Friday after Pentecost 1195. Her remains were first interred at Polongey, but after the destruction of that monastery were removed to the abbey of Boulencourt.

3. **Bl. Richildis,** lived many years as a recluse in a small cell adjoining the church of the monastery at Hohenwart in Upper Bavaria and received her eternal reward in 1100.

4. The two **Austrian** Congregations—that of the Immaculate Conception and that of St. Joseph—were established on August 23, 1889, on which day their Constitutions were approved by Pope Leo XIII.

24

1. **Bl. Theoderic,** abbot of St. Hubert at Andaine in the diocese of Liege, was the son of the knight Gonzo, and was born at Lerna near Thuein in Hainaut in 1007. While his father preferred to see his son adopt the calling of a knight, his mother prayed that he might serve God in the sanctuary. It was not before two accidents had happened to Theoderic, that he was permitted to follow his mother's choice. Being still a child, he received his elementary instruction from his sister Ansoaldis, a nun at Maubeuge; but when he was ten years of age, his mother offered him to the abbey of Lobbe, which was then ruled by the saintly abbot Richard. The abbot observed the piety and industry of the boy and was so well pleased with his progress and exemplary life that he permitted

Wilmer: Mab.
Altigianus: Mab.; Stadler calls his associate Hilarinus.
Ascelina: Goswin; Henriquez; Boll.
Richildis: Raderus.
Austr. Cong.: St. and Mitt. 1889; Familiae Confoed.

him to be professed and had him ordained a deacon.   His abilities and accomplishments were of no mean order, for he was at once appointed to direct the monastic school.   In 1037 he was ordained priest,—a distinction which only roused him to love and serve God with increased fervor.   He always wore a hairshirt, ate little, allowed himself no comforts and prayed and studied incessantly.   His success as a master induced abbots Poppo of Stablo, Walleram of Verdun and Rudolph of Mouson to secure his aid in improving the schools at their monasteries.   While on a pilgrimage to the Holy Land he visited Rome, where he met the canon Anselm of Liege, who persuaded him to return to the monastery of his profession, Lobbe.   He was about to assume direction of the schools at Fulda, when the death of abbot Adelard of St. Hubert's was reported.   No one was found better qualified to succeed him; Theoderic accepted reluctantly, but applied himself diligently to the task although he met with obstinate resistance in some quarters.   After making several other pilgrimages to Rome his last illness befell him; summoning the brethren to his bedside he exhorted them, blessed them, absolved them of all offences against the Holy Rule and expired on this day of the year 1087.

2.   Bl. Sandrad, abbot of Gladbach, diocese of Cologne, had been a monk at St. Maximin's in Trier and was appointed abbot of Gladbach by archbishop Geron.   Sandrad justified the esteem in which he was held by this prelate, but under the latter's successor, Warinus, was charged with being more devoted to the bishop of Liege than to him, and was replaced as abbot by one Meginhard. Sandrad fled for protection to the empress Adelheid, who made him one of her spiritual advisers.   Through her influence he was appointed abbot of Weissenberg, but resigned that charge to resume the government of Gladbach after Meginhard's retirement.   His day's work closed in 985.

3.   The American Cassinese Congregation under the patronage of the Holy Guardian Angels owes its establishment chiefly to the zeal and energy of Abbot Boniface Wimmer (†1887), a monk of Metten in Bavaria, who founded the monastery of St. Vincent in Pennsylvania in 1846 and procured the establishment of the Congregation through Brief of Pope Pius IX, dated August 24, 1855.   The Statutes originally observed were those of the Bavarian Congregation.

25

1.   St. Gregory, abbot at Utrecht and bishop, was the son of the noble Alberic and first saw St. Boniface at Pfalzel at the age of fourteen years.   The missionary zeal of the great Apostle impressed the boy so strongly that he refused to listen to the objections of his relatives and shared Boniface's privations and labors.   When in the course of years Boniface had assured himself of Gregory's sterling qualities and the firmness of his character, he appointed him abbot of the monastery at Utrecht about 750.   After the death of St. Boniface, Gregory was appointed to administer the episcopal see of Utrecht.   He did not take episcopal consecration; nevertheless he endeavored to provide for the suit-

Theoderic: Mab.; Boll.
Sandrad: Mab.
Amer. Cass. Cong.: Enchiridion Ben.; Album Ben. 1881.

able training of the clergy, for the preaching of the word of God and for the proper care of the poor. In his private life, he was a model of all virtues; he met his calumniators with the weapons of silence and prayer, and refused to avenge himself upon the slayers of his brother. He was about seventy years of age when Heaven sent him a severe trial; his left side was completely paralyzed and caused him much inconvenience, although it left him free to fulfil the greater part of his duties. When death drew nigh, he requested his brethren to carry him into the church, where he received the holy Viaticum and died on this day about 776.

2. **St. Marcian,** abbot of St. Eusebius in Provence, was the son of wealthy parents, but preferred to follow Christ in poverty. An inner impulse moved him to leave his paternal home and make his abode in a solitude, where he devoted himself to the practices of the contemplative life. The same spirit that had impelled him to this step, now directed him to found a monastery in honor of St. Eusebius. He was joined by six companions, with whose aid he built suitable cells and an oratory. As the foundation still lacked revenues, he did not disdain to beg for food. The report that he had raised from the dead the son of a widow at Apt, increased his popularity and the number of brethren grew daily. He died while returning from Apt to his monastery in 1010, and was buried in the cathedral at Apt in recognition of his sanctity.

3. **St. Gurloesius,** abbot of Quimperle in Brittany, had been a monk at Redon in the diocese of Vannes, and ruled as abbot from 1029 to 1057. Since it is generally stated that he governed his monastery for twenty-five years, he may have retired three years before his death to spend the decline of his days in communion with God alone. After his death in 1057 he was venerated as a Saint at Quimperle.

4. **St. Hunegundis,** a nun at Homblieres in Vermandois, was of illustrious birth and early in life made a vow of virginity. Having been forced by her parents to consent to a marriage with a young noble, Eudald, she persuaded him to make a pilgrimage with her to Rome, for she hoped that God would dispose all for her welfare and that of her spouse. Availing herself of a canonical privilege she took the veil from the hands of the Pope. This step angered her husband, who from that day abandoned her, leaving her to her own resources in a foreign country. After many hardships she succeeded in returning home, and entered the monastery of Homblieres, which she endowed with her patrimony. By her incessant prayers she brought about a complete change of heart in Eudald, who administered the temporalities of the monastery for many years to the day of his pious death. Hunegundis died about 690. Her remains were raised in 946.

5. **St. Ebba, the Elder,** abbess of Coldingham in Scotland, was of the royal blood of Northumberland, a sister of kings Oswald and Oswy. Early in

Gregory: St. Ludger. Butler.
Marcian: Mab.
Gurloesius: Mab.; Migne-Petin calls him Ureles or Urloux and gives as the Latin equivalent Garlaesius. Stadler.
Hunegundis: Bernier, abbot of Homblieres.

life she took the veil from the hands of Bishop Finan of Lindisfarne. To escape abduction by the Scottish prince Aidan, who wished to marry her, she fled to Coldingham, where she subsequently became abbess of the double monastery. With means furnished by her brother she also founded a monastery on the Derwent in the diocese of Durham. St. Cuthbert was a valued friend of Ebba and at her request was accustomed to visit the abbey and instruct her community in the ways of Christian perfection. St. Adamnan was a monk in one of her monasteries. Rich in merit she died in 683.

6. The Order or Congregation of **Fiore**, founded by Bl. Abbot Joachim (May 29), was approved by Pope Celestine III in 1196. In 1570 it was united with that of Citeaux.

26

1. **Bl. Margaret** of Faenza, Vallombrosan abbess of St. Salvius at Florence, was born at Faenza about 1230 and early placed herself under the guidance of St. Humilitas in a monastery of her native city. St. Humilitas went to Florence to establish a monastery; her companions were Margaret and two other sisters, with whom she struggled against the difficulties in the way of a new foundation without resources or encouragement. During the three years that passed before the monastery stood finished, they begged not only their daily food but also money to defray the cost of construction of the buildings. Under such circumstances the soul of Margaret attained to remarkable heights of perfection and contemplation. After the death of Humilitas in 1310, Margaret, although bearing the burden of fourscore years, was elected her successor. She governed the monastery of St. Salvius, as the house founded by Humilitas was called, for twenty years, during which she enjoyed many remarkable spiritual favors. When she was a hundred years of age, her spiritual director, the Franciscan Peter of Florence, who had known her many years, requested her to tell him of some of her graces and visions. She consented upon condition that this information be kept secret during her life-time. Her death occurred in 1330.

2. **Bl. John Bassandus**, Provincial of the Celestine Order, was born at Besancon in Burgundy in 1350, and at the age of eighteen years joined the Canons Regular at their monastery of St. Paul, of which he was several years later chosen prior. Urged by a desire for greater perfection, he entered the Celestine abbey of Notre Dame at Paris in 1390. Fifteen years later he was elected subprior three years later, prior at Amiens, in 1410 prior at Paris and in 1411 Provincial of the Order for a term of three years, to which office he was five times re-elected. He led his brethren ably by deed and word, and achieved more by service than by commanding. If he chanced to arrive at a monastery at a late hour, he would, even if hungry and fatigued, molest no one, but partake of a slight refection and retire for the night. Pope Martin V offered to confirm him in his office for life, but he declined such an honor. Affairs at the monastery of Collemadio in Italy claimed his attention in 1443. Although eighty-three years

---

Ebba: Capgrave; Stanton.   Butler says she is also called in English St. Tabbs, and that the monastery she founded in the Derwent was called Ebchester.
Cong. of Fiore: Boll.
Margaret: Peter of Florence.

of age, he undertook a journey to Italy, visited the monastery, effected a wonderful revival of religious fervor in its religious and governed it in person. A year later he was taken ill on the eve of the feast of the Assumption, and died on Aug. 26, 1445. St. John Capistran, who had visited him shortly before his death, delivered the funeral discourse.

3. **Ven. Herluin,** founder and abbot of Bec in Normandy, originally was a knight and had distinguished himself on several occasions by feats of arms. For this reason, and no less for his integrity and nobility of soul, he was regarded with high favor by duke William of Normandy. At the age of thirty seven years, however, his heart was turned heavenward; he began to lead a devout life, observed many fasts and endeavored to escape the favors of men. Finally he withdrew from the world altogether, built a monastery, in the construction of which he toiled with his own hands, and, although forty years of age, was not too proud to learn the elements of grammar and to study Sacred Scriptures. Bishop Herbert of Lisieux clothed him with the religious habit and ordained him a priest. As abbot, Herluin shared the poor and toilsome life of his monks. The original place on which the community settled proved unsatisfactory, and Bec was chosen in preference. Herluin's wisdom and virtue attracted a number of able men to Bec,—it will suffice to mention Lanfranc and St. Anselm. He died in 1087.

4. Establishment of the **Bavarian Congregation** of the Holy Guardian Angels, approved by Pope Innocent XI in 1648, and endowed with the privileges of the Cassinese and Swiss Congregations.

27

1. **St. Ebbo,** archbishop of Sens in France, was descended from a distinguished family at Tonnerre and was born about 665. For a time he administered the estates he inherited from his parents but finally renounced all his rights, and became a monk at St. Pierre-le-Vif in a suburb of Sens. When Abbot Aigilenus of that house died, Ebbo's reputation for solid virtue was already so firmly established that he was chosen to succeed him, and in 710 was elected archbishop of Sens in succession to his uncle Guerricus. When the city was threatened by the Saracens in 731, he had recourse to prayer, and personally led the forces that scattered the invaders. At an advanced age he retired into a solitude, where he spent the week in prayer and penances, returning to the city for the services on Sunday. Edifying all men by his bright example, he passed to a better life about 744 and was buried in the church of St. Peter at Sens.

2. The meritorious **Alexander III,** Pope, formerly known as Orlando Bandinelli, was born at Siena. After being professor of canon law at Bologna and canon at Pisa, he became a Cistercian monk in the monastery of Claravalle near Milan. Pope Eugene III, also a Cistercian, summoned him to Rome and cre-

John: Boll.
Herluin: Gislebert Crespin of Westminster.
Bav. Cong.: Bullarium Magnum.
Ebbo: Mab.; Boll.

ated him cardinal and papal chancellor. In 1159 he was elected to succeed Pope Adrian IV. The eighteen years of his pontificate were an almost uninterrupted struggle with emperors and anti-popes. He died in 1181 and is praised in his epitaph as "the light of the clergy, the ornament of the Church, the father of his city and of the world."

28

1. **St. Alfric**, archbishop of Canterbury, had previously been a monk and, probably, abbot of Abingdon. From that position he was promoted to be bishop of Wilton, which see he governed till he was elevated to the primatial see of Canterbury. He ruled his church in a most exemplary manner for eleven years, during which occurred the Danish invasion, and was called to the reward of his labors at Abingdon in 1006. In the reign of King Canute his remains were transferred to Canterbury.

2. **Egward**, a bishop in Silesia, and former monk of Hirschau, was appointed to an episcopal see by Otto I. God put to shame the holy prelate's enemies by restoring life to a drowned man at his intercession, on which account Egward was popularly known as the "man of God." He died about 965.

3. **Ven. Herman**, abbot of Marienberg in Tyrol, was slain by Ulric of Matsch while defending the rights of his monastery in 1303.

4. **Emmo**, monk and guest-master at Luxeuil, was wont to receive all guests without distinction as if each were Christ, and thus gathered rich merits. He died in 580.

29

1. **St. Mederic**, abbot at Autun, was of illustrious descent, and at the age of thirteen years devoted himself to the service of God at St. Martin's in Autun, although his parents yielded their consent with much reluctance. His heart was aglow with the fire of divine love and no power on earth was strong enough to check his fervor. He is said to have taken food but twice a week, and to have subsisted on bread only. After the abbot's death, the monks and the people of the surrounding country demanded that Mederic be abbot. The bishop yielded to their wishes, and blessed and installed him without delay. Fearing that in the midst of his solicitude for the welfare of others, he should neglect his own, he left the community and settled in a neighboring forest. The sorrowing brethren made search for him in every direction and when they finally found him pressed him to return with them to the monastery. He refused at first, but eventually yielded when the bishop threatened him with excommunication. Although bowed by age he made a pilgrimage to Paris, where he lived as a re-

Alexander: Baronius; Lives of Popes.
Alfric: Wm. of Malmesbury; Harpsfield.
Egward: Mab.
Herman: Monuments of Marienberg. This abbot's name was Herman von Schauenstein.—
    (Benediktinerbuch. 1880).
Emmo: Mab.

cluse in a cell near the church of St. Peter for two years and nine months to the day of his death about the year 700. His remains were interred in that church, which was later renovated and called by his name.

2. **St. Sebbi,** monk in London, succeeded his father Seward as king of Essex in the year of the great pestilence, 664. Although dwelling in a palace, he lived as modestly as a religious. It was said that such a man should have been a bishop rather than a king, for it was his wish for many years to lay down his sceptre and become a monk. His wife refused her consent, and it was not until he had reigned thirty years and was seized with a sickness which evidently betokened his approaching death, that she yielded. Sebbi received the religious habit from Bishop Waldhere of London, while his wife took the veil in a convent. In his humility he feared lest at his last moments he might be betrayed into some want of conformity to the Divine Will, and asked that no one might be present, save the bishop and two attendants. Three days before his death he was consoled by a vision assuring him that he was about to be summoned to his reward. He died in 694 and was buried in St. Paul's cathedral.

3. **Walburga** Diepolder, of the Congregation of St. Ottilien, while engaged in missionary work in the apostolic vicariate of Dar-es-Salaam in East Africa, was put to death by rebellious natives in 1905.

30

1. **St. Agilus,** abbot of Rebais, was one of the first disciples of St. Columban at Luxeuil, and received his education under abbot Eustasius. His knowledge and prudence qualified him to be the teacher and guide of the brethren. When Columban had been sent into exile and the royal decree forbade the monks of Luxeuil to leave the enclosure of their monastery, the newly elected abbot Eustasius deputed Agilus to treat with the king for a revocation of the order. The decree was revoked. In 613 King Clothair convoked a synod of bishops, who decreed that Eustasius and Agilus should preach the Gospel among the most benighted people of the realm. The two missionaries preached along the banks of the Seine and the Doux, where they found many pagans and not a few adherents of the heresy of Photinus and Bonosus. Having converted many of these, they pushed forward as far as Bavaria. When Audoenus founded the monastery of Rebais in 634, he selected Agilus for its first abbot; two years later the monastery and church were dedicated and Agilus installed. Under his prudent rule the foundation grew in numbers and in good repute. He died about 650.

2. **St. Bononius,** abbot of Lucedio in Piedmont, was born at Bologna, and in his youth entered the monastery of St. Stephen, where he excelled in all the virtues of a good religious. With leave of his superior, he passed over to Egypt and renewed the fervor of the monks he found in that country. He also

Mederic: Mab.; Stad.; Butler (St. Merri); Migne-Petin (St. Merry).
Sebbi: Bede; Stanton; Butler (Sebbi or Sebba).
Walburga: Heimbucher; Kath. Missionen.
Agilus: Mab.; Boll.; Butler says he is commonly called St. Aile.

labored as a missionary and effected the ransom of several prisoners, including Bishop Peter of Vercelli. For some time he journeyed through the Holy Land and lived as a hermit on Mount Sinai. When the abbey of Lucedio became vacant, Bishop Peter of Vercelli believed he could find no one worthier to fill the place, and sent messengers to Mount Sinai, inviting him to accept the appointment. Bononius reluctantly assented, but encountered difficulties that obliged him to withdraw from the monastery for a while. Eventually all differences were adjusted and he ruled his flock in peace to the day of his death in 1026.

31

1. **St. Amatus**, bishop of Nusco in the former kingdom of Naples, was born at Nusco in 1104 and from earliest youth evinced a pronounced inclination for a virtuous life. At the age of fourteen he lost his parents, and devoted the greater part of his inheritance to the relief of the poor. After he had been ordained a priest the bishop made him archpriest, or vicar general, in which capacity he excelled among the clergy by his devotion, zeal for souls, in administration of sacraments and every other kind of good works. Attracted by the fame of St. William of Monte Vergine, who inhabited the monastery of S. Salvator near Nusco, he applied for admission to his community. William received him with pleasure and soon found him to be his most valuable associate in his undertakings for the spread of God's kingdom. After William's death in 1124, Amatus founded the monastery of Fontiliano where, among others, he gave the religious habit to a youth to whom he had restored speech. The see of Nusco became vacant in 1152 by the death of its bishop, and William was chosen for the see by the united acclaim of clergy, prince and people. Having appointed as his successor in the monastery the monk whose speech he had restored, he reluctantly accepted episcopal consecration. He built a cathedral which was dedicated to St. Stephen, assiduously preached the word of God, prayed much during the night, founded the monastery of Maria Nova and built a church in honor of St. Lawrence. He died on this day in the year 1193 while at prayer after Holy Mass. Nusco recognizes him as its patron saint.

2. **St. Cuthburga**, abbess of Winburn in England, was espoused to Aldfrid, son of Oswy of Northumberland, but with his consent separated from him to follow a higher vocation. She became a nun at Barking in Essex, and was instructed in the religious life by St. Hildelida, the second abbess. Later she undertook the foundation of Winburn, a double monastery, which she ruled as abbess to the day of her death in 724.

3. **St. Eanswida**, abbess of Folkestone in the ancient kingdom of Kent in England, was the daughter of Eadbald, king of Kent; and her mother was Emma, daughter of the king of Austrasia. With her father's consent she retired to the newly-founded monastery at Folkestone and became its abbess, ruling the house to the day of her death about 636. In the Danish wars the monastery

Bononius: Mab.; Boll.; Roman Martyrol.
Amatus: Felix Renda. Also in the Roman Martyrology.
Cuthburga: Capgrave; Stanton; Butler.

was destroyed. Her remains formerly rested in the church of St. Peter at Folkestone.

4. **Bl. Albertin,** general prior of the Order of Fontavellana, died on this day in 1285 and is venerated in the church of Santa Croce at Fontavellana.

5. At Bobbio the Translation of the relics of SS. Columban, Bobolen, Congel (abbots), and Meroveus, Agibod, Theobald, Blidulf, Baudachar, etc., took place on this day in the year 1482.

Eanswida: Capgrave; Stanton.
Albertin: Jacobillus; Dorgan; Boll. Placid Donati, who wrote a life of Bl. Albertin in 1905, places the date of death at 1294.
Columban etc.: Mab.

September

1

1. **Bl. Aegidius** was a Cistercian in Spain, who, having been an abbot at Castaneda in Asturia, retired into a solitude and spent the remainder of his days in communion with God. Many sought him to confess their sins to him and to receive salutary guidance. He died about 1203, and was buried at Casajo, where he was venerated.

2. **Bl. Juliana**, abbess of S. Blasius and Cataldus at Venice, was a scion of the distinguished family of Collalto and was born 1186. At the age of ten years she was clothed with the religious habit in the convent of St. Margaret at Salarola near Padua. When Beatrice of Este left that convent in 1222 to organize a new community at Demola, Juliana was one of her associates. Beatrice died four years later and Juliana succeeded her as abbess. After some time she removed her community to Venice, where she established herself in a house near the church of SS. Blasius and Cataldus and spent her life in the exercises of piety to the day of her death in 1262. Her body was found incorrupt after thirty-five years and at that time was translated.

3. The devout **Agnes**, abbess of S. Salvator at Venosa in Apulia was converted from the ways of the world by discourses of St. William of Monte Vergine, and died, ruling her house in holiness, about the year 1160.

4. The Venerable **Hereswitha** was the daughter of Ereric, the son of St. Edwin, King of Northumbria, and was the wife of King Anna of the East Angles who reigned only one year and was killed in war in 655. Hereswitha sanctified her widowhood by entering the religious state at Chelles near Paris, where she persevered to the time of her death about 664.

5. The **French Congregation** was established principally through the efforts of Abbot Prosper Gueranger of Solesmes and received the approval of the Holy See on this day in 1837 by the Apostolic Letter "Innumeras inter" of Pope Gregory XVI.

2

1. **St. Nonnosus**, prior of a house on Monte Soracte north of Rome, was, although positive proof is lacking, a Benedictine monk and always received veneration in the Order. The calm peace of his life in the monastery was clouded at times by the harshness of his abbot, but he bore all with the greatest charity

---

Aegidius: Manrique; Chalemot; Henriquez.
Juliana: Boll.; Seeboeck. Her veneration was approved by Pope Gregory XVI.
Agnes: Schindele; Bucelin.
Hereswitha: Mab.; Stanton (who says she was the wife of Ethelhere).
French Cong.: Acta Greg. XVI (Rome 1091) vol. II. pp. 222–236, where the Constitutions may also be found.

and patience. He died about 560, and was translated to Freising in Bavaria by Bishop Nitger in the pontificate of Pope Leo IX.

2. The devout **Anthony de Winghe,** abbot of Liessies in Hainaut, was a man in whom all virtues existed in most perfect harmony. The Bollandists regard him as one of the earliest promoters of their undertaking, for he voluntarily promised to support the assistant of Fr. Bolland when the latter found the task of compiling the "Acta Sanctorum" an excessive demand on his strength. He died in the odor of sanctity in 1637.

3. The devout **Hugo,** monk of Cluny, had been a duke of Burgundy, but laid aside that dignity to become a religious under abbot Hugo. His distinguishing virtue was his humility; he delighted in performing the lowliest services, and even begged leave to do them that thus he might be more conformable to his Divine Master who had humbled Himself for our sake. Pope Gregory VII is said to have entertained a high regard for this servant of God. Hugo died in 1093.

3

1. **St. Aigulph,** abbot, and SS. **Troncharius** and **Frongentius,** monks of Lerins, died as martyrs to duty and Christian virtue about 675. Aigulph was born about 630 at Blois, embraced monastic life at Fleury and was sent by Abbot Mummolus to Monte Cassino to secure the remains of St. Benedict and remove them to France. Having been successful in this mission, he was invited to rule the abbey of Lerins, where he established admirable order and regularity, yet not without causing dissatisfaction. Several of the brethren conspired against him; he succeeded in appeasing them after some time, but their evil passions finally conquered them; they seized the abbot and the few monks that remained faithful to him, placed them aboard ship and massacred them on the island of Capraja off the coast of Tuscany. Their remains were carried to Lerins.

2. **St. Remaclus,** bishop of Mastricht, was born in the province of Aquitaine about 618, and educated under the supervision of SS. Sulpitius and Eligius. When the latter had founded the abbey of Solignac in 637, he selected Remaclus as its first abbot. Remaclus within a short time was surrounded by a community of 150 monks and both he and his monastery were spoken of in terms of the highest commendation. In 642 he was summoned to the court of King Sigebert III; he was ordained priest by the Bishop of Metz and appointed abbot of Cougnon in Luxemburg. In 650 he was chosen as successor of St. Amandus in the see of Mastricht, of which he took possession in 651 and which he adorned by the splendor of his eminent virtue. Under his guidance a number of youths received an education that fitted them for the most responsible offices in the church. When King Sigebert had founded the monasteries of Stablo and Malmedy, the saintly bishop was commissioned to rule them. Having governed

Nonnosus: St. Gregory the Great.
Anthony: Boll.
Hugo: Mab. Also commemorated on Sept. 18.
Aigulph: Adrewald; Mab.; Boll. Stadler calls the associate Trucharius.

the see of Mastricht ten years, he retired to Stablo and devoted himself to the interests of that house which enjoyed a marvellous growth under his rule. He died in 664.

3. At Glanfeuil in the diocese of Mans was formerly commemorated the **Dedication** of the **Church** and the **Translation** of the **relics** of SS. Antonius and Constantinian, disciples of St. Benedict and companions of St. Maurus when the latter was sent into France. They assisted St. Maurus for several years, and after the monastery had been established, returned to Monte Cassino, where they died burdened with years and merits about 590. When the church at Glanfeuil was dedicated by Pope Calixtus II in 1119, the relics of the two companions of St. Maurus were brought from Monte Cassino and were venerated down to the time of the religious revolt when they were thrown into the Loire by the Calvinists.

4

1. The devout **Gerbert**, abbot of Fontenelle, was sent by Divine Providence in the hour of sore need to edify the faithful and to revive the ardor of spiritual life and religious discipline in monasteries. He ruled his monastery twenty-one years and died, regarded as a Saint, in 1089.

2. The venerable **Simon**, formerly abbot of the Benedictine abbey of St. Peter at Caziac in the diocese of Soissons, was such an ardent admirer of St. Bernard that he wished to become a monk at Clairvaux. St. Bernard counselled him to remain where he was but foretold him that his wish to die in Clairvaux would be fulfilled. After St. Bernard's death, Simon resigned his abbacy, retired to Clairvaux and there spent the last seven years of his life in the exercise of religious virtues, in the spirit of his holy model. He died in 1160.

5

1. **St. Bertin**, abbot of Sithiu in Artois, was born near Constance about 597, and, following the example of his cousin Audomar, dedicated himself to the service of God at Luxeuil, where he and his friends Mommolen and Ebertran became professed monks. When Audomar had been made bishop of Terrouanne, abbot Walbert sent him his three friends—Bertin, Mommolen and Ebertran—who founded a monastery at St. Omer, of which Mommolen was the first abbot. So numerous were the devout souls who applied for admission to the community that it was found necessary to found another house at Sithiu, for which the noble Adrowald granted the lands. For some time Mommolen governed both houses, but after his promotion to the see of Noyon and Tournai in 659, Bertin succeeded him in the abbatial office. Under his prudent administration, both establishments prospered and the revenues were increased. The noble Heremar granted Bertin the estate of Wormhout, where he founded a monastery at first known as St. Martin's but later as St. Winoc's. Count Walbert, after his conversion, made Bertin a grant of his estates at Arques near St. Omer and

Remaclus: Boll.; Mab.
Gerbert: Aderic; Mab.
Simon: B. de Brito; Manrique; Stadler ("Simeon").

Poperingue near Ypres, and placed himself and his wife under the Saint's spiritual direction. Their son became a monk at Sithiu and was an exemplary religious. Feeling the weight of years and infirmities, Bertin in the year 700 appointed the monk Rigobert in his place, and dwelt in a hermitage near the cemetery, where he died in 709.

2. **Bl. Albert,** abbot of Pontida in Italy, in his youth pursued a military career, but, once when he suffered from a severe wound, vowed to serve God alone, if he recovered. When his health was restored, he made a pilgrimage to Compostella with a certain Herman of Cremona, at his return divided his patrimony with his brother and retired to one of his estates at Pontida, where he built a small chapel, and later a splendid church and a monastery. A monk from Cluny was invited to organize a religious community. After some time Abbot Hugo of Cluny arrived and installed Albert as abbot. Abbot Albert's life was spent in doing good; he won the respect of the great and the love of the poor and died after a holy, edifying life in 1095. In the fourteenth century his remains were translated to the church of Our Lady at Bergamo.

3. **Bl. Jordan,** abbot-general of the Order of Pulsano, was the successor of the founder, St. John of Matera, in 1139, being elected to that office by the unanimous voice of his brethren, who deemed him best qualified for that important office. King Roger summoned him to render the customary homage and Jordan was pressed by the brethren to comply, but he set little value upon the favor of men, and sent some of the brethren instead. It is related that the king, far from taking the abbot's action amiss, esteemed him the more and commended himself to the prayers of the Order. Jordan died in the year 1152.

6.

1. **St. Chagnoald,** bishop of Laon, was the son of Chagneric, a noble of Brie, and brother of St. Faro, bishop of Meaux, and of St. Fara, abbess of Ebory, or Faremoutier. The same good spirit that animated his brother and sister, impelled him to renounce all and to seek God alone. He became a monk at Luxeuil and accompanied St. Columban into exile. After spending some time at Bobbio, he returned to Luxeuil, and was sent to Ebory at the request of St. Fara to found a monastery. Heaven blessed the undertaking, and most excellent discipline prevailed in the new foundation. Chagnoald, now far famed for his virtue and ability, was made bishop of Laon and died after a life of meritorious service in the year 632.

2. **St. Magnus,** abbot at Fuessen in the Allgaeu, was a companion of the devout priest Willimar and became a disciple of St. Gall. He was sent by his master to Bobbio to make inquiries concerning St. Columban's death and returned bearing with him that Saint's crozier (or staff), which was regarded as a dear keepsake by his northern followers. After St. Gall's death, Magnus was chosen to perpetuate his good work at the cell over which the Saint had pre-

Bertin: Six ancient lives of Saints.
Albert: Guarneri; Teutald of Cluny.
Jordan: Boll.
Chagnoald: Boll.

sided. Subsequently Magnus, accompanied by the monk Theodore and in possession of Columban's staff, set out in the direction of Kempten to preach the message of salvation and remission of sin through the merits of our Blessed Redeemer. Having built a chapel at Kempten, which he left in charge of Theodore, he pushed onward into the mountainous country and founded the monastery of Fuessen on the banks of the Lech. Here he died about 660, and was always venerated as a Saint and as a protector against noxious vermin.

3. **St. Faustus**, abbot of St. Lucy at Syracuse in Sicily, is remembered as the spiritual father and teacher of St. Zosimus and died about 607.

4. **St. Limbania**, nun and recluse at Genoa in Italy, was born on the island of Cyprus and became a nun at Genoa. After her virtue had been well tried, she was permitted to live as a recluse in a cell beneath the church, where she at first subsisted on bread and vegetables, but later received no nourishment but the Holy Eucharist. She was found dead with outstretched arms and kneeling, in the year 1294.

7

1. **SS. Alchmund** and **Tilbert**, both at one time monks in a monastery founded at Hexham, in England, by St. Wilfrid, were successively bishops of that see—Alchmund from 767–780 and Tilbert from 871–789. Over 250 years after his death St. Alchmund appeared to a pious priest at Hexham, and ordered that his body should be translated to a more honorable place in the same church, which was done with great pomp on the 4th of August.

2. **St. Madelberta**, abbess of Maubeuge, was the daughter of Saints Vincent and Waldetrudis, and was early in life entrusted to the pious care of her aunt, St. Aldetrudis, foundress and abbess of Maubeuge. The graces received in Baptism and Confirmation produced wonderful fruit and gave her joy in walking the thorny path of perfection. After her aunt Aldetrudis and her own sister Aldegundis had died as abbesses, Madelberta was chosen to rule the godly community, which she continued to edify by her example to the time of her death about 705. Her remains were translated to Liege.

3. **St. John**, bishop of Gubbio, in Italy, was born at Lodi about 1026 and spent his boyhood in his baptismal innocence. In his studies he progressed so satisfactorily that his elegance of style merited for him the surname of *Grammaticus*; yet he despised all conceit and affectation and practiced self-abnegation to a degree surprising in one of his years. Attracted by the fame of St. Peter Damiani's sanctity, he became at the age of forty a member of the community at Fontavellana. His zeal in the discharge of his religious duties and in the practice of every virtue was so remarkable, that he appeared to be completely strange to the pleasures of sense and to move in the realm of spirit only.

Magnus: Boll.; Mab.
Faustus: Oct. Cajetanus.
Limbania: Boll.; Breviary.
Alchmund: Stanton.
Madelberta: Mab.; Boll.

In compliance with the direction of St. Peter Damiani he presented himself for ordination to the holy priesthood, and in 1072 he succeeded the Saint in the government of the community. He was requested to mitigate the severity of the Rule in some particulars but declined to do so; yet in all his intercourse with the brethren was a mirror of humility, occasionally falling down on his knees before them to confess his faults and ask their forgiveness. He was already eighty years of age when he was promoted to the episcopal see of Gubbio, and was consecrated by Pope Pascal II. Death called him from the new scene of labor several months after in the the year 1106.

4. The pious **Humbert**, abbot of Igny, entered the Cistercian Order and edified the community of Clairvaux by his holy life during fifty years as a simple monk. He was esteemed by St. Bernard, who often sought his advice in matters of consequence. Humbert died, reputed a Saint, in 1148.

5. The pious **Ansteus**, an abbot of St. Arnulph's at Metz, was remarkable for his great fidelity and constancy in religious observance. He prepared his own tomb and there spent many hours in meditating upon the vanity of the transitory things of time and the joys of eternity. He died in 960.

8

1. **St. Disibod,** bishop and abbot, was an Irish monk who labored for the salvation of his own soul and the souls of others both in his native land and in France and parts of Germany. He crossed over to the Continent in 652 and preached and ministered as a regionary bishop; his zealous exhortations, enforced by the weight of his example, produced wonderful fruit in all places blessed by his presence. After spending ten years in apostolic labors he founded a monastery, later called Diesenberg, on a hill near Mainz, and ruled his monks with great prudence and holiness. In order to shield the brethren from temptation and to prevent relaxations in regular observance, he built a cell at the foot of the hill for the entertainment of guests and the relief of the poor. While he was kind and gentle in his treatment of others, he was severe with himself, and observed a stricter rule than that of St. Benedict, although he had introduced the latter for his religious. He died on the present day about the year 700.

2. The Ven. **Gisla,** lay-sister at Marcigny in Burgundy, had brought her body into such perfect subjection to her spirit that she served God with singular fidelity. Without practicing any conspicuous external austerities, she was intent upon conscientiously performing every one of her daily duties. She so completely forgot the world that she never set a foot beyond the convent gate. Her devout soul took its flight heavenward about 1099.

John: Boll.
Humbert: Mab.
Ansteus: Mab.
Disibod: St. Hildegarde.
Gisla: Mab.

9

1. St. Corbinian, first bishop of Freising and patron saint of the diocese of the same name in Bavaria, was born in 680 at Chatres in the diocese of Paris, and lived a quiet, devout life with several other pious persons near his native place. When their number had grown so great that it was deemed expedient to provide some kind of government for them, he founded a monastery which was known as St. Germain-les-Chatres. As the fame of his sanctity was spread abroad and many had recourse to him for guidance or counsel, he left the monastery and made a pilgrimage to Rome about 716, and lived for some time in a cell adjoining St. Peter's church. He was discovered by Pope Gregory II, who drew him from his obscurity, consecrated him bishop and commissioned him to preach the Gospel. From France, where his words found willing ears, he proceeded to Suabia, and Bavaria, where he converted a great number of idolaters. Dukes Theodo and Grimoald urgently requested him to remain in Bavaria, but Corbinian continued on his way to Rome where he hoped to find rest in a monastery. But Pope Gregory II sent him back to Bavaria. Corbinian obeyed, but lingered for some time at Mais near Meran, till duke Grimoald begged him to take up his abode at Freising. The Saint upbraided the duke for his scandalous marriage with his sister-in-law Plectrudis, who sought for his life. Corbinian was informed of her wicked design and fled to Mais, where he remained till 726 when Grimoald died and Plectrudis was taken to France. In the course of his apostolic labors he never relaxed his diligence in prayer and meditation; he frequently joined the brethren in choir in the monastery of St. Stephen, which he had founded at Freising. He also built a monastery in honor of St. Benedict near his cathedral. He offered the Holy Sacrifice for the last time on September 8, 730; returned to his residence, partook of a slight refection, made the sign of the Cross and expired on the present day of the year above mentioned.

2. St. Audomar, bishop of Terrouanne, was born at Guldenthal near Constance about the year 595. The thoughts of his parents, Friulph and Domitilla, were all centered on him and his education was their chief care. After the death of his mother Domitilla, both his father and he, having disposed of their temporal possessions, were received as monks by St. Eustasius, abbot of Luxeuil. The humility, obedience, meekness and purity of heart, which shone forth in everyone of Audomar's actions, distinguished him among his brethren. He was remarkable for his proficiency in Sacred Scripture and his reputation spread over the whole kingdom. In 637, King Dagobert designated him bishop of Terrouanne, the capital of the ancient Morini in Belgic Gaul, at the suggestion of St. Acarius, bishop of Noyon and Tournai. Upon receiving the message with a severe command to obey without demur he cried out: "How great is the difference between the secure harbor in which I now enjoy a sweet calm, and that tempestuous ocean into which I am thrust, against my will, and destitute of experience!" The country was still full of idolaters, many of whom the Saint converted by his preaching. Among the converts was the noble Adrowald, who had no children and granted all his possessions to the bishop for charitable purposes. On one of the estates, Sithiu, he founded a monastery in 648, to which

Corbinian: Aribo of Freising; Butler.

he was wont to withdraw for rest and devotion. The town that sprang up about the monastery was subsequently known as St. Omer. St. Austreberta, whom her parents wished to compel to marry, took refuge with Audomar and received the veil from his hands. In his old age, Audomar suffered the loss of his eyesight; he selected the priest Drausio to assist him in his work and continued to preach and instruct the people. While engaged in a missionary journey he was seized with a fever at Wavrans and felt that his end was not far distant. One day after celebrating Holy Mass and addressing the faithful, he was led back to his house where he died shortly after on the present day in 670. His remains were interred at Sithiu.

3. The venerable **James ab Herculano,** a laybrother at St. Severin's in Naples, was always cheerful and practiced the most eminent degree of mortification by exact observance of the Rule and statutes without doing anything to attract attention or comment. After his death in 1619, many experienced relief through his intercession.

10

1. **St. Theodard,** bishop of Mastricht and martyr, was the son of French nobles and born in the reign of Clothair II. Under the prudent guidance of St. Remaclus, then an abbot, he learned the principles of Christian perfection, and progressed so rapidly that he won not only the full confidence of his master, but the esteem of all that knew him. Remaclus was promoted to the episcopal see of Mastricht in 650 and intrusted to Theodard the government of the two monasteries of Malmedy and Stablo, and when he retired to Stablo after twelve years spent in the discharge of the episcopal office, he proposed Theodard for the see of Mastricht. As bishop, Theodard was deeply impressed with the responsibilities of his office, and was solicitous for the training of zealous clergy to cooperate with him in the spread of the kingdom of God. Among his most famous pupils was St. Lambert, who also became one of his successors in the see adorned by his virtues. Several encroachments had been made upon the rights of the see by powerful nobles and little had been done to check them, for it was feared that vigorous opposition would only make matters worse. Finally Theodard courageously made certain demands, and when these were not complied with, he appealed to the Austrasian King Childebert II, who at the time was residing in one of his castles on the Rhine. When his enemies were made aware that he had gone to court, they pursued him and overtaking him in a forest between Speier and Strassburg, reddened their hands in his guiltless blood, hacking the body to pieces in their blind fury. One of the bishop's servants who had succeeded in escaping gathered up the remains and buried them. This happened in the year 668. Later St. Lambert caused them to be taken to Mastricht, and some time later they were translated to Liege.

2. **Ven. Ambrose Barlow** was the son of an illustrious confessor of the faith and was born at Manchester in England. He became a monk at Douay, and after he had been professed and ordained, returned to labor in the English

Audomar: Mab.; Boll.
James: Armellini:.
Theodard: Sigebert of Gemblours.

mission. He was imprisoned several times and was just recovering from a severe illness when he was arrested for the last time. Having been sentenced to death, he devoutly thanked God and prayed for his persecutors. On his way to execution he bore in his hands a cross of wood and with this he walked thrice around the gallows reciting the Psalm *Miserere*, whereupon he gave himself up to the executioners. He suffered death on September 10, 1641.

3. **Francis Leuthner,** priest and monk of the Missionary Congregation of St. Ottilien, was engaged in missionary work in the apostolic vicariate of Dar-es-Salaam, East Africa, and was slain by rebellious natives in 1905.

11

1. **St. Bodo Leudinus,** bishop of Toul in Lorraine, was the son of the noble Gondoin and a brother of St. Salaberga. When the saintly monks Eustasius and Agilus were sojourning in the house of Gondoin, they blessed the youth Bodo and his brother Folculf. Several years later Bodo married a lady, Odila, by whom he had a daughter named Teutberga. After some years both Bodo and his wife following the example of Salaberga, embraced the religious state at Laon and served God with great zeal and devotion. Bodo's sanctity was so generally recognized that he was appointed bishop of Toul. He founded a monastery for women—Bodon-moutier—in the Vosges mountains and appointed his daughter Teutberga its first abbess. Leaving behind him a blessed memory of his virtues and benefactions, he passed to his reward about the year 670. His remains were first interred in the church of St. Mansuetus, but were later translated to the abbey of St. John at Laon.

2. **St. Adelphius,** abbot of Remiremont in Lorraine, was the son of a noble, whose wife Asselberga was a daughter of St. Romaric. The mother sent her son and his sister Tetta, or Gebetrude, to her father, St. Romaric, to be educated at Remiremont. Adelphius also received a part of his education in the house of St. Arnulph, bishop of Metz, and then became a monk at Remiremont, where he shone as a pattern of every virtue. After Romaric's death, he was chosen to succeed him as abbot, while Gebetrude ruled the nuns. Adelphius survived the holy founder, Romaric, only a few years. When he perceived that the day of his dissolution was not far distant, he went to Luxeuil to prepare himself for rendering an account of his stewardship. Abbot Ingofred received him with great joy, and appointed the monk Emmo to attend him, to whom he was as considerate and affectionate as to a brother. One morning he suffered an apoplectic stroke; he called out thrice "Christ help me!" and died on this day about 670. His remains were interred at Remiremont.

3. **St. Sperandea,** abbess of St. Michael's of the Congregation of Bl. Sperandeus and Bl. Santuccia, was born at Gubbio about the year 1216, and was probably a sister of Bl. Sperandeus. Even as a child she practiced remarkable austerities, and as she advanced in years, she progressed in knowledge,

Ambrose: Stanton.
Francis: Kath. Missionen; Heimbucher.
Bodo: Mab.; Boll.
Adelphius: Mab.; Boll.

piety and in the spirit of mortification. For several years she dwelt in lonely places and seized every opportunity to exhort the people to do penance. She spent the holy season of Lent in recollection and austerities which stronger natures could not have borne. Eventually she entered the Congregation of Sperandeus and Santuccia, in 1265 built the convent of St. Michael at Cingoli and was made its abbess. She died in 1276; in 1497 her remains were found to be incorrupt. The March of Ancona honors her as one of its patron saints.

12

1. **Bl. Wifred,** abbot at Marseilles, restored the decayed abbey of St. Victor in that city and laid the foundations of its prosperity. The most precious fruit of his labors was the training of St. Ysarnus who also was his successor. Wifred died in the year 1021.

2. **Bl. Thesaurus Beccheria,** General of the Order of Vallombrosa and cardinal, was born at Pavia. Pope Alexander IV created him cardinal and employed him in negotiations to allay the partisan strife of the Guelphs and Ghibellines. In obedience to the command of the Pope he repaired to Florence and undertook to reconcile the conflicting parties, but fell a victim to the steel of assassins in 1258. His remains were carried to Vallombrosa and exposed for the veneration of the faithful.

3. **Ven. Venerius,** Camaldolese monk and hermit, was scorned as a simpleton and contemptuously treated in his monastery, and on this account left and lived in solitude six years. St. Romuald visited him and asked him under whose guidance he was living. Venerius replied that he recognized no superior and regulated his life and actions as he himself saw fit. Wherupon Romuald said: "If you wish to bear the Cross of Christ, you must not cast off the obedience of Christ." And at the same time he advised Venerius to return to his abbot and order his life according to the superior's will and with his sanction, that obedience might perfect what good will had begun. Venerius obeyed and with the leave of his abbot returned to a secluded life in an almost inaccessible cavern where he lived in contemplation four years, subsisting on such food as he found in the forest. He was found dead about the year 1000, kneeling before the altar in the little chapel built for him with the bishop's approval.

13

1. **St. Amatus,** bishop of Sion in the Swiss Canton of Wallis, had spent his youth in faithful observance of the commandments of God and was made bishop about the year 670. Although he toiled with the zeal and unselfishness of an apostle, his character was aspersed by calumniators in the time of Thierry III, and he was, without being given an opportunity to clear himself of the charges brought against him, exiled to the abbey of St. Furseus at Perronne,

---

Sperandea: Boll.
Wifred: Mab.
Thesaurus: MS. of Vallombrosa; Boll.; Chev. (Beccaria).
Venerius: Peter Damiani; Ferrari.

where St. Ultan was abbot. Amatus suffered in patience and silence, his only regret being, that his flock was in the mean time at the mercy of a hireling. After Ultan's death, his successor Maurontius sent Amatus for some time to Hamay near Marchiennes, later to Breuil, which he had founded. Maurontius deemed no one better qualified to establish regular discipline in this new house and therefore appointed Amatus its first abbot. After the community had been firmly established and God's blessing evidently rested upon the monastery, Amatus shut himself up in a cell near the church and came forth only on Sundays to preach the word of God to the people. On the last day of his life his sorrowing brethren were at his bedside; he consoled them, dismissed them when the sign for choir was given, and while they were at prayer yielded his spirit into the hands of his Creator in 690. During the Norman invasion his remains were first carried to Soissons, and in 870 to Douai.

2. Another St. Amatus, abbot of Remiremont, was born of illustrious parents about 670 at Grenoble in France, and at an early age was sent to the monastery of St. Maurice at Agaunum in Switzerland, where he was also professed and where he lived as an exemplary religious for thirty years. Longing for more intimate communion with God, he entered a solitude, where he was discovered three years later by St. Eustasius, abbot of Luxeuil, then on his way to Italy. At his return in 614, he persuaded Amatus to accompany him to Luxeuil, where he lived not only as an exemplary monk, but was also sent out to preach the Gospel in the surrounding country. Among those whom his zeal won for Christ was the noble Romaric, who renounced the world and entered the monastery of Luxeuil. Romaric had reserved for himself a large estate called Habende in the Vosges mountains, where he built a double monastery— Remiremont—the government of which he entrusted to Amatus in 620. Romaric himself became a member of the community. Towards the end of his life he frequently retired to a grotto from which he issued on Sundays to preach. A year before his death, he made a general confession of all his faults in the presence of the brethren, put on a coarse hair shirt and fervently exhorted the brethren to persevere in their struggle for perfection. On his deathbed he had the epistle of Leo I to Flavian read, and publicly professed his adherence to the faith expounded in that letter. He died in 625.

3. St. Columbin, abbot of Lueders, or Lure, in Alsace was the godchild of St. Deicolus, founder of that monastery, and governed it with prudence and holiness to the year 640 when he was summoned to his eternal reward.

4. The devout Martin, abbot general of the Order of Camaldoli, died in the Lord in 1259. His tomb was visited frequently by devout petitioners.

5. The devout Leutberta, nun at Faremoutier and disciple of St. Fara, lost her speech for some time during her final illness, but recovered it, and died praying in the year 650.

Amatus: Boll; Gallia Christiana;
Amatus: Boll.; Mab.
Columbin: Mab.
Martin: A. Florentinus.
Leutberta: Mab.

14

1. The feast of the **Exaltation of the Holy Cross**. St. Benedict is said to have possessed a fragment of the true Cross of Christ and to have given three particles to St. Maurus who deposited them at Glanfeuil. Other particles passed into the possession of the monastery of Elnon in the Netherlands, Moelk in Austria, Scheyern and Oberalteich in Bavaria, Wiblingen and Weingarten in Suabia, Kalenberg in Poland, and Gellon in Languedoc.

2. The devout **Leoteric**, monk and hermit at Cormery near Tours, was born at Sancey near Sens and renounced all prospects of temporal advancement to go in pursuit of the treasure of eternal life. Putting aside his armor, he made a pilgrimage to Rome. After his return he dwelt as a hermit in Lorraine and made a second pilgrimage, from which he returned poor. He was recognized at Cormery and presented to Abbot Guido, who invited him to join his monks. After being professed, Leoteric was appointed almoner, but was for a time permitted to lead a more contemplative life at Anchy, a dependency of the abbey of Cormery, where roots and herbs were his sole nourishment. At the abbot's request he changed his abode to Vontes where he was visited by many distinguished personages, including several bishops and cardinals, and where he died, regarded as a Saint, in 1099. He was buried in the chapel of St. Nicholas at Cormery.

15

1. **St. Aicard**, abbot of Jumieges in Normandy, was the son of Anschar, a high court official of King Clothair II, and was reared in the spirit of true Christian piety by his parents. His school training he received at a monastery in Poitiers. At the age of sixteen he was to go to the court of the King, but he preferred the service of his Heavenly Lord and entered the monastery of Jouin in Poitou. His pious parents about this time founded the abbey of Guincay near Poitiers and entrusted its government to St. Philibert who, in order to escape the tyranny of the major-domo Ebroin, had recently fled from his abbey of Jumieges into Normandy. Philibert selected Aicard to govern the new foundation and prepared to return to Jumieges. Circumstances, however, rendered his return impossible; hence he remained at Guincay and sent Aicard to Jumieges, which at that time harbored a community of nine hundred members. The new abbot's piety, knowledge and dignified bearing impressed all, every word he spoke had the weight of authority. The secret of his successful rule was his own example and prayer. In a vision he was told that one third of all his monks was to die within three days. He prepared them all with the greatest care. His own death, he was informed, was to follow within three years. When the hour of his dissolution drew nigh, he delivered a final exhortation to his brethren, blessed them and gave them the kiss of peace, whereupon he calmly expired about the year 687. During the Norman invasion his relics were removed to Hapres, a place between Cambrai and Valenciennes.

Exaltation of Cross: Mab.
Leoteric: Mab.
Aicard: Surius; Mab.; Boll.

2. **St. Rithbert**, abbot of St. Valery in the diocese of Amiens, was distinguished for his piety and learning. He is the author of a life of St. Walaric, first abbot of the monastery (which was originally known as Leuconaus), and died before the year 700. His relics are venerated with those of SS. Walaric, Blithmund, Sevold and Volganius.

3. The devout **John of Caramola**, a Cistercian monk of St. Maria di Saettatore in the former kingdom of Naples, led such a mortified life that he is said never to have been seen asleep or to have been heard speaking. He died meditating in 1339.

4. The **Octave** of the **Nativity** of the **Blessed Virgin** is said to have been first celebrated by Bl. Eberhard, archbishop of Salzburg, on accasion of a synod celebrated at Regensburg in 1150. Pope Innocent IV in 1243 extended the feast to the Universal Church.

16

1. **St. Edith**, nun of Wilton in England, was the daughter of King Edgar and Wulfrida and was still in her tender infancy when her mother carried her to the monastery of Wilton, to which place she herself retired to pass the rest of her days. From her first years Edith exhibited every token of the divine predilection, by the sweetness of her disposition, her humility, her angelic purity and her singular charity towards the sick and the poor. Whenever she set about her work, she signed herself with the sign of the Cross, a practice which highly edified St. Dunstan. She built the church of St. Denis at her monastery and St. Dunstan came to celebrate its consecration. He was seen to shed tears at the altar, and afterwards explained that he had a vision, in which it was revealed to him that within six weeks she would be called hence to Paradise. She died forty days after, at the age of twenty-three years in 984, and was buried in the church she had built.

2. **St. Eugenia**, second abbess of Hohenburg in Alsace, was a daughter of Duke Adelbert of Alsace, and a niece of St. Odilia, whose pious example she ·strove to copy in her own life. After ruling her community fifteen years by her word and example she died in the odor of sanctity in 735.

3. **Bl. Victor III**, Pope, was descended from the dukes of Beneventum and was born in 1027. His baptismal name was Dauferius, which was later exchanged for that of Desiderius. From his earliest years he displayed most singular piety. Ignoring all the allurements of honor and pleasure, he fled from home in the twentieth year of his age, after the death of his father, and received the religious habit from the hermit Santari. He was discovered, taken back to Beneventum and remained at his home for a year, without, however, renouncing his intention to become a religious. His uncle Duke Guaimar sent him to

Rithbert: Boll.; Mab.
John: Boll.
Octave: Pez.
Edith: Wm. of Malmesbury; Capgrave; Stanton.
Eugenia: Abbe Grandidier.

the monastery of Cava, from which he was removed by other relatives to the monastery of St. Sophia at Beneventum. At his own earnest request he was permitted to enter a monsatery on the island of Tremiti in the Adriatic Sea. The abbot was so completely charmed with his excellent qualities that he offered to resign in his favor, but no sooner was Desiderius aware of this than he returned to the mainland and joined the hermits at Majella. He had been three months in this devout company, when in 1053 a messenger from Pope Leo IX ordered him to return to Beneventum, where he became seriously ill, partly in consequence of his austerities and partly for grief at being compelled to live in a monastery in his birthplace. Two years later he obtained leave of Pope Victor II to enter Monte Cassino. Not many months passed before he was made prior of a house at Capua, and in the same year, 1057, he was chosen abbot of Monte Cassino. On March 6, 1059 Pope Nicholas II ordained him priest, at the same time created him a cardinal, and on the following day made him abbot of Monte Cassino, although he was but thirty-two years of age. When Pope Gregory VII was at the point of death in 1085, he recommended abbot Desiderius as his successor. He was elected, but declined to accept the dreadful responsibility; he fled to Monte Cassino, hoping that events would shape themselves otherwise. Finally he was compelled to yield, and was crowned at Capua as Pope Victor III. He held a council at Beneventum against the anti-pope Guibert, ratified the decrees concerning investitures and died on this day in the year 1087. At Monte Cassino, Cava and Beneventum his feast is celebrated *sub ritu duplici* with permission of Pope Benedict XIII.

4. The devout **Bruno,** abbot of Scheyern, although connected by ties of blood with the reigning house of Bavaria, left the world to become a monk at Hirschau in the days of the abbot William. When the Countess Haziga, wife of Count Otto II of Scheyern, secured a colony of monks from Hirschau, Bruno was appointed their superior. They first settled at Margarethenzell, after some time removed successively to Fischbachau and Petersberg, and finally were quartered in the castle of Scheyern in 1113. Here Bruno governed his community with great prudence and holiness and died in 1127 or 1128.

17

1. **St. Lambert,** bishop of Mastricht and martyr, was a native of that city and early in life passed into the hands of St. Theodard, who took pains to train him in all the virtues of a Christian. Lambert did not disappoint his saintly teacher and shone like a bright light among the secular and regular clergy of the country. When Theodard had fallen at the hands of assassins in 669, Lambert was elected his successor in the see of Mastricht. In this capacity, he suffered much during the unsettled condition of affairs under Childeric II, Theodoric II and Clothair III. As he remained loyal to Childeric, he was, after the latter's death in 673, driven from his see to make place for an intruder by name of Faramund. Lambert withdrew to Stablo and lived there like the plainest of the monks. One night he rose from his pallet and happened inadvertently to make a noise with his sandals. The abbot, unaware of the identity of the in-

Victor: Mab.; Lives of Popes.
Bruno: Chron. of Scheyern.

nocent offender, at once ordered him to pray at the foot of the cross before the church. Lambert meekly obeyed and remained kneeling where he was told, for several hours during the cold night, for it was winter. When the monks were all assembled in the cell where they usually warmed themselves after matins, the abbot inquired whom he had sent to the cross. Learning that it was Lambert, he fell at the holy prelate's feet, but Lambert heartily forgave him and praised him for doing what he had done. When Pepin of Heristal became major-domo after the assassination of Ebroin, Lambert was permitted to return to his see, where he resumed his toil with redoubled effort. He took occasion to rebuke Pepin for his unlawful relations with Alpais and thus made an enemy of the woman. One morning while the Saint was returning from matins at Liege, Dodo, a relative of Alpais, met him with an armed force. Lambert at once divined their purpose, forbade his companions to offer resistance and fell pierced by a lance in the year 708. His remains were carried to the church of St. Peter at Mastricht; in 721 Bishop Hubert translated them to Liege, whither the see of Mastricht had also been transferred. The city of Liege chose him as its patron saint.

2. St. Columba, nun and martyr, was born at Cordova and was induced to embrace a life of renunciation when she saw the holy example of her sister Elizabeth. The latter and her husband Jeremias had founded the double monastery of Tabane and had, together with their children and several devout friends, consecrated themselves to the service of God by embracing the religious state. Columba entered the monastery ruled by her sister and soon excelled in the practice of all the virtues that adorn the true religious. When the Moors dispersed the inhabitants of Tabane, they fled to Cordova and found shelter in a house near the church of St. Cyprian. While many other Christians placed their lives and fortunes in safety by renouncing their faith, Columba burnt with a desire to suffer martyrdom. Boldly she appeared before the judges and loudly professed her faith in Christ. She was at once imprisoned and beheaded on this day in the year 853. She was interred in the church of St. Eulalia, but later a part of her relics were translated to a priory that bore her name.

3. St. Roding, abbot of Beaulieu in France, was a native of Ireland and joined the monks of Tholey in the diocese of Trier. So many thronged to see and consult him that he left that monastery and, accompanied by several brethren, removed first to Verdun and finally into the forest of Argonne, where he founded the abbey of Beaulieu. Having governed the community as its abbot for thirty years, he retired to a lonely cell, from which he came forth only on Sundays, and in which he died in the year 680, at the age of 86 years.

4. St. Hildegardis, abbess at Bingen, was descended as some say from the counts of Spanheim and was born in 1098. At the age of eight years she was placed in the monastery on the Diesenberg, where she was educated under the direction of her cousin Jutta. Hildegard was favored with visions and ecstasies, some of which she describes in her writings. She wrote, apart from

Lambert: Gottschalk of Liege; Stephen of Liege.
Columba: Eulogius.
Roding: Menard; Mab.

her revelations, a life of St. Disibod, of St. Rupert of Bingen and a brief commentary on the Holy Rule.   Although elected abbess after Jutta's death, and necessarily in frequent contact with the outer world, she never ceased to be in intimate communion with God.   In 1148 she organized the monastery of Rupertsberg at Bingen, and later that of Eibingen.   She died in the eighty-second year of her age in 1179.   During the Thirty Years' War her remains were removed to Eibingen in 1632.   No formal canonization has ever taken place, but her name is in the Roman Martyrology.

18

1.   **St. Richardis**, empress and foundress of the monastery of Andlau in the diocese of Strassburg, was born 862 and was espoused by emperor Charles III.   By mutual consent they lived together like brother and sister.   In 880 Richardis founded the monastery of Andlau and endowed it with several of her estates.   Her honor having been assailed by calumniators, she publicly proved her innocence, and then bidding farewell to the world, she withdrew to Andlau, devoting herself exclusively to prayer and works of charity.   Although she wrote a body of statutes for the nuns, it cannot be proved that she was a nun of the Benedictine Order.   She died in 896.   Pope Leo IX translated her remains in 1049 and wrote several hymns in her honor.

2.   At Mons the raising of the remains of **St. Winoc**, abbot of Wormhout in Flanders in the year 900 at the request of Count Balduin of Flanders.

3.   The **Order of Pulsano** was founded by John of Matera at Pulsano, a monastery on Monte Gargano in Apulia in the year 1120, but disappeared in the course of centuries, being incorporated in other reforms of the Benedictine Order.

19

1.   **St. Pomposa**, nun and martyr of Cordova, the child of devout parents who devoted all their earthly resources to the foundation and endowment of the monastery of San Salvador at Pinna-Mellaria, consecrated herself to God by taking the veil of religion in that house.   When she was informed of the glorious martyrdom of St. Columba, she burnt with a desire to sacrifice her life in the same cause.   One morning after matins, finding the convent gate open, she interpreted this as a token that Divine Providence favored her design, and making her way to Cordova, she loudly proclaimed the divinity of the Christian religion and the falsehood of that of Mahomet.   She was seized by order of the Moorish judges, sentenced to death and executed in 853.   Her body was thrown into the river by her executioners, but was recovered by some Christians and interred in the church of St. Eulalia.   At Cordova her memory is celebrated on the twenty second of the present month.

Hildegardis: Theodoric, abbot of St. Tron; Cave; Martene; C. E.
Richardis: Grandidier.
Winoc: Mab.
Order of Pulsano: Boll.
Pomposa: Eulogius.

2. **St. Arnulph,** bishop of Gap in Dauphine, was born at Vendome and became a monk in a monastery founded in that town by Count Godfrey. By reason of his modesty and regularity he was highly esteemed by his abbot Odericus, whom he also accompanied on a journey to Rome. Pope Alexander, delighted by his conversation and commendable traits of character, detained him at his court for some time, and in 1063 appointed him bishop of Gap to fill the place of the simoniacal bishop Ripert. He received episcopal consecration in Rome, and labored with edifying zeal at a time when much disedification was given by those in high places. One of his enemies—probably a sympathizer of the previous occupant of the see—attacked him and inflicted a wound upon his right arm. Arnulph died shortly after in the odor of sanctity about 1079. He is commemorated both at Gap and Vendome.

3. **St. Acca,** bishop of Hexham, England, was brought up in the school of St. Bosa, bishop of York and his whole life gave evidence of the virtuous and learned training he had received. He was with St. Wilfrid in Friesland and Rome, and it was to him the Saint confided the vision which he had, when sick at Meaux, predicting his restoration to his see. On the death of St. Wilfrid, Acca succeeded him as bishop of Hexham and greatly added to the splendor of that church by the erection of chapels in honor of the Saints whose relics reposed there. For some reason not disclosed in history, he was banished from his diocese; nor does it appear that he ever returned. On his death, however, in 740, he was most honorably buried in his own church.

4. The devout **Simeon,** priest, monk and hermit of Camaldoli, was distinguished for his ardent love of God and complete detachment from all creatures. Blessed Humiliana beheld his soul radiating a bright light even during his life time. He died a holy death in 1292 and was long remembered for his eminent and exemplary virtue.

5. **Ven. Louis Barbo,** abbot and bishop of Treviso, had been a canon regular at Alga in Venice. Desirous of reforming the Benedictine Order, he was appointed abbot of St. Justina at Padua and founded the celebrated Congregation of St. Justina, which eventually became known as the Cassinese Congregation. Pope Eugene IV recognized his distinguished services to the Church by appointing him bishop of Treviso. Bishop Barbo was papal nuncio at the Councils of Pisa, Basel and Florence and died in 1443. He was interred in the monastery of St. Justina at Padua.

20

1. **Ven. Anno,** bishop of Worms had been a monk at St. Maximin's in Trier and attracted the attention of all by his good qualities. At the suggestion of emperor Otto I he was appointed abbot of St. Maurice at Magdeburg; from this dignity he was promoted several years later to the see of Worms. His meritorious life closed in the year 974.

Arnulph: Boll.; Mab.
Acca: V. Bede; Stanton.
Simeon: Fortunio; Boll.
Louis: Pez; Armellini
Anno: Mab.

2. **Bl. John Eustachius,** was the first abbot of Jardinet in Belgium. In his youth he became an Augustinian at Mons, but later he entered the Cistercian Order and was professed at Moulins. So exemplary was his life that he was selected to reform a monastery of nuns at Jardinet. His efforts in this direction were apparently not appreciated, for he dismissed the three remaining nuns and organized a monastery of monks with the assistance of a monk from Moulins and three clerics. They contended with poverty for a long time, yet were all content and prospered beyond all expectation with the blessing of Heaven. A number of other houses adopted his reform. After resigning his office, abbot John lived in retirement four years and died at the age of 78 years in 1441.

3. The Congregation of Beuron in Germany is the creation of two brothers, Dom Maurus and Dom Placidus Wolter. The former received the abbatial benediction on this day in 1868 and was the first abbot of Beuron after its restoration. The members devote themselves largely to literature and ecclesiastical art.

21

1. The devout **Paul,** a deacon, monk of Monte Cassino, entered the Order while Abbot Theobald presided over that monastery, and was sent by him to rule a dependency at Capua. He had already served God faithfully many years, when a bishop from France, on a pilgrimage to Monte Gargano, passed through Capua and lodged for the night at the church of St. Lawrence. Rising at night for prayer, he saw a bright light above the monastery. While gazing at it and wondering what it might be, he heard the passing bell that announced the death of a brother. In the morning he learned that the soul of Paul had taken its flight heavenward. Paul's death occurred in 1033.

2. **Ven. Martin,** Cistercian monk and cardinal, is mentioned in terms of praise by St. Bernard in his treatise *"De Consideratione."* Martin, returning from an embassy to Denmark, is said to have travelled in such poverty, that he was barely able to pursue his journey to Florence. The bishop of that city presented him with a horse that he might continue on his way and meet St. Bernard at Pisa. Being involved in litigation, the bishop expected Martin's support in view of the gift, but Martin declined to be bought and preferred to see justice take its free course. St. Bernard is said to have exclaimed: "Would that there were many such men." Martin died in the year 1134.

22

1. **St. Salaberga,** abbess at Laon, in France, was the daughter of the noble Gondoin and of his wife Saretrudis. She was born blind, but her sight was restored by St. Eustasius, who with his companion Agilus was one day the guest of her parents. She was married to a young gentleman of rank who died

John: J. Wimes. J. de Assigny; Henriquez.
Cong. of Beuron: This date is arbitrarily chosen.
Paul: Leo Marsicanus; Peter the Deacon.
Martin: St. Bernard: Henriquez.

two months later, and now resolved to devote herself to a life of recollection and prayer. Not daring, however, to oppose the wishes of King Dagobert I, she was married for a second time, in this instance to a court dignitary by the name of Blandin. The fruit of this union were five children, two of whom—Baldwin and Anstrudis—are venerated as Saints. After the birth of the fifth child she received the consent of her husband to realize her former desire, and began to build a monastery, probably that of Poulangey. As this monastery was too much exposed to warlike incursions, she removed to Laon with her sisters and was welcomed by Bishop Attilo of that city. She there built a great monastery which soon sheltered three hundred nuns, who were divided into several choirs, so that the praises of God were sung almost continuously day and night. Among her sisters was her sister-in-law, Odila, who had been permitted by her husband Bobo, Salaberga's brother, to embrace the religious state. It would have been difficult to find a more perfect religious than Salaberga. In her humility she served her sisters in the kitchen and at table. When the sun of her days drew near its setting, Bishop St. Ansericus of Soissons appeared to her in a vision and announced the approach of her death. She now redoubled her fervor in prayer, her charity and self-abnegation; on her deathbed exhorted her sisters to persevere, and died in the year 665.

2. Bl. Mauritius, a Cistercian abbot of St. Martin's, in the diocese of Quimper in Britanny, was remarkable for his virtue and supernatural gifts and died in the odor of sanctity in 1215.

3. The devout Homodeus, a Vallombrosan monk and hermit, led a life of self-denial and austerity for forty years and died at the age of ninety years in 1519.

23

1. St. Adamnan, an abbot of Iona, was born in Ireland about 624, was educated by the Columban monks and became a novice at Iona in 650. He was made abbot in 679. During his rule he paid three visits to Ireland; on the third he assisted at the Synod of Tara (697). He introduced the observance of Easter according to the Roman custom and wrote a life of St. Columba. Adamnan is described as being "tearful, penitent, fond of prayers, diligent and ascetic, and learned in the clear understanding of the Holy Scriptures of God." He died in 704.

2. Otto, bishop of Freising, was a son of Leopold, duke of Austria and received his education at the university of Paris. On his way back to Austria, he enjoyed the hospitality of the Cistercian monks at Morimond, and was so powerfully struck by the sanctity of their lives that he resolved to remain and become a monk. On account of his knowledge, zeal and ability he was made abbot of the monastery. But he was not to remain in this seclusion very long, for he was appointed bishop of Freising in Bavaria, and in this capacity accom-

Salaberga: Anon. author.
Mauritius: Manrique.
Homodeus: Armellini.
Adamnan: Ven. Bede; C. E.

panied emperor Conrad III on a Crusade to the Holy Land.   On his return he ruled his diocese with great zeal and devotedness, encouraged studies and left behind him a universal chronicle down to the year 1146 and some notes on the history of his times.   Feeling the approach of his dissolution, he withdrew to Morimond and died in the arms of his brethren on September 22, 1148.   The anniversary of his burial is celebrated at Freising on the present day.

24

1.   **St. Gerard Sagredo,** bishop and martyr, was born in Venice about the year 1000 and at an early age consecrated himself to God in a monastery. With permission of his superiors, he made a pilgrimage to the Holy Land; on the way he met King Stephen of Hungary, who was so well pleased with his bearing that he invited him to remain in his kingdom.   Gerard consented and lived in a retired spot seven years with his companion Maurus, after which King Stephen invited him to preach the Gospel to his people.   Two years later Gerard was appointed bishop of Csanad near Temesvar.   He continued his apostolic labors with increased zeal, usually travelled on foot, compassionated and relieved the distressed, instructed the neophytes, provided for the care of the sick, built churches, prayed to God for his people and commended them to the protection of the Blessed Virgin.   When in 1042 an attempt was made to depose Stephen's successor Peter and Gerard was expected to crown the intruder, Gerard not only declined but also sternly rebuked him for his unlawful assumption of authority.   Four years later, King Andrew was permitted to ascend the throne on condition that he would restore idolatry.   Gerard with three other bishops went to the king to induce him to withdraw his sinful promise. Gerard had a presentiment that they were, with the exception of one, to die as martyrs.   When they were about to cross the Danube they were overtaken by duke Vatha and a band of ruffians; Gerard was stoned and pierced with a lance. He died praying for his enemies.   Two of the other bishops—Bezterd and Buld —suffered death with him, while the remaining one was rescued by the new king.   Thus was shed the blood of the Apostle of Hungary in the year 1046. For a long time his body reposed in the cathedral at Csanad; later it was removed to the church of Our Lady at Murano.

2.   **St. Geremar,** founder and abbot of St. Germer de Flay near Beauvais in France, was born of distinguished parents at Warde near Beauvais about 610, received an appointment at the court of King Dagobert I, and espoused the lady Domana, who bore him three children.   Geremar's domestic life was peaceful and truly Christian; his delight was to do good and to serve God.   A deed for which he deserved to be remembered was the foundation of the monastery of Isle or St. Pierre-aux-bois.   In 648 he received the consent of his wife to consecrate himself exclusively to the divine service; he was clothed with the religious habit by St. Audoenus, instructed by him in the principles of monastic life and installed as abbot of Pentalle.   Although he was a capable ruler and a kind father to his monks, some of them bore him ill-will and plotted to take his

Otto: Menard; Meichelbeck; Stadler.

Gerard: Surius; Mab.; Stad.; Butler.   On Sept. 25, 1901, the remains of St. Gerard were placed in a reliquary of crystal presented by the Bishop of Csanad.

life. He discovered the knife which was to be the instrument of his death, and on the following day begged the brethren to suffer him to go into retirement, a step to which they assented with reluctance. He withdrew to a cavern, and, having been ordained priest by Audoenus, passed his days in prayer and mortification. In 654 he was informed of the death of his son; he mourned his decease, but thanked God for having kept the youth in the path of virtue and duty. As he now re-entered into possession of all his property, he built a church over the tomb of his son, and a monastery at Flay, the direction of which he undertook in person. He governed this house for less than four years and died in 658.

3. St. Ysarnus, abbot of St. Victor at Marseilles, was born about 990 at Pamiers near Toulouse, and became a monk at St. Victor's, where he made such progress in virtue that he was appointed prior and in 1020 abbot of that monastery. Everyone marvelled at his boundless benevolence and charity to the poor, for whom he collected clothing from the simple wardrobe of the brethren. He was mortified in his life, though he cleverly concealed the fact from the eyes of men, and spent many hours of the night at prayer in the church, even during winter. It was the opinion of St. Odilo that Ysarnus possessed all virtues in such a high degree, that any one of them would suffice to make one perfect. When the Moors had invaded the island of Lerins in 1046 and carried off a number of its monks, the Saint, although ailing at the time, travelled to Spain and secured the liberation of the prisoners. He lived four months after his return to Marseilles and died in peace in 1048.

25

1. St. Ceolfrid, abbot of Weremouth and Jarrow in England, was born of noble parents and from his early years devoted himself to the practice of virtue. At the age of eighteen he entered the monastery of Gilling, of which his kinsman Tunbert, afterwards bishop of Hexham, was then abbot. While visiting St. Botulph, he was invited by St. Benedict Biscop to assist him in founding a monastery at Weremouth. When the abbey of St. Paul at Jarrow was founded, Ceolfrid was selected to govern it, as was Esterwin to govern that of Weremouth, both houses remaining under the superior authority of St. Benedict Biscop. The latter shortly before his death appointed Ceolfrid to succeed him in the government of both houses, an office which he filled for twenty-eight years (688–716). Much is related of the sanctity of his life and his zeal for religious observance. The venerable Bede was the brightest ornament of the monastery during Ceolfrid's wise and holy administration. At length, desirous of being set free from the cares of government, he resolved to resign his office and to end his days near the tombs of the Holy Apostles in Rome. Having recommended the monk Hubert as his successor, he set out on his last pilgrimage in 716. At Langres in France he was taken sick, and there God called him to his reward in the same year. He was interred in a church at Langres, but later was translated to Jarrow and thence to Glastonbury.

Geremar: Mab.; Butler (Germer).
Ysarnus: Mab.
Ceolfrid: Bede; Stanton; Butler.

2. **St. Ermenfrid,** prior at Cusance in Burgundy, was a son of the noble Ermenric, and early in his life was attached to the court of King Clothair. Heeding the voice of grace summoning them to a higher calling, Ermenfrid and his brother Wandalen resolved to leave the world and retired to the deserted monastery of Cusance, which had been founded by their grandfather Iserius. Shortly afterwards, Ermenfrid entered the monastery of Luxeuil and, after growing proficient in the principles and practices of religious life, was sent back as abbot to his monastery at Cusance. By his prayer and exhortations he preserved his brother from a sad fall; later he foresaw the latter's death and buried him in the monastery. Under his rule the number of brethren grew to three hundred, He caused his monastery to be incorporated with that of Luxeuil and died about 650.

3. The venerable Martyrs—Theodoric, abbot, Asker, prior, Lethwin, subprior, Elfget, deacon, Savinus, subdeacon, Egelrod and Vulrich, acolytes —fell victims to bloodthirsty Danish invaders in the year 870, in the monastery of Croyland in England. On the same occasion many other monks of that monastery were slain, but their names--with the exeption of two centenarians, Grimkeld and Agamund—have not been preserved. The shrine of St. Guthlac was profaned, and the holy place left in a state of complete desolation.

4. **St. Gingurian,** a laybrother in a monastery at Ruiz, in the diocese of Rennes in Brittany, attained a high degree of perfection under the guidance of the Abbot Felix. He foreknew the day of his death and suffered severely during the last year of his life. He could neither turn on his pallet nor move a limb, yet he never lost his cheerfulness or the peace of his soul to the day of his blessed death in the year 1030.

26

1. **St. John de Meda,** founder of the Order of the Humiliati, descended from the family of the Oldradi at Como, in Italy, was born about 1100 and was ordained priest in his native country. In consequence of the wars in which Lombardy was involved with the German emperors a number of noblemen had been reduced to poverty, and in order to subsist had formed a pious confraternity for charitable purposes. Men and women lived in groups in separate houses and devoted themselves largely to the manufacture of woolen goods, which they sold to obtain means to relieve the poor and support themselves. St. John gathered a number of the men, founded the monastery of Rondenario in a suburb of Como for them, and prescribed the rule of St. Benedict for their observance, while he acted as their superior. He was eager to promote the honor of God, preached with great success in various cities throughout Italy, brought back many sinners to the path of virtue and founded a number of houses of his institute. Generous in his efforts to relieve the distress of the needy, Divine Providence wonderfully succored him in times of embarrassment. While visiting Milan in 1159 and staying in a house of the Humiliati in that city, he was seized with an illness and died in the year aforesaid. His remains were carried to Como.

Ermenfrid: Mab.; Boll.;
Theodoric etc.: Mab.; Stanton.
Gingurian: Mab.; Boll. (Sept. 27).
John: Anon. member of the Order in the Boll.; Stad.

2. **Bl. Meginhard,** abbot of Hersfeld (or Hirschfeld) in Hessia, died in the odor of sanctity in the year 1059.

3. The venerable abbot **Hedda** and eighty-four of his monks died at the hands of the Danes in 870 in the monastery of Medeshamstede (later called Peterborough) in England. On this occasion the invaders destroyed the altars, broke open tombs, scattered the remains of the holy virgins SS. Kyneburga, Kyneswitha, and others, and devastated the monastery.

27

1. **St. Bonfilius,** bishop of Foligno in Italy, was born about 1040, and in his boyhood was placed in the care of the monks of S. Maria de Storaco to be educated for the sacred ministry. He became a monk in that monastery, was ordained priest and shortly afterwards appointed prior of a dependency in the diocese of Foligno. In 1070 he was elected abbot of S. Maria de Storaco and was compelled to accept notwithstanding his unwillingness to assume such a responsibility. The report of his virtue prompted the clergy of Foligno to choose him to succeed the deceased bishop Azo. When messengers arrived with news of the election, he protested and remonstrated, but was eventually compelled to yield. Gregory VII personally conferred upon him episcopal consecration. In 1096 he accompanied the Crusaders to the Holy Land, visited many of the holy places, and lived an eremitical life in a cavern for ten years, disposed to end his days in that remote solitude. In a vision, however, he was advised to return to Italy. First he visited Rome, where Pascal II was surprised to see him, for he had been reported dead a number of years. At Foligno he was received with great rejoicing, but he resigned his claim to the see—a successor, Andrew, had been appointed in 1099—and retired to his monastery, where he occupied a cell and prepared himself for the journey to his heavenly home. He appears to have had some authority in the house, for some of the brethren, offended by his serious exhortations in chapter, acted so offensively towards him that he deemed it expedient to seek for rest elsewhere. He fell upon his knees before the abbot and the brethren, humbly kissed their feet, begged them for forgiveness and, bent as he was with age, retired to a solitude at Fara near Cingoli. There he spent several years in prayer, fasting and vigils, at the same time instructing those who came to him for counsel. Having died in 1115, his remains were translated. to Cingoli in 1681, and buried in the church of the Silvestrines.

2. **St. Hiltrudis,** nun of Liessies in Hainaut, was the daughter of Count Wibert of Poitou, who later settled in Hainaut, where Pepin the Short granted him the domain of Liessies, and where Wibert founded a monastery of which his son Guntard was the first abbot. Hiltrudis was to be married to a nobleman, but preferring to lead a life of virginity fled into a forest. Only when she had learned that her sister Bertha had become the wife of the nobleman intended for her, she returned to her home and from that time met with no hindrance to

---

Meginhard: Mab.
Hedda: Mab.; Stanton (Apr. 9).
Bonfilius: St. Silvester Gozzolini.

her pious wishes. Theodoric, bishop of Cambrai, gave her the veil, and from that hour she consecrated herself to the service of God. Like St. Scholastica, she was instructed by her brother, abbot Guntrad. She was never seen to laugh, never spoke of idle things and at all times maintained perfect recollection. After spending seventeen years in the exercises of piety and in the practice of virtue she died about the year 790, and was interred at Liessies.

3. **Bl. Conrad,** abbot of Mondsee in Austria, was slain at Oberwang while acting in defence of the rights of his monastery on January 14, 1145. Since his translation took place on the present day in 1745, it was annually commemorated.

28

1. **St. Thiemo,** archbishop of Salzburg, was a descendant of the counts of Medlingen in Bavaria, received his education in the abbey of Niederaltaich, but was overpowered by discouragement and took his departure. In a forest he met a priest, who gently remonstrated with him and persuaded him to return. Thiemo humbly obeyed saying: "I shall return in humility to the house from which pride drove me!" and he begged to be punished for his rash action. After he had been professed and given many proofs of his virtue and prudence, he was made abbot of St. Peter at Salzburg in 1079. Several years later he accompanied archbishop Gebhard into exile. He retired to the abbey of Hirschau where he observed the rule of the Order like the least of the monks. Three years later he returned to Salzburg, but in order to escape the attentions of the intruded bishop, Berthold, he withdrew to the abbey of Admont. After that prelate's death, Thiemo was elected as his successor. He was consecrated in 1090 by Bishop Altmann of Passau, after whose death he administered that diocese and gave it a worthy bishop in the person of the provost of Augsburg. In 1095, he attended the Council of Piacenza. He was disturbed in the quiet possession of his see by partisans of Henry IV, who were bent upon deposing him and installing the favorite Berthold in his place. A bloody feud followed, in which the imperial party was victorious. Thiemo was compelled to flee, but was captured, carried to Friesach and imprisoned. He bravely resisted all attempts to win him over to the imperial cause, and remained loyal to the Church and the Pope. Five years after his imprisonment, he was liberated by Conrad, a monk of Hirschau, betook himself first to Bishop Gebhard of Constance, and later joined Duke Guelph and abbot Gislebert of Admont in a journey to the Holy Laud to support the Crusaders. Treacherous guides furnished by the Greek Emperor Alexius led the party into a desert, called Corizana, where they fell into the hands of the Turks and were slain, confessing their faith, on September 28, 1101.

2. **St. Lioba,** abbess of Bischofsheim, was born in Wessex in England, and was consecrated to the service of God by her devout mother Ebba. She received her training under abbess Tetta in the monastery of Winburn and displayed marvelous gifts both of nature and of grace. She was so familiar with

---

Hiltrudis: Mab.
Conrad: Chronicles of Mondsee.
Thiemo: Paul of Bernried; Otto of Freising; Rader.   Also called Theodemar.

Latin that she wrote verses in that language. St. Boniface, who maintained correspondence with her, requested her bishop and her abbess to send Lioba and several other nuns to found monasteries for women in Germany. Abbess Tetta reluctantly consented to part with such a priceless jewel but made the sacrifice. Lioba arrived in Germany in 748, and St. Boniface entrusted her with the government of a house, which came to be known as Bischofsheim on the Tauber. Under her circumspect rule the monastery prospered and became the motherhouse of several other foundations. After the death of St. Boniface, she retired to the monastery of Schornsheim founded by her near Mainz, and devoted herself to prayer and mortification. Charlemagne entertained high regard for her, and his queen Hildegard several times asked her advice in difficulties. Lioba's holy life closed in the year 779, and she was buried near the tomb of St. Boniface.

29

1. **St. Ludwin**, archbishop of Trier, was the son of Gerwin, a noble of the court of Childebert III, and of his wife Gunza, sister to St. Basinus, archbishop of Trier. He had spent several years at court, when the fire of divine love burning within him urged him to leave the world and retire to the monastery which he had founded at Mettlach on the Saar. But his stay here was not to be forever; he was in 698 elected to succeed his uncle as archbishop, in which high office he spent himself in labor for the welfare of souls and for the embellishment of churches, at the same time showing singular devotion to the sick and the poor. This holy and deserving prelate died about 713 and was buried at Mettlach.

2. **St. Alaric**, monk of Einsiedeln, in Switzerland, was the son of duke Burkard II of Suabia and of his wife Regulinda, both generous patrons of that celebrated monastery and pilgrimage. Desiring to save his soul by leading a spiritual life in retirement, he withdrew to the island of Ufnau in the Lake of Zurich and dwelt there several years as a solitary. His mother, after the death of her second husband, also came to Ufnau for the purpose of devoting the rest of her days to prayer as a preparation for death. Alaric about this time decided that it would be more pleasing to God if he were to live under the obedience of a superior, and became a monk at Einsiedeln. But after his mother's death, he returned to the island, resumed his former manner of life and died on this day about 973. Einsiedeln chose him as one of its patron saints.

3. **Bl. John de Montmirail** (*de monte mirabili*), a Cistercian monk of Longpont, diocese of Soissons, was the son of the wealthy nobles Andrew de Montmirail and of his wife Hildiard de Oissy, and was born about 1166. At the age of twenty six years he took to wife Helvidis de Dampierre, who bore him six children. During the reign of King Philip Augustus he was one of the bravest soldiers in that monarch's service and was a star at all the tournaments. A conversation with the zealous Augustinian Walter of the monastery of St. Jean de Vigne gave his thoughts and ambitions a new direction; he no longer

Lioba: Rudolph of Fulda; Butler.
Ludwin: Theoderic of Echternach. Also called Leodewin.
Alaric: Annals of Einsiedeln; Mab. At Einsiedeln he is known as St. Adelrich.

found delight in the pleasures and festivities of the world, but began to serve the sick and the poor, built an hospital and placed it in charge of an organization of pious women. In 1210 he took the Cistercian habit at Longpont with the consent of his wife. Abbot Gaucher declared that he had never, in the course of forty-seven years since his profession, seen a religious who excelled John in humility, poverty and contempt of the world. It appears that his humility and patience were sorely tried by slights and insults from relatives and former dependents. Rich in merit, he died in 1217. In some martyrologies he is styled Joannes Humilis.

30

1. **St. Simon** of Crespy and Valois, monk of the congregation of Cluny, was the son of Count Rudolph of Crespy and of his wife Adela, and distinguished himself in his youth by valiant feats of arms. The sight of his father's corpse, who had been slain in the act of assisting in the unjust seizure of a castle, gave him such a profound shock that he made a pilgrimage to Rome and sought for advice how he might repair the wrong and aid the soul of his father. He persuaded his bride to enter a monastery, and in 1077 took the religious habit at St. Claudius in the Jura. Simon edified all by his prompt obedience and self-denial. His abbot could find no terms to express his amazement at his mortifications, and assigned him a higher place than was due him in the order of profession. Nothing was more distasteful to Simon than to be preferred to others, hence he obtained leave to dwell in retirement. Accompanied by several brethren he betook himself to a quiet spot in the diocese of Besancon, established a monastic settlement and lived in simplicity and poverty with his associates. One day a wayfarer begged for something to eat, and the steward gave him the last loaf in the house. When the brethren returned from the fields and sat down at table, the steward said: "There is nothing left but wild fruit; I have given all the bread that was left to the poor." Simon thanked God and entered the church to pray. In the meantime a stranger appeared at the gate and brought them a copious supply of bread. Abbot Hugo of Cluny sent him on several missions, once to meet King Philip I at Compiegne, and another time to effect a reconciliation between William the Conqueror and his son Robert. Subsequently he was sent to Rome, where Gregory VII received him warmly and commissioned him to treat with Robert Guiscard. Simon was successful in his task, and returned to Rome, where he died shortly after, on this day in 1080. He was first buried in Rome, later his remains were translated to the monastery of St. Claudius.

2. **St. Eusebia**, abbess of the monastery of St. Cyricus at Marseilles, during an invasion by the Saracens, in order to preserve her virtue, disfigured her countenance and was followed by forty of her nuns. Nevertheless all of them were foully massacred on this day about 732. At Marseilles their feast is observed on the second Sunday of October.

John: Anon. monk of Longpont; Boll.
Simon: Boll.; Mab.
Eusebia: Mab.; Boll.

October

1

1. **St. Bavo**, or Alowinus, second founder and monk of St. Peter's at Ghent in Flanders, was born of illustrious parents in Brabant, and in vain strove for complete happiness in the pursuits of the world. After his wife's death he sought bishop Amandus, confessed his sins and devoted his fortune partly to the relief of the poor and partly to the support of churches and religious houses, particularly of the church of St. Peter, which Amandus had reared on the site of a pagan temple and to which he had added a monastery. Here Bavo received tonsure and the bishop adopted him among his clergy. With the bishop's leave Bavo visited a number of monasteries to derive edification from the lives of the religious. On his return to Ghent, the abbot Florbert permitted him to live in a cell near by, where he practiced remarkable mortifications, subsisted on bread and water, wept almost unceasingly and longed to be dissolved and to be with the Lord. When the hour of his death was at hand, he summoned the priest Domlinus from the distant monastery of Turnhout and expired in his presence in the year 654.

2. **St. Dodo**, abbot of Lobbe, in the diocese of Liege, received his education in letters and in the fear of God from St. Ursmar. Obedient to an interior call of grace, he bestowed all his earthly wealth on the church of St. Peter attached to the monastery of Waslere, took the religious habit in that house and for some time was its abbot. After laboring for the sanctification of others he resolved to provide for the welfare of his own soul and for this purpose caused a cell to be built in which he lived as a recluse to the year 737. After the destruction of the monastery of Waslere, his relics were translated to Lobbe.

3. **St. Virilus**, abbot of San Salvador at Leira in Navarra, lived in the reign of King Inigo in the ninth century. His remains were venerated for a long time, but little is known of his life and virtues.

4. Anniversary of the consecration of the church of Monte Cassino by Pope Alexander II in 1071, in the presence of a great number of bishops and an immense throng of the faithful.

5. On the same day Monte Cassino celebrates the discovery and solemn elevation of the bodies of a number of Saints, including those of Guinizo, Januarius, Carlmann, Constantine and Simplicius, in the year 1628 under abbot Simplicius II.

Bavo: Mab.; Boll. Also called Alloynus. Butler.
Dodo: Fulcuin in Mab.
Virilus: Boll.; Yepez.
Monte Cassino: Mab.; Boll.

2

1. **St. Leodegar,** bishop of Autun and martyr, was born in 616 and received his training in the school of his uncle, the bishop of Poitiers. The latter also appointed him archdeacon of the church of Poitiers, in which dignity he distinguished himself by his prudence and persuasive eloquence. For six years he was abbot of the monastery of St. Maxentius, and in 659 was made bishop of Autun, which had been vacant and neglected for two years. After the death of King Clothair III, bishop Leodegar declared his adherence to that King's lawful successor Childeric, and became one of the latter's councillors. Notwithstanding the fact that the king lavished favors and honors upon him, Leodegar boldly reprimanded him for certain scandalous actions. The result was that Leodegar was banished to Luxeuil, where he remained four years until the unfortunate death of the king, when he was permitted to return to his see. He was not to enjoy peace very long, for Ebroin set up an alleged son of Clothair III to contest the rightful claims of King Theodoric and sent an army into Burgundy to enforce allegiance to the usurper. Bishop Leodegar spent a season in fasting and prayer with his people and was resolved to lay down his life, if it were demanded, for the true king. The besieging army demanded that the bishop be delivered to them; he left the city privately and presented himself before his enemies, who put out his eyes and cut off his lips and part of his tongue. Through the efforts of a kindhearted nobleman, he was permitted to pass three years in the monastery of Fecamp in Normandy, whence he wrote to his mother Sigrada, then a nun at Soissons, to forgive their enemies and to pray for them without ceasing. Finally he was summoned before a council of bribed prelates and asked to plead guilty of being an accomplice in the death of King Childeric. He asserted his innocence of the crime, whereupon they degraded him and delivered him into the hands of Chrodobert to be privately executed. This bloody deed was done in 678, and the remains of the Saint were carried to the abbey of St. Maxentius in Poitiers.

2. **Bl. Godfrey,** a Cistercian monk at Villers in Brabant, had been a monk at St. Pantaleon in Cologne, but, believing that he could attain perfection with greater security as a Cistercian, entered that Order and edified his brethren by his singularly virtuous conduct as a priest and sacristan to the time of his death in 1170.

3. **Bl. Godfrey,** another Cistercian monk at Villers in Brabant, was called Pachomius on account of his virtues and miracles. He was a native of Louvain, and as a youth became a canon regular at St. Gertrude's in that city. Later he entered the Order of Citeaux, which at the time was still in its first fervor and was attracting wide attention. He spent forty-seven years at Villers, steadily progressing in virtue and merit. Like St. Bernard, he was a devout client of the Blessed Virgin. He died in the year 1197.

Leodegar: Monk of St. Symphorian. Butler. French form: St. Leger.
Godfrey(1): John d'Assigny; Caes. of Heisterbach. Also called Godfridus.
Godfrey(2): Aubert Le Mire; Arnold de Raisse.

3

1. **St. Gerard**, abbot of Brogne in the diocese of Namur in Belgium, was the son of an Austrasian nobleman. While attending Count Berengar of Namur, he was one day returning from the chase and paused to say a prayer in the church at Brogne, where a vision directed him to renovate that church and enrich it with the relics of St. Eugene. Shortly after, he chanced to be in Paris on affairs of state and while attending the offices at St. Denys heard the reader of the martyrology announce that the remains of St. Eugene reposed in that venerable sanctuary. To his question how he might come into possession of these relics he was told that they could be purchased for.no earthly price. He understood and became a monk at St. Denys, and though advanced beyond the years of youth learned the elements of the Latin language like a schoolboy. Ten years later he was ordained priest, and now he submitted his request for the relics of St. Eugene, which were given him for the monastery of Brogne. He introduced the Rule of St. Benedict into that house, for a short time instructed the brethren in monastic observance, then retired to a cell to devote himself to the concerns of his own soul. He was not allowed to remain hidden long, for at the request of Duke Gilbert he proceeded to reform the canons regular at St. Guislin, a task which he accomplished by turning it into a Benedictine monastery. At the instance of Duke Arnold he undertook the general supervision of all the monasteries of Flanders, in all of which he restored exemplary discipline. His beneficial influence extended even to Lorraine, Champagne and Picardy. For twenty-two years he was unceasingly active in the prosecution of the noble work for which he had been chosen. Finally he made a pilgrimage to Rome to secure the approval of his reform. He revisited all his monasteries, and then retired to a cell where he remained to the day of his holy death in 959. His remains rest at Brogne.

2. **St. Froilan**, bishop of Leon in Spain, was a native of Lugo in Galicia. At the age of eighteen he entered a monastery in which he spent several years in the study of the spiritual life, then dwelt several years in a solitude and preached to the people. His fame was spread abroad and a number of disciples gathered about him to be instructed in the warfare of the spirit. King Ramirus of Leon requested him to build a monastery and pray for the welfare of the country in those distracted times. He founded Tabara and, somewhat later, Morerola, where he ruled a community of two hundred monks. At the instance of King Veremund he was elected bishop of Leon, which see he governed sixteen years to the day of his death in 1095.

3. **Bl. Utto**, first abbot of Metten in Bavaria, came from Italy and devoted himself to the exercises of perfection under the direction of the pious priest Gammelbert, who subsequently sent him to minister to the faithful at Michelsbuch. The wars at that time waged by Charlemagne in those regions compelled him to leave and fix his abode across the Danube. There Charlemagne found him, and encouraged him to establish a monastery, for which that prince is said to have furnished the means. This was the beginning of the mon-

Gerard: Mab.; Boll.; Butler.
Froilan: Mab.; Boll.

astery of Metten, of which Utto was the first abbot in 792. He ruled the monastery for thirty-six years and passed to his reward about 828. His veneration was approved on August 25, 1909. Metten was suppressed in 1803, but restored in 1830 and is the mother-house of the American-Cassinese Congregation of Benedictines.

4

1. **St. Donatus,** a disciple of St. Benedict, suffered martyrdom in Sicily together with St. Placidus, whose feast is celebrated on the fifth of October.

2. **St. Aurea** was appointed abbess of a monastery founded by St. Martial at Paris in 631 and piously ruled a large community. A year previous to her death she received a premonition to prepare herself and her sisters for their approaching end. She was stricken by a pestilence and died, together with many of her sisters, on this day in the year 666. The city of Paris owes many favors to her intercession.

3. **Herveus,** a Cistercian abbot of Ourchamps, was of the blood of the Frankish kings and even as a child was deeply attached to St. Bernard, who foretold his future sanctity. Herveus became a monk at Ourchamps and made such praiseworthy progress in virtue that he was elected to succeed abbot Valeranus. He died in 1124.

4. **Mary,** first abbess of the Cistercian monastery of S. Maria at Carrizo in Spain, was of royal descent and induced many members of the nobility to follow her example in choosing a life of poverty and obscurity. At her own expense she built the abbey, of which she was made abbess, and ruled it to the day of her death in 1177.

5

1. **St. Placidus and his Companions,** disciples of Our Holy Father St. Benedict, were slain by corsairs at Messina, Sicily, on this day in the year 542 or 546. Placidus was a descendant of the noble Roman family of the Anicii and was in his early boyhood confided to the care of St. Benedict by his father Tertullus. Pope Gregory the Great relates that one day when the boy Placidus was on the point of drowning, St. Benedict sent to his rescue the monk Maurus, who walked upon the waters, drew out the child and brought him safe to the shore. Like Maurus, he was one of the most beloved disciples of our Holy Father, who, although Placidus was but twenty-six years of age, sent him to Sicily to organize a monastery on estates granted by Tertullus. While engaged in this peaceful enterprise he was attacked by pirates, who slew all the monks and destroyed the monastery by fire in the year aforesaid. Among his companions were his sister Flavia, and the monks Eutychius, Victorinus, Donatus, Firmatus and Faustus.

Utto: Boll.; Album Ben.
Donatus: Ferrari.
Aurea: Audoenus; Quetif; Butler.
Herveus: Gaufrid; Vincent of Beauvais.
Mary: Seguin. Stadler calls the monastery Curico.
Placidus: Greg. Magnus; Mab.; Butler.

2. **St. Aymard,** abbot of Cluny and successor of St. Odo in 941, is described as a man distinguished for simplicity and regularity. Under his rule Cluny prospered both in numbers, fame and wealth; even bishops placed themselves under the obedience of the abbot. Although afflicted with blindness towards the end of his life, he never murmured. Having, with the consent of the brethren, designated Majolus as his assistant in 948, he lived in retirement to the time of his death in 964.

3. **St. Attilanus,** bishop of Zamora in Spain, was born at Tarazona in Spain in 939 and entered a monastery near that city when he was fifteen years of age. Attracted by the reputation of St. Froilan, he was permitted by his abbot to join this saintly solitary. After Froilan had built the monastery of Morerola, he appointed Attilanus as its prior. Both abbot and prior had won the esteem of the Spanish clergy in such a degree that Froilan was elected bishop of Leon, and Attilanus bishop of Zamora, which he governed for ten years. Fearing that he was unworthy to be a bishop, he left Zamora and wandered about for the space of two years begging his daily bread, till an inner voice ordered him to return to his see, which he continued to rule eight years, after which he died in the seventieth year of his age in 1009. He was canonized by Pope Urban II, about 1095.

4. **Bl. Gwerwich,** descended from an illustrious family in Westphalia, severely wounded his friend Count Theobald of Vohenberg in a tournament and to atone for his careless life entered the monastery of Siburg. Subsequently he and his friend Theobald founded the monastery of Waldsassen and introduced the Cistercian rule. Gwerwich died as a monk of Waldsassen about the year 1200.

6

1. **St. Pardulph,** abbot of Gueret in France, was the son of peasants and was born at Sardene. As a child he was temporarily blind. Urged by a strong desire to attain perfection, he left his home and for some years lived in a solitude. When Count Lanthar of Limoges had founded the monastery of Gueret, Pardulph was selected to govern the community, in which he maintained perfect discipline, edifying the brethren by his mortification and charity to the poor. When the Moors began to make bloody raids into the district in which his monastery lay, he ordered his religious to seek a place of safety, while he remained to face the invaders. The latter laid waste the country round about but spared the monastery. At the age of eighty he was prostrated by an illness, of which he died about the year 740.

2. **St. Adalbero,** bishop of Augsburg, was descended from the Counts of Dillingen and became a monk at Ellwangen. He succeeded Hatto as abbot and in 887 was elected bishop of Augsburg. Emperor Arnulph confided to him the education of his son Louis, and authorized him to reform the monastery of

---

Aymard: St. Odilo; St. Peter Damiani.
Attilanus: Sandoval; Mab.; Boll.
Gwerwich: Bruschius.
Pardulph: Mab.; Boll.

Lorsch. The report of his virtues and valuable services to the Church reached far beyond the bounds of the country. He was a benefactor of many monasteries and twice visited St. Gall's. According to some of his biographers, he excelled all his contemporaries in music. After ably and faithfully ruling his diocese twenty years he died in 909. His remains rest in the church of SS. Ulric and Afra in Augsburg.

3. **St. Epiphania,** a nun at Pavia, was the daughter of the Lombard King Rachis, but scorned the honors of this life to serve her heavenly Lord in humility and obscurity. She passed to her eternal reward about 795.

4. The Statutes of the (extinct) **Bohemian Congregation** were approved by Pope Clement XI in 1714.

7

1. **St. Ositha,** the daughter of the Mercian prince Frithwald and of his wife Wilburga, was brought up in the monastery of Aylesbury, and was promised in marriage by her parents to King Sighere of Essex. The marriage rite was performed, but when Sighere learned that she had previously resolved to embrace the religious life, he allowed her to carry out her purpose and gave her a place called Chich for the establishment of a monastery. Here Ositha established herself and formed a community, which she governed till about the year 653, when Danish pirates plundered the convent and, on the firm refusal of Abbess Ositha to abjure her faith, struck off her head and thus added the crown of martyrdom to that of virginity.

2. **St. Martin,** Cistercian abbot of Valparaiso in Castile and a disciple of St. Bernard, even as a child renounced all earthly advantages and pleasures, and strove to please God by observing the evangelical counsels. One day King Alphonse saw him take the discipline in a cavern, and was so deeply moved that he decided to built a monastery, of which he appointed Martin abbot. He was the father of many spiritual children and maintained such edifying discipline in his monastery that the place truly deserved to be called Valparaiso, or Vale of Paradise. He died in 1152.

3. **Ven. Fingenius,** abbot of St. Felix at Metz, was a native of Ireland, and came to Germany in the days of emperor Lothair. Bishop Theodoric detained him in Metz, where he became a monk. He was made abbot of the monasteries of St. Felix and St. Symphorian at Metz and of St. Victor at Verdun and died after a meritorious life in 1004.

8

1. **St. Theodefrid,** bishop of Amiens, was so splendidly endowed with high gifts of mind and heart, that at the instance of Queen Bathildis he was ap-

Adalbero: Mab.; Boll.
Epiphania: Ferrari.
Ositha: Boll.; Stanton; Butler.
Martin: Le Mire; Seguin.
Fingenius: Mab.

pointed first abbot of Corbie, which she had founded. He was a monk of Luxeuil at the time. Having ruled his abbey successfully several years he was promoted to the see of Amiens and died about 690.

2. Bl. **Badilo**, an abbot as to whose identity little is known, since there are several bearers of the name, is buried in the monastery of Leuze, in the diocese of Cambrai and is venerated on this day.

3. Bl. **Compagni**, a Camaldolese monk at Padua, shone by his virtue throughout his life, and his sanctity is attested by the preservation of his body and by numerous miracles wrought at his tomb. He died in the year 1264.

9

1. St. **Gislenus**, abbot of the monastery of Zell in Hainaut, was born in Athens, in Greece, and received his education in that famous home of learning. He became a Basilian monk, and, after he had been ordained priest, obtained leave to make a pilgrimage to Rome. On his way a vision instructed him to go to a country, called Hainaut, there to build a church in honor of SS. Peter and Paul and to dwell near it to the end of his days. He did not delay to obey the directions, and travelled to Hainaut with two companions, Lambert and Bellirius. Under the direction of Bishop Amandus, he cleared a place for a cell, but subsequently chose to settle at Ursidong, where with permission of Bishop Autbert of Cambrai he built a church in honor of SS. Peter and Paul. King Dagobert granted him some lands for a monastery. His holy life edified the people, many of whom, including Waldetrudis and her sister Aldegundis and their daughters Aldetrudis and Waldeberta, placed themselves under his spiritual guidance. Blessed by the poor and the afflicted whom he had befriended, he died in the monastery which he had dedicated to the Apostles and which was later called St. Gislin, in the year 681.

2. St. **Deusdedit**, fifteenth abbot of Monte Cassino, had governed that house six years when it was invaded by the tyrant Sicard, duke of Beneventum. As the abbot could not or would not deliver the money demanded by Sicard, he was thrown into a dungeon, where after suffering for a long time from cold and hunger, he died in 834.

3. St. **Guenther**, monk and hermit at Niederaltaich in Bavaria, was of illustrious descent, but spent the years of his youth in frivolity and sin. Having been touched by the grace of God, he prostrated himself at the feet of abbot Gotthard of Hirschfeld and confessed his faults. He accompanied that abbot to Niederaltaich, there completed the work of his conversion, but did not take the religious habit before he had made a pilgrimage to Rome. His progress in virtue was so rapid that his superiors were filled with amazement. Having been permitted to embrace the eremitical state, he first made his abode at Ran-

Theodefrid: Mab.
Badilo: Mab.
Compagni: Boll.
Gislenus: Mab.
Deusdedit: Mab.

zing near Altaich, and afterwards penetrated deeper into the forest and built a chapel and a monastery for the brethren who had followed him. Ere long the fame of his sanctity reached even foreign lands. King St. Stephen of Hungary three distinct times sent envoys inviting him to come to his court. Guenther finally acceded to the pressing invitation, and induced the king to make a number of pious foundations. On his return, he placed his monks under the jurisdiction of the abbot of Oberaltaich and entered farther into the forest to resume the life of a solitary. When the monks of Brewnow desired to make him their abbot, he fled to a distant hill and lived for some time near the Bohemian village of Dobrawoda where he met duke Brzetislav, to whom he warmly commended the monastery of Brewnow. Shortly after, he said: "To-morrow I shall die; see to it, that I am buried at Brewnow." He died as he had foretold, in 1045, at the age of ninety years. His tomb was destroyed during the Hussite Wars.

4. **Bl. Sibylla of Gagis,** a Cistercian nun and faithful attendant of St. Lutgardis, died in the year 1246. One day she grew weary of her work and was on the point of seeking for a change in employment, when an inner voice spoke: "I am not come to be served but to serve," whereupon she took fresh courage and persevered to the end. The present day is that of the elevation of her body and was celebrated at Aviers at Brabant.

10

1. **St. Paulinus,** archbishop of York, a monk from the monastery of St. Andrew on the Caelian Hill in Rome, was one of the missionaries whom Pope St. Gregory the Great sent to aid St. Augustine in the conversion of England. In 625 he was made bishop of Northumbria, but his labors progressed slowly for the reason that King Edwin, though favorable to Christianity, hesitated to ask for baptism. Finally, on Easter Sunday 627, he also baptized the king and the conversion of the people followed rapidly. At York a church of wood had been hastily erected for the baptism of the king, and a stone edifice was erected to take its place. At Lincoln he conferred episcopal consecration and the pallium on archbishop Honorius of Canterbury. Paulinus had already received the pallium from Pope Honorius and was the first archbishop of York. After the battle of Hatfield Chase, in which King Edwin was killed, Paulinus was compelled to leave his see and return to Kent to place queen Ethelburga under the protection of her brother Eadbald. At the request of the latter he undertook the administration of the vacant see of Rochester, and in this charge death found him in the year 644.

2. **St. Telechildis,** first abbess of Jouarre in the diocese of Meaux, was descended from the Frankish kings and was a disciple of St. Columban. She ruled a community of religious women for many years and rested from her pious labor about the year 680.

Guenther: Arnulph of St. Emmeran. Also called Guntherus.
Sibylla: Arnold de Raisse.
Paulinus: Bede; Stanton; Butler.
Telechildis: Mab.; Menard.

2. **St. Aldrich**, archbishop of Sens, was of noble descent and revealed a pronounced inclination to a life of prayer from boyhood. Heedless of the allurements of the world, he became a monk at Ferrieres in Gatinois—then called Bethlehem—where he received his education from the celebrated Alcuin and the abbot Singulf. On account of his proficiency in the sacred sciences he was ordained priest by Bishop Jeremias of Sens, and emperor Louis the Pious invited him to his court. For a short time he was abbot of Ferrieres, but in 830 was promoted to the archiepiscopal see of Sens. Wearied by ten years of devoted service he was about to resign his charge and return to Ferrieres, when he was summoned to his eternal reward in 840 or 841. His remains were carried to Ferrieres.

4. The monastery of **St. Vincent** in the Duchy of Beneventum celebrated the memory of nine-hundred monks, who shed their blood for Christ during the Norman and Saracen invasions in the year 881.

11

1. **St. Paldo**, first abbot of St. Vincent on the Voltorno in the former kingdom of Naples, was born at Beneventum and left home with his two cousins Taso and Tato, to make a pilgrimage for the welfare of his soul. Without informing their parents of their departure, they first journeyed to Rome, then, after having been trained in the monastic life according to the Benedictine Rule by Abbot Thomas of Farfa, they proceeded to a secluded spot near the sources of the Voltorno, where they were soon joined by a number of disciples eager to take part in their pious exercises. Paldo established a monastery for them and during the years of his rule was so evidently blessed by Heaven in his work, that he would say to his brethren: "He that perseveres to the end in tl house, will never be lost, but will have eternal life." He governed the original monastery from 707 to the time of his death in 720, and was succeeded in its government by Taso and Tato, both of whom are also numbered among the Saints.

2. **St. Ethelburga**, first abbess of Barking, in England, was the sister of St. Erkonwald, bishop of London, who founded for her the abbey of Barking. Here Ethelburga became the spiritual mother of many great servants of God, her chief assistant being St. Hildelita. In the year of the great pestilence a number of monks and nuns of Barking were carried off by death. Ethelburga envied them but consoled herself with the reflection that if she lived longer, she should have more time to cleanse and perfect herself. The Lord summoned her to the heavenly nuptials about the year 705.

3. **St. Juliana**, abbess of Pavilly, in the diocese of Rouen, was the child of humble parents employed in the service of the monastery, and begged in vain for a number of years to be admitted as a nun. When, finally, she was received,

---

Aldrich: Mab.
St. Vincent: Mab.
Paldo: St. Autbert.
Ethelburga: Bede; Butler; Stanton.

she proved to be so devout, zealous and prudent that after the abbess's death she was chosen to fill her place. Her life, rich in merit, closed about the year 740. Her remains repose in the monastery of Montreuil.

4. **Bl. Roderic,** a Cistercian novice of Morerola in Spain, was so pleasing to God by the fervor of his striving for perfection that he was summoned to receive the crown of eternal life before the day of his religious profession.

12

1. **St. Wilfrid,** archbishop of York, entered the monastery of Lindisfarne when only fourteen years of age. He soon perceived the defects of the Scottish tradition in ecclesiastical matters and resolved to visit Rome to seek for information at the source. He left England in company with St. Benedict Biscop, was detained for some time at Lyons, and at length reached the capital of Christendom, where he studied some months under the archdeacon Boniface. On his return he was again detained at Lyons, and spent three years there, until the death of the bishop left him at liberty to return to his own country. In Northumbria he was welcomed by Alchfrid, the son of King Oswy, who gave him the monastery of Ripon which he had lately founded. Shortly afterwards, Wilfrid was ordained priest by bishop Agilbert, whom he also accompanied to the celebrated conference of Whitby (or Streaneshalch), where he pleaded eloquently for the abolition of the peculiar usages introduced by the missionaries from Iona. Bishop Tuda of Lindisfarne died about a year later and by unanimous consent Wilfrid was named his successor. He went to France for consecration, which he received from the same Agilbert who had ordained him priest and who was now bishop of Paris. After some delay he returned to England and found that King Oswy had in the mean time placed St. Chad in the see of Northumbria. He was therefore unable to take possession until the arrival of St. Theodore, who as metropolitan investigated the matter and decided in Wilfrid's favor. He first established his see at York, but was again and again expelled and each time restored by the Holy See, to which he appealed. He had incurred the hostility of two kings, Egfrid and his brother Aldfred, and found himself opposed by men of eminent sanctity, such as St. Theodore of Canterbury, St. John of Beverley and others, who considered it more conducive to the service of God that the vast diocese should be divided, while he considered it his duty to preserve the integrity of the church committed to his care. Failing to accomplish anything by his resistance, he travelled to Rome and on his return spent some time in the missions of Friesland, and in the conversion of Sussex and the Isle of Wight. He was in every sense a great and munificent prelate; the edifices erected by him were the most splendid of those times, notably the churches of Ripon, York and Hexham. He was also zealous in establishing the Rule of St. Benedict in all the monasteries subject to him. The last four years of his life he spent as bishop of Hexham, having been restored to that portion of his former diocese by the Synod of Nidd. His last illness overtook him at Oundle, while visiting a monastery there. He died there April 24, 709 at the

Juliana: Mab.
Roderic: Aybert.

age of seventy-five years. His remains, which originally reposed at Ripon, were removed to Canterbury in 959.

2. **St. Harlindis**, abbess of Eick in the Netherlands, was, like her sister Relindis, adorned with unusual gifts of grace. Both were brought up in the fear of God by their parents, and trained in the convent at Valenciennes in all the accomplishments of noble young ladies in that age. Wishing to devote themselves to God's exclusive service, they persuaded their parents to found a monastery for them. The holy bishops Willibrord and Boniface installed them as abbesses and frequently visited the monastery. A goodly number of aspirants joined them, and the blessing of Heaven visibly rested upon the house. The nuns were not only exemplary in observance, but also accomplished in the manufacture of artistic ornaments for churches. The two abbesses copied the Psalms of David in letters of gold, also the four Gospels and other books with their own hands. Harlindis died about the year 745.

3. **Bl. Rodulph**, abbot and fourth General of the Camaldolese Order, had previously been an obscure and humble hermit of that Order. He established the female branch of the Order in 1086 and died in 1106.

13

1. **St. Simpert**, bishop of Augsburg, was educated in the monastery of Murbach in Alsace, and made such progress in piety and in learning, that after the death of Bishop Tosso in 778 he was made bishop of Augsburg. Ten years later he was also entrusted with the government of Murbach. He was a lover of the interior life and was content to leave the administration of external affairs to others that he might gain time to do the work of God. He restored the church of St. Afra, which was in a ruinous condition, renewed and built a number of other edifices and restored the abbey of Fuessen. Immediately after his death in 807 he was venerated as a Saint, and was canonized by Pope Nicholas V in 1450.

2. **St. Chelidonia**, abbess, was born in Calabria and became a nun at Subjaco. She was elected abbess of a monastery near by, but yielding to an inner impulse, left the monastery and served God in solitude by a life of prayer and mortification. She died October 13, 1152. Her name was perpetuated in that of the monastery which she had ruled.

3. **Reginbald**, bishop of Speier, was one of the twelve Benedictine monks whom Bishop Bruno of Augsburg secured from Tegernsee in 1012 to replace the chapter of secular canons at St. Afra in Augsburg. Bruno was their abbot, ruling and edifying them by his humility, charity and devotion. He reformed the monasteries of Ebersberg in Bavaria and of Lorsch in the diocese of Worms. In 1033 he was made bishop of Speier, and from that time devoted all his energy

Wilfrid: Eddi Stephen; Stanton; Butler.
Harlindis: Mab.
Rodulph: Menard.
Simpert: Adilbert, prior of St. Ulric.
Chelidonia: Arnold of Douai; Wion.

to the service of God, instructed his people, gave clergy and laity the example of an upright, stainless life and was a model bishop. He died in 1039.

14

1. **St. Burkard**, first bishop of Wuerzburg, was of noble descent and born in England. At the request of St. Boniface he left his native land to assist him and St. Lullus in preaching the Gospel in Germany. His apostolic fervor received recognition by his elevation to the new see of Wuerzburg, in which he labored with such unremitting zeal that in ten years no pagan was to be found within the limits of his diocese. Longing for repose after such a devoted day's work, he resigned in favor of Megingaudus, a disciple of St. Wigbert, and withdrew to Hohenburg, a quiet place in his diocese, and lived with six monks, devoting himself to prayer, study and mortifications. He died on Feb. 9, 752 and was buried by the side of St. Kilian in the monastery of St. Andrew, which he had built on the Marienberg. His body was raised and translated on the present day in 983 by Bishop Hugo. He is the patron saint of Worms and is also mentioned in the Roman Martyrology.

2. **St. Angadrema**, abbess at Beauvais, was the daughter of Count Robert, a high official at the court of King Clothair III, and had already been betrothed to a noble, by the name of Ansbert, when she was afflicted with a malady which disfigured her. Both now agreed to cancel the promise of marriage and devote themselves to the service of God. Ansbert eventually became archbishop of Rouen, while Angadrema received the veil at the hands of St. Audoenus, bishop of Beauvais, and founded a monastery, which she ruled to the day of her death, towards the close of the seventh century. During the Norman invasion, her remains were removed to the church of St. Michael. The city of Beauvais chose her as its patron saint.

3. **St. Dominic**, called *Loricatus*, a monk of Fontavellana, from childhood seemed to be destined for the religious life. His parents, who placed no difficulties in his way, are said to have offered the bishop a present that he might ordain the youth. The Saint, who detested simony, fled into the wilds of the Apennines and resolved never to undertake an ecclesiastical function. For some time he dwelt in a solitude at Luceolo, but subsequently made his way to a secluded spot near Montefeltre, where he led an austere life under the direction of a hermit. In 1042 he joined the hermits of Fontavellana, who were at the time governed by St. Peter Damiani. He always wore a steel corselet next to his skin, scourged himself while reciting the Psalter and otherwise mortified himself. After reciting Matins and Lauds with the brethren he died on this day in 1060.

15

1. **St. Thecla**, abbess at Kitzingen on the Main, in the diocese of Wuerzburg, was a native of England and had consecrated herself to God in the mo-

Reginbald: John of Mutterstadt.
Burkard: Mab.; Gropp; Butler.
Angadrema: Mab. Also called Angadrisma.
Dominic: St. Peter Damian; Butler.

astery of Winburn. St. Boniface invited her to come to Germany and second his efforts to spread the kingdom of God in that country. It is probable that she arrived in Germany with St. Lioba, about 748. She was for a time a nun in Lioba's convent at Bischofsheim, and was appointed by St. Boniface to preside over the monastery at Ochsenfurt. She succeeded Hadeloga as abbess of Kitzingen, where she completed her earthly course about 750.

2. **St. Hedwig,** duchess of Silesia and Poland, and foundress of the monastery of Trebnitz, was the daughter of Count Berthold of Andechs, and was educated by the nuns at Kitzingen. She induced her husband, Duke Henry, to found a monastery for Cistercian nuns at Trebnitz and to endow it with resources sufficient to maintain a thousand persons. She herself continued to live in her palace, but in her dress, fare and devotion copied the life of the nuns. Although of delicate constitution, she always wore a hairshirt, ate neither fish nor flesh for forty years, usually went barefooted to church and slept on the floor. She maintained her interior calm in the midst of sorrows and sufferings and was favored with ecstasies. After her husband's death in 1238, she took the habit at Trebnitz and lived under the rule of her own daughter, the abbess Gertrude, although she was never professed. She foretold the day of her death, asked for the Sacrament of Extreme Unction at a time when no one expected that her end was at hand and died in 1243. Pope Clement IV canonized her in 1266, and Pope Innocent XI ordained October 17 for her feast.

16

1. **St. Gall,** first abbot and founder of St. Gall's in Switzerland, was born in Ireland about 560, was trained by St. Columban and accompanied him to France about 585. He assisted Columban in founding the monasteries of Anegray, Luxeuil and Fontaines on the boundary of Lorraine and Burgundy. When Columban was banished by King Thierry, Gall accompanied him into the territory of King Theodebert and thence up the Rhine into the country about the Lake of Zurich, where they preached so powerfully against the impiety of idolatry, that they suffered much persecution. When Columban departed for Italy, Gall was sick and was prevented from following his master, but having been nursed back to health by the priest Willimar, he selected a place for a monastery and marked it with a cross. Here the foundations for a great religious house were laid about 614. Gall continued his preaching and converted a great number to the faith of Christ. Having delivered Frideburga, the daughter of Duke Gunzo, from an evil spirit, Gall was offered the see of Constance, but he declined, although pressed by clergy and people to accept, and suggested the deacon John for that honor. He likewise declined to meet the wishes of the monks of Luxeuil, who desired to make him their abbot. He died in 646 and was buried at St. Gall. The city which grew up in the shadow of the famous monastery bears his name to this day—St. Gallen.

2. **St. Mummolen,** bishop of Noyon and Tournai in France, was born at Constance and in his youth entered the abbey of Luxeuil, where he was or-

Thecla: Willibald; Mab.; Butler; Stanton.
Hedwig: Engelbert:; Cromer; Butler (Oct. 17).
Gall: Walafrid Strabo.

dained priest. With permission of the abbot, Mummolen and two companions
offered their services to bishop Audomar of Terouanne and, after assisting him
in the evangelization of the country for nine years, in 648 took up their abode
in the abbey of Sithiu, which the bishop had built for them. Mummolen, who
was made abbot, excelled all the rest in his mortifications, and is said to have
taken no other nourishment than bread and water. After the death of St.
Acharius in 659 he was chosen bishop of Noyon and Tournai, which he governed
faithfully to the end of his mortal career in 685.

3. **St. Lullus,** archbishop of Mainz, was born in England and received
his early education at Jarrow under the direction of Ven. Bede. He crossed
over to Germany in 732, where St. Boniface gladly received him, gave him the
religious habit and conferred on him the order of deaconship. He now accompanied St. Boniface on his missionary journeys and contributed his share to the
spread of the faith by his powerful and fearless preaching of the word of God.
In 751, St. Boniface ordained him priest and sent him to Rome to consult Pope
Zachary on matters concerning the missions. On his return to Germany, he
was appointed to succeed St. Boniface in the see of Mainz. Boniface resumed
his missionary work in the north and did not return alive; Lullus governed the
church committed to his charge for thirty-four years. He attended many
councils, maintained an extensive correspondence and founded the abbeys of
Bleidenstadt and Hirschfeld. When his health and strength began to fail, he
went to seek a little rest in the abbey of Hirschfeld, and it was there that he was
called to receive the reward of his faithful stewardship on November 1, 787.

4. **St. Anastasius,** a hermit, was born at Venice about 1020 and became
a monk at St. Michel in Normandy. After his abbot had been convicted of
simony, Anastasius retired to a neighboring island, but was recalled by Abbot
Hugo of Cluny. Pope Gregory VII sent him to preach the Gospel to the Moors
in Spain. After his return he was appointed to teach the monks. In his old
age he withdrew into the Pyrenees to lead a contemplative life, but was summoned to return to his monastery and died on the way at Doydes, in the diocese
of Rieux, in 1085.

17

1. **St. Anstrudis,** abbess of St. John at Laon, was sought in marriage by
a young nobleman, but preferred the example of her saintly mother Salaberga,
who had embraced the religious state. She entered the convent over which her
mother presided, received the monastic habit from her, and succeeded her in
the government of the community. Anstrudis was notable for her scrupulous
observance of the Holy Rule, her charity, zeal and purity of heart, that shone
forth in every word and action. When her brother had been slain by assassins
and she was threatened with a similar fate, she put her trust in God and did
not yield to fear. Her serenity made to naught the wickedness of her enemies.
On the day of her death, she called the sisters to her bedside, begged forgiveness
of all, and died on the present day in 688.

Mummolen: Folcard; Mab.; Butler.
Lullus: Wm. of Malmesbury; Mab.; Stanton; Butler.
Anastasius: Mab.
Anstrudis: Mab.; Butler, who says she is commonly called Austru.

2. **Gilbert the Great,** or the Theologian, eighth abbot of Citeaux, and formerly abbot of Ourchamp, is by some supposed to have been a native of England. He was a poet, philosopher and historian, and governed the Order of Citeaux but one year and four months, and died in 1165.

18

1. **Ven. Benno,** or Benedict, bishop of Hamburg and successor of St. Reginbert, is called the fifth Apostle of the Wends and died in the peace of the Lord in 1190.

2. **Guichard,** a monk at Clairvaux, walked in the path of religious perfection under the guidance of St. Robert of Brugges and received his reward about 1170.

3. Commemoration of the establishment of the Order of **Celestines** by Pope Celestine V; its rule was approved by Pope Gregory XI in 1374.

19

1. **St. Theofred,** abbot of Carmeri, was the son of a government official at Orange and led a devout life in the midst of the distractions of the world. Whenever he heard of the virtues of his uncle Eudo, abbot of Carmeri, he felt an impulse to follow his example. He eventually obeyed this heavenly call and became a monk, although his father reluctantly consented. Abbot Eudo on his deathbed expressed a wish that Theofred be chosen his successor, and the monks heartily agreed to have him as their father. When the Saracens moved upon Carmeri, he told his monks to seek safety in the forest while he remained kneeling before the altar. The invaders entered the chapel and beat him almost to death. When, on the following day, he rebuked them for their wild feasting, they maltreated him so cruelly that he died from the effects on this day in 728.

2. **St. Frideswida,** abbess at Oxford in England, was the daughter of the prince Didanus and his wife Safrida and was placed in charge of Algiva, supposed to have been an abbess in Winchester, by whom she was to be educated. After she had been professed as a religious, a certain prince, called Algar, was bent on making her his wife and threatened to destroy Oxford if her parents did not deliver her up to him. But his impiety was speedily punished by heaven with the loss of sight. To escape this persecution, Frideswida fled to a place on the banks of the Isis, where she remained concealed for three years, after which she ventured to approach nearer to Oxford and took up her abode at Binsey. Her father is said to have built the monastery in Oxford and made his daughter abbess, but she for the most part resided in a solitary spot called Thornbury, where she died about 790. She was the patroness of Oxford.

Gilbert: A. Manrique; Boll.
Benno: Krantz; Bucelin. Also called Benedict.
Guichard: Manrique.
Celestines: Papebroch.
Theofrid: Mab. Also called Thietfrid.
Frideswida: Wm. of Malmesbury; Butler; Stanton. Stadler gives various forms of her name;
    e.g. Frevisse.—In the Roman Martyrology she is called Fredeswinda.

3. **St. Desiderius,** abbot of Longret, was of noble lineage, became a monk at Longret under abbot Sigirannus, and was ordained priest. The number of monks having grown too great for the resources of the monastery, he was sent with several brethren to establish the abbey of Ruriac and to be its abbot. After the fame of his sanctity had attracted a great number of religious, he built an oratory in honor of St. Martin and took up his abode in a cell and lived in communion with God. He distributed the offerings he received to the poor and died in 679.

4. The venerable Servant of God, **James de Graffi,** a monk of the Cassinese Congregation, was distinguished both for his piety and his learning. His life was one of angelic purity and his devotion to the Blessed Virgin was so tender that he never grew tired of speaking in her praise and was wont to say that heaven and earth would pass away before any faithful client of Our Lady should be lost. On account of his learning he was appointed grand penitentiary and *censor librorum* for the kingdom of Naples. He declined an appointment as abbot, but was created a titular abbot by Pope Paul V, and died in the odor of sanctity in 1620.

5. **Elizabeth of Spalbeke,** nun at Herkenrode in the Netherlands, was favored with ecstasies while contemplating the sufferings of Our Lord, and bore the stigmata like St. Francis of Assisi. Her ecstasies are said to have occurred daily during the seven canonical hours of prayer. She died in 1304.

20

1. **St. Vitalis,** bishop of Salzburg and successor of St. Rupert, was selected for that see during the lifetime of his predecessor and strove to emulate his zeal and piety. As the inhabitants of the Binzgau, in Austria, were still living in the darkness of paganism, he did not rest till he had brought them all into the fold of Christ. Hence is he called the Apostle of Binzgau. He was noted for his charity and his success in reconciling enemies, and died in the year 645. His intercession is invoked for the preservation of monastic discipline.

2. **St. Wendelin,** abbot of Tholey in the diocese of Trier, was of royal Scottish blood, but ignored the nobility of his descent to become a humble follower of Christ, for which purpose he left his home and established himself as an anchorite in the diocese of Trier. One day a noble reproached him for leading such an indolent life, whereupon Wendelin served him as a shepherd. Having suffered severe temptations from internal and external enemies, he entered the monastery of Tholey, which King Dagobert had founded in 627, but he was permitted to live in a hermitage near by, where he led such a holy life that he was chosen to succeed abbot Pirminius after the death of the latter. Although of delicate constitution and much troubled with illness, he was an example of virtue for all the brethren. Shortly before his death, which occurred in 1015,

Desiderius: Menard.
James: Armellini.
Elizabeth: Blosius; Stadler (who styles her Blessed).
Vitalis: Hansiz; Canisius.

he disclosed the secret of his illustrious descent.   According to another tradition, he was the first abbot of Tholey and died in 650.

21

1.   St. Wimo, bishop of Bremen and apostle of the Goths, was a monk of Corbie in Saxony, who was singled out for his learning, prudence and piety to govern the see of Bremen.   He preached the faith in Denmark, and induced prince Harald, though not a Christian at the time, to protect the churches and missionaries in that country.   With an escort from the same prince he visited the islands off the eastern shore of Denmark, which had not hitherto been visited by missionaries, and then proceeded to Sweden, where he fell ill and died on September 17, 936.   His remains were interred at Birka, where he died.

2.   St. Gebizo, a monk of Monte Cassino in the days of abbot Desiderius, edified his brethren by his humility and other virtues.   By his prayers he effected the conversion of a good friend in the world, who was straying from the path of righteousness.   He died in the year 1090 and has for a biographer Paul the Grammarian.

3.   St. Condedus, monk and hermit at Fontenelle, was born in England and served as a missionary for several years in France.   After spending some time at St. Valery in Caux, he was attracted by the sanctity of the abbot Lambert of Fontenelle, by whom he and several companions were received as monks into that community.   Under Abbot Lambert's direction he settled on the island of Belcinac which King Theodoric had granted to him and where he built two churches.   After transferring his possessions to the monastery of Fontenelle, he died peacefully in 685.

22

1.   St. Bertharius, abbot of Monte Cassino and martyr, was of noble descent, received an excellent education, but was still more illustrious for virtue and piety and consecrated himself to God's service in religion.   He was elected to succeed abbot Bassutius in 856, and ruled the monastery at a period when it suffered much from Saracen incursions.   He is the author of commentaries on the Old and the New Testament, of poems and of treatises on grammar and medicine.   At the foot of the mountain he founded the city of St. Benedict, later called San Germano and at present Cassino.   He was slain by Saracen invaders in 884 while at prayer at the altar of St. Martin.

2.   St. Moderamnus, bishop, and abbot of Berceto near Pavia, was born in France about 650 and was elected bishop of Rennes in 703.   After governing that see for sixteen years with great zeal and energy, he set out on a pilgrimage

---

Wendelin: Mab.   Stocker gives as the year of his death 560; Loeffler, in the C.E., "about 617".
      Not in the Roman Martyrology.
Wimo: Mab.; Wion; Stadler.   Also called Unni, or Wenni,.
Gebizo: Peter the Deacon; Mab.
Condedus: Mab.
Bertharius: Peter the Deacon; Leo Marsicanus.

to Rome. He was bearing with him certain relics of St. Remigius and when he arrived in the territory of Parma, it was impossible for him to proceed on his way till he had left a part of them at the monastery of Berceto. When King Luit-prand had heard of this occurrence, he granted him that monastery. On his return from Rome, he arranged for the appointment of a successor at Rennes, then settled at Berceto, where he died in 719 or 730.

3. The devout **Henry**, a Cistercian laybrother of Villers in Brabant, was a native of Brussels, and was about to marry, when he chanced to visit some relatives in the monastery at Villers and was so powerfully captivated by their edifying life that he decided to remain. He was not spared temptations, but perseveringly triumphed over them all. God overwhelmed him with spiritual delights and consolations. Once while at prayer he heard a voice that said: "If thou wouldst share my consolations, thou must drink with me the chalice of suffering. Choose: wouldst thou rather bear moderate and long, or short but violent sufferings with me?" He replied: "Short but violent sufferings." He had his wish: he was beset by the world, the flesh and the devil, but persevered manfully in the struggle and received the crown of life in the thirteenth century.

23

1. **St. Benedict** was a monk whose memory is celebrated at Poitiers, but of whose life and virtues no written record is extant.

2. **St. Leothadius**, bishop of Auch in France, had been abbot at Moissac but was so eminent for learning and piety that he was made bishop of Auch and primate of Gascony. After governing his diocese faithfully for twenty-seven years, he received his eternal reward in 720.

3. **St. Bernard**, a Cistercian abbot, was bishop of Vich in Catalonia, Spain, and labored zealously not only for the welfare of the faithful but also in the conversion of the Moors. As he was not content to rule docile hearts, but also was bent upon checking the malice of evil men and extirpating infidelity, he personally, as was customary in those days, led troops against the Moors and captured several cities which they had occupied. In his private life he was very austere, guarded the purity of his heart, was charitable and had the gift of miracles. He died in 1243.

4. **Ven. Romuald of Fabriano**, a monk of Camaldoli, though not possessed of any remarkable degree of human learning, was distinguished for his holy simplicity and spiritual unction. He is said never to have offended God with a grievous sin. One day, when he fell into the hands of highwaymen, who bound him to a tree, he calmly said: "Do what God permits; I had as lief die today as tomorrow." In his bearing he was always cheerful and serene, and died smiling in the year 1579, after having lived in the monastery fifty-six years.

Moderamnus: Ferrari; Mab. According to Gams (Ser. Ep.) he was bishop of Rennes 793-720.
Henry: Arnold de Raisse; J. d'Assigny.
Benedict: Menard.
Leothadius: C. Robert; Menard.
Bernard: A. Vincent; Alvarez; Manrique.
Romuald: A. Florentius.

5. **Gauzelin,** a monk of Clairvaux, spent forty years in that monastery in uninterrupted communion with God and in internal peace and joy, that was reflected in his countenance and bearing.

24

1. **St. Martin,** abbot of Vertou in Brittany, was born about 527 at Nantes and early devoted himself to the clerical life. His bishop Felix sent him out even as a deacon to preach the Gospel to the heathens. Since his labors apparently bore no fruit and the city of Herbadille near Poitou, where he had preached, was devastated by a flood, he felt profoundly humbled and voluntarily went into exile. He travelled through a great part of Europe and studied the best features of the religious houses which he had an opportunity to visit. On his return to Brittany, he built a hermitage, but so many pious souls gathered about him that he was prompted to found a monastery for them. He presided over it as a kind, solicitous father to the year 601, when he entered into his rest. For many years after his death, the monastery stood in high repute for its excellent discipline; later it was reduced to the rank of a priory and was a dependency St. Jouin des Marnes.

2. **Bernard,** a Cistercian monk of Sauve-majeur in France, renounced earthly rank to serve the Lord in poverty. Having been appointed infirmarian, he treated those committed to his care with as much love and attention as if in each he saw Christ himself. The more repulsive a malady, the more tender was his solicitude for the comfort of the sufferer. Shortly before his death it was revealed to him that he would enter the heavenly mansion prepared for him. The year of his death is not stated.

3. **Mansuetus,** a Cistercian monk, was one of the brethren who assisted St. Stephen in founding the Order of Citeaux and foresaw its wonderful growth He died in the beginning of the twelfth century.

25

1. **St. Dulcard** was abbot of Ambiliac in France, and in the days of Bishop St. Sulpitius Pius of Bourges shone by the light of his virtue and led many on the path of salvation. He died about 640.

2. **St. Hildemarca,** abbess of Fecamp in Normandy, for some time presided over a community near Bordeaux, but later repaired to Rouen, where she placed herself under the spiritual guidance of St. Wandregisil. The latter appointed her abbess of a monastery founded by St. Vanning at Fecamp, where she ruled a great number of sisters, who were divided into choirs in such manner that the praises of God might be heard at all hours. She died in 670.

Gauzelin: Seguin.
Martin: Mab.
Bernard: Manrique; Rusca.
Mansuetus: Seguin.
Dulcard: Menard.
Hildemarca: Menard; Mab.   The Elenchus calls her abbess of Fontenelle.

3. **Dionysius l'Argentier,** Cistercian abbot of Orval in the Netherlands, was noted for his wisdom; piety, zeal for the honor of God and many
other virtues. He died in 1624 and appeared to the pious Bernard Montgail-
lard radiating joy and happiness.

26

1. **St. Albuin,** bishop of Fritzlar, was a native of Ireland and a monk of
Iona, but was urged by the apostolic zeal burning within him to cross over to
the Continent and preach the Gospel in Germany. He was appointed bishop
of Fritzlar and was intimately acquainted with St. Boniface and St. Lullus.
While praying for the grace of a happy death for the latter, Albuin was himself
summoned to take possession of the place prepared for him in the kingdom of
his Heavenly Father in 787. Archbishop Lullus had his remains carried to
Hirschfeld abbey.

2. **Bl. John,** Cistercian abbot of Aune, in the diocese of Liege, was slain
together with the brother sacristan by wicked men in 1338.

3. **Congan,** an abbot in Ireland, at the suggestion of Bishop Malachy of
Armagh became a Cistercian monk and died a holy death about 1150.

4. **Bernard,** bishop of Maurienne, in Savoy, was a Cistercian monk,
whose conscientious discharge of his religious duties marked him as qualified to
shed lustre upon a higher station. He ruled the see of Maurienne with great
solicitude, while in his private life practicing all the austerities of a monk, and
died about 1190.

27

1. **St. Tetta,** abbess, governed the double monastery of Winburn in
England so ably that both communities were renowned for the sanctity of their
lives. She was so rigorous in enforcing enclosure in the monastery for the nuns,
that not even prelates were allowed to enter. At one time the number of nuns
under her direction was five hundred. She was the spiritual mother of SS.
Lioba and Thecla and maintained correspondence with St. Boniface. The day
of her death, about 760, is not known; some calendars keep her memory on the
twelfth of August, others on the seventeenth of December.

2. **Verdino,** an abbot at Otranto in Italy, had the gift of prophecy and
wrote a commentary on the opening of the sixth seal of the Apocalypse. His
guardian angel revealed to him the day of his death, which occurred in 1278.

Dionysius: L. de la Roche.
Albuin: Mab.
John: Henriquez; Boll.
Congan: Seguin.
Bernard: B. de Montalbo.
Tetta: Stanton (Sept. 28); Rudolph of Fulda.
Verdino: Ben. Annals. Stadler calls him Werdinus.

3. **Mefred,** Cistercian prior at Ebersbach near Mainz, strove hard to preserve discipline in the monastery during the controversies between popes and emperors. The evil spirit beset him with horrid images and menaces, against all of which he defended himself with the sign of the Cross. He died about 1200.

4. **Armand Jean Le Bouthillier de Rance,** founder of the Reformed Cistercians, or Trappists, was born in Paris on January 9, 1626 and made such progress in his studies that he is said to have excelled even Bossuet. As early as 1637 he became a canon of Notre Dame at Paris and abbot of La Trappe and several other houses, which yielded him considerable revenue. The archbishop of Tours, his uncle, ordained him priest in 1651, but this did not produce much of a change in the young man's worldly inclinations and habits. Several incidents in his career, however, made him pause and ponder seriously upon the importance of providing for the salvation of his soul. He resigned all his benefices, declined the co-adjutorship offered him, took the Cistercian habit at Persaigne and after his profession in 1664 returned to his abbey of La Trappe, where he introduced the reform known by the name of that house. In his own life he exemplified the rules which he prescribed for others. He had already directed the reform for thirty-four years and was at death's door, when some one remonstrated gently with him for exacting such austerities from his monks. He ordered the brethren to attend him at his bedside and asked them if the reform were too strict. All without exception answered: No. He died in the year 1700. His remains lie in the monastery of La Grande Trappe.

28

1. **Egbert,** a Cistercian laybrother of Villers in Brabant, took delight in studying and emulating the lives of the monastic fathers. But as the kingdom of Heaven cannot be obtained without suffering and sorrow, Egbert was destined to bear his share, for which he was ever thankful. He was at all times pleasant, charitable to the poor, and compassionate with the distressed. Three days before his death he had a vision in which Our Lord revealed the approach of his entrance into eternal glory. The year is not recorded.

2. **Briolaya** was a Cistercian nun in Portugal, who declined to marry, as her parents had wished, and became a nun at Evora. She maintained perpetual silence and was blessed by Heaven with extraordinary gifts of grace. While assisting at the Holy Sacrifice of the Mass she frequently saw angels hovering above the altar, and beheld Christ either as a child or as crucified in the place of the consecrated host; at times the priest appeared to be covered with blood, or to be crowned with flowers while the altar was enveloped in a dazzling light. Despite these heavenly favors she always was humble and unassuming and died with sentiments of humility and resignation to the divine will about the year 1500.

Mefred: Henriquez. According to Chevalier the name is also written Ensfridus (Ensfrai) and the year of his death 1246.
De Rance: Life by Le Nain; Cath. Enc.
Egbert: Book of Models of Virtues at Villers.
Briolaya: B. Brito.

29

1.   **St. Elfleda,** third abbess of Ramsey in England, was the daughter of Earl Ethelwold, who founded Ramsey in the time of King Edward the Elder. The latter interested himself in the pious enterprise and induced St. Merwenna to govern the house and form a community of holy women.   Elfleda became one of her first disciples and in due time was chosen her successor.   Having acquired a reputation for eminent sanctity she died about 930 and was buried in the abbey church.

2.   **Bl. Margaret,** prioress at Rupertsberg near Bingen, flourished under the guidance of St. Hildegard and also persuaded her own sister, Ida of Spanheim, to embrace the religious life.   She died in the year 1190.

3.   **Peter of Catalonia,** Cistercian monk at Clairvaux and a disciple of St. Bernard, faithfully employed the graces which he received from Heaven in striving for religious perfection and died in the course of the twelfth scentury.

4.   **Beringer,** first abbot of Formbach, was distinguished for his charity to the poor and his condescension to the lowliest.   He died in the year 1113.

5.   The constitutions of the **Camaldolese Order** were approved in 1072 by Pope Alexander II.   This new body grew so rapidly, that in a short time it was necessary to divide it into four Congregations,—that of Camaldoli, Venice, Monte Corona and of Notre Dame.   In 1550 it absorbed the Order of Fontavellana.

30

1.   **St. Egelnothus the Good,** archbishop of Canterbury, is said to have been baptized by St. Dunstan, and was promoted to the archiepiscopal office after the death of archbishop Livingus in 1020.   He enjoyed the favor of the Danish ruler of England, King Canute, and used the latter's influence in the service of religion.   Egelnoth went to Rome for the pallium, which was conferred on him by Pope Benedict VIII, and on his return carried with him some relics of St. Augustine from Pavia.   He governed the church of Canterbury for eighteen years and was called to his reward in 1038.

2.   **Rainer,** a Cistercian monk of Villers in Brabant, though afflicted with bodily infirmity, had a courageous spirit and manfully struggled upward to the heights of perfection.   He suffered much from temptation, but issued unscathed from the long and painful combat.   Although a subdeacon, he delighted in performing the lowliest kinds of work.   He died saying "Praise the Lord."

Elfleda: Wm. of Malmesbury; Stanton.
Margaret: Trithemius; Arnold of Brescia.
Peter: Henriquez.
Beringer: Bucelin.
Camaldolese: Bullarium Mag.
Egelnothus: Mab.; Stanton (Ethelnoth, Egilnoth) on Oct. 29.
Rainer: Arnold de Raisse.

3. On this day was celebrated the feast of all the Saints whose **Relics** are deposited in the churches of our holy Order to remind us that if we would share their happiness we must walk in their footsteps. The feast was first observed, it is said, by abbot Reginbert of Echternach in Luxemburg.

4. Commemoration of the remarkable **Vision** in which our holy Father St. Benedict, in 541, saw the world before his eyes, collected, as it were, under a single ray of the sun, and saw the soul of Germanus, bishop of Capua, carried to heaven by angels, as it is related by St. Gregory the Great in his Second Book of Dialogues (c. 35).

31

1. **St. Wolfgang,** bishop of Regensburg, was a native of Suabia, and as a boy was sent to the monastery of Reichenau, where he enjoyed the intimate friendship of a youth named Henry. Later both went to Wuerzburg, and when Henry had been made archbishop of Trier, Wolfgang followed him to that city, where he first taught children and then ruled a religious community. After archbishop Henry's death he spent some time with archbishop Bruno of Cologne, after which he retired to Einsiedeln where he was ordained priest. Burning with a desire to spread the knowledge of the name of Christ, he sought the permission of the abbot to preach the Gospel in Hungary. He labored as a missionary for some time after 972, but was summoned from this field of labor to govern the see of Regensburg, As Bishop he preached with unflagging zeal and energy and eradicated abuses. He died at Puppingen in 994 and was interred in the monastery of St. Emmeram at Regensburg. He was canonized by Pope Leo IX in 1052.

2. **St. Foilanus,** monk at Nivelle in the diocese of Liege, was, as some authorities suppose, the son of Fyltan, king of Munster in Ireland, and heeded the advice of his brother St. Fursey to embrace the religious state. Fursey entrusted him with the government of the monastery of Knobbersbury in East Anglia, but in 650, after Fursey's death, Foilanus and his brother Ultan passed over to France, and lived as monks in a monastery at Nivelle under the direction of St. Gertrude. Even after Ultan had gone to found the monastery of Fosse, Foilan remained at Nivelle and devoted himself to instructing the people. In 655 he set out with three companions to visit his brother, but was slain on the way. His remains were interred at Fosse.

3. **St. Notburgis,** nun at Cologne, was of distinguished parentage and in order to escape importunate suitors, went into a solitude with her cousin Plectrudis. Another tradition says that she entered the convent of Our Lady at Cologne. But when her relatives and friends did not cease to urge her to return to the world and take a husband, she prayed that God might take her unto Himself. Her prayer was heard about the year 700.

Feast of Relics: Mab. This feast has been transferred recently to May 13.
Vision of St. Benedict: Gregory the Great.
Wolfgang: Mab.; Butler.
Foilan: Boniface, a contemporary. Compare the life of St. Ultan on May 1.
Notburgis: Menard; Stadler (Noitburgis).

November

1

1. **St. Genesius,** bishop of Lyons in France, was so zealous in the observance of discipline as a monk, that he edified not only his brethren but also the faithful of the surrounding country. Queen Bathildis appointed him her almoner, since she recognized him to be a man who knew how to treat the poor in whom Christ is served. After his elevation to the metropolitan see of Lyons he labored very successfully both by word and deed, and after his death in 668 was venerated as a Saint. His remains reposed in the abbey of Benedictine nuns at Chelles near Paris.

2. **St. Florbert,** abbot of Mont Blandin at Ghent in Flanders, was one of the worthiest disciples of St. Amandus, the Apostle of Flanders, and was his successor in that abbey and in his zeal to evangelize the people. It was he that received St. Bavo as a member of that community and aided him in the pursuit of perfection. After governing the monastery of Mont Blandin and that of St. Peter in the city of Ghent from 640 to 660, he died in the year last mentioned.

3. **St. Severin** was a monk at Tivoli, in Italy, of whose life no record is extant. He flourished about the year 700 and was always honored as a Saint. His remains repose in the cathedral of Tivoli.

4. **Spinela,** a nun at Aruca in Portugal, attained a high degree of perfection and flourished towards the end of the thirteenth century.

2

1. The **Solemn Commemoration** of the Souls of all the Faithful Departed was first celebrated by Abbot St. Odo of Cluny in 998 and was gradually adopted everywhere.

2. **St. Beuno,** (or Benno), a Welsh priest and monk, descended from the prince of Powis, was the uncle of St. Winifreda and became a monk,—perhaps at Bangor. After receiving Holy Orders he founded the monastery of Clynnog Fawr and that of Clynnog Fechan, and on the island of Anglesey the monasteries of Aberfraw and Trefdraeth. He died at Clynnog Fawr about 620.

3. **St. Lautenus,** abbot of Beaume, was descended from illustrious Burgundian stock, and received his training under Abbot Lawrence in the abbey of

Genesius: St. Antonine; Trithemius.
Florbert: Mab.
Severin: Ferrari.
Spinela: Brito.
Beuno: Menard. "The ancient day of his commemoration is not known, but the 21st of April was assigned to it by Pope Pius IX. in favor of the College of the Society of Jesus, near St. Asaph."—Stanton.

SS. Peter and Paul at Beaume. After that abbot's death, Lautenus was chosen to succeed him. Abbot Lautenus was a model religious and superior, was given to austerities and is said to have partaken of food only twice a week in Lent. He died in the tenth century.

4. **Peter Dagnini**, a Camaldolese monk, was one of the most beloved disciples of St. Romuald, the founder of that Order. In 1016 he was appointed prior of Camaldoli by Romuald, and discharged the burdensome duties of that office with the greatest solicitude and conscientiousness. After receiving the last sacraments, he devoutly kissed the crucifix and died in the year 1051.

5. This is also the anniversary of the death of several monks of St. Mary's of Grumain near Breslau, who suffered death at the hands of the Hussites rather than renounce their faith.

3

1. **St. Pirmin**, bishop, was at first a monk and after he had learned the art of ruling others by governing himself and by obeying, was chosen to rule others. He is said to have been a missionary bishop, while some writers assign as his see the fortress of Meltis—now Medelsheim—near Zweibruecken in the Palatinate. From this missionary centre he went forth to preach the Gospel along the upper Rhine and crowned his labors by founding the abbey of Reichenau. Having been driven from this place by duke Theobald in 727, he appointed Heddo to rule that house, from which issued founders and restorers o many monasteries. Pirmin himself restored the monasteries of Schuttern, Gengenbach, Schwarzach, Marmoutier and Neuweiler, and in 727 settled near Colmar, where he laid the foundation of the monastery of Murbach. In 740 he founded Hornbach; according to credible traditions he also founded Ober- and Niederaltaich and Pfaffenmuenster, Mondsee, Pfaefers and Amorbach. He died in 758 and was venerated as a Saint immediately after his death. In 1777 his relics were translated from Innsbruck to St. Blasien.

2. **St. Winefrid**, abbess and martyr, was the daughter of a nobleman in North Wales, but from her infancy showed an inclination for the religious state. She was one of the most eager disciples of St. Beuno, from whose hands she received the veil. With several other ladies of a similar disposition she led a religious life in a house presented her by her father at Holy Well. She left this place after the death of Beuno, for some time lived under the guidance of St. Deifer, but later entered the monastery of Gutherin, of which she was elected abbess after the death of the abbess Theonia. Caradoc, a son of the ruling prince, is said, to have slain her about the year 700 for refusing to violate her vows. In 1138 her remains were removed from Gutherin to Shrewsbury.

Lautenus: Menard.
Peter: A. Florentius.
Grumain: Le Mire; Cochlaieus.
Pirmin: Warmann; Henry of Calw. The Roman Mart. calls him Meldensis Episcopus.
Winefrid: Robert of Shrewsbury; Stanton. The Roman Mart. has the name Wenefrida.
    Other forms: Wennefrida, Winfrida, Guenfrida. Butler (Wenefride).

3. **St. Amicus,** a monk of Monte Cassino, was born at Camerino about 1000 and contrary to the wishes of his parents embraced the clerical state. After his ordination he became a monk at Monte Cassino, where he soon excelled all in piety and observance. With the permission of his abbot he dwelt for three years in a secluded spot, but was discovered. His hermitage now became a resort of many devout persons who came to ask his advice or to commend themselves to his prayer. He was prevailed upon to abandon his solitude and make his abode near the church of St. Peter at Avellano, where he continued to edify the people by his austerity and to soften the hearts of sinners by his kind but earnest admonitions. He died in 1045 and was ever since that time honored as a Saint.

4

1. **St. Modesta,** abbess of St. Symphorian in Trier, was the sister of St. Willibrord. She lived in spiritual communication with St. Gertrude of Nivelle, although she had never seen the latter. One day while she was at prayer, the Blessed Virgin appeared to her and announced that Gertrude was dying. Modesta followed her into the regions of eternal light about 680.

2. **St. Berthila,** abbess of Chelles near Paris, was born in Soissonais about 620, and with the consent of her parents and the blessing of St. Audoenus, entered the monastery of Jouarre in Brie, which had recently been founded by Ado, the brother of St. Audoenus, and had been committed to the charge of St. Telechildis. In this house Berthila laid the foundation of religious perfection by the practice of humility. On account of this and other eminent virtues she was given the charge of the guest-house, the sick and the children that were educated in the monastery. After queen Bathildis had restored the monastery at Chelles in 646, the community placed in it was drawn from Jouarre with Berthila as the first abbess. Such was the renown of the house during her rule that even two queens, Hereswida and Bathildis, took the veil at Chelles. Berthila governed the community forty-six years and died in 692.

3. **St. Girard,** monk and prior at Brossay, from his childhood led a retired, innocent life, became a monk at St. Albin in Anjou and strove to deserve the name of a son of St. Benedict by cultivating every virtue of a monk. He always wore a hairshirt, slept but a few hours, subsisted on fruit and vegetables and was an ardent client of the Blessed Virgin. The power and unction of his words drew hardened sinners from the brink of the precipice and led them to ·God. His eyes and hands raised heavenward he died in 1123.

4. **Henry,** prior at Ochsenhausen in Suabia, led his brethren by the power of his virtuous example and died in 1240.

Amicus: Peter the Deacon.
Modesta: Menard. Also in the Roman Martyrology.
Berthila: Menard; Butler (Bertille).
Girard: Menard.
Henry: Canisius; Henriquez.

5. The Order of **Monte Vergine** was approved on this day in the year 1197 by Pope Celestine III. An account of the founder, St. William, may be found June 25.

5

At Monte Cassino in Italy is commemorated on this day the Dedication of the church of St. Stephen and discovery of the bodies of Blessed Paulin and Augustine, disciples of St. Benedict. Abbot Oderisius in 1103 translated their remains to the church of St. Andrew.

1. **St. Fibitius**, an abbot, of whom little is known beyond the name, is venerated on this day at Trier. He is supposed to have died about 511.

2. **St. Malachy**, archbishop of Armagh in Ireland, learned the elements of spiritual life under the guidance of the hermit Imar. He was ordained priest by archbishop Celsus at the age of twenty-five and at once began to rouse the faithful from their religious torpor by the vigor of his apostolic preaching. In order that he might study ecclesiastical discipline in other lands where it had been maintained through the influence of the Holy See, he obtained leave to visit Bishop Malchi of Lismore, and on his return was appointed superior of the famous abbey of Bangor. At the age of thirty he was elected bishop of Connor, an office which he accepted only at the instance of Celsus and Imar. When the city of Connor was devastated by the King of Ulster, Malachy with one hundred and twenty of his disciples went to Munster, where he founded the monastery of Ibrak. Archbishop Celsus on his deathbed designated Malchi to succeed him and Malachy was recognized by the clergy as the new archbishop. He encountered difficulties in maintaining the see of Armagh, which for a part of the time was in the hands of an intruder. He journeyed to Rome in 1139 to apply for the pallium, and while on his way visited Clairvaux, made illustrious by the virtues of St. Bernard. Here he would fain have stayed for the rest of his days, and while at Rome he petitioned Pope Innocent II to grant him this favor, but the Pontiff sent him back north as papal legate. On his return journey Malachy again paused at Clairvaux, where he left four companions who were to profess in the Cistercian Order and transplant it to Mellifont in Ireland. Having returned to Ireland, he celebrated several synods and accomplished much for the welfare of souls. In 1148 he undertook to revisit France and there to confer with Pope Eugene III, whom he, however, did not meet. After his arrival at Clairvaux he was seized with a violent fever, and died on November 2.

6

1. **St. Winoc**, abbot of Wornhout in Flanders, was a native of Brittany. His earliest years were marked by singular innocence and piety, and a desire to embrace a life of Christian perfection. He gained over to the same views sev-

Monte Vergine: Bullarium
Monte Cassino: Mab.
Fibitius: Menard; Rom. Mart.
Malachy: St. Bernard; Butler (Nov 3.).

eral companions of high rank and passed over to England, but after a while they returned to the Continent and put themselves under direction of St. Bertin at Sithiu. Seeing that the strangers were called to a more retired life than that in a great monastery, he allowed them to build a little dwelling for themselves on a spot later known as Berg St. Winoc. Here they lived together till obedience called Winoc to another field of labor. St. Bertin had accepted from a certain rich man a gift of lands at Wornhout, and Winoc was commissioned to assume the charge of building a monastery and a hospice at that place. To this work he devoted the remainder of his days, laboring with his own hands so diligently, that all beholders were filled with amazement. He was called to his eternal rest in 717. At the time of the Norman ravages in the ninth century, his relics were translated to St. Omer, and at a later period to Berg.

2. **St. Appian,** a monk and hermit, was born in the Italian province of Liguria in the eighth century and lived a devout life at the monastery of St. Pietro *in cielo aureo* at Pavia. His abbot sent him to Comacchio to supervise the salt works owned by the abbey. During the summer he devoted himself to the development of that industry, and during the winter lived as a recluse near by, fasting, praying, meditating to the edification of the faithful. Here he died lamented by the poor.

3. **St. Condeluc,** priest and monk at Rennes in Brittany, was distinguished for his simplicity and candor. He always guarded the purity of his heart and shed many tears at prayer. When the garden was entrusted to his charge, he cultivated it with his own hands. One season a host of caterpillars threatened to destroy the vegetables; he bade them in the name of Christ to leave and they were seen no more. After he had lived many years in holiness, God revealed to him the day of his death, and he exchanged this life for a better in 870.

7

1. **St. Willibrord,** first bishop of Utrecht, was born about 658 in Northumbria and received his education at the monastery at Ripon. After his profession he was sent, in the twentieth year of his age, to Ireland, to his fellow-countrymen, St. Egbert and St. Wigbert, under whom he rapidly advanced in the way of holiness, and after spending eleven or twelve years in their company, felt himself inspired with the same ardor for the apostolic missions, which had long inflamed their breasts. Having been ordained a priest, he left in 690 with Suitbert and ten other companions to preach the Gospel to the Frisians. Willibrord journeyed to Rome to receive the license and blessing of the Roman Pontiff for his undertaking and returned to his chosen field of toil. Within six years the number of converts had grown to such an extent, that Pepin of Heristal proposed that Willibrord receive episcopal consecration. Once more the Saint crossed the Alps, was consecrated by the Pope and received the name of Clement. At the same time the pallium was conferred on him and he was

Winoc: Mab.; Stanton; Rom. Mart.; Butler.
Appian: Mab. Stadler (Mar. 4) gives other forms: Apianus, Apuanus.
Condeluc: Life of St. Convoyon.

authorized to select a see in Frisia. He selected Utrecht and built a cathedral in honor of the Most Holy Redeemer. Two years later he founded the abbey of Echternach in Luxemburg and reserved its chief direction for himself. At Utrecht he founded another monastery, for which he appointed Gregory as the first abbot. His influence over Pepin of Heristal was so great that he prevailed upon that magnate to be reconciled with his lawful wife Plectrudis before his death. He extended his missionary activity beyond the limits of Frisia into Denmark. When in 719 Radbod, king of that part of Frisia which the Franks had not yet subjugated, died, Willibrord encountered no more opposition to the spread of Christianity in that region. Alcuin thus describes Willibrord: "In his external demeanor he was pleasant and dignified, he was always cheerful and gentle in company, prudent in counsel, indefatigable in his apostolic labors and at the same time ever intent upon nourishing and strengthening his soul by prayer, reciting the Psalms, vigils and fasts." When old age rendered the performance of his manifold duties impossible, he committed the charge of his see to a coadjutor and retired to prepare himself for the journey into eternity. He died in 738 at the age of eighty years and in the forty-third year of his episcopate. He was interred in the abbey of Echternach.

2. St. Wilgis, father of St. Willibrord, led a devout life in the world, until, feeling himself called to a higher state, he retired to a promontory on the banks of the Humber, where he lived for some time as a hermit, serving God with prayers, fastings and vigils. Eventually the king and others joined in endowing his cell with certain lands, and with means to build a church, which he dedicated to Our Blessed Lady. A small community gathered around him, over which he presided until his happy passage to a better life. Neither the day of his death is known, nor the year in which he died. Alcuin, who has written a notice of his life, tells us that he himself was at one time prior of the monastery founded by St. Wilgis.

3. St. Tetta, or Gebetrudis, abbess of Remiremont, continually struggled to obtain the one thing necessary, and devoted herself exclusively to God's service and the sanctification of the souls in her care. For the edification of posterity she caused the life of St. Adelphius to be written. Tetta died in 680.

8

1. St. Willehad, bishop of Bremen, and apostle of the Saxons, was a Northumbrian and received a careful religious training in his childhood. When he had been ordained a priest he received permission, in 772, to preach the Gospel in Frisia. He began his missionary activity at Dokkum, where St. Boniface had been slain eighteen years before, and in a short time saw his labors blessed with numerous accessions to the Christian fold. As he penetrated farther into the country, however, he found his progress retarded by the bitter opposition of idolatrous priests, but he escaped their violence and commenced to preach in the neighboring province of Drente. Here, too, his life was beset with dangers and he once barely escaped death by defending himself with a reliquary. Next

Willibrord: Alcuin; Bede; Rom. Mart.; Butler.
Wilgis: Stanton; Menard.
Tetta: Mab.

he betook himself to Bremen, where he preached seven years to the Saxons, until the latter, in 782, rebelled against Charlemagne and killed several missionaries. To escape this danger, Willehad journeyed to Rome, submitted to Pope Adrian a report on the state of the missions and spent two years in retirement at the abbey of Echternach, where he copied the Epistles of St. Paul and other writings. At the same time he collected his fellow-missionaries who had been driven out of Saxony, and after Wittekind, the Saxon king, had been baptized, returned to his former scene of labor and took up his abode at Wigmar. Having been consecrated bishop of the Saxons on July 15, 787, he selected Bremen for his residence. Here he labored not only for his own salvation but also for that of his flock, ate little, abstained from intoxicating drink, delighted in reading Holy Scripture, was moved to tears while offering the Holy Sacrifice of the Mass and performed the functions of his office despite the weakness that came upon him with the advance of years. He died in 789 and was buried at Bremen. During the Reformation his relics were lost; gradually, too, his feast was forgotten, but the Sacred Congregation of Rites in 1901 authorized its celebration to be re-introduced in the dioceses of Muenster, Osnabrueck and Paderborn and to be observed on a vacant day after the eighth of November.

2. **St. Godfrey,** bishop of Amiens, at the early age of five was placed in charge of his godfather, Godfrey, abbot of Mont St. Quentin, who trained him in the practices of piety and instilled into him such a love of prayer, that he was known to spend nights in contemplation. Although reluctant, he was ordained priest at the age of twenty-five years by the bishop of Noyon, and shortly after was made abbot of Nogent in Champagne, which acquired such an excellent reputation that two abbots entered his community and took their place in the ranks of the plain religious . In 1103 he was appointed bishop of Amiens; accepted when he saw that no heed was paid to his remonstrances, and made his entrance into his episcopal city barefooted. At his table he daily fed thirteen poor persons and washed their feet; he valiantly resisted unjust and unwarranted aggressions of the powerful, corrected abuses among the clergy and effected the reform of the abbey of St. Valery. While on a journey to Rheims, he was attacked by illness in the abbey of St. Crespin at Soissons and died there in the year 1118.

3. **Bl. Gregory,** abbot of Einsiedeln, a native of England, and, as some say, a son of King Edward the Elder, left his betrothed bride and accompanied by two other youths, fled to Rome where he lived for several years as a monk on Mount Coelius. In consequence of several visions, he betook himself to Einsiedeln, where his life was so edifying that he was elected to succeed the deceased abbot Thietland. This saintly abbot at the request of Bishop Gebhard of Constance sent monks from Einsiedeln to establish the monastery of Petershausen, and was one of the teachers of St. Wolfgang. His meritorious career came to a close in the year 996.

4. One hundred and sixteen monks of **Marmoutier** near Tours fell victims to the invading Normans in the year 853.

Willehad: Life by St. Anschar; Surius; Mab.; Rom. Mart.; Butler.
Godfrey: Nicholas of Soissons; Rom. Mart. (Godefridus); Butler.
Gregory: Herman Contractus; Trithemius.
Martyrs oj Marmoutier: Mab.

9

1. Ven. Henry, bishop of Luebeck, was a native of Brabant and for some time presided over the abbey of St. Aegidius in Braunschweig. While accompanying Duke Henry of Braunschweig on a journey to Palestine, he delivered an eloquent discourse in the presence of the Greek emperor on the procession of the Holy Ghost. On his return from the East, he was made bishop of Luebeck, which church he ruled very ably for fifteen years. He also founded the monastery of St. John at Luebeck and died 1184.

2. Ven. Fulcard, third abbot of Diessenberg in the diocese of Mainz, ruled his abbey as a model of all religious virtues eight years and died in 1136.

3. Nicholas, a Cistercian laybrother at Villers in Brabant, herded the cattle of his monastery and made wonderful progress in virtue. Though short of stature, he was great of soul. He ate but once a day, always wore a hairshirt and rested his head on a block of wood instead of a pillow. The year of his blessed death, after fifty years spent in religion, is not recorded.

4. Albero, second abbot of the Cistercian monastery of Dunes in France, was a grandson of Count Thierry of Alsace, and spurned the honors and riches of the world to secure the pearl of great price. He was made abbot in 1153, but gladly and without a regret resigned that office two years later and died as a plain monk at Clairvaux towards the end of the twelfth century.

5. Commemoration of the establishment, at Rome, of the pious Confraternity of SS. Benedict and Scholastica, which enjoyed the singular privilege of annually securing the pardon of a criminal condemned to death. It was founded in 1615 and enriched with numerous indulgences by Popes Paul V and Gregory XV.

10

1. St. Justus, archbishop of Canterbury, had been a monk at St. Andrew's in Rome, and accompanied St. Mellitus when the latter was sent to aid St. Augustine in converting England. Three years after his arrival, he was appointed bishop of Rochester. After St. Augustine and King Ethelbert had been called to their reward, great calamities befell the infant church, and both Justus and Mellitus thought it best to retire to the Continent. Before long, however, the conversion of King Eadbald made possible their return, and Justus resumed the government of his church which he continued to hold until he was chosen archbishop of Canterbury on the death of Mellitus. From Pope Boniface he received letters of encouragement and the pallium. He sent Paulinus to spread the faith in Northumbria and appointed St. Roman bishop of Rochester. Justus lived long enough to hear of the first successes which fol-

Henry: Kranz; Trithemius.
Fulcard: Bucelin; Dodechin.
Nicholas: C. Henriquez.
Albero: Bucelin.
Confrt. of St. B.: Bullar. Mag.

lowed the baptism of King Edwin, but his labors were then nearly at an end. He died in 627 and was buried in the abbey church of SS. Peter and Paul.

2. **St. John,** bishop of Mecklenburg and martyr, was a Scot by birth, early in life embraced the religious state in a monastery in Ireland and came to Germany to preach the Gospel to the Wends and the Saxons. By his zealous preaching he led many pagans to the knowledge of the one true God and after he had been consecrated bishop of Mecklenburg made provisions to ensure the permanency of his conquest. He had labored many years in the service of his Heavenly Master, when he was seized by a pagan mob who beat him with clubs, dragged him from one place to another, and finally cut off his hands, feet and head in the year 1066.

3. **St. Bundlinus,** bishop of Alessandria della Paglia in Italy, was born at Forli in the reign of the Lombard King Luitprand; after the death of his parents disposed of all his wealth for the benefit of the poor and became a member of the Congregation or Order of the Humiliati. He was a remarkable lover of silence, prayer and mortification. The bishop of Alessandria chose him as his co-adjutor, and Bundlinus succeeded to the see after the bishop's death. He flourished about 1220.

4. **Bl. Godfrey,** monk at Corvey in the diocese of Paderborn, was venerated as a saint from the time of his death in 1009.

<h1 style="text-align:center">11</h1>

1. **St. Martin,** bishop of Tours, whose feast is celebrated by the Church on this day, was one of the Saints honored by our Holy Father who, as St. Gregory relates, built a chapel in honor of St. Martin on the site of the temple of Apollo on Monte Cassino.

2. **Sergius,** archbishop of Damascus, having been driven from his see by the Saracens, sought refuge with the common father of the faithful, the Roman Pontiff Benedict VII, who received him with great kindness and placed at his disposal the church of SS. Boniface and Alexius. It is uncertain, whether he had been a monk before he was consecrated bishop; at all events, he governed a community at Rome and died a holy death in 981.

3. **Henry,** abbot of Heisterbach, early escaped from the distractions of the world to strive for evangelical perfection in the Order of Citeaux, but was subject to severe trials before he was privileged to make his profession, for his brothers strained every effort to draw him back into the world. As abbot of his monastery, he governed his monks with great care and solicitude, ever mindful

Justus: Bede; Stanton; Rom. Mart.; Butler.
John: Kranz; Trithemius.
Bundlinus: Menard; Ferrari.
Godfrey: Mab.
Martin: S. Greg. Mag.; Butler.
Sergius: Menard.

of a vision in which the Blessed Virgin handed him the pastoral staff. The year of his holy death is not known.

12

1. **St. Emilian,** abbot of San Millan de Cogolla in Spain, and hermit, in his youth was a shepherd. One day while herding his flock and playing on his lute, he fell asleep and a had vision that beckoned him to the pursuit of higher things. He placed himself under the spiritual tutorship of a hermit named Felix, at Najara, and made rapid strides in holiness. Having returned to his native place in Aragon, the bishop of Tarragona ordained him priest and appointed him pastor of Vergege, where he was so charitable to the poor, that his brethren of the clergy complained to the bishop of his unreasonable liberality. This induced him to leave his pastoral charge and return to solitary life where he might continue to care for the poor without hindrance. During Lent he remained locked up in his cell and saw no one but the brother who supplied him with food. He died at the age of nearly one hundred years in 574. From his epitaph it seems to be established that he followed the Rule of St. Benedict. By many he is considered the first Benedictine in Spain.

2. **St. Anastasius** was bishop of Colocza in Hungary. When St. Adalbert, bishop of Prague, at the instance of archbishop Willigis of Mainz was commanded by Pope Gregory V to return from Rome to Prague, he brought with him six monks of the monastery of SS. Boniface and Alexius. Among them was Anastasius. Adalbert founded and endowed the monastery of Braunau in Bohemia and appointed Anastasius as its abbot. He and his monks led such exemplary lives, that Adalbert at frequent intervals visited Braunau to gather new strength and fervor in their midst. When Adalbert was compelled to abandon his see a second time, Anastasius and his monks directed their course towards Hungary, where they were welcomed by King St. Stephen. He built the monastery of Eisenberg, or St. Martin, which the king liberally endowed. Ten bishoprics were erected in Hungary under the auspices of King Stephen, and Anastasius was selected for the see of Colocza. When Sebastian, archbishop of Gran, was stricken with blindness, Anastasius was promoted to that see, but withdrew three years later, when his predecessor's eyesight was restored. He then continued to govern the see of Colocza to the time of his death in 1007.

3. **SS. Benedict, Matthew, John, Isaac and Christian,** disciples of St. Anastasius, whose career has just been described, fled from Braunau after the death of archbishop Adalbert and settled in a secluded spot, pointed out to them by Adalbert's brother Gaudentius. When Prince Mesco heard of their edifying life he one day visited them while they were at prayer and was so deeply moved, that he sent them a considerable sum of money as alms. They promptly sent it back, but wicked men who had not heard of the return of the

---

Henry: Caesarius of Heisterbach.
Emilian: Braulio, the bishop of Saragossa, is mentioned by the Roman Martyrology as the author of a life of St. Emilian (Aemilianus).—He is also called *Cucullatus.*
Anastasius: Mab.; Dubrow; Also called Astricus.

money, fell upon the monastery and murdered the monks above named about the year 1000. Their remains were interred at Gnesen.

4. **Bl. Rudolph**, General of the Order of Vallombrosa, was sent out as missionary by St. John Gualbert. By command of Pope Alexander III he appeared at a Roman Council convoked to try Bishop Peter of Florence, who had been accused of simony. Rudolph died in the year 1076.

13

1. The **Feast of All Saints of the Benedictine Order** is celebrated on this day with the approval of Pope Paul V, that the memory of the thousands who have fought the good fight under the standard of St. Benedict may inspire his spiritual children with fresh courage to engage in the spiritual combat.

2. **St. Paternus**, a monk of Bray-sur-Seine, in the diocese of Sens, began early in life to practice mortifications and became a monk at Avranches, where he spent nights in prayer and partook of food but once a week. God rewarded his piety with such unusual spiritual gifts that he began to fear for his humility and fled first to Yonne, and then to the monastery of St. Pierre-le-Vif. Here, too, being the object of much curiosity and his prayers being requested by persons of every station, he set out on his way back to Yonne, but was slain by highwaymen in 726.

3. **Bl. Eugene**, bishop of Toledo, in Spain, had been a monk at St. Encratis at Saragossa. He was possessed of considerable learning, wrote several works, celebrated some synods and vigorously combatted the prevalent heresies. He died in 658.

4. **St. Abbo**, abbot of Fleury, and martyr, was a native of Orleannais, and consecrated himself to God in the monastery of Fleury (S. Benoit sur-Loire), of which he became a professed monk. His piety was enhanced by his learning, for which reason Bishop Oswald of Worcester secured his services for the monastic school of Ramsey in England. Several years later he was elected abbot of Fleury and shed lustre upon that celebrated house by his eminent virtue and prudence. In 1003 he restored the abbey of Reole in the diocese of Bazas, which had been destroyed by the Normans. While on his second journey to that house, a quarrel broke out between his companions and some Gascons. Abbo endeavored to pacify the latter by laying the blame upon his own escort; nevertheless one of the Gascons pierced him with a lance in the year 1004.

Benedict etc.: Mab.; Dubrow; Cromer. The Roman Martyrology calls the last named of these
    martyrs *Christinus*.
Rudolph: Boll.
All Saints: Breviary.
Paternus: Mab.
Eugene: Mab.; Rom. Mart.
Abbo: Aimoin, a disciple of Abbo.

14

1. The Solemn Commemoration of **All Souls** of the Benedictine Order was first introduced by Abbot St. Odilo of Cluny in the eleventh century.

2. **St. Sidonius,** abbot of Saint Saens in Normandy, was a native of Ireland and was so highly edified by the brethren whom St. Philibert, abbot of Jumieges, had sent to Ireland, that at their return he accompanied them and became a monk at Jumieges. When archbishop Audoenus of Rouen founded a monastery in the district of Caux in 674, he found no one better qualified to be its abbot than Sidonius, whom he honored with his most intimate confidence. Sidonius governed the monastery in great holiness and died 689. The monastery was subsequently named for him, St. Sidonius, or S. Saens.

3. At Ely in England a great number of **Nuns** were slain by the Danes in the year 870.

4. The venerable **Desiderius** (Didier)de la Cour, prior at Verdun and founder of the Congregation of St. Vannes, was born at Montreuil in 1551, and at the age of fifteen became a monk at Verdun. After completing a course in philosophy and theology at Pont-a-Mousson, he returned to his monastery and was sent to Rome on business of his community. While sojourning in Rome, he taught theology in the house of the Minims. On his return to Verdun he expected a reform to set in, but when he saw that no change was likely to take place, he entered the Order of the Minims, which, however, he left shortly after. He went back to his monastery, prevailed upon his bishop, who was at the same time commendatory abbot of St. Viton at Verdun, to authorize a reform, and in 1596 was made prior of that house. He distributed most of the monks among other houses and with four novices inaugurated an observance that was gradually adopted by a number of other monasteries and was known as the Congregation of St. Vannes. Didier died in 1623.

15

1. **St. Paduinus,** abbot at Mans in France, in his youth retired into a solitude, that he might serve God undisturbed, but he was drawn from this obscurity and appointed prior of St. Vincent's at Mans. Bishop Domnolus of Mans founded a monastery between the river Sarthe and the demesne of Beauge and made Paduinus its first abbot. In this position the Saint was more vigilant than ever over his own actions, prayed unceasingly and maintained calmness of soul under all circumstances. He was summoned to his reward about 580.

2. **St. Fintanus,** a recluse at Rheinau in Switzerland, was a native of the province of Leinster in Ireland. In his youth he performed a heroic act of charity by rescuing his sister who had been enslaved by the Normans. Later,

Sidonius: Menard.
Nuns of Ely: Ingulf of Croyland.
Desiderius: Bucelin; Heimbucher.
Paduinus: Mab.

he was himself captured, but on one occasion fought so bravely in defence of his master, that the latter promised to release him. The ship having landed at an island, Fintan made a vow to visit the tombs of the Apostles, leaped into the sea and swam to the shore of Scotland. Here he remained two years, then proceeded to fulfill his vow. On his return from Rome he crossed the Alps, for some time dwelt in the monastery of Pfaefers and for four years was hospitably entertained in the castle of Count Wolfen, one of the founders of the abbey of Rheinau near Schaffhausen. In 851, he entered as a monk at Rheinau, where by his exemplary humility, obedience and purity of heart he contributed much to the maintenance of regular discipline. He was a pattern of charity and self-denial. During the first year of his monastic life, he devoted one fourth of the loaf that fell to his share to the relief of the poor; during the second year and third year each another fourth and thus subsisted upon only one fourth of his allowance. Five years after entering the monastery, he felt an impulse to go into a solitude. The abbot built him a cell which adjoined the monastery; it had two windows, one towards the church and the other towards the Rhine. Through the latter opening he was wont to receive offerings, which he distributed among the poor. Thus he lived nearly thirty years as a recluse, teaching and consoling the faithful that thronged to see him. His abbot commissioned him to bear the relics of St. Blasius to the newly founded monastery of St. Blasien in the Black Forest. Shortly after his return to Rheinau, Fintan died, in the year 878. He was venerated as a Saint immediately after his death and was canonized in the eleventh century.

16

1. **St. Othmar,** abbot of St. Gall's in Switzerland, was a native of Suabia and early in life found opportunity to pursue studies under the patronage of Count Victor. He entered the monastery of St. Gall and was ordained a priest. Several years after (720), he was sent to minister to the faithful at Remosch in the canton of Grisons. After he had labored here for some time, Waltram of Thurgau appointed him abbot of the monks at the cell of St. Gall. These monks still followed the rule of St. Columban and did not live under one roof until Othmar collected them and introduced the cenobitic manner of life. To the monastery he added a hospital, or hospice, and a school, and at the instance of Pepin substituted the Rule of St. Benedict for that of St. Columban. Othmar performed the responsible duties of an abbot according to the heart of St. Benedict; taught by his word and his living example, observed strict fasts, and was solicitous for the welfare of the poor. Many a time he came to the monastery from a visit to the poor without his outer garments. His liberality was amply repaid by donations of lands and moneys. Counts Warin of Thurgau and Rudhart of Baar seized a part of the possessions of the abbey, and when Othmar set out to lay his grievance before Pepin, these rapacious nobles seized him and bribed the monk Lambert to lodge monstrous charges against the Saint. Bishop Sidonius of Constance, before whom the venerable abbot was tried, passed sentence against him and ordered him to be thrown into prison. For some time he was confined in the castle of Bodman, where he should have died of starvation, had not a monk secretly supplied him with food; subse-

Fintanus: Mab. Also called Findanus.

quently he was taken to an island in the Rhine, where he died in 759, six months later, at the age of sixty-eight years. Ten years later his body was found incorrupt and was translated to St. Gall's.

2. **St. Emilian** was first abbot of the monastery known by his name near Bordeaux. He professed as a monk at Saligny and was by reason of his kindness and affability appointed cellarer. He was a faithful and conscientious official, but, for reasons God alone knows, was accused of squandering the substance of the monastery. He begged permission of his abbot to leave and establish a new monastery elsewhere. Shortly he found himself at the head of a numerous community, even wealthy and highly respected persons seeking his holy guidance. He died in the year 767.

3. **St. Simeon**, the fifth abbot of Cava in Italy, ruled that abbey during the period of its highest prosperity and fame, and died in 1141.

4. **SS. Benedicta and Cecilia** were abbesses of Susteren in the former principality of Juelich. They are said to have been the daughters of King Zuentebold, who founded the monastery of Susteren, and were abbesses after the first Abbess, Amalberga.

5. **SS. John and Benedict**, Camaldolese monks and martyrs, were disciples of St. Romuald. When the latter, at the request of King Boleslaus of Poland, promised to send missionaries to that country, John and Benedict at once offered their services. They journeyed to Poland, learned the language of the country and began their apostolic toil. When the king intimated a desire to send them to Rome to negotiate some affair of the state, they declined on the ground that they had come to labor in the interest of God's kingdom. Evil-minded men who had heard that the king had advanced them a sum of money to cover the expenses of the embassy fell upon them by night and slew them in the year 1004. A splendid church was built over their tomb.

17

1. **St. Gertrude the Great**, a nun of Helfta (or Helpede), in Saxony, was born in Germany on January 2, 1256, but the exact place of her birth is not known. As a child of five years of age she was placed with the nuns of Helfta, and in particular care of St. Mechtilde. From the first she had the gift of winning hearts and her biographer gives many details of her exceptional good qualities, which matured with advancing years. Throughout her life in the monastery she was favored with unusual spiritual gifts, visions and ecstasies, some of which she committed to writing. Most of the time she seemed to be living in heaven rather than upon earth. Outwardly, says one of her recent biographers, her life was that of the simple Benedictine nun, of which she stands forth pre-eminently as the type. Her boundless charity embraced rich and poor,

Othmar: Walafrid Strabo; C. E.   Latin Form: Audomarus.   Rom. Martyrol.
Emilian: Mab. (Aemilianus).
Simeon: Monum. of Cava.
Benedicta: Menard.
John: St. Peter Damian.

learned and simple; it was manifested in tender sympathy towards the souls in purgatory, in a great yearning for the conversion of sinners and in a vehement zeal for the perfection of souls consecrated to God. Her humility was so profound that she wondered how the earth could support so sinful a creature as herself. Gertrude was in the forty-sixth year of her age, when she was summoned to enjoy forever the vision of God in the year 1301 or 1302. Her name was placed in the Roman Martyrology in 1677. At the instance of the king of Spain she was declared patroness of the West Indies, and in Peru her feast is solemnly celebrated.

2. **St. Hilda,** an abbess in England, was the daughter of Hereric, the nephew of St. Edwin, and received baptism from St. Paulinus when she was thirteen years of age. When she was thirty-three years old, she resolved to retire to the monastery of Chelles near Paris, but before she could leave the country to carry out her resolve, St. Aidan invited her to establish a religious community in Northumbria. At first she ruled only a few nuns in a house on the north bank of the Wear, but after a year went to the monastery at Hartlepool, was its superior for a short time and finally removed to Whitby, where she founded a great double monastery, from which proceeded such eminent and holy personages as Wilfrid the Younger, St. John of Beverley, Caedmon, and St. Elfleda, daughter of King Oswin. Hilda was afflicted with an illness which she bore with admirable patience and holy joy. About day-break on the seventeenth of November, 680, she was fortified with the Holy Viaticum, and after exhorting her sisters to charity, slept in peace. Her abbey was destroyed during the Danish invasion, and her remains were removed to Glastonbury.

3. **St. John,** a Roman monk and disciple of St. Gregory the Great, was one of the associates of St. Augustine in the conversion of England and was ·arded the crown of life in 620.

4. **St. Hiltrudis,** a nun at Bingen, was the daughter of Count Meginrad of Spanheim. Her virtues elicited praise from St. Hildegard. She died in the year 1177.

18

1. **St. Odo,** abbot of Cluny, was born of distinguished parents in 879, at the age of nineteen received tonsure and was awarded a canonicate at Tours. It was at this time that his thoughts began to take a serious direction; he laid aside the pagan authors whom it had hitherto been his delight to read and confined himself to the reading, exclusively, of Holy Scripture and other books that are conducive to edification and compunction. After completing his course in theology at Paris, he lived a retired life at Tours. Here he chanced to find a copy of the Rule of St. Benedict; he read it and at once decided to enter a monastery, but encountered opposition from his guardian, Count Fulco of Anjou. Three years later he resigned his canonicate and in 909 took the religious habit

Gertrude: Dom Mege; Cave; C. E. Rom. Martyrol. Butler (Nov. 15).
Hilda: Bede.
John: Menard.
Hiltrudis: Menard.

at Beaume from the hands of abbot Berno. Odo brought with him a collection of one hundred books, which was an enviable possession at that time. After the death of Abbot Berno, who had governed Cluny since 910, Odo was chosen to rule not only that monastery but also those of Massay and Deols. In all the monasteries subject to his jurisdiction he introduced the primitive observance of the Rule of St. Benedict, and laid special stress upon silence, obedience, humility and self-denial. He may be considered the originator of the celebrated Congregation of Cluny, which existed to the time of the French Revolution. In his treatment of his brethren he was charity itself; though severe towards himself he was kind to others, and was wont to say that if he was to be condemned at the judgment he had rather be condemned for leniency than for excessive severity. As he had a filial devotion to St. Martin, he had the brethren convey him to Tours during his final illness. There he exchanged this life of trial and suffering for that of endless bliss in 942.

2. **SS. Anselm, Eucherius, Vincent, Sylvanus** and **Amandus** were holy abbots of the monastery of Lerins, whose memory is celebrated on this day. Amandus is said to have ruled over three thousand monks and to have died about 708.

3. **St. Mumbolus**, abbot of Lagny in the diocese of Paris, disheartened by the ceaseless strife that resulted in a weakening of discipline, left the house and served as a missionary in the diocese of Noyon, of which St. Eligius then was bishop. Mumbolus passed to his eternal reward in the year 675.

4. The venerable **Durandus**, bishop of Clermont in France, had been abbot of Chaise-Dieu, and was distinguished for his great learning and piety. He died on the first day of the Council of Clermont in 1095. Pope Urban II and two hundred bishops attended his burial.

19

1. **Bl. Totto**, abbot of Ottobeuren, was descended from a noble Allemanian family, received a sound Christian education and joined the clergy of the city of Vienne. In 764 his parents founded the monastery of Ottobeuren; Totto was selected to govern the first community, which consisted of twelve monks. He was a model of charity and kindness, and of every virtue that a true monk ought to possess; he was regular in the choir service and generous to the poor. He ruled the monastery forty-eight years to the day of his death in 815. Abbot Isengrin in 1163 raised his remains and placed them beneath the altar of the choir, but during the Peasant War in the sixteenth century they were scattered. Such parts as were subsequently recovered, were placed in a niche with other relics near the altar of St. Martin.

2. **St. Mechtildis**, nun of Helfta, was born in 1240 and was of the noble family of Hackeborn. At the age of seven years, she was sent to the monastery

Odo: John, a disciple. Rom. Martyrol.
Anselm: Monum. of Lerins.
Mumbolus: Mab.
Durandus: Mab.
Totto: Monum. of Ottobeuren.

of Rodalsdorf in the diocese of Halberstadt, where her sister Gertrude was a nun. She was so well pleased with all that she saw and heard, that she obtained leave of her parents to follow the example of her sister. When the latter, now abbess, in 1258, removed the community from Rodalsdorf to Helfta, Mechtildis accompanied her to the new home. From early childhood she had learned to despise earthly vanities and keep the brightness of her soul unstained; as a nun she attained heights to which few souls are conducted by Divine Providence. Such was her obedience that she no longer seemed to have a will of her own, and such her humility that she always strove to hide the good she was doing. She died in the year 1298.

20

1. **St. Bernward,** bishop of Hildesheim, was of noble descent and was educated under the supervision of Bishop Osdag of that city. As he was both studious and pious he was received among the diocesan clergy, but received all the major orders from bishop Willigis at Mainz. After his ordination, he spent some time with his grandfather, the count-palatine Adelbert, and with his uncle, bishop Volkmar of Utrecht. Next he was selected to act as tutor to the youthful Otto III, and when the see of Hildesheim became vacant by the death of Bishop Gerdag (992), Bernward was appointed to that see and received consecration at the hands of Bishop Willigis. Although daily occupied with the manifold duties of his charge, he devoted his nights to study and prayer. He was a friend of the poor, eradicated abuses, restored ecclesiastical discipline, and built churches and monasteries. During the last five years of his life he was prostrated by illness, which he bore with exemplary resignation. Having given all his personal possessions to the abbey of St. Michael, which he had founded at Hildesheim, he received the habit of the Order and died a year later on Nov. 20, 1022. He was canonized by Pope Celestine III in 1193.

2. **St. Eudo,** abbot of Carmeri, in the diocese of Geneva, learned the elements of Christian perfection while a monk of Lerins and was sent from that monastery with a small colony of brethren to establish Carmeri. The holiness of his life induced his nephew Theofred to follow in his footsteps and emulate his virtues both as monk and abbot. Eudo died about 700.

3. **St. Leo,** abbot of Nonantula, had enjoyed the peace and calm of monastic life in that monastery for several years, when he was made its abbot, though he was reluctant to assume the responsibility and believed that it was the greatest calamity that could have befallen him. He resigned his office after two years and retired to Rome, where he lived as a plain monk in the monastery of SS. Boniface and Alexius on the Aventine. He died about the year 1000.

4. **St. Bertrand,** a Cistercian abbot of Grandselve near Toulouse, was one of the bright luminaries in the ecclesiastical firmament of his age and not only led his own monks to the summit of perfection by word and example but

Mechtilids: L. Blosius.
Bernward: Tangmar; Brower.
Eudo: Mab.
Leo: Mab.

exercised a beneficent influence far beyond the walls of his monastery. So complete was his detachment from the world that he rarely spoke of worldly affairs or even of his relatives. He died about 1170 and was venerated as a Saint ever since that time.

21

1. The feast of the **Presentation of the Blessed Virgin** was first celebrated in the monastery of St. Nicholas in Normandy about 1374; it was subsequently adopted by the churches of Saxony and Sicily and in 1585 was enjoined upon the Universal Church by Sixtus V.

2. **St. Columban,** founder and abbot, was born in 543 in Ireland, received his early training from St. Sinellus at Cluain-Inys, and received the religious habit from the hands of abbot St. Congall at Benchor on the coast of Down, where he lived as a monk for several years. Inflamed with a desire to spread the kingdom of Heaven in distant parts, he requested his abbot to permit him to devote himself to the missions. With twelve associates he departed from Benchor in 585 and passed over to Gaul, where at the invitation of King Guntram he built a monastery at Anegray in the Vosges mountains, and, when this proved too small for the numbers that sought for admission, that of Luxeuil, about eight miles distant, and, shortly after, that of Fontaines. For these three houses he composed a Rule which was characterized by austerities that were calculated to repel rather than to attract lovers of religious life. Prayer and recollection were emphasized; but one meal was taken a day, and that towards evening; even the slightest transgression of the rule was severely punished. He had achieved much good in France in twenty-five years, when he incurred the king's displeasure and was sent into exile. He travelled up the Rhine with several brethren and preached the Gospel in Switzerland. In consequence of his vehement preaching against idolatry, the pagans threatened to take his life, but he escaped to Argon and in 613 made his way across the Alps to Lombardy, where he was kindly received by King Aigulf, who furnished him means to found the monastery of Bobbio. Two years after his arrival he died, in 615, in a cell to which he was wont to retire for fasts and penitential exercises.

3. **Gelasius O'Cullenan,** a Cistercian abbot of Boyle in Ireland, was born of a family in Connaught remarkable for its piety. He studied at Louvain and in Rome, and soon after his return to Ireland entered the Cistercian Order. While abbot at Boyle in the reign of Elizabeth, he was arrested in Dublin in 1580 and imprisoned. Many inducements were held out to him to abandon the Catholic faith, but he remained unmoved. The executioners crushed his fingers, arms and legs with blows of a hammer, and finally hanged him November 21, 1584. The historian of the Cistercian Order, Henriquez, styles him "the ornament of the Cistercian Order, the light of the century, and the glory of all Ireland." While he was on the way to the scaffold, five hundred persons were converted to the Catholic faith by the sight of his constancy.

Bertrand: Manrique
Presentation: Wion.
Columban: Jonas, a disciple; Butler.
Gelasius: Manrique; Hartry; Murphy: Our Martyrs.

22

1.   Anniversary of the consecration, at Rome, of St. Willibrord, the first
bishop of Utrecht and Apostle of Frisia by Pope Sergius on the vigil of the feast
of St. Clement in 697.

2.   Bl. John Thorne and Roger James, treasurer and under-treasurer of
the abbey of Glastonbury, suffered with their Abbot Richard Whiting in the
year 1539.   An attempt was made to charge them with stealing or concealing
some of the church plate, but the real reason for which they were condemned
was because they denied the king's supremacy in the Church.   Their veneration as Blessed was sanctioned by Pope Leo XIII on May 13, 1895.

3.   Ven. John Rugg and William Eynon monks of Glastonbury, also
suffered in 1539 on the same day as abbot Richard Whiting.   They were both
priests and exercising parochial duty in the town of Reading.

4.   Henry de Marcy, cardinal bishop of Albano, at an early age entered
the Cistercian Order, and in due course of time was made abbot of Hautcombe
in the diocese of Geneva.   He declined the mitre of Toulouse, but was obliged
to accept the election to the abbatial chair of Clairvaux.   Pope Alexander III
created him a cardinal, and Henry would in all likelihood have succeeded Pope
Urban III, if he had not declined on the plea that he had decided to preach a
Crusade.   He died in 1187 or 1188.

5.   Alphonse Henry, first king of Portugal, and knight of the Order of
Ala, founded about one hundred and fifty churches and monasteries and died
with a high reputation for sanctity in the year 1185.

6.   The Congregation of St. Ottilien in Bavaria was founded in 1884 and
was affiliated to the Benedictine Confederation by Pope Pius X on this day in
1904.   Its members devote themselves chiefly to foreign missions.

23

1.   St. Guido, abbot of Casauria in Italy, was a monk at Farfa and was
appointed abbot of Piscaria at the suggestion of Emperor Henry II.   Guido
tried to evade the honor; neither tears nor protests moved his abbot, who had
given his consent.   The brethren of Piscaria without a dissenting voice elected
him and he could not but accept.   Ere long he perceived the true nature of the
task imposed upon him; everything was in a disorderly condition, and most of
the possessions of the monastery were in the hands of rapacious neighbors.
After a long struggle, in which his most effective weapons were patience and

Willibrord: Menard.
John Thorne: Acta S. Sedis 1895.
John Rugg: Acta S. Sedis 1895.
Henry: Ughelli; Kranz.
Alphonse: A. de Vasconcellos; B. Brito.
Cong. St. Ottilien: Fam. Confoed.; Heimbucher.

prayer, he recovered all that the monastery had lost. In the midst of all these worries, he continued to be a model of every virtue to his brethren. He breathed forth his soul in the year 1045 in the presence of his sorrowing brethren on the feast of St. Clement, having ruled the monastery twenty-one years and six months.

2. **St. Wilfetrudis,** abbess of Nivelle, in Brabant, progressed so rapidly on the way of·perfection that at the age of only twenty years she was appointed to succeed her spiritual mother, St. Gertrude, as abbess. Filled as she was with the fear of God, which is the beginning of wisdom and lends strength to the soul, she led her sisters firmly and securely; she was gentle towards the obedient, firm and inflexible towards the wayward. The will of God was her guide in all her undertakings, and since she paid little heed to the opinions of men, she was not spared trials and opposition. But in the end she triumphed by her patience and constancy. She was called to receive the reward of her faithful service in the year 670.

3. Ven. **Aligerno,** a monk educated in the monastery of St. Paul outside the walls of Rome and subsequently prior at Monte Cassino, was elected abbot of the latter monastery on Oct.25,949. The monastery, which had been restored by Petronax in the eighth century, was oppressed and harrassed by the barons of the surrounding country and by the dukes of Beneventum, and was sacked and burnt by the Saracens in the ninth century, so that at the time of Aligerno's arrival it was little more than a heap of ruins. The fields lay waste, and their tenants had been dispersed. Aligerno went about the work of restoration with a heavy heart but trusting in God. He firmly resisted the usurpations and unlawful claims of the barons, and introduced new tenants with whom he agreed upon equitable terms of lease. When the country had been once more settled, he prepared to rebuild the monastery and its church. It was during his administration that the Basilian abbot Nilus the Younger of Grotta Ferrata with his monks was hospitably received and permitted to occupy the monastery at Valleluce for fifteen years. After ruling his monastery wisely and guiding it through calm and troubled waters for thirty-seven years, Aligerno rested from his labors in 986.

4. The Congregation of **St. Justina of Padua** was founded by Abbot Luigi Barbo in 1408, and was approved by Pope Eugene IV in 1432. After Monte Cassino had entered the congregation, it was called the "Cassinese Congregation of the Observance."

24

1. **St. Marinus,** hermit and martyr at the monastery of St. Savin in Poitou, in his boyhood was placed in the care of a certain bishop Ellidius in or near Rome, by whom he was ordained long before he had attained the canonical age. After Ellidius' death the people chose Marinus as his asuccessor, but he

Guido: Mab.
Wilfetrudis: Mab.
Aligerno: Mab.
Cong. St. Justina: Bullar. Mag.; Annales O.S.B. (1909).

fled during the night and went to France. In the Jura he came upon a great monastery, probably Condate. The edifying lives of the monks impelled Marinus to beg leave of abbot Erilius to remain in their midst for some time. The abbot not only granted this request but also invited Marinus to remain in the community permanently and teach the younger brethren. A year later, Marinus decided to remove to a solitude, for he had grown so popular that people came from all quarters to see and hear him. With the blessing of the abbot he went to Maurienne, where he lived in obscurity four years and is said to have been supplied with food by two bears. While he was in hopes that he might live undisturbed at this place for years, pagan invaders surrounded his cell. He came forth and preached the name of Jesus to them, but they bound him, led him before their chieftain, who ordered him to be thrown into a stove, and, when the flames failed to injure him, ordered him to be beheaded for the steadfast profession of his faith, in the year 731. His remains were removed to St. Savin.

2. **St. Mary**, nun and martyr at Cordova, in Spain, emulating the heroism of her brother Walabonsus, a monk of the monastery of St. Felix, boldly appeared before the Moorish judges and professed that she was a Christian. The judge ordered her to be cast into prison, from which she was taken after a long time and executed in the year 851.

3. **Balsamus**, abbot of Cava, in Italy, was indeed a sweet smelling balsam that spread its odor far and wide. He was the tenth abbot of that monastery, governed it twenty-four years and died in 1232.

25

1. **St. John Francardus**, Celestine monk and prior at Aquila in the Abruzzi, was a man of remarkable mortification and wrought miracles even before his death, which occurred in 1478.

2. **Bl. Bernold**, monk and priest at the monastery of Ottobeuren in Suabia, lived in the eleventh century and was a remarkable model of self-denial and austerity. Since his tomb was visited by the faithful and miracles were said to have been wrought through his intercession, his remains were raised by Bishop Udalschalk in 1189, and assigned a place near those of SS. Hatto and Benno. As the day of his death is apparently unknown, the present day being that of the translation is observed as his feast.

3. **Bl. Tussanus**, prior at Cluny, in France, was born at Amiens and was a relative of Bl. Coleta. In his life he exemplified the virtues of a monk in the most glorious days of the Order. He is said to have had great devotion to St. Catherine of Alexandria; hence he was privileged to die on her feast in the year 1420 under the rule of Abbot Odo II.

Marinus: Mab.
Mary: St. Eulogius; Rom. Martyrol.; Butler.
Balsamus: Monum. of Cava.
John: Menard:.
Bernold: Braun.
Tussanus: Martyrol. Gallic.

4. **Conrad,** a Cistercian monk of Heisterbach, served fifty years as the soldier of an earthly prince, and spent as many years in the honorable service of the King of Kings as an humble monk. When a brother told him of a vision which had foretold his approaching end, he said: "I have no fear; I wish I were already dead," and died on the day following. The year is not known.

5. **Jerome of Corsica,** an Olivetan monk of Florence, was a soldier in his youth and was distinguished for his fidelity in service. At the age of twenty he laid aside his armor and entered the monastery of San Girolamo de Agnano, where he lived an edifying life for the space of thirty years. He died in 1479.

6. In France the anniversary of the approval of the Reform of the Order of **Fontevrault** by Pope Sixtus IV in 1474 or 1475, at the instance of the Abbess Marie, sister of Francis II, duke of Bretagne.

26

1. **St. Silvester Gozzolini,** abbot and founder of the Order of Silvestrine Benedictines, was born in 1177 at Osimo, fourteen miles from Loreto in Italy. On account of his learning and exemplary conduct he was appointed to a canonicate at Osimo, and shone as a preacher. The frankness with which he rebuked his bishop for certain irregularities made him the object of persecution, which he bore with heroic equanimity. When he was forty years of age, the sight of the corpse of a gentleman who had been much admired for the external graces of his person impressed him. He was so profoundly stirred that he left Osimo and entered a solitude some thirty miles distant, and in 1231 founded a monastery on Monte Fano near Fabriano, in the march of Ancona. He adopted the Rule of St. Benedict, and added several statutes which received the approval of Pope Innocent IV in 1248. His foundation encountered many difficulties, but he persevered, confiding in the protection and intercession of Our Blessed Lady, for whom he cherished a tender devotion. He passed to his eternal reward in 1267 and was canonized by Pope Paul V in 1617.

2. **St. Martin,** priest and monk at Corbie in Picardy, was distinguished for his virtue and prudence, and was domestic chaplain to Charles Martel. He died in 726; his relics are preserved at St. Priet near Limoges.

3. **Adelbert,** prior at Oberaltaich in Bavaria, was descended from the counts of Haigerloch and spent his youth in indulging his passions with his equals in age. God's grace opened his eyes to the perils into which he was running headlong, and he resolved to save his soul by embracing the religious state. Several monasteries in which he applied for admission declined to receive him. Finally he entered Oberaltaich and led a life that strongly contrasted with the unbridled career which he had abandoned. He would punish the most trivial fault which he committed and would confess it before the brethren with such

Conrad: Caesarius of Heisterbach.
Jerome: And. Volaterranus.
Fontevrault: Pragm. Hist. of Rel. Orders.
Silvester: Fabrini; Butler.
Martin: Mab.

contrition as if he had been guilty of a grievous sin. He displayed such seriousness and good judgment that he was appointed confessor, then novice-master and finally prior of his monastery. He died in 1131.

27

1. **St. Virgilius,** archbishop of Salzburg, was a native of Ireland and like so many of his countrymen came to preach the Gospel on the European Continent. For two years he remained in the country of King Pepin and when the see of Juvavia, or Salzburg, fell vacant was recommended for the see by that prince, who was a brother-in-law to duke Odilo of Bavaria. Virgil dreaded the responsibility of an office for which he felt himself so little qualified and left most of his episcopal functions to Dobad, an Irish bishop whom he had brought with him from Ireland, reserving for himself the office of preaching and instructing, till he was compelled by his colleagues to receive episcopal consecration in 766 (or 767), twenty-one years after his appointment. He rebuilt the abbey of St. Peter, of which he was abbot and translated the body of St. Rupert to the church, which he made his cathedral. His apostolic zeal prompted him to preach the Gospel to the Wends and to send missionaries to Carinthia, two dukes of which country he baptized; he also dedicated the church at the famous pilgrimage of Altoetting and was instrumental in the foundation of the abbey of Kremsmuenster. Wishing to assure himself of the success of the preachers of the faith in Carinthia he visited that country and penetrated as far as the junction of the Drave and the Danube. Shortly after his return from this expedition, he was seized with an illness and died in the year 780. Pope Gregory IX canonized him in 1232. Virgil was a man of considerable erudition and taught that the earth is round. In connection with this teaching he was accused of holding certain views contrary to Catholic faith and was drawn into an unpleasant controversy. Virgil, however, succeeded in clearing himself of the suspicion cast upon his orthodoxy.

2. **St. Acharius,** bishop of Noyon in France, was one of the most zealous disciples of St. Eustasius, successor of St. Columban as abbot of Luxeuil, and was raised to the see of Noyon in 621. He was at the same time bishop of Tournai, in the administration of which see he was supported by the holy bishop Amandus, who was a regionary bishop. Acharius enjoyed the favor and protection of King Dagobert and extended his missionary activity as far as Ghent in Flanders. After eighteen years of unselfish and prosperous service he entered into his rest in 639 and was succeeded as bishop by St. Eligius.

3. **St. Apollinaris,** the fourteenth abbot of Monte Cassino, ruled that house during fifteen years of prosperity and trials and died in 828.

4. **St. Bilhildis,** foundress of the monastery of Altmuenster in Mainz, was born at Hochheim of noble parents in 625 and had two sisters, Hildegard and Renildis, who consecrated their virginity to God. Bilhildis was piously

Adelbert: Pez.
Virgilius: Mab; Canisius; Butler; C. E. (Vergilius); the Rom. Martyrol.
Acharius: Mab.
Apollinaris: Mab.

brought up by her cousin at Wuerzburg, and was married to the pagan duke Hettan. The latter died in battle; shortly after her only child died, and then, free from all ties, she devoted herself to God's service in the religious state. She founded Altmuenster, in which she spent the remainder of her days. The year of her death is uncertain.

5. **Garcias de Cisneros,** abbot of Montserrat in Catalonia, was born in 1455 and was a nephew to the celebrated Cardinal Ximenes. Originally a monk at Valladolid, he was appointed abbot of Montserrat in 1493 and introduced the reform of Valladolid into that monastery. He was a distinguished lover of the spiritual life and contributed to ascetical literature the well-known "Exercitatorium Vitae Spiritualis." Abbot Garcias inculcated the value of silence as an indispensable element to the maintenance of discipline and cherished a tender devotion to Our Lady. He died on this day in 1510.

28

1. On this day took place the Elevation of the relics of **SS. Germanus** and **Rudolph,** priests, and **Isthmius** amd **Isthmido,** deacons, of the monastery of Taloire, in the diocese of Geneva, by St. Francis de Sales in 1621. St. Germanus—whose feast is celebrated on December 31—was the first prior of Taloire, which was founded 1029, The year of his death is unknown. Of St. Rudolph nothing seems to be known but that he was a monk of Taloire. Isthmius and Isthmido also lived in the eleventh century.

2. **St. Baltherius** was a priest who led the life of an anchorite in Northumberland. His hermitage was on a solitary rock encompassed by the sea. He rested in the Lord on March sixth, 756. In the reign of Canute, the Dane, the relics of this Saint were translated to Durham.

3. **Gunfrid,** a disciple of St. Bernard and abbot of Clairmarais in Belgium, became a monk at Clairvaux, and made such wonderful progress in perfection that he was appointed prior of his monastery and was subsequently commissioned to establish the Cistercian abbey of Clairmarais, where he died about the middle of the twelfth century.

4. **Haimodis,** abbess of Gandersheim, was descended from the dukes of Saxony, and was of a very religious and serious disposition from early childhood. Her parents reluctantly consented to her entrance into the monastery of Herford, where her worth was soon recognized. She was made abbess of the newly founded monastery of Gandersheim, which he governed in an exemplary manner to the time of her death at the age of only thirty-four years in 874.

Bilhildis: Gropp; Stadler.
Garcias: Hierarchia Bened.; Stadler; Buchberger.
Germanus etc: Mab.; Stad.
Baltherius: Stanton.
Gufnrid: Seguin.
Haimodis: Pez.; Andrew of Bamberg; Bruschius. Also called Hathmoda.

29

1. **St. Radbod,** bishop of Utrecht, was partly of Frankish and partly of Frisian descent, his grandfather on his mother's side having been Radbod, the last king of Frisia. After receiving a careful education in his tender years from his uncle Bishop Guenther of Cologne, he was sent to the court of Charles the Bald and of Louis the Stammerer, where he found opportunity to perfect himself in the sacred sciences as well as in the various branches of human knowledge. Among the evidences of his gifts are some poems in honor of SS. Martin, Livinus and Suitbert and some discourses in prose. He deemed himself unworthy to be received among the clergy of Utrecht, and was with difficulty persuaded to accept the appointment to the episcopal see of that city in 906. As most of his predecessors had been monks, he also took the monastic habit and practiced the mortifications of a monk, occasionally fasting for the space of two or three days in succession. During the invasion of Frisia by the Danes, he was compelled to flee to Deventer, where he continued to reside to the end of his life in 918.

2. **Bl. Robert,** abbot of Clairvaux, was closely related to St. Bernard and was instructed by that Saint in the elements of religious perfection. While humbling his spirit in prayer and keeping the flesh in subjection by austerities, he lost courage, left the Cistercians and entered Cluny where a less strict observance was prescribed. St. Bernard deeply regretted his departure and prayed that he might reconsider the step he had taken. Robert eventually returned and after St. Bernard's death was chosen abbot of Clairvaux (1153), which he governed to the time of his death in 1190.

3. The devout **Gerard,** abbot of Fontenelle, in Normandy, was educated under Fulbert, bishop of Chartres, and became a monk at Lagny, where he was esteemed by all for his conscientious observance of the Rule and for his cheerful yet sedate behavior. After he had been made abbot of Crespy, he had occasion to visit duke Richard of Normandy. The latter invited him to revive the declining abbey of Fontenelle. Having been informed of the true state of affairs, Gerard took upon himself the arduous task of restoring discipline, but his well-meant efforts drew upon him the ill-will of some malcontents, one of whom slew him in the year 1031.

30

1. **Bl. Angelus Senesius,** abbot, was a native of Catania in Sicily, and became a monk at the abbey of San Nicolas de Arena in the same island. He was made abbot of San Martino delle Scale at Palermo and restored both the buildings and discipline of that monastery. Noted for his boundless charity, zeal and humility, he passed to a better life in 1380 and was buried beneath the altar of St. Michael in the abbey church.

Radbod: Mab.; Butler.
Robert: William of St. Thierry; Barnabas de Montalbo.
Gerard: Mab.
Angelus: Oct. Cajetan; Schindele.

2. Bl. Joscio, a monk of Sithiu, was a devout client of Our Lady and is said daily to have recited, on his knees, five Psalms in her honor, each beginning with one of the five letters of her name (MARIA).   He died about 1163.

3. Bl. William, abbot of Maniaco in Italy, died about 1315, leaving behind him the memory of a saintly and edifying life.

4. Bl. Bernard, a laybrother at Clairvaux, and disciple of the great St. Bernard, was a man of unusual humility and meekness, who never was seen to be out of temper and was in the habit of at once praying for any one that offended him.   He died in the twelfth century.

5. Bl. Rufinus, abbot of Citeaux and general of the Cistercian Order was distinguished for admirable purity of life and piety.   He was the twenty-eighth abbot of Citeaux.

Joscio: Menard; Stadler.   Also called Jossio and Josbert.
William: O. Cajetan.
Bernard: Seguin.
Rufinus: Manrique.

December

1

1. **St. Hereswida**, widow of King Ethelbert, was a nun at Chelles. After her husband's death in war in 655 she crossed over to France and consecrated herself to God in the monastery of Chelles near Paris, where she was professed and where she remained to her death in 647, after a life of intimate communion with God by prayer, humility and self-denial.

2. **Bl. Richard Whiting**, the last abbot of Glastonbury, in England, was a professed monk of that monastery and its abbot since 1525. When the royal visitors appointed by Henry VIII arrived at Glastonbury they could find no scandal to complain of; the only pretext they could allege for their proceeding was that the abbot most resolutely persisted in rejecting the king's pretensions in religious matters. The answer sent from the court was that the Abbot, who was feeble and advanced in years, be sent to London. When his company had reached Wells, he heard that a court was then sitting, which he had been summoned to attend, and accordingly he proceeded to take his place in the assembly when to his amazement he was called upon to answer the charge of high treason. He could scarcely persuade himself that their intention was serious, even when the sentence against him was pronounced, until he perceived that he was taken past his abbey without being allowed to enter. He then begged for a few days to prepare for death and to take leave of his brethren. Even this was refused and he was forthwith dragged on a hurdle to the top of the Tow, a hill near the monastery, and there hanged and quartered on November 15, 1539.

3. **Bl. Hugh Faringdon** was elected abbot of St. James at Reading in England in 1520, and his extant letters show that he was distinguished by learning and piety. When the royal commission demanded the surrender of his abbey, he refused and at the same time rejected the spiritual supremacy of the king. For this he was convicted of high treason and was hanged, drawn and quartered at Reading on the same day that Richard Whiting suffered, in the year 1539.

4. **Bl. John Beach** was abbot of the monastery of St. John at Colchester in England, was educated at Oxford and in 1530 was elected abbot. He had the courage to preserve his conscience free from reproach amidst the snares laid to entrap him and resolutely refused to surrender his abbey into the hands of King Henry VIII, or to acknowlege his supremacy in things spiritual. For this he was attainted of high treason and suffered death by hanging at Colchester on December 1, 1539.

Hereswida: Mon. of Chelles; Menard; Stanton.
Richard: Stanton; C. E.
Hugh: Stanton.
John: Stanton.

5. **Oddo** was called, with several other brethren of the monastery of St. Savin at Poitiers, to restore discipline at the priory of Anzy-le-Duc in the diocese of Autun and was a model for every member of his community. After the canonical hours he was wont to remain in the oratory and to pray and weep tears of compunction for his sins and those of others. He died about 895.

6. **Hugo,** Cistercian abbot of the monastery of SS.Vincent and Anastasia in Rome, was a native of France. Pope Eugene III created him cardinal and bishop of Ostia for his valiant services to the Church in combatting the errors of the Arnoldians and the Henricians. He died in the odor of sanctity in the pontificate of Adrian IV about 1158.

7. **Luke Manzoli,** a prior of the Humiliati, was bishop of Fiesole in Italy, and was created a cardinal by Pope Gregory XII in 1408. St. Antoninus of Florence praised him as a man of rare discernment, an able teacher of theology, a man of high reputation and sterling worth. He died on September 14, 1411.

2

1. **Bl. Oderisius,** abbot of Monte Cassino, and cardinal, was descended from the counts of Marsi and entered Monte Cassino while St. Desiderius—later Pope Victor III—was its abbot. On account of his learning and other eminent qualifications, he was made prior of the abbey, and Pope Nicholas II created him cardinal. This elevation changed nothing in his manner of life, which was always one of monastic simplicity. When Pope Victor III, who had retained the government of the abbey, was at the point of death, he appointed Cardinal Oderisius to succeed him in the abbatial dignity in 1087. Oderisius followed in the footsteps of his predecessor, completed the buildings the latter had begun and insisted upon conscientious observance of the Rule. In his public career he was invariably loyal to the Roman Pontiffs in their struggles with antipopes. He died in peace in the year 1105.

2. **Bl. Robert,** first Cistercian abbot of S. Maria de Mataplana in Spain, not only himself struggled to attain the height of religious perfection but also by his word and example animated the brethren to persevere in the way of holiness. He died about 1195.

3. **Anselm,** a Cistercian monk of Hemmenrode, was distinguished for his meekness, zealous in observance of the Rule, and void of all self-esteem. So little did he rely upon the quality of his goodness that he often begged the brethren to pray for him. One day brother Henry, who was praying for him, heard a voice saying: "You are praying for Anselm: he ought to be praying for you." The time at which he lived is not stated.

Oddo: Mab.
Hugo: Manrique.
Luke: Wion; Stadler.
Oderisius: Peter Diaconus.
Robert: Manrique.
Anselm: Seguin.

3

1. **St. Sola,** (Solus), monk and priest was a native of England, followed St. Boniface to Germany and was by him ordained a priest and clothed as a monk. His attraction, however, was for a life of solitude and prayer, and in this St. Boniface seconded his design and approved of his settlement on the banks of the Altmuehl near Eichstaett, at a spot since called Solenhofen. Notwithstanding his humility and his strong desire to live in obscurity, the holiness of his life was widely spoken of and even reached the ears of Charlemagne, who made him a free gift of the district in which his cell was erected. Although he was obliged to accept the gift at the time, he soon turned it over to the abbey of Fulda, which was then ruled by Abbot Rhabanus. After the glorious martyrdom of St. Boniface, Sola continued to enjoy the friendship of SS. Willibald and Wunibald, who frequently visited him and derived much edification from his discourse. What would have tempted a less perfect man, was to the Saint an opportunity to practice greater mortification; he would accept no gifts from his clients and would tell them to thank God, the source of all favors. Sola died at an advanced age, in 700. In 830 his remains were raised and with the authorization of Pope Gregory IV exposed for public veneration.

2. **St. Eloquius,** abbot of Lagny, was one of the associates of St. Furseus, founder of that monastery, and succeeded him in its government. He emulated the virtues of his predecessor and died with the reputation of sanctity in 675. At the request of Count Eilbert, his remains were translated to the abbey of Vasour.

3. **St. Galganus,** hermit of the rule of Citeaux, was born in a village near Siena in Italy and in his youth gave little serious thought to the eternal interests of his soul. His parents selected a bride for him; one day while riding to pay her a visit, his horse stood still in the road and refused to advance a step. He interpreted this as a sign from Heaven to enter the service of Christ. Near the place where he had paused, he built a cell in which he led a very austere life. God favored him with many heavenly gifts; he saw distant things as if they were present; he saw the future, drove out evil spirits, healed the sick and died in the year 1181. The burial was attended by the bishops of Massa and Volaterra and several abbots. A church and an abbey bearing his name were built near Siena. Galganus was canonized by Pope Alexander III.

4. **Bl. Abbo,** bishop and abbot at Auxerre, died about 860.

4

1. The **Translation** (Illatio) of the Relics of **St. Benedict** was observed in France on this day. There were two translations: that from the Church of

Sola: Canisius; Mab.; Stanton; Butler.
Eloquius: Menard; Molanus. Also called Eulogius.
Galganus: Ferrari; Stadler; Roman Martyrol.
Abbo: Mab.

St. Peter at Fleury to the church of Our Lady at Orleans in 653, and that from Orleans back to Fleury in 883.

2. **St. Cyran**, abbot of Lonrey in France, was born in the district of Berry of noble parentage, received a suitable education and was appointed to an honorable office at the court of King Clothair II. At court he lived a life almost as retired as that of a monk. Repelled rather than charmed by the worldly, thoughtless life of the courtiers, he resolved to cut himself off from the world and all its tempting prospects. He journeyed to Tours, conferred with the pious Bishop Modegisil and was soon received among the clergy of the diocese. As archdeacon he labored zealously for the honor of God, but incurred the displeasure of the governor, who had him imprisoned as a madman. After his release he resigned his office, distributed his possessions among the poor, made a pilgrimage to Rome in the company of an Irish bishop named Fulvius and on his return to France founded the monasteries of Meaubec and Lonrey, the latter of which he governed to the time of his holy death in 655.

3. **St. Maurus**, monk of Martinsberg and bishop of Pecs in Hungary, lived in the days of King Stephen, was noted for the purity and sanctity of his life, and died in 1070.

4. **St. Bernard**, cardinal and seventh General of the Order of Vallombrosa, was of the noble Florentine family of the Uberti, and early in life entered the Order of Vallombrosa. His virtue and ability were recognized when he was chosen to the office of abbot and subsequently to that of general of his Order. Pope Urban II created him a cardinal and thus secured a bold supporter in the struggle against the vice of simony. After he had reconciled the city of Parma with the Holy See, he was appointed bishop of that city by Pope Pascal. As bishop, Bernard lived as plainly as a monk and always had several brethren about him with whom he led a community life. He died in their arms in 1133 and was canonized.

5

1. **St. Gerard**, archbishop of Braga in Portugal, was born at Cahors in France and was even before his birth offered by his parents for the service of God. Early in life he entered the abbey of Moissac, which belonged to the Congregation of Cluny. Here he excited the admiration of all by the purity of his life and his conscientious observance, as well as by his unusual mental endowments and progress in study. Bishop Bernard of Toledo appointed him to the office of cantor at his cathedral, from which position he was elevated to the archiepiscopal see of Braga. Gerard was a zealous preacher, maintained discipline in the monasteries and was so liberal in his alms that he was called the father of the poor. Yet in his private life he was so mortified as if he were living in a cloister. He died in 1109.

Translation of Relics: Mab.
Cyran: Mab.; Labbe; Stadler.   Latin form: Sigiranus.   Butler (Siran or Sigirannus).
Maurus: Mab.
Bernard: Ciaconi; Roman Martyrol.
Gerard: Yepez.   Also called Geraldus and Giraldus.

2. **Joanna,** a Cistercian nun in Belgium, was the daughter of Count Baldwin of Flanders, first Latin emperor of Constantinople. After her father's death she had to endure much harsh and unjust treatment. She was married first to Ferdinand, son of King Sanchez of Portugal, and after his death to Thomas, brother of the duke of Savoy. At the same time she ruled Flanders as a wise and just princess, was charitable to the poor, and founded the monastery of Marquette, to which she often retired for practices of devotion. In the course of time her yearning for the religious life grew so strong that she obtained the consent of her husband to enter a monastery. She retired to Marquette but shortly after her admission was summoned to receive the crown of life in 1244.

3. Establishment of the Congregation or Union of **Bursfeld** in Saxony in 1432, largely due to the efforts of abbot John von Rhode of Trier and John Dederoth. The first impulse to this movement was given by the Council of Basel. The union was formed in 1430, included the principal monasteries of Germany and at the period of its greatest prosperity numbered two hundred houses. It flourished to the time of the Protestant Reformation.

6

1. **St. Gertrude,** widow, and abbess of Hamai, after the death of her husband was intent upon one thing only—to save her soul. Fort his purpose she devoted all her wealth to charities, founded the monastery of Hamai, near Marchiennes, and became a religious and abbess there, leading her sisters prudently and in all humility and serving them in preference to being served by them. She died about 650 and was buried at Marchiennes.

2. **Bl. Nicholas,** third abbot of Vaucelles, in the diocese of Cambrai, is praised for his rare virtue and eloquence. Delicate health and an inclination to a retired life prompted him to resign his office and to live as a plain monk, intent exclusively upon the salvation of his soul. He died in 1163. As numerous miracles were wrought at his tomb, his body was raised from its tomb by order of Pope Alexander III and exposed for public veneration.

3. **Bl. Henry,** abbot of Pontida, in the diocese of Bergamo in Italy, flourished about the year 1100.

4. **Gerard,** prior of Cluny, and cardinal-bishop of Ostia, was a faithful companion of St. Ulric of Cluny and a man of such remarkable piety, learning and firmness of character that he attracted the attention of the Supreme Pontiff, Alexander II, who created him a cardinal and bishop of Ostia as successor to St. Peter Damiani. He was sent to France as papal legate and presided at a council which issued important legislation regulating the life of the clergy. Pope Gregory VII also sent him on a mission to Spain. Having been despatched

Joanna: Meyer; Bucelin; Henriquez.
Cong. of Bursfeld: Wion; C. E.
Gertrude: Mab.
Nicholas: Le Mire; A. de Raisse.
Henry: Mab.; Stadler.

on an embassy to emperor Henry IV, he was imprisoned for some time, but never wavered in his loyalty to the Head of the Church. He died in 1077 and was regarded as one of the strong pillars of the Church in the days of persecution.

7

1.   **St. Fara,** foundress and abbess of Faremoutier, in the diocese of Meaux, was the daughter of Agneric, a noble of the court of King Theodebert II.   While St. Columban was visiting her parents in 610, he blessed the child Fara.   Her father wished to give her in marriage to a young noble, but she persisted in her desire to consecrate herself to God, and when her father urged her to comply with his desire, she was seized with an illness, of which she was cured by the blessing of Columban's successor, St. Eustasius.   Finally her father relented, and she took the veil at the hands of Bishop Gondoald of Meaux in 614. Her progress in the religious life pleased her father so highly that he built a monastery for her at the confluence of two streams, the Aubelin and the Morin, and furnished it with a sufficient endowment.   It was originally called Brige, was later known as Evory and, after Fara's death, Faremoutier *(Farae Monasterium)*.   Despite her youth, she was elected abbess and presided over the monastery with great prudence and conscientiousness.   The rule observed was that of St. Columban; the religious abstained from wine, and, during Advent and Lent, also from milk, examined their conscience three times a day and revealed to their superior every emotion of the heart.   Her words and example induced her brothers Faro and Chagnoald to embrace the religious state.   Fara governed her large community thirty-nine years and entered into the joy of the Lord in 655.

2.   **Sebastian of Villoslado,** abbot of St. Martin's at Madrid, was born of an illustrious family in Spain and received an excellent education.   One day he was challenged to a duel at Alcala; he waited four hours for the appearance of his opponent and while waiting God's grace called him to abandon the world and its vanities.   He became a monk at St. Mary's at Valvenaria and was a model of monastic virtue.   He was given to remarkable austerities and was at all times so recollected that he seemed to be completely estranged from creatures.   Once on the feast of the Ascension he fell into an ecstasy and his countenance grew so radiant that no one could bear to look upon it.   He regarded himself as the last and least of the brethren and wished to be treated as such. Honors and dignities had no attraction for him, and he resolutely declined an appointment to a bishopric.   Eventually he was induced to rule several monasteries,—those of Our Lady at Buesso, St. John de Podio, and St. Martin's at Madrid,—and was appointed visitor general of the Spanish Congregation.   He died in 1597.

3.   **Jerome Arminius,** monk of San Martino delle Scale at Palermo in Sicily, in a wonderful degree possessed the gift of prayer, and never ceased either by day or by night to implore the grace and mercy of God.   He was at

---

Gerard: Mab.   Also called Gerald.
Fara: Jonas of Bobbio.   Also Phara or Burgundofara; Butler.   The Roman Martyrol. calls her Phara.
Sebastian: Gonzalez; Menard.

all times a lover of humility and poverty, and declined honors and preferences of every description. He died at Parma, Italy, in 1626.

4. Approval of the Congregation of **Salzburg** in 1641. Its chief promoter was the archbishop of Salzburg, Paris Lodron (1619–1653).

8

1. The feast of the **Immaculate Conception**, which the whole Church observes on this day, was first introduced in Spain by St. Ildephonse of Toledo and accepted throughout the Order through the efforts of St. Anselm of Canterbury.

2. **St. Romaric**, abbot of Remiremont, was of illustrious parentage, occupied an honorable position at the royal court, but suffered none of these things to lead him away from God. Among the worthy men he numbered among his friends was St. Arnulph, who subsequently became bishop of Metz. Romaric's attachment and devotion to King Theodebert led to his banishment. Upon his return he distributed among the poor all his earthly possessions with the single exception of the castle of Habende in the Vosges mountains, which was destined to be a monastery. St. Amatus, a monk of Luxeuil, established and ruled the first community, which professed the rule of St. Columban. Romaric himself entered the ranks of the brethren and after the death of Amatus in 627 was elected abbot. For twenty six years he shone as a model of humility and charity, and died in 653, lamented by all that knew him. The monastery was, after his death, named for him Remiremont; it was destroyed in the tenth century, but rebuilt at the foot of the hill on which the original buildings had stood.

3. **Bl. Guntard**, first abbot of Liessies in Belgium, was the son of Count Wipert of Poitou, who founded that monastery in honor of St. Lambert in the days of Pepin. He was the brother of St. Hildetrudis, and died about 780.

4. **Bl. Hunechildis**, abbess in Thuringia, is said to have accompanied St. Lioba to Germany at the invitation of St. Boniface. From a letter written to her by the holy bishop, it appears that she had been a worthy and useful instrument in propagating the kingdom of God and religious life. She died in the year 760.

9

1. **St. Balda**, abbess of Jouarre, in the diocese of Meaux, was an aunt of St. Telechildis, first abbess of that house, and of St. Aguilberta, the second abbess. Balda succeeded Aguilberta and died rich in merit in the year 700.

Jerome: Armellini.
Cong. of Salzburg: Chronicle of Salzburg.
Immac. Conception: Mab.
Romaric: Mab.; Butler; Roman Martyrol.
Guntard: Mab.
Hunechildis: Mab. Also called Chunichildis.
Balda: Mab.

2. **St. Wulfhildis,** abbess of Barking in England, was of a noble family and with her own estate endowed the abbey of Horton in Dorsetshire. When Barking was restored after the Danish wars, Wulfhildis was appointed its abbess, and her rule was so successful that the house again flourished in its primitive perfection, in observance and the holy lives of the religious. In the troubles that followed the death of King Edgar, she was expelled by queen Elfleda, but was restored by Ethelred. She died about the year 990.

3. **Ven. Angelrannus,** the Wise, abbot of Centula at Ponthieu, early in life began the pursuit of holiness in that monastery and also made remarkable progress in his studies. He finished his education under the tuition of the celebrated Fulbert of Chartres. After the death of abbot Engelhard, he was elected to succeed him, but hid himself in a forest to escape the dignity. Having been discovered and persuaded to comply with the wishes of the brethren and of the king, he entered upon the discharge of his duties. He insisted upon strict observance of the Rule encouraged studies and the transcription of books, resisted all aggressions upon the rights of his house, was a father to the poor, and after edifying his community for a number of years by the sanctity of his life, he departed in peace in 1045.

4. **Witmar,** monk of Corvey in Saxony, was a faithful companion of St. Anschar, Apostle of the North, and entered into eternal rest after a life of devoted labor about the year 870.

5. **Egbert,** archbishop of Trier, had been a monk at St. Martin's in the same city and had been singled out for his eminent qualities to preside over that metropolitan see. Beneath his episcopal insignia he bore the humble heart of a monk; he encouraged good discipline in religious houses and was a distinguished patron and benefactor of the monastery of Egmont.

10

1. **St. Thomas,** abbot of Farfa in Italy, a native of Savoy, made a pilgrimage to Rome and to Jerusalem, remaining three years in the latter city and praying for light to know for what kind of life he was called by God. One night while praying at the Holy Sepulchre, he had a vision in which Our Lady told him to go to Italy and to establish a religious community near a church beside which stood three cypresses and which was dedicated to her honor. He found the place that had been shown him in the vision and did as he had been ordered. Among his spiritual pupils were SS. Paldo, Taso and Tato, for whom he selected the site for the monastery of St. Vincent on the Voltorno. After ruling his community wisely and faithfully for thirty-five years he entered his rest in the year 715.

Wulfhildis: Stanton; Wm. of Malmesbury; Butler.
Angelrannus: Mab. Also called Ingelrannus.
Wilmar: St. Rembert.
Egbert: Mab.
Thomas: Mab.

2. **St. Herbert,** bishop of Rennes, previously was a Cistercian monk in the monastery of Clermont. He governed his see by word and holy example for fourteen years and was summoned to his eternal reward in 1198.

3. **St. Fulgentius,** first abbot of Afflighem in Brabant, was a native of that province, and became a monk at the monastery of St. Agericus in Verdun, but was driven from that city by its bishop with whom neither he nor any member of the community would have intercourse, since he was under excommunication. In casting about for a new home, he was attracted by the excellent reputation of a young community that had come into existence about six years before at Afflighem. He became one of their number and they elected him as their first abbot. A short distance from his monastery he organized one for women, and soon had under his direction a community of two-hundred members. He is said to have foretold the death of St. Anselm of Canterbury and of St. Hugo abbot of Cluny, and followed them into the region of light in 1122.

4. **Ven. John Roberts,** also called de Mervinia, because he was a native of Merionethshire in Wales, was born in 1575 or 1576. He received part of his education at Oxford, then for a time studied law, and finally was a student in the English College at Valladolid in Spain, from which he passed to the Spanish Benedictine Congregation and was professed at Compostella. In 1601 he was ordained priest and sent on the English mission. Nothing could be more admirable than his perseverance in his holy work, and his charity was notably manifested during a severe visitation of the plague in London. He contrived to render assistance to multitudes of the infected and was the means of converting many of them from their vices and misbelief. Four times he was arrested and sent into banishment, but he always returned and resumed his former course of life. At length he was seized for the fourth time when vested for Mass, and, without being allowed to put off the sacred vestments, was hurried away to a filthy dungeon. He was condemned solely for his priestly character and for refusing the proposed oath, and was hanged, drawn and quartered at Tyburn on this day in the year 1610. The introduction of the cause of his beatification was approved by Leo XIII, 1896.

5. **Bl. Meinrad,** abbot of Sassovivo, founder of that monastery and of the Congregation of the Holy Cross of Sassovivo, was equally distinguished for his learning and godliness and was active in suppressing the schism growing out of the opposition of Antipope Cadalous to Pope Alexander. He died in 1095.

6. **Witgar,** abbot of Ottobeuren and bishop of Augsburg, at all times had in view the honor of God. Hence he never looked back to see how much he had done, but rather strove to attain what lay before him. Having ruled his monastery for several years, and presided over the see of Augsburg from 858-887 he set out to preach the Gospel in the Swiss canton of Grisons, where he died in 902.

Herbert: C. Robert; Menard.
Fulgentius: Mab.
John: Bucelin; Camm: Life of Dom John Roberts.
Meinrad: Armellini (who calls him Maynardus).
Witgar: Monum. of Ottobeuren; Stadler. Also called Wigger.

11

1. **St. Hildeman,** bishop of Beauvais in France, was at first a monk at Corbie under Abbot Adalard, upon whose recommendation, with the consent of clergy and people, he was made a bishop. During St. Adalard's last illness, Hildeman visited him and administered to him the sacrament of Extreme Unction. He also officiated at his burial. He attended several councils,—in 829 that of Paris, in 835 that of Thionville and in 844 that of Beauvais. After Adalard's death he continued to rule his diocese for twenty years, was unjustly accused of siding with Lothair against Emperor Louis, contributed to the re-instatement of that emperor and died with the reputation of sanctity in 846.

2. **St. Wulfer,** priest and monk of the monastery of Reome, was a man noted for his cheerful spirit and was possesssed of considerable skill as a physician. Once on the first Sunday after Pentecost he had a vision during Holy Mass: he saw the souls of many who had fallen fighting against the Saracens ascend to heaven out of purgatory and heard them say that others were about to follow, among whom he believed himself to be. Five months later he was sent to the monastery of St. Germain at Auxerre to prescribe medicines for several sick brethren, and died there in 1018.

3. **St. Fitweten,** monk of Redone in Britanny, was born in England and joined the community of St. Convoyon at Redone. He edified the brethren by his wonderful self-abnegation, but believed that he could better ensure his salvation by living as a solitary. When on the point of leaving the monastery the brethren besought him with tears and prayers to abide with them, and he remained with them to the day when he was called to his reward in eternal life in 868.

4. **St. Tato,** third abbot of St. Vincent's on the Volturno and a brother of SS. Paldo and Taso, was distinguished for his paternal affability and kindness and was a wonderful example of austerity and self-denial for his brethren. Although he labored with the brethren, he spent many nights in prayer and afflicted himself with long fasts. He died in the year 739.

5. **Bl. Ida** of Nivelle, a Cistercian nun of the monastery of Rameige in southern Brabant, was born at Nivellon, and at the early age of nine years went about begging for the poor. After she had taken the veil, the rare gifts of grace with which Heaven had endowed her came to light. Her heart was continually burning with love of God, and in order to relieve those who suffered temptation and distress, she offered to take upon herself their sufferings. Many souls were rescued from purgatory through her fervent prayers. She saw into the future, read the secrets of the human heart and several times beheld Our Lord and His Blessed Mother in visions. At the same time she regarded herself as the lowliest and unworthiest of all creatures. She died at the age of thirty two in 1231.

Hildeman: Mab.
Wulfer: Mab.
Fitweten: Mab.
Tato: Mab.
Ida: Molanus; Stadler.

6. **Ven. Richerius,** abbot of the monastery of Monte Cassino, was professed in Niederaltaich in Bavaria, and summoned to be abbot, successively, at the monastery of Leno in the diocese of Brescia, and of Monte Cassino, for which he recovered the possessions wrested from the monks by the Normans and inaugurated a new period of prosperity. In the midst of all his achievements, he was humble, and patiently bore the humiliations that fell to his share. He promoted the spread of the Order in Hungary and died at Pescara in the former kingdom of Naples in 1055. The monks who were with him at the time, buried him in the monastery of San Liberatore, in the county of Chieti.

12

1. **St. Walaricus,** abbot of a monastery that afterwards bore his name in Picardy, was born in Auvergne about 550 and in his boyhood was a shepherd. As soon as he was able to read he began to study the Psalms. After surmounting numerous obstacles, he was admitted into the monastery of Autumon, or Autoin, where he shone by his piety and humility. Aiming at still greater perfection, he passed to the monastery of Luxeuil, and after St. Columban, its abbot, had gone into exile, governed it while St. Eustasius, the second abbot, was absent in Italy. On the return of Eustasius, St. Walaric accompanied by St. Waldolen went forth to preach the Gospel in several adjacent provinces and in Vimeux established a monastery which became the centre of a notable missionary activity. Walaric, who was its abbot, observed long fasts, slept on a couch consisting of twigs, performed manual labor and distributed the proceeds of the sale among the poor. He died in 622; the monastery and the town which grew up about the latter, were called St. Valery.

2. **St. Gregory,** monk at St. Stephen's, Terracina, and disciple of Our Holy Father St. Benedict, was sent by the latter to found a monastery at Terracina, and in a dream received directions how to construct the buildings. In a vision he also saw the death of his brother St. Speciosus. Gregory died about 540.

3. **St. Vicelinus,** bishop of Oldenburg, had been a monk at Siburg on the Rhine and was promoted to the episcopal office on account of his exemplary life and his learning. He labored zealously not only within the limits of his diocese, but also preached the Gospel to the Wends, Slavs and the inhabitants of Holstein, among whom he obliterated the last traces of heathenism. He passed to his reward in 1154.

13

1. **St. Jodocus,** priest and hermit at Ponthieu, in the diocese of Amiens, was the son of an Armorican lord, and was requested by his brother, who had assumed the title of king after his father's death, to rule in his stead. Jodocus considered the proposition for a week, then decided to embrace the ecclesiastical

Richerius: Chron. of Niederaltaich; Tosti.
Walaricus: Mab. Also called Valery. Butler.
Gregory: Greg. the Great in the IV Book of Dialogues.
Vicelinus: Helmold: Kranz.

state. After his ordination he presided seven years over the chapel of Haymo, count of Ponthieu, and afterwards spent eight years with a disciple named Wulmar in the solitude of Brahic, or Ray; whereupon both went to Runiac at the mouth of the Canche, where they built a chapel in honor of St. Martin and dwelt thirteen years in prayer and practices of austerity. Terrified by the bite of a serpent, Jodocus and his companion left their solitude, made a pilgrimage to Rome, and again betook themselves to Runiac, where Count Haymo built for them a handsome church in honor of St. Martin. Here Jodocus remained to the end of his mortal career in 668. The hermitage eventually grew to be a monastery and was called S. Josse-sur-Mer.

2 St. Odilia, abbess of Hohenburg in Alsace, was the daughter of Adalric, duke of Alsace and his wife Bereswinda. As she was born blind, she was removed from court, for some time was reared in a private family and finally was placed in the monastery of Beaume-les-Nones at Besancon. At her Baptism she recovered her eyesight. Nevertheless her father continued to ignore her; hence she decided to cast her lot with the nuns. When, some time after, her father deigned to acknowlege and receive her, he intimated that she marry a certain young nobleman of his choice; but she prevailed upon him not to press the proposition, as she preferred to consecrate herself to God in religion. He consented and in 680 made her a gift of the castle of Hohenburg together with its revenues for the establishment of the first religious house for women in Alsace. During the ten years that elapsed before the buildings stood finished, she gathered about her a fervent community of sisters. Odilia fared on barley bread and vegetables; rarely drank anything but water and rested on a hard couch. At the foot of the hill on which the monastery stood, she built a house for the guests and the poor, and as a dutiful child often visited her aged parent who lived near by and consoled him in the hour of greatest need, unmindful of the treatment she had received in her childhood. In the garden of the monastery there was a chapel known as the "Chapel of Tears," where she wept frequently over the death of her father. As the sisters wished to participate in her charitable work, she built another monastery, called Niedermuenster, at the foot of the hill and adjoining the hospice. After many years of faithful service Odilia died on the feast of St. Lucy in 720 or 722.

3. St. Elizabeth, surmaned Rose, abbess of Rosoy, was a nun of the monastery of Chelles near Paris, but was permitted to live as a solitary. Gradually she was joined by other devout souls, for whom she established a monastery and whom she ruled to the day of her death in 1130.

4. The celebrated John Tritheim (Trithemius), abbot of St. James at Wuerzburg, and previously at Spannheim in the diocese of Mainz, was born near Trier in 1462 of poor parents and at the age of fifteen learned how to read in a very short time—some say in the space of a month. His desire to be educated met with much opposition from his parents; therefore he left home and in the course of his aimless wandering stopped at the monastery of Spannheim,

---

Jodocus: Mab. French form: Josse. Butler; Rom. Martyrol.
Odilia: Mab.; Butler (Othilia).
Elizabeth: Mab.

where he decided to enter. He received the Benedictine habit in 1482 and as early as July 28, 1483 was elected abbot. A controversy that broke out in the monastery grew so bitter that he withdrew from Spannheim in 1505. A year later he was made abbot of St. James at Wuerzburg, where he continued his literary activity and died in 1516.

14

1. **St. Agnellus,** an abbot at Naples, was the only child of his parents and the fruit of earnest prayer to Our Blessed Lady. At the age of fifteen he resolved to embrace the religious state, and made a beginning by living, as did St. Benedict, in a cavern.which he did not leave before the death of his parents. With the wealth that fell to his share he built a house for the poor and strangers whom he served with great charity. In the course of time the number of visitors grew so great that he concealed himself in a remote locality in the mountains and there remained till an inner voice urged him to go back and serve the poor. Seven years later he was chosen abbot of the monastery established by the African bishop Gaudiosus near Naples, and introduced the Rule of St. Benedict. Here he died in 596 and was buried by bishop Fortunatus. Naples owes so many favors to his holy intercession that it has conferred on him the title of *Pater Patriae*.

2. **Bl. Adam,** monk of Monte Cassino, was sacristan and discharged the duties of that office faithfully and fearlessly. When prince Pandulph of Capua demanded the delivery of the treasure stored up in the sacristy, Adam refused. Some of the brethren fearing that some dreadful things might happen, endeavored to persuade the sacristan to yield, whereupon he laid the treasure upon the altar of St. Benedict saying: "Let every one take from that place what he pleases." God signally punished all that dared to lay sacrilegious hands upon the pious offerings of the faithful. Adam died about 1030.

3. **Arduin,** margrave of Ivrea, at one time king of Italy, found rest for his soul in the monastery of Fructuaria, of which he had been a distinguished benefactor. He died a holy death as a monk of that house in 1018.

15

1. **Bl. Raynald,** bishop of Nocera in Umbria, was descended from a noble German family that had acquired possessions in Italy from the emperors. Early heeding the voice of grace, he entered the monastery of Fontavellana, where his growth in virtue was so conspicuous that after the death of Bishop Hugo he was made bishop of Nocera. One of the principal objects of his solicitude was the welfare of the poor. In his private life he was given to austerities, slept on the floor, partook of the plainest kind of fare and devoted many hours of the night to meditation. His demeanor was invariably calm: no one ever saw him laugh,

John Tritheim: Ziegelbauer; C. E.
Agnellus: Mab.
Adam: Mab.
Arduin: Mab.

yet he never was either sad or morose. He had adorned the see of Nocera three years by his virtues when the Lord called him to his reward in 1225. He was chosen patron saint of Nocera.

2. **Marinus,** seventh abbot of Cava in Italy, succeeded Falco in the government of that monastery in 1147 and ruled as a wise and just superior to the end of his days in 1170.

3. **Candidus Furlong,** monk at Nogales in Spain, was a native of Ireland, but being desirous to serve in the mission among his persecuted brethren in the faith, he crossed over to the Continent, made a pilgrimage on foot to Rome and became a monk at Nogales. After his ordination, he was, according to his wish, sent to Ireland. Before entering upon his apostolic career, he prepared himself by a long season of prayer and fasting. Such was the force and unction of his preaching, that the enemies of the faith were enraged by his boldness. Great numbers of the faithful thronged about him to hear him or to receive his blessing. By his prayer he healed the sick, restored speech to the dumb and called the dead back to life. King James I summoned him to England that he might see this prodigy. Thomas Madden, Furlong's companion, relates that as many as a thousand persons were relieved by him in a day, and that he converted some four thousand. Still greater is the number of those whom he strengthened in the profession of their faith. He died in the year in 1616.

16

1. **St. Ado,** archbishop of Vienne, was descended from one of the oldest families in Gatinois, in France, was born in 800 and was educated at the monastery of Ferrieres. His talent, supported by unusual docility and diligence, was of a high order. To escape the importunities of his friends, who strained every effort to win him for the world, he took the religious habit and irrevocably consecrated himself to the service of his Divine Master. In the monastery of Pruem, whither he was sent to instruct the monks in the sacred sciences, he aroused remarkable enthusiasm among his eager pupils, yet always taught them to preserve humble hearts, for his motto was, in the words of the Apostle, "to be wise unto sobriety." After the death of abbot Marquard he became a victim to calumny, left the monastery and made a pilgrimage to Rome where he spent five years satisfying his devotion at the tombs of the Apostles and holy martyrs. Thence he went to Ravenna, where he compiled the Martyrology that bears his name, and wrote lives of SS. Desiderius and Theuderius. From Ravenna he passed to Lyons, where the archbishop appointed him pastor of the church of St. Roman with the sanction of his abbot. After the death of archbishop Remigius of Vienne no one was found worthier than Ado to succeed to that important see (860). He received episcopal consecration, but continued to live as simply as a monk; he was a zealous preacher of the word of God, struggled against abuses and provided for the training of his clergy. For the poor, who were his special wards, he built several hospices. He energetically

Raynald: Ferrari.
Marinus: Monum. of Cava.
Candidus: F. de Vivar; Stadler.

opposed the divorce of emperor Lothair and his wife Thietberga, and was highly respected by kings and popes. After governing the church of Vienne for fifteen years he entered into his rest in 875.

2. **St. Adelaide,** empress and wife of Otto I, was always a patron and benefactress of religious, and founded or endowed a number of monasteries. Towards the end of her life she betook herself to the monastery of Selz in Alsace to prepare herself for her voyage into eternity. She would frequently exclaim with the Apostle: "Who shall deliver me from the body of this death?" (Rom. 7, 24), and as her end drew nigh, she said: "I wish to be dissolved and to be with Christ." She died in 999.

3. **Helinward,** bishop of Minden, was a monk of a monastery whose name is unknown, but it is recorded that he was made a bishop on account of his eminent virtues and that he died a holy death in 958.

17

1. **St. Sturmius,** abbot of Fulda, was born in Bavaria and educated under the supervision of St. Boniface, whom he accompanied in his apostolic journeys, till they reached Fritzlar, where he was left in charge of abbot Wigbert. He had scarcely attained the canonical age when he was promoted to sacred orders and commissioned to preach the Gospel. He spent three years in this employment, when he asked leave of St. Boniface to retire into a solitude. The Saint consented and appointed two brethren to accompany him. They entered the great forest of Buchonia and after wandering about for three days, paused at a place called Hersfeld. Sturmius informed St. Boniface of the choice he had made, but was directed to select some other place as Hersfeld was exposed to incursions of the Saxons. He continued his search and finally found a suitable locality on the present site of Fulda. At the instance of St. Boniface, King Carlmann and several nobles made a grant of lands for a monastery. Sturmius here laid the foundations of the future abbey of Fulda on March 12, 744. Encouraged and blessed by St. Boniface, he cleared the land of shrubs and trees and built a monastery which soon sheltered a large community. A year later St. Boniface visited the new foundation. Sturmius and several other brethren were sent to Italy in 748 to study the discipline and traditions of the principal Benedictine houses, particularly of Monte Cassino. On their return, two years later, Sturmius was solemnly inducted into office as the first abbot by St. Boniface, and a year later Pope Zachary granted Fulda complete exemption. The peace and growth of Fulda was unfortunately disturbed by the machinations of spiteful men; several of the brethren denounced Sturmius as a traitor to the cause of Pepin and accomplished his banishment to Jumieges, much to the grief of all well-meaning brethren. In 758, Sturmius was permitted to return and from that time ruled the monastery without difficulty. He was already feeble and advanced in age when Charlemagne in 878 commissioned him to instruct and baptize the Saxons. He was seized with an illness on the way,

---

Ado: Mab.; Butler.
Adelaide: Odilo. Also called Adelheid or Alice. Butler.
Helinward: Kranz.

caused himself to be carried back to Fulda and died on this day in 779. He was canonized by Pope Innocent II in 1139.

2. **St. Begga**, widow and abbess in Brabant, was the daughter of Pepin of Landen and the sister of St. Gertrude of Nivelle. After her husband Ansegisus had been killed in the chase, she renounced the world, made a pilgrimage to Rome and on her return built a monastery at Aden on the Maas, for which she secured nuns from Nivelle. She governed them as a wise and loving mother for fifteen years, and entered through the gates of eternal life in 698.

3. **St. Vivina**, prioress of Bigarden at Brussels, was of illustrious parentage and destined to be the bride of a young nobleman. But she persuaded him to renounce his prospects and devote himself to the service of God in solitude. With the aid of count Godfrey, called the Bearded, she built the monastery of Bigarden, professed as a nun there in 1133 and was an example of humility, obedience and self-denial to her sisters. She died at an advanced age in 1170.

4. **William Longue-Epee** (Long Sword), duke of Normandy and son of Rollo, first duke of that country, early aspired to the religious life, but as he was prevented from carrying out his pious design, he wore the religious habit secretly, always hoping for the day when he might become a religious. He was assassinated by minions of his adversary Count Arnulph of Flanders in 944, and was buried at Rouen.

18

1. The church of Spain on this day commemorates an **Apparition of Our Lady** in the cathedral of Toledo, of which occurrence an ancient chronicle says: When St. Ildephonse the archbishop was as usual repairing to the church with his clergy for the night offices, they were all dazzled by the brightness that filled the interior and they ran out in bewilderment. Ildephonse advanced to the sanctuary and there on the archiepiscopal throne sat Our Lady, who gave him a white Mass vestment, with these words: "Servant of God, accept this gift, because you have ever been my faithful servant and spread my praise amongst the faithful. Use this garment as long as you live; in Heaven you shall have another out of my treasure." In token of reverence for the throne upon which Our Lady sat, neither Ildephonse nor any of his successors dared to occupy it ever since that memorable apparition.

2. **St. Wunibald**, abbot at Heidenheim, in the diocese of Eichstaett, was the son of the Anglo-Saxon prince Richard, and the brother of SS. Willibald and Walburga. In 722 he accompanied his father and his brother on a pilgrimage to Rome, and remained in that city seven years to prepare himself for the holy priesthood, while Willibald continued on his way to Jerusalem. After his ordination, Wunibald returned to England, then made a second pilgrimage to

Sturmius: Aegil of Fulda.
Begga: Mab.; Butler.
Vivina: Molanus; Mab.
William: Arnold of Douai; Menard.
Ildephonse: Mab.

Rome and there received the religious habit. When St. Boniface visited Rome in 728, he induced Wunibald to accompany him to Germany and join his brethren on the mission in that country. In his new field of labor he was given charge of seven churches. After his brother Willibald had been made bishop of Eichstaett, he invited Wunibald into his diocese to establish a monastery for monks at Heidenheim. This monastery prospered in a short time, which encouraged him to found a monastery for women at the same place to be governed by his sister St. Walburga. Wunibald was much afflicted with sickness and finally decided to resign his office as abbot and to retire to Monte Cassino, but the brethren by their tears and prayers prevailed upon him to change his resolution. As the hour of his death approached, he assembled all the brethren in his chamber, absolved them from transgressions of the Rule, encouraged them to abide in faith and charity and slept in peace in the year 760. Sixteen years after, his brother Willibald raised the remains and laid them in a costly tomb.

3. Ven. **Oderisius Pierius,** monk of Monte Cassino, was one of the glories of the Church in the seventeenth and eighteenth century. Pope Clement X commissioned him to labor for the re-union of the schismatic Greeks on the islands of the Mediterranean Sea. On this mission he toiled with great patience and perseverance. Pope Innocent XI appointed him vicar apostolic and dispatched him to the Peloponnesus, where he induced the inhabitants of Bracia di Maina to make their peace with the Church. Oderisius returned to Monte Cassino, where he lived a calm, retired life and died in 1704.

19

1. **St. Berard,** bishop of Teramo in Italy, was descended from the family of the Orsini, at an early age saw the emptiness of earthly fame and became a monk at Monte Cassino, He was sent to preside over a dependency of that abbey, St. John at Lanciano, where he was so conspicuous for the sanctity of his life that he was chosen bishop of Teramo. He was a tender and solicitous father to the poor and the orphan and died in 1122.

2. **Bl. Urban V,** Pope (William de Grimoard) was the son of the knight Grimoard of Grisac and was born at Toulouse about 1310. After he had been educated in a manner suited to his rank, he became a monk at the priory of Chirac, where he was also ordained. He continued his studies at Toulouse and Paris, and received the degree of doctor in 1342. The Pope conferred on him the abbeys of S. Victor at Marseille and S. Germain at Auxerre, and employed him on several important diplomatic missions to Italy. On October 23, 1362, he was elected Pope at Avignon, although he was not a cardinal. During his pontificate, which was mostly spent at Avignon, he provided a thousand students with an opportunity to study at one of the universities at his own expense, was lavish in his kindness to the poor, while he always lived as a monk and on days of fast partook of nothing but bread and water. Deaf to all representations made by the court of France, he resolved to put an end to the exile of the

---

Wunibald: Mab.; Canisius; Stanton (Winebald); Butler.
Oderisius: Armellini.
Berard: Ughelli. Also called Eberhard.

Popes and returned to Rome, where he was given a royal welcome on October 23, 1367. Two years later he was visited by the Greek Emperor John V Palaeologus who came to beg for aid against the infidels and abjured the schism. The apparently peaceful condition of Italy which had induced Urban to return to the capital of Christendom soon came to an end; repeated revolts of cities discouraged him and he decided to go back to Avignon despite the remonstrances of St. Bridget, who came to Rome from Montefiascone and told him that if he returned to Avignon he would shortly die. Not long after his arrival at Avignon he was seized with a fatal illness, and died on December 19, 1370. He was interred at the abbey of St. Victor in Marseille.

3. **Catherine,** a nun in the monastery of St. Margaret at Milan, displayed heroic indifference to danger and to repulsive sights during a pestilence. She mortified her sense of taste by adding salt or water to her food. One day when her duties prevented her from receiving Holy Communion with the other sisters, the Holy Eucharist was conveyed to her in a miraculous manner. She died in 1529 at the age of forty years, most of which she had spent in the monastery.

20

1. **St. Dominic,** abbot of Silos in Spain, was born in the village of Cannas in Navarra, spent his youth herding his father's cattle and finally prepared to enter the clerical state. After his ordination he was intent, above all things, upon his own sanctification and for this purpose went into a solitude, where he communed with God alone for the space of eighteen months. Fearing, however, that he might go astray without a guide, he became a monk at St. Millan de Cogolla. The abbot of this house sent him to restore the monastery of St. Mary, and Dominic was delighted that he was obliged to contend with poverty. After his return to San Millan he was appointed prior of that house. While he was holding this office, King Garcias commanded him to deliver a certain sum of money, but met with a determined refusal from the Saint, who, in consequence, was sent away by his abbot to preside over a small monastery with only three cells. But the King pursued him and renewed his former claims, whereupon Dominic fled into Castile, where King Ferdinand IV made him abbot of Silos (Exilium), a decayed monastery, which rose to new life under Dominic's fostering hand and prayers and became one of the principal monasteries of the realm. St. Dominic received the reward of the faithful servant in 1073.

2. **St. Ursicinus,** a monk of Luxeuil and disciple of St. Columban, for many years lived a holy life at a place later known as St. Ursiz in the diocese of Basel, and by his word and example led many others heavenward. He died about 630.

3. **Bl. Ilduara,** nun at Cella nueva in the Spanish province of Gallicia, was the mother of Bishop St. Rudesind of Duma and of the abbess Adalsinda

---

Urban: Panvini; Lives of Popes; C. E. Veneration approved Mar. 5. 1870.
Catherine: Armellini.
Dominic: Yepez.
Ursicinus: Mab.; Stadler.

of Cella nueva. Ilduara had founded this monastery out of her own means. She became a nun there and lived under the rule of her own daughter. Such was her love of poverty that she never wore footgear of any description and by no outward sign betrayed the station she had abandoned to serve in the ranks of a sisterhood. She died in 962 and was buried by her son, St. Rudesind.

4. **Hogerus**, archbishop of Bremen, was formerly a monk at Corvey and had been selected by the aged and infirm archbishop Adalgar to assist him in the discharge of his duties. He succeeded Adalgar as archbishop, and in that capacity was ever watchful lest ecclesiastical discipline suffer harm. While visiting Hamburg, he rose during the night and made his way to the church to hear the monks chanting the divine offices. His diocese was much harrassed by neighboring tribes that made frequent incursions into Bremen and Hamburg and devastated churches and monasteries. Hoger died in 915 and was buried by the side of his predeccessor.

21

1. The feast of St. Gregory is celebrated at Utrecht this day. A notice of his life will be found on August 25.

2. **St. Onnenus**, a monk, probably of St. Malo in Armorica, was venerated in the village of Santonnes. No particulars regarding his life and virtues are extant.

3. **Baudacharius**, a monk at Bobbio in Italy, had charge of the vineyard of that monastery. One day, it is said, he fed thirty brethren with one fowl and they acknowledged they had never before fared better. The biographer at this point observes that faith supplied the lack of nourishment. He died about 650.

4. **Thomas**, a Cistercian monk at Arnsburg in the diocese of Mainz, shone among his brethren by his devotion and innocent life. Once while prostrated by illness he felt such an intense devotion to Our Blessed Lady that he left his bed and went into the garden. There he had a vision: the holy virgins Agnes and Catherine appeared to him one after the other, singing, and after these Our Lady accompanied by a choir of angels, whose songs entranced him so that he fell to the ground, where he was found after Matins. After he had been carried back to his cell, he was obliged to confess what had happened to him. His love of God and of Our Lady steadily grew from this day to that of his death about 1200.

5. **William**, surnamed Bardus, a Celestine monk at Paris, was distinguished for his piety, and once while sunk in contemplation was favored with a vision of Christ on the Cross.

Ilduara: Yepez.; Menard
Hogerus: Adam of Bremen.
Onnenus: Boll.
Baudacharius: Mab.
Thomas: Caesarius of Heisterbach.
William: Menard.

22

1. **St. Jutta,** abbess of Diesenberg near Mainz, the daughter of Count Stephen II of Sponheim and the sister of Count Meginhard, was the spiritual mother of St. Hildegarde. Jutta entered the monastery in 1112 accompanied by three other candidates, one of whom was St. Hildegarde and the other Hiltrudis, while the name of the third has been forgotten. She died in 1136 after ruling her monastery prudently for twenty-four years. For some time before she was elected abbess, she had lived near the monastery as a recluse.

2. **Bl. Notingus,** bishop of Constance, had been a monk at St. Gall's in Switzerland, distinguished himself among his brethren by his piety and purity of life, and was the teacher of St. Conrad, the future bishop of Constance. He left some writings, among them a commentary on the Gospel and several hymns in honor of Saints. From 920 to 930 or 935 he ruled the see of Constance during a period when the country was overrun by barbarous hordes. The Lord called him to the reward of his toil in 935.

3. **Bl. Engelbert,** Cistercian laybrother at Zulpich in the former principality of Juelich, was born blind, but favored by Heaven with internal illuminations. As a pilgrim and guided by a child, he went from one holy place to another, lived in extreme poverty, never slept in a bed, and finally applied for admission among the Cistercians. While he was lying on his deathbed, his mother who had been sick nine years, was disconsolate, but he said: "Mother, the Blessed Virgin will help you." He died, in 1190, and his mother recovered.

4. **Amaswind,** abbot of Sylva de Malaga in Spain, is described by writers as a meek and pleasant man and an enemy to every kind of bodily comfort. He died in 982.

23

1. **St. Ventila,** monk and hermit at the church of Our Lady of Pugin near Orense in Spain, was renowned for his austerities and died in 890.

2. **Bl. Hartman,** bishop of Brixen, in Tyrol, had been a monk at St. Peter's in Salzburg and was on account of his piety and tried ability selected to rule the see of Brixen. He died in 1165.

3. **Bl. John Zurita,** a Cistercian abbot in Portugal, at first served as a soldier in the wars against the Saracens, then withdrew from the world and took up the life of an anchorite. Having met some of the monks whom St. Bernard had sent to Spain, John joined them and received the Cistercian habit at Tarouca in Portugal. After the death of Adelbert, the second abbot, John Zurita

Jutta: Trithem.; Mab.   Also called Juttha, Juda.
Notingus: Ziegelbauer; Bruschius.
Engelbert: Seguin.
Amaswind: Morales; Sandoval.
Ventila: Morales.
Hartmann: Hundt; Arnold of Douai.

was elected his successor. He wrote a rule for the military Order of Avis, of which he is considered the founder or organizer (1162). He is said to have had the spirit of prophecy and to have read the human heart. Yearning to serve God in seclusion, he resigned his office as abbot and as grandmaster of the Knights of Avis and withdrew to the monastery of St. Christopher, where he lived three and a half years longer. On his deathbed he intoned the "Te Deum" and died at peace with God and man in 1164. The Order of Avis was later united with that of Calatrava.

4. **Agnes,** wife of emperor Henry III, after her husband's death entered the monastery of Fructuaria (Frudelle) near Turin in Piedmont and took the veil, although she was not professed. Later she went to Rome, and lived a holy life at the church of St. Petronilla. She made a general confession to St. Peter Damiani, her spiritual adviser, and, as one of her biographers relates, afflicted her body excessively with vigils and fastings, and died in the year 1077.

24

1. **St. Irmina,** abbess of Ohren at Trier and daughter of King Dagobert II of Austrasia, was born about 660 and was betrothed to a certain count Herman. After the unexpected death of the latter, she renounced all earthly ties and was supplied by her father with means to build the monastery of Ohren about 675. Once when an infectious disease raged in the monastery, she called for St. Willibrord, who offered the Holy Sacrifice of the Mass and sprinkled the sick with holy water, whereupon all recovered. As an expression of gratitude for this favor, she granted him certain lands, on which the monastery of Echternach was later built. This and similar grants for religious purposes bear witness to her pious liberality. She died about 720. The greater part of her relics was in the monastery of Weissenburg in the diocese of Speier.

2. **St. Adela,** widow and abbess at Pfalzel on the Moselle, was a sister of St. Irmina and was espoused by the noble Alberic. Their only son became the father of St. Gregory, abbot at Utrecht. Desiring to promote the honor of God by establishing a house in which God's praises should be sung day and night, she founded the monastery in which she took the veil after her husband's decease. She governed her sisters in holiness both by word and example and died about 734.

3. **Bruno,** a laybrother at Ottobeuren, first a monk and then a recluse, centered all his thoughts on God and bestowed no part of his affections on creatures. He died in the reputation of sanctity about 990.

25

1. **St. Adelsindis,** nun at Marchiennes, was the daughter of St. Adalbald and St. Rictrudis. Like her parents, she strove to please God above all and be-

---

John: Manrique.
Agnes: Albert of Stade; Krantz.
Irmina: Mab.
Adela: Mab.
Bruno: Khamm.

came a nun at Hamay, or Marchiennes, which had been founded by her aunt St. Gertrude and was governed by her sister Eusebia. Adelsindis died in the year 680.

2. **Bl. Matthew,** cardinal bishop of Albano, was born of a distinguished family at Rheims, held a canonicate at the cathedral in that city, and entered the Cluniacensian monastery of St. Martin des Champs near Paris, of which he was appointed prior. His love and solicitude embraced all the members of the community and was at all times combined with seasonable firmness. His fidelity and success in maintaining exemplary observance induced Abbot Peter the Venerable to appoint him prior at Cluny. Having been sent to Rome on business of the Order, he found so much favor with Pope Honorius II that the latter created him cardinal and bishop of Albano. Beneath his purple he preserved the simplicity and humility of a monk, and lived as plainly as if he were in a monastery. The Pope repeatedly employed him on diplomatic missions and found in him a trusty supporter in the days of dissension and schism. The saintly cardinal died after an illness of several months on Christmas of the year 1134. Pope Innocent II and the cardinals kissed the hands and feet of the deceased prelate as if he were a Saint.

3. **Bl. Peter Mauritius,** called the Venerable, was descended from the counts of Auvergne, and was born at the chateau of Montboissier about 1092. Early in life he was conspicuous for his piety and rare talent. He entered the monastery of Cluny and after the death of Abbot Pontian was chosen his successor. His charity, prudence and extensive learning won for him the appellation of Venerable. While intent upon the progress of his monastery, he took an active part in the affairs of the Church; he combatted the errors of Peter de Bruys, induced Abelard to retract his erroneous teachings and wrote a treatise refuting the errors of the Jews and of the Koran. On several occasions he was an effectual peacemaker: he reconciled the Pope with the King of France, and Roger of Sicily with the emperor. For the purpose of reforming his abbey, he adopted a number of salutary provisions from the Rule of Citeaux and died in peace in 1157.

4. **Bl. Fulco,** bishop of Toulouse, was first a monk at Grandselve, of which house he was also elected abbot. As bishop of Toulouse, he was active in combatting the errors of the Waldenses and the Albigenses. His earthly reward for these services was persecution and exile. He was a friend of St. Dominic, the founder of the Order of Preachers, and died 1232.

26

1. **Bl. Stephen,** was a monk of San Martino delle Scale at Palermo in Sicily, of whose life no details are known.

Adelsindis: Mab.; Stadler (Adalsindis).
Matthew: Peter the Venerable; Menard.
Peter: Radulf; Baronius.
Fulco: Menard.
Stephen: Oct. Cajetan.

2. **Ven. Adelhard,** a monk of Hirschau in Wuerttemberg, was born in 846 and was educated and professed in that monastery under Haderard, its fourth abbot. God sent His servant a severe trial. Adelhard suffered intense headaches for two years and as a result became blind. As he was in every other respect physically sound, he resolved to draw as much spiritual profit as possible from the affliction that barred him from external occupations. He scrupulously avoided every distraction and put out of his mind all temporal concerns; never spoke a trivial or thoughtless word; spent his time in prayer and meditation, and wept tears when he heard the brethren read the Passion of Our Lord. He foretold his death three years before it actually occurred and also the destruction of the monastery eighty years before the event, and died in 924.

3. At **Luxeuil** in France a great number of monks, together with their abbot **Mellinus,** were slain by the Saracens in the year 732.

4. **Thiagrinus,** bishop of Halberstadt in Saxony, had been a monk at Corvey, where he and his brother Hildegrin, his predecessor in the see of Halberstadt, had consecrated themselves to the divine service by monastic profession. He ruled the diocese with great zeal and fidelity and entered into his rest 840.

5. **Francis Levorot,** monk at Montserrat in Catalonia, was a priest at the time of his entrance into that monastery, and was distinguished by his fervor in prayer and penitential practices. He partook of food but once a day, and although he had spent the greater part of the day in the confessional, he was regular in attendance at the night offices, after which he would remain in meditation before a crucifix until morning. He died at the age of eighty years during the night following Christmas. The year is not stated.

27

1. **St. Alvitus,** bishop of Leon in Spain, had previously been monk and abbot at Sahagun. While occupying the see of Leon, he transferred the relics of St. Isidore of Seville to his cathedral at Leon. Leaving to posterity a memory of a pious and zealous life he departed in peace in 1063.

2. **St. Adamnan** was a monk of great sanctity and austerity at Coldingham in Scotland. It is not certain whether he was a native of Scotland. In his youth his life was all but edifying, however when the grace of God had touched his heart he was moved with a desire to do penance for his sins. He lived for many years at Coldingham and was made one of the priests of the monastery. He prophesied the destruction of the monastery and died about 700.

3. **St. Edburga** was the daughter of King Edward the Elder and his wife Edgiva. In her early childhood she was considered to have given a striking

Adelhard: Trithemius.
Mellinus: Mab.
Thiagrinus: Bruschius. Also called Thiatgrim.
Francis: Yepez.
Alvitus: Yepez.
Adamnan: Mab.; Barrett (Jan. 31).

proof of a religious vocation. She was only three years of age, when her father one day calling her to him, placed before her on one side bright jewels, bracelets, and other ornaments and on the other side a book of the Gospels and offered her the choice of whatever she pleased to take. To the admiration of all, she pointed to the book of the Gospels. She was carefully educated in all the learning and accomplishments of the age, and entered the monastery at Winchester, where she gained the hearts of her sisters in religion by her sweet disposition and singular humility. She would rise in the night, silently take the sandals of the nuns from their bedside, cleanse them and replace them before daylight. She died, as she had lived, in the odor of sanctity in 985

4. **Bl. Balto,** abbot of Wessobrunn iu Bavaria, was noted for his austerity and self-denial, and governed that monastery from 1129 to the time of his death in 1157. At his own request his remains were buried at the entrance of the chapel of St. Nicholas; in 1282 they were removed to a more conspicuous place.

5. **Bl. Hugo,** a Cistercian monk of Tennebach in the diocese of Constance, was so completely oblivious of earthly things and intent upon the concerns of the soul, that his greatest delight consisted in speaking the holy names of Jesus and Mary. A scrupulous observer of the Holy Rule, he attained such a high degree of perfection, that he could in truth say: "Not I live but Christ liveth in me." (Gal. 2, 20). He died reputed a Saint in the twelfth century.

6. **Godfrey,** a monk at Winchester in England, was born at Cambrai in France. He was both learned and pious, and enjoyed some reputation as a writer both in prose and verse. While prior of the monastery, he maintained exemplary order and observance, and built a house for the accommodation of guests. After a long illness he was called to receive the reward of his toil in 1141.

28

1. Two devout brothers, **Herman** and **Otto,** led a holy life in a hermitage near the abbey of Niederaltaich in Bavaria and edified the people living about them by prayer, word and example. They possessed the remarkable gift of reading the hearts of men, led many sinners to do penance and exhorted the virtuous unto perseverance. Herman died in 1326, Otto in 1334.

2. **Hucbald,** monk of St. Peter's at Orbains, diocese of Soissons, suffered much from the invading hordes from Hungary, who laid waste the eastern provinces of France in 937. Having several times failed in attempts to take his life, they considered him a charmed being and held him a captive until he was ransomed by a bishop who restored him to his monastery, where he died in the course of the tenth century.

Edburga: Wm. of Malmesbury: Stanton (June 15). Also called Eadburga.
Balto: Hundt; Stadler. Also called Waltho.
Hugo: Seguin.
Godfrey: Wm. of Malmesbury.
Herman: Monum. of Niederaltaich.
Hucbald: Mab.

3. Establishment of the Congregation of **Melida** by the venerable Chrysostom Calvini, a Cassinese monk of St. Geminiano, in 1548 with the approval of Pope Paul III. It consisted of the monasteries of the Dalmatian archipelago in the Adriatic Sea.

29

1. **St. Ebrulf**, abbot of Ouche in the diocese of Lisieux, was descended from a distinguished family at Bayeux, where he was born in 517. He held important offices at the court of Childebert I, and led a virtuous wedded life. Both husband and wife consented to separate and enter religious communities. His wife carried out her resolve without delay, while her husband had some difficulty in securing the approval of King Childebert. After all obstacles had been removed, he sold all his possessions, distributed the proceeds among the poor and entered the monastery of Deux Jumeaux which St. Martin, the abbot of Vertou, had just founded in the diocese of Bayeux. Seeing that he was shown too much deference on account of his former exalted station, he left with three of the brethren, penetrated into the depths of the forest and established himself at Ouche, where he was soon surrounded by a number of pious persons who sought his spiritual guidance. Ebrulf was a lover of charity and peace and was the servant of the least member of his community. For forty-seven years he was almost continually afflicted with illness and his only nourishment was the Holy Eucharist. He founded as many as fifteen monasteries and died at the age of eighty years in 596. The monastery which he founded at Ouche was named for him and at a later period was incorporated in the Congregation of St. Maur. At Evreux his feast is celebrated on January 16.

2. **St. Thomas a Becket**, archbishop of Canterbury and martyr, though not a Benedictine by virtue of monastic profession, nevertheless wore the habit like the canons of his cathedral, and while living in exile associated with the brethren at Sithiu and Pontigny in the exercises of monastic life. He was slain in defence of the rights of his church, at the foot of the high altar in Canterbury cathedral in 1170 and was canonized by Pope Alexander III in 1173.

3. **Bl. Pontius**, bishop of Puy-en-Velais, had been abbot of Chaise Dieu and merited by his well-tried virtue to be adorned with the episcopal dignity. He died shortly after his return from a pilgrimage to Jerusalem in 1130. He was interred in the priory of Roque Paule in Dauphine.

4. **Ven. Regimbert**, founder and abbot of St. Blasien in the Black Forest, was descended from the barons of Seldenburen and had been honored with the friendship and confidence of Otto I, in whose service he lost a hand in battle. Regimbert, who seems to have become a monk either at Einsiedeln or Rheinau, governed St. Blasien to the end of his days in 964.

Cong. of Melida: Armellini.
Ebrulf: Mab.   French form: Evroul; Butler.
Thomas a Becket: John of Salisbury; Stanton; Butler.
Pontius: Mab.
Regimbert: Boll.; Murer.

30

1. **St. Egwin,** bishop of Worcester in England, is said to have been of royal descent, but from his early youth to have been inspired with better thoughts than those of worldly greatness. Having renounced the most brilliant temporal prospects, he embraced the clerical state and in 692 was elevated to the see of Winchester. As bishop he preached zealously against prevalent vices, but his apostolic fearlessness provoked the ill-will of some who prejudiced the mind of the king and of the archbishop aginst him and obliged him to withdraw from his diocese. Considering that he now had a favorable opportunity, he resolved to visit Rome and explain his case to the Pope. The latter was convinced of his innocnce, sent him back to England with much honor and ordered him to be re-instated in his see in 701. On certain lands granted him by King Ethelred he founded the abbey of Evesham. Having settled all things in good order, he accompanied the two princes, Kenred and Offa, who had resigned their thrones for the love of God, on their pilgrimage to Rome. When he believed that the time had come to gratify his earlier longing, he resigned his episcopal charge and went to end his days at Evesham, where he died on this day 717.

2. **St. Elias,** fourth abbot of Sainte-Foi de Congues in France, died about 900 and was always honored as a Saint at his monastery.

3. **St. Marnoch,** a Cistercian monk and, according to some, an abbot, whose sanctity was attested by miracles before and after his death, was translated from Portmanor to the monastery of Our Lady at Dublin early in the sixteenth century.

4. **Bl. Radulph,** first abbot of Vaucelles near Cambrai, was a native of England, and in the course of a journey on the Continent visited Clairvaux, where he derived so much edification from the lives of the disciples of St. Bernard that he begged to be received among their number. Shortly after his profession he was selected by St. Bernard to establish the monastery of Vaucelles. Radulph was noted for his kindness, generosity to the poor and sincere detestation of every form of sin and wrong. He died in 1151 and his public veneration was authorized by the III Council of the Lateran in 1179.

5. **Bl. Herman,** abbot at St. Pantaleon in Cologne, was a count of Zutphen and a brother of St. Irmengard. He was remarkable for his great humility and condescension, and died in 1120.

6. **Bl. Richard,** a Cistercian monk in the monastery of Our Lady at Altwoerth in Frisia, shone by his exemplary life and virtues in the twelfth century.

Egwin: Mab.; Stanton.
Elias: Mab.
Marnoch: C. Henriquez.
Radulph: Le Mire; Chev. (calls him St.).
Herman: Mab.
Richard: Molanus; Brito.

7. **Lothair**, Frankish king and emperor, sanctified the close of his career by taking the religious habit and living as a monk at Pruem. He died 855.

31

1. **Bl. Peter**, abbot of Subjaco, presided over that abbey in the days of Pope Silvester II (999–1003) and contributed to its prosperity and name by writings, by embellishing the church of the abbey and by increasing its resources. He was captured by enemies of the monastery and imprisoned in the castle of Monticelli. He escaped, but was recaptured and kept in duress because he refused to surrender one of the possessions of the abbey. According to some accounts he was deprived of his eyesight, and died in prison in the year 1103.

2. **Ven. Gunthar**, bishop of Regensburg, had been a monk of St. Emmeram's in that city. The see of Regensburg was vacant and emperor Otto I resolved to appoint the first ecclesiastic he should meet in the morning to fill that see. It happened that the first to meet him was the monk Gunthar, who opened the door of St. Emmeram's to admit the monarch to the church. Otto asked the monk what he would give if he were made bishop. Gunthar smilingly said: "My shoes." When the election was to take place, the emperor related the incident and the monk Gunthar was chosen to fill the vacancy. Six months after assuming the burden of the episcopate, he lay on his deathbed; he caused himself to be laid upon the floor and to be bestrewn with ashes while he said with patient Job: "With hearing of the ear, I have heard thee, but now my eye seeth thee; therefore I reprehend myself and to penance in dust and ashes." (Job XII, 5–6). Weeping tears of compunction he died in 938.

3. **Luitfrid**, third abbot of Muri in Switzerland, had been a monk at St. Blasien in the Black Forest, and was noted for his purity of heart. As abbot of Muri he labored for the material and spiritual growth of his monastery and died on Dec. 31, 1096, in the thirtieth year of his profession.

Lothair: Mab.
Peter: Baronius; Stadler (calls him St.).
Gunthar: Dietmar of Merseburg.
Luitfrid: Annals of Muri.

Supplement

Feb. 20. The *Belgian* Congregation under the title of the Annunciation of the Blessed Virgin was erected by papal decree of February 20, 1920.—(Fam. Conf.).

June 25. *Peter Deforis*, a Maurist monk, was born at Montbrison in 1732. In 1760 he was summoned to Paris by his superiors to assist in preparing a new edition of the Councils of Gaul commenced by Dom Hervin. He begged to be relieved of this work that he might devote himself exclusively to the defence of the Catholic faith against the infidelity of the age. He was a zealous religious and raised his voice in protest against a faction of his brethren who introduced certain relaxations in monastic observance. He was accused by some journalists of being the author of the civil constitution of the clergy, but vindicated himself by a public letter. He was arrested, condemned to death by the revolutionary committee and after lingering for some time in Parisian prisons was executed June 25, 1794. He begged to be executed last that he might have an opportunity to sustain the courage of the others who were to die on the same occasion.—(Feller, Bio. Universelle.)

Sept. 2. Dom *Ambrose Augustine Chevreux*, last General of the Congregation of St. Maur, was born Feb. 13, 1728, and professed as a monk May 14, 1744. He succeeded Dom John Peter Chartree in the office of General in 1788 and was one of the clerical deputies in the States General. As he was unwilling to take the oath to the civil constitution of the clergy, he was condemned to death and fell as one of the victims in the massacre in the church of the Carmelites in Paris in 1792. The cause of his beatification was introduced in 1916.—(Acta Ap. Sedis, 1916).

Sept.—Dom *Louis Barreau de la Touche*, monk of the Congregation of St. Maur and nephew of Dom Ambrose Chevreux, the General, was sentenced to death for refusing to swear to the civil constitution of the clergy and was slain by revolutionaries at the Carmelite church in Paris in 1792.–(Acta Ap. Sedis, 1916).

Sept.—Dom *Renatus Julian Massey*, monk of the Congregation of St. Maur, fell a victim to the fury of the French Revolution together with a number of other Benedictine monks in Paris in 1792.—(Acta Ap. Sedis, 1916).

Sources

The principal authorities consulted in preparing the original (where only the name of the author is given) are:

Adam of Bremen (11th cent.). *Gesta Hamburgensium Pontificum.*
Alberic of Monte Cassino (1088). Writings.
Albert of Stade. O.S.B., (13th cent.). *Chronica.*
Alcuin of Tours, *Opera* (in Migne, P. L.).
Anastasius Bibliothecarius, *Liber Pontificalis.*
Armellini, Mariano. *Catalogus virorum sanctitate illustrium e Congreg. Cassinensi.* Assisi. 1733.

Baillet, Adrian, *Vies des Saints.* 4 vols. Paris. 1656.
Barnabas de Montalbo, *Chronica de la Orden de Cistertio.* 2 vols. Madrid, 1601.
Baronius, Caesar, *Annales Ecclesiastici* (35 vols.).
Barralis, Vincent, *Chronicon Sanctorum Insulae Lirinensis.* Lugduni. 1613.
Beda Venerabilis. *Hist. eccles. Gentis Anglorum etc.*
Bernard de Brito, *Chronica de Cistertio.* Lisboa, 1602.
Bollandists *Acta Sanctorum.*
Bonanni, Philip. S.J., *Ordinum Religiosorum*.......*Catalogus.* 2 vols. Rome 1738, 1741.
Bonnefons, A. *Les Fleurs des Vies des Saints.* Paris. 1556.
Bruschius, Caspar, *Chronologia monasteriorum Germaniae.* Ingolstadii, 1551.
Bucelinus, G., *Menologium Benedictinum.* 1655.
Bugatti, Caspar. O.P., *Istoria della Terra di Meda.*
Bulteau, Louis, *Abrege de l histoire de l'Ordre de S. Benoit,* 1684.
Butler, A. *Lives of the Saints.* (German translation).

Caesar of Heisterbach, *Opera.*
Cajetanus, Octavius, *Vitae Sanctorum Siculorum.* Panormi, 1657.
Calzolari, Peter, *Historia Monastica.* Firenze, 1561.
Canisius, Peter, S.J., *Martyrologium.*
Capgrave, John, *Nova Legenda Angliae,* Londinii, 1516.
Caraccioli, A. *De Sacris Ecclesiae Neapolitanae monumentis.*
Chalemot, Claude, *Series Sanctorum Ord. Cist.* Bruxellis, 1623.
Chenu, John, *Historia chronol. episcoporum*......*Galliae.* Paris, 1621.
Cherle, Benedict. *Menologium Benedictinum.* Augsburg, 1714.
Ciaconius, A., O. P. *Vitae*......*Summorum Pontificum Romanorum et S. R. E. Cardinalium.* Rome, 1601-2.
Colgan, John, *Acta SS. veteris Scotiae seu Hiberniae.* Lovanii, 1645.

D'Achery, Luke. *Acta Sanctorum O.S.B.* (ed. by Mabillon).
Domenec, A., O. P. *Historia Universalis Sanctorum Cataloniae,* 1602.

Esterl, Francis. *Chronik des Frauenstiftes Nonnberg in Salzburg,* 1841.
Eulogius, St. (9th cent.) *Memoriale Sanctorum.—*

Ferrari, Philip, *Catalogus Sanctorum Italiae.* Milan, 1613.
Feyerabend, Maurus, *Saemmtliche Jahrbuecher von Ottobeuren.* 4 vols. 1813.
Flaminius, C. *Hagiologium Italicum,* 2 vols. Bassano, 1773.
Florence of Worcester, (12th cent.) *Chronicon ex chronicis.*
Fortunatus, A. *Historiarum Camaldulensium* libri III. Florence, 1575.
Fortunatus Venantius, *Opera.*

Ghesquierius, Jos. *Acta SS. Belgii.* Bruxellis, 1783.
Goldast, M. *Rerum Alemanicarum Scriptores.* Frankfurt, 1696.
Gonzales Davila, A, *Theatro ecclesiastico de las Iglesias de las dos Castillas,* 3 vols. Madrid, 1645-50.
Guilliman, F. *De Episcopis Argentoratensibus.* Friburgi, 1608.

Hansiz, Marcus, S.J., *Germania Sacra.* 3 vols. 1727-55.
Harpsfield, Nich., *Historia anglic. ecclesiastica,* Duaci, 1682.

Henriquez, Chr., *SS. Ord. Cistert.* Bruxellis, 1623—
Henry of Huntingdon., *De Sanctis Angliae.*
Herman Contractus (11th cent.) *Chronicon.*
Hess, Gerard., *Catalogus Abbatum Monast. Weingartensis*, Aug. Vindel, 1781.
Hundt, W., *Metropolis Salisburgensis*, Ingolstadii, 1680.

Jacobilli. L., *Vite de ' Santi e Beati dell' Umbria.* 1647.
Jonas of Bobbio (7th cent.) *Vitae of S. Columban. Attala etc.*

L'Hermite, M., S.J., *Histoire des Saints de la Province de Lille*, Douay, etc. (17th cent.).
Le Nain, Pierre, *Essai de l'histoire de l'Ordre de Citeaux.* 9 vols. Paris. 1696.
Locatelli, E., *Vita del'glorioso Giovanni Gualberto.* 1632.

Mabillon, J., *Acta Sanctorum O.S.B.*
Mabillon, J., *Annales O.S.B.*
Manrique, A. de., *Cisterciensium annalium* tomi 4. Lyons, 1642–59.
Marieta, J., *Historia de todos los Santos de Espana.* Cuenca. 1596.
Martene, Edmund, *Thesaurus novus Anecdotorum.*
Menard, H. *Martyrologium O.S.B.* Paris, 1629.
Meyer, Jacob, *Chronicon Flandriae.*
Miraeus (or Le Mire). A., *Chronicon Cist. Ordinis.* Coloniae., 1614.
Molanus, J. *Usuardi Martyrologium* (annot.) 1568.
Mombritius, B., *Sanctuarium, seu Vitae Sanctorum* (15th cent.).
Murer, H., *Helvetia Sancta.* Luzern, 1648.

Raderus, M., *Bavaria Sancta.* 3 vols. 1615.
Raisse, Arnold, *Belgica Christiana.* Duaci, 1634.
Ram, F. X., *Hagiographie......Louvain.*
Rambeck, Aegidius, *Calendarium Annale*, Augsburg, 1675.
Razzi, Silvano, *Vite de Santi e Beati del ordine de Camaldoli.*—Firenze 1600.
Rinaldus, Jac., *Flores Galliae Sanctae*, Divione, 1643.
Rusca, Robert, *Origine del s. ordine Cisterciense*, Milano, 1598.

Sander, Ant., *Batavia Sacra*, Bruxellis, 1714.
Sander, Ant., *Hagiologium Flandriae*, Antverpiae, 1625.
Sandoval, Prud., *De fundationibus monasteriorum O.S.B.*
Sartorius, A. *Cistercium bis-tertium*, Pragae, 1700.
Saussay, And., de, *Martyrologium Gallicanum.* Paris, 1638.
Schindele, R., *Benedictus redivivus.*
Schindele, R., *Chronologia Benedictino-Mariana.*
Serarius, N. *Moguntiacarum rerum* libri V. 1604.
Stengelius, C. Numerous *"Vitae."*
Surius, L., *Vitae Sanctorum.*, 6 vols. 1570–75.

Tamajo, J., *Comment .SS. Hispanorum*, Lugduni, 1651.
Tamajo, J., *Martyrologium Hispanum*, Lugduni, 1651–9.

Ughelli, Ferd., *Italia Sacra*, 9 vols. Romae, 1644–62.

Wicelius, George., *Hagiologium*, Coloniae, 1554.
Wion, Arnold, *Lignum Vitae*, Augsburg, 1507.

Yepez, Ant., *Cronica general de la Orden de S. Benito.* Valladolid, 1607–21.

Ziegelbauer, M. *Historia Rei Literariae O.S B.*, 4 vols. Augustae Vind., 1754—

To the above list may be added the following sources consulted by the revisor:

Acta Apostolicae Sedis, 1909–
Acta Sanctae Sedis, 1864–1909.
Barrett, M., *A Calendar of Scottish Saints*, Ft. Augustus, 1904.
Buchberger, M., *Kirchliches Handlexikon*, 2 vols. Muenchen, 1907.-
Burgener, L. *Helvetia Sancta*, 2 vols. Einsiedeln, 1860.

Catholic Encyclopedia, 16 vols. New York, 1907.

Chevalier U. *Repertoire des Sources historiques du Moyen Age.—Bio-Bibliographique*, 2 vols. Paris, 1905—

Dunbar, A. B. C., *A Dictionary of Saintly Women* ,2 vols. London, 1994.

Fleming, W., *Complete Calendar of English Saints and Martyrs*. London, 1905.

Gallia Christiana 16 vols. Paris, 1870—

Heimbucher, M., *Die Orden u. Kongregationen der Kath. Kirche*, 3 vols. 2d. edition, Paderborn, 1907—

Montalembert, *Monks of the West.*

O'Hanlon, J., *Lives of the Irish Saints.* (Jan.–Sept. only) 9 vols. Dublin, 1875—

Petin (Migne), *Dictionnaire Hagiographique*, 2 vols.

Stadler (and Ginal), *Heiligen Lexikon*, 5 vols. Augsburg, 1858.

Stanton, R., *A Menology of England and Wales*, London, 1892.

Studien u. Mitteilungen aus dem Ben. Orden, Bruenn, 1880—

Wetzer u. Welte, *Kirchenlexikon*, 12 vols., 2d ed. Freiburg 1882—

Index

American Cassinese Congregation, 215.
Amicus, St., 274.
Amnichadus, St., 28.
Amor, St., 209.
Amulwinus, 38.
Anastasius, St., of Colocza, 281.
Anastasius, St., of Cordova, 156.
Anastasius, St., of St. Michel, 262.
Andrew, Bl., of Clairvaux, 94.
Andrew, of Clairvaux, 56.
Andrew, St., of Elnon, 36.
Andrew de Strumis, Bl., 68.
Angadrema, St., 260.
Angelrannus, Ven., 305.
Angelus al Aquapagana, Bl., 45.
Angelus de Masatio, Bl., 175.
Angelus, of Monte Cassino, 178.
Angelus Senesius, 296.
Angilbert, St., 48.
Anno, Ven., of Micy., 6.
Anno, Ven., of Worms, 239.
Ansbald, St., 181.
Anschar, St., 31.
Anselm, St., of Canterbury, 106.
Anselm, St., of Lerins, 287.
Anselm, St., of Lucca, 75.
Anselm, St., of Nonantula, 61.
Anselm, of Hemmenrode, 299.
Ansbert, St., 38.
Ansegisus, St., 188.
Ansfried, Bl., 119.
Ansoaldis, Ven., 184.
Ansologus, 30.
Ansteus, St., 228.
Anstrudis, St., 262.
Ansuerus, St., 183.
Ansuin, 136.
Anthony de Winghe, 224.
Anthony, St., of Monte Cassino, 17.
Anthony, St., of Rome, 16.
Antimus, St., 10.
Antonia of Orleans, 109.
Antonine, St., 44.
Apollinaris, St., of Monte Cassino, 294.
Apollinaris, Ven., of Monte Cassino, 190.
Apparition at Toledo 313.
Appian St., 276.
Ardagnus, St., 41.
Ardo Smaragdus, St., 65.
Arduin, 310.
Argimirus, St., 168.
Armand J. de Rance, 269.
Arnaldus de Catani, Bl., 40.
Arno, 22.
Arnulph, St., of Gap, 239.
Arnulph, St., of Metz, 290
Arnulph, St., of Soissons, 207.
Arnulph, Bl., of Villers, 170
Ascelina, St., 214.

Asker, 244.
Attala, St., 67.
Attalus, St., 91.
Attilanus, St., 253.
Atto, St., 136.
Audomar, St., 229.
Augustine, St., 140.
Aunofledis, 60.
Aurea, St., of Cuteclara, 187.
Aurea, St., of Paris, 252.
Aurea, St., of St. Millan, 69.
Aurelian, St., 173.
Auremund, St., 178.
Austreberta, St., 40.
Austrian Congregation (old), 193.
Austrian Congregations (new), 214.
Aymard St., 253.
Azo, 97

Babolenus, St., of St. Maur, 167.
Babolenus, St., of Malmedy, 167.
Badilo, Bl., 255.
Bainus, St., 161,
Balda, St., 304.
Balderic, Bl., of Montfaucon, 210.
Balderic, of Salzburg, 5.
Baldwin, Bl., 213.
Balsamus, 292.
Baltherius, St., 295.
Balto, Bl., 321.
Bardo, St., 153.
Barking, Nuns of, 81
Barnard, St., 21.
Barontus, St., 82.
Bartholomew, St., of Durham, 165.
Bartholomew, St., of Marmoutier, 53.
Bartholomew, of Poblete, 54.
Basilissa, St., 135.
Bathildis, St., 27.
Baudacharius, 316.
Bavarian Congregation, 218.
Bavo, St., 249.
Beatrice of Este, Bl., Jan. 18, 17.
Beatrice of Este, Bl., May 10, 126.
Beatrice, Ven., nun of Nazareth, 194.
Bede, St., 141.
Begga, St., 313.
Belgian Congregation, 325.
Bellendis, St., 33.
Bellerius, St., 127.
Benedict and Scholastica, Conf. of 279.
Benedict, St., Founder, 78.
Benedict, St., Translation of, 300.
Benedict, St., of Albenga, 42.
Benedict, St., of Braunau, 281.
Benedict, St., Camaldolese monk, 285.
Benedict, St., of Chiusa, 145.
Benedict, St., of Monte Cassino. 47.
Benedict, St., of Poitiers, 266.

J. O. G. D.

* 9 7 8 1 9 6 5 3 0 3 6 4 1 *